PENGUIN BOOKS

RACING IN THE STREET:
THE BRUCE SPRINGSTEEN READER

Born in Glasgow, Scotland, June Skinner Sawyers has written extensively about music, travel, history, and popular culture. She contributes regularly to the *Chicago Tribune* and the *San Francisco Chronicle* and is an adjunct lecturer at the Newberry Library in Chicago. She is the author of numerous books, including *Celtic Music: A Complete Guide*, and has edited several literary anthologies, including *Dreams of Elsewhere: The Selected Travel Writings of Robert Louis Stevenson; The Greenwich Village Reader;* and *The Road North: 300 Years of Classic Scottish Travel Writing*. She lives in Chicago.

RACING IN THE STREET

The Bruce Springsteen Reader

FOREWORD BY MARTIN SCORSESE

EDITED BY

June Skinner Sawyers

PENGUIN BOOKS

To
Asbury Park . . .
and, of course, the fans

PENGUIN BOOKS
Published by the Penguin Group
Penguin Group (USA) Inc., 375 Hudson Street, New York, New York 10014, U.S.A.
Penguin Books Ltd, 80 Strand, London WC2R 0RL, England
Penguin Books Australia Ltd, 250 Camberwell Road, Camberwell, Victoria 3124, Australia
Penguin Books Canada Ltd, 10 Alcorn Avenue, Toronto, Ontario, Canada M4V 3B2
Penguin Books India (P) Ltd, 11 Community Centre,
Panchsheel Park, New Delhi – 110 017, India
Penguin Books (N.Z.) Ltd, Cnr Rosedale and Airborne Roads,
Albany, Auckland, New Zealand
Penguin Books (South Africa) (Pty) Ltd, 24 Sturdee Avenue,
Rosebank, Johannesburg 2196, South Africa

Penguin Books Ltd, Registered Offices: 80 Strand, London WC2R 0RL, England

First published in Penguin Books 2004

1   3   5   7   9   10   8   6   4   2

LIBRARY OF CONGRESS CATALOGING IN PUBLICATION DATA
Racing in the street : the Bruce Springsteen reader / edited by June Skinner Sawyers ;
foreword by Martin Scorsese.
p.   cm.
Includes bibliographical references (p.) and index.
ISBN 0-14-200354-9
1. Springsteen, Bruce. 2. Rock musicians—United States—Biography.
I. Sawyers, June Skinner, 1957–
ML420.S77R33 2004
782.42166'092—dc22
[B]   2003062414

Printed in the United States of America
Set in New Calendonia • Designed by Alice Sorensen

Contents

◾

The Springsteen Musical Family Tree   xi

Foreword by Martin Scorsese   xiii

Acknowledgments   xv

A Note on Selections   xvii

Chronology   xix

"Newark by the Sea" by Gene Lazo   xxv

Maps   xxviii and xxix

INTRODUCTION   1

◾ *Part One* ◾
GROWIN' UP

PETER KNOBLER,
WITH GREG MITCHELL
**Who Is Bruce Springsteen and Why Are We Saying
All These Wonderful Things about Him?**   29
  Crawdaddy!

PAUL WILLIAMS
Lost in the Flood   40

JOHN ROCKWELL
Springsteen's Rock Poetry at Its Best   47
  New York Times

DAVE MARSH
Bruce Springsteen: A Rock "Star Is Born"   50
  Rolling Stone

MAUREEN ORTH, JANET HUCK,
AND PETER S. GREENBERG
Making of a Rock Star   53
  Newsweek

JAY COCKS
Rock's New Sensation: The Backstreet Phantom of Rock   64
  Time

LESTER BANGS
Hot Rod Rumble in the Promised Land   74
   CREEM

ARIEL SWARTLEY
The Wild, the Innocent and the E Street Shuffle   78
   from *Stranded: Rock and Roll for a Desert Island*

DAVE MARSH
Thunder Road   86
   from *Born to Run: The Bruce Springsteen Story*

▪ *Part Two* ▪
GLORY DAYS

ROBERT HILBURN
Out in the Streets   93
   Los Angeles Times

DON McLEESE
Abdicating the Rock 'n' Roll Pedestal:
Bruce Springsteen Gets Down   99
   Chicago Reader

GREIL MARCUS
The Next President of the United States   103
   New West

GEORGE F. WILL
Bruuuuuce   107

T. CORAGHESSAN BOYLE
Greasy Lake   110
   from *Greasy Lake & Other Stories*

BOBBIE ANN MASON
   from *In Country*   120

JAMES WOLCOTT
The Hagiography of Bruce Springsteen   126
   Vanity Fair

SIMON FRITH
The Real Thing—Bruce Springsteen   130
   from *Music for Pleasure*

KEVIN MAJOR
   from *Dear Bruce Springsteen*   140

JEFFERSON MORLEY
Darkness on the Edge of the Shining City:
Bruce Springsteen and the End of Reaganism   146
    New Republic

JACK RIDL
Video Mama   154

ANDREW M. GREELEY
The Catholic Imagination of Bruce Springsteen   155
    America

ROBERT SANTELLI
Twenty Years Burning Down the Road:
The Complete History of Jersey Shore Rock 'n' Roll   166
    from Backstreets: Springsteen—The Man and His Music

CHARLES R. CROSS
The Promise   178
    Backstreets

DAVE BARRY
Glory Days   182
    Miami Herald

ELIZABETH WURTZEL
    from *Prozac Nation: Young and Depressed in America*   185

NEIL STRAUSS
Springsteen Looks Back but Keeps Walking On   190
    New York Times

HOPE EDELMAN
Bruce Springsteen and the Story of Us   196
    Iowa Review

JUDY WIEDER
Bruce Springsteen: The Advocate *Interview*   211
    The Advocate

BRYAN K. GARMAN
The Ghost of History: Bruce Springsteen,
Woody Guthrie, and the Hurt Song   221
    Popular Music and Society

JIM CULLEN
Tom Joad's Children   231

The Bars of Graceland   235

    from *Born in the U.S.A.: Bruce Springsteen*
    and the American Tradition

TOM PERROTTA
from *The Wishbones*   241

NICHOLAS DAWIDOFF
The Pop Populist   246
New York Times Magazine

MIKAL GILMORE
Bruce Springsteen's America   266
from *Night Beat: A Shadow History of Rock & Roll*

R. C. RINGER
Asbury Park   284
from *Shore Stories: An Anthology of the Jersey Shore*

SHERI TABACHNIK, JOSEPH SAPIA,
AND KELLY JANE COTTER
Father of Bruce Springsteen Dies at 73   292
Asbury Park Press

▪ *Part Three* ▪
REBIRTH

PELLEGRINO D'ACIERNO
Roll Over, Rossini: Italian American Rock 'n' Roll   297

*After the Long Good-bye: From Frank Zappa
to Bruce Springsteen and Madonna*   300

from *The Italian American Heritage*

WILL PERCY
Rock and Read: Will Percy Interviews Bruce Springsteen   305
DoubleTake

NADINE EPSTEIN
Asbury Park, My Hometown   321
Christian Science Monitor

FREDERICK REIKEN
from *The Lost Legends of New Jersey*   325

SAMUELE F. S. PARDINI
Bruce Springsteen's "American Skin"   329
Artvoice

BOB CRANE
from *A Place to Stand: A Guide to Bruce Springsteen's
Sense of Place*   337

NICK HORNBY
Thunder Road   347
  from *Songbook*

COLLEEN SHEEHY
Springsteen: Troubadour of the Highway   352

ALAN LIGHT
The Missing   358
  The New Yorker

A. O. SCOTT
**The Poet Laureate of 9/11: Apocalypse and Salvation
on Springsteen's New Album**   362
  Slate

KEVIN COYNE
His Hometown   366
  New Jersey Monthly

ERIC ALTERMAN
  from *It Ain't No Sin to Be Glad You're Alive:*
  The Promise of Bruce Springsteen   371

CHRISTOPHER PHILLIPS
The Real World   376

AFTERWORD BY ROBERT SANTELLI   382

Appendix   389
Web Sites   415
Credits   417
Bibliography   419

The Springsteen
Musical Family Tree

The Castiles
(*1965 to 1966*)
Bart Haynes: drums[1]
Frank Marziotti: bass
Paul Popkin: guitar/vocals
Bruce Springsteen: guitar/vocals
George Theiss: guitar/vocals

The Castiles
(*1966 to 1968*)
Bob Alfano: organ
Curt Fluhr: bass
Vinny Maniello: drums
Paul Popkin: guitar/vocals
Bruce Springsteen: guitar/vocals
George Theiss: guitar/vocals

Earth
(*1968*)
Bruce Springsteen: guitar/vocals
John Graham: bass
Michael Burke: drums

Child
(*1969*)
Bruce Springsteen: guitar/vocals
Danny Federici: organ
Vini Lopez: drums
Vini Roslin: bass

Steel Mill
(*1970*)
Bruce Springsteen: guitar/vocals
Danny Federici: organ
Vini Lopez: drums
Steve Van Zandt: bass

Steel Mill
(*1971*)
Bruce Springsteen: guitar/vocals
Danny Federici: organ
Vini Lopez: drums
Robbin Thompson: guitar/vocals
Steve Van Zandt: bass

Dr. Zoom and the Sonic Boom
(*1971–1972*)
Bruce Springsteen: guitar/vocals
Kevin Connair: mc
Danny Federici: organ
Danny Gallagher: Monopoly
Vini Lopez: drums
David Sancious: keyboards
Southside Johnny: harmonica
Garry Tallent: bass
Bobby Williams: drums
Steve Van Zandt: guitar/vocals
The Zoomettes: vocals

The Bruce Springsteen Band
(*1971*)
Bruce Springsteen: vocals/guitar
Harvey Cherlin: trumpet
Francine Daniels: vocals
Barbara Dinkins: vocals
Bobby Feigenbaum: saxophone
Danny Federici: organ
Delores Holmes: vocals
Vini Lopez: drums
David Sancious: keyboards
Garry Tallent: bass
Steve Van Zandt: guitar/vocals

The E Street Band
(*1972–1974*)
Bruce Springsteen: vocals/guitar
Clarence Clemons: saxophone
Danny Federici: organ
Vini Lopez: drums
David Sancious: keyboards
Garry Tallent: bass

The E Street Band
(*1974*)
Bruce Springsteen: vocals/guitar
Ernest "Boom" Carter: drums
Clarence Clemons: saxophone
Danny Federici: organ
David Sancious: keyboards
Garry Tallent: bass

The E Street Band
(*core members 1974–1984*)
Bruce Springsteen: vocals/guitar
Roy Bittan: piano
Clarence Clemons: saxophone
Danny Federici: organ
Garry Tallent: bass

Steve Van Zandt: guitar/vocals
Max Weinberg: drums

The E Street Band
(*core members 1984–2000*)
Bruce Springsteen: vocals/guitar
Roy Bittan: piano
Clarence Clemons: saxophone
Danny Federici: organ
Nils Lofgren: guitar/vocals
Patti Scialfa: vocals
Garry Tallent: bass
Max Weinberg: drums

The E Street Band
(*core members 2000–current*)
Bruce Springsteen: vocals/guitar
Roy Bittan: piano
Clarence Clemons: saxophone
Danny Federici: organ
Nils Lofgren: guitar/vocals
Patti Scialfa: vocals
Garry Tallent: bass
Steve Van Zandt: guitar/vocals
Max Weinberg: drums

For a detailed description of Springsteen's musical history, see "The E Street Family Tree" in *Backstreets: Springsteen—The Man and His Music,* Charles R. Cross and the editors of *Backstreets* magazine (New York: Harmony Books, 1989; Crown, 1992), pp. 32–33.

Note
1. Haynes died in Vietnam.

Foreword

∎

Martin Scorsese

There's an epic vision at the heart of Bruce Springsteen's music. It's evident in the breadth of American experience he covers in his songs, in the rich and colorful landscape of his music, in the unadorned beauty of his words. It's there in that voice of his, an instrument which has only grown more eloquent as the years have gone by. And that epic vision is there in the amazing range of emotions in his songs—exhilaration, tragedy, desire, sorrow, hope, resignation, anger, betrayal, longing.

I heard Springsteen for the first time in the mid-'70s. Like a lot of people, I was knocked out. There was no one else like him around at the time. The punk and New Wave explosions were happening here and in England, but that was a different kind of music—anarchic, relentlessly abrasive. Springsteen was something else—deeply romantic, even extravagantly so. But he was also genuinely compassionate—here was a guy who really had a rock-solid commitment to working-class America and a feel for the lives of ordinary people: he gave their dreams and hopes the grandeur that they deserved. He was also a great showman, one of the greatest, as anyone who has ever seen one of his concerts can tell you. With the exception of solo projects like *Nebraska* and *The Ghost of Tom Joad,* every album seemed to encompass the entire history of rock and roll. Listen to *Born to Run* or *Darkness on the Edge of Town* or *The River* and you'll hear blues, R&B, garage rock, folk, country, Motown, Phil Spector, pure pop, and more. Springsteen possesses an amazing generosity—in the music, in the legendary performances, in his sense of social justice and his political outspokenness—that's almost unmatched.

During the '70s, the word "epiphany" was used quite often by certain film critics—referring to those moments when everything breaks through, when the audience finds itself delivered to a new and unexpected place by the artist, be it a filmmaker, a poet, a musician, or a writer. Springsteen, with his amazing E Street Band or off on his own, has given us many such moments. *Born to Run* is loaded with them. There was a time in 1975 when you could hear those songs blaring from car radios and apartment windows, and no matter how many times you listened to them, they never lost their edge: the moment in the title song when the band seems to push through to a new place, and Springsteen screams, "The highway's jammed with broken heroes on a last chance power drive"; Randy Brecker's mournful horn over the quietly tragic "Meeting Across the River"; the soaring climax of "Jungleland." Springsteen had already made two beautiful albums before *Born to Run,* but that was the one that put him on the map, and it still has the same wild grandeur it had when it first hit the airwaves (and the turntables) almost thirty years ago.

There are many more artistic peaks, from *Darkness on the Edge of Town's* surprisingly quiet "Racing in the Street" to the heartbreaking "Valentine's Day" from *Tunnel of Love,* a very underrated album, to the haunting song about 9/11, the title tune from *The Rising.* You'll read about many of these songs in this book, and if you weren't around when they came out, you'll find out what they meant to people, why they felt so special and so important, and so eternally fresh.

Simply put, Bruce Springsteen is a major American artist, and this wonderful book is a fitting tribute.

Acknowledgments

■

I consider *Racing in the Street* to be a public service, a gift if you will, to Springsteen fans, scholars, and anyone with even a cursory interest in the singer's life and music. It was both a pleasure and a privilege putting it together.

This anthology could not have been completed in as timely or as thorough a fashion without the invaluable assistance of Cheryl Besenjak, Joe Besenjak, and Sherry Hoesly at the Permissions Group. I wish also to thank Elaine Wong and Matthew Bradley for their research assistance—without them it would have been much more difficult—Rick Selin for last-minute computer assistance, and Amelia Janes for the exquisite New Jersey maps. I offer my gratitude to Robert Santelli; Adel Hauck; Meg McCarthy; George Francis for the reminiscences he shared with me on Asbury Park; Bob Crane; Deirdre Harrison; Richard Schickel; Brian K. Garman for his generosity; Bobbie Ann Mason for her cooperation; Alessandro Portelli; Samuele Pardini for his various suggestions; Mark Allister; Kevin Major; Eric Alterman; Joseph Albini for referring the Michael Bader piece that ran in the December 2002 issue of *Tikkun* and, alas, was cut at the last minute; Fred Gardaphé; my agents, the late Jane Jordan Browne and Scott Mendel and Danielle Egan-Miller; Jennifer Ehmann, my editor at Penguin; and Gene Lazo for permission to reprint his poem, "Newark by the Sea," that opens the book and hopefully sets the mood for what is to follow.

A word of thanks is extended to all the writers, agents, and lawyers who granted permission to reprint the selections here. I would especially like to thank Charles Cross, the founder of *Backstreets*, and Christopher Phillips, its editor, for their support and generosity.

And thanks always to Theresa Albini.

A Note on Selections

So much has been written about Bruce Springsteen over the last few decades that it was difficult to know where to begin, or end. I wanted to include as representative a sampling of selections as possible and, with that in mind, I chose articles from the mainstream press, essays from academic journals, interviews, reviews, a poem or two, excerpts from novels and short stories, as well as articles that inspired Springsteen's work. There's certainly enough material to warrant a second volume. When appropriate, I have also added endnotes either for clarification purposes or as corrections to factual errors that appeared in the original pieces.

As always when compiling an anthology, some things got away. Sadly, I was unable to obtain permission to reprint "Growing Young with Rock and Roll" by Jon Landau that ran in the May 22, 1974, issue of *The Real Paper*, probably the most famous piece written about Springsteen (certainly the most quoted). Nor, for the most part, was inclusion of *Rolling Stone* articles and interviews possible since, as any true Springsteen fan knows, the magazine published *Bruce Springsteen: The Rolling Stone Files* in 1996. Of course, I think *Racing in the Street* is a terrific companion piece to that work and should be an indispensable item in any Springsteen collection.

I hope that what does remain provides hours of enjoyment and edification. It was certainly fun putting it together.

Chronology

September 23, 1949 Bruce Frederick Springsteen is born in Long Branch, New Jersey, the firstborn child of Douglas, a third-generation New Jerseyan, and Adele Springsteen. His sister Virginia is born in 1950, followed by Pamela in 1962.

1955 Springsteen enters St. Rose of Lima School.

1964 Springsteen joins his first band, the Rogues.

1965 Springsteen joins the Castiles. They play their first professional gig at the Woodhaven Swim Club in Woodhaven, New Jersey. The four band members and manager Tex Vinyard split the evening's take of $35 five ways.

May 18, 1966 Springsteen, as a member of the Castiles, records "Baby I" and "That's What You Get"—cowritten by Springsteen and the Castiles' lead singer, George Theiss—at Mr. Music, Inc., in Bricktown, New Jersey.

June 19, 1967 Springsteen graduates from Freehold High School.

September 1967 Springsteen enrolls at Ocean County Community College in Toms River, New Jersey, but drops out shortly thereafter. Before leaving, he does manage to publish several poems in the school's literary magazine.

November 3, 1967 Springsteen meets guitarist Steve Van Zandt at the Hullabaloo Club in Middletown, New Jersey.

1968 The Castiles break up.

Summer 1969 Springsteen fails his army physical exam. Graded 4-F, he is deemed "unfit" partly due to injuries sustained from a motorcycle accident two years earlier and his intentionally chaotic and confusing answers on the army questionnaire.

Springsteen's family moves to San Mateo, California, but he stays behind in New Jersey.

Winter 1969 Springsteen moves to the Jersey Shore town of Asbury Park.

January 13, 1970 Springsteen and his new band, Steel Mill, perform at the Matrix in Berkeley. Critic Philip Elwood in the *San Francisco Examiner* writes a highly favorable review calling Steel Mill's ninety-minute performance "one of the most memorable evenings of rock in a long time. . . . I have never been so overwhelmed by an unknown band." He adds that Springsteen "is a most impressive composer."

February 22, 1970 Springsteen and Steel Mill record three demos for legendary impresario Bill Graham, "Going Back to Georgia," "Guilty (Send That Boy to Jail)," and "The Train Song" at Fillmore Recording Studios in San Francisco. But they refuse Graham's offer of a recording contract, proclaiming the $1,000 advance to be too low.

July 1970 Racial riots engulf Asbury Park for five nights.

February 1971 Steel Mill disbands.

March 1972 Springsteen signs a management contract with independent producer Mike Appel on the hood of a car in an unlit parking lot.

May 2–3, 1972 John Hammond arranges a demo session, for which Springsteen records twelve songs, including "It's Hard to Be a Saint in the City," "Mary Queen of Arkansas," "Growin' Up," "Does This Bus Stop at 82nd Street?," "The Angel," "If I Was the Priest," "Cowboys of the Sea," and "Arabian Nights."

June 9, 1972 Hammond signs Springsteen to a contract with Columbia Records; Springsteen receives a $25,000 advance.

November 12, 1972 First show attributed to Bruce Springsteen and the E Street Band, in York, Pennsylvania.

January 5, 1973 Springsteen's debut album, *Greetings from Asbury Park, N.J.,* is released to mostly critical acclaim, but the public largely ignores it.

June 14–15, 1973 Springsteen opens for the band Chicago at Madison Square Garden, New York. It's a disaster; the Chicago fans do not appreciate Springsteen's brand of music.

September 11, 1973 Springsteen's second album, *The Wild, the Innocent & the E Street Shuffle,* is released. Again, the critics applaud and again the public fails to be won over.

April 9–11, 1974 Springsteen plays Charley's Bar in Cambridge, Massachusetts, where he meets rock critic Jon Landau.

May 9, 1974 Music critic Jon Landau reviews Springsteen's performance at the Harvard Square Theater in Cambridge, Massachusetts, where he proclaims that he has seen "rock and roll future and its name is Bruce Springsteen." It runs in his "Loose Ends" column in *The Real Paper,* on May 22.

August 1974 Ernest "Boom" Carter and David Sancious leave the E Street Band to form their own jazz-rock fusion outfit, Tone. Springsteen places an ad in the *Village Voice* for replacements.

September 1974 Pianist Roy Bittan and drummer Max Weinberg join the E Street Band. Vocalist Patti Scialfa also auditions but is rejected.

May 1975 Steve Van Zandt joins the E Street Band.

August 13–17, 1975 Springsteen and the E Street Band begin a ten-show stand at the Bottom Line in New York's Greenwich Village.

August 25, 1975 *Born to Run* is released.

October 27, 1975 Springsteen appears on the covers of *Time* and *Newsweek* simultaneously.

April 28, 1976 Springsteen and the E Street Band become reportedly the first rock band to play the Grand Ole Opry in Nashville.

July 27, 1976 Springsteen fires manager Mike Appel and sues him in federal court in Manhattan for fraud and undue influence.

July 29, 1976 Mike Appel countersues Springsteen in New York State Supreme Court. Judge Arnold L. Fein issues a preliminary injunction preventing Springsteen from recording with new manager Jon Landau while the case is being pursued. It drags on for ten months.

1977 *Thunder Road,* the first Springsteen fanzine, is founded by Ken Viola and Lou Cohan.

May 28, 1977 Springsteen and Appel settle the lawsuit.

June 2, 1978 *Darkness on the Edge of Town* is released.

September 1979 Springsteen performs in the antinuclear Musicians United for Safe Energy (MUSE) concerts at Madison Square Garden in New York City.

April 17, 1980 The General Assembly of New Jersey proposes to bestow the title of "New Jersey Pop Music Ambassador to America" on Springsteen, calling for the adoption of "Born to Run" as "the unofficial rock theme of our State's youth." It is not passed.

October 10, 1980 *The River* is released.

November 8, 1980 "Hungry Heart," Springsteen's first top-five single, is released.

September 20, 1981 Springsteen organizes a benefit concert for the Vietnam Veterans of America in Los Angeles.

January 3, 1982 Springsteen records *Nebraska* on a Teac four-track cassette machine in his New Jersey home.

September 20, 1982 *Nebraska* is released.

May 1984 Steve Van Zandt leaves the E Street Band to pursue his own music.

June 1984 Nils Lofgren, whose past gigs include stints with Neil Young, joins the E Street Band. Patti Scialfa also is hired.

June 4, 1984 *Born in the U.S.A.* is released; it eventually sells more than 20 million copies.

October 1984 Springsteen meets model/actress Julianne Phillips.

February 1985 Springsteen records "We Are the World" as a member of USA for Africa, which also features Bob Dylan, Stevie Wonder, Lionel Richie, Paul Simon, Smokey Robinson, Ray Charles, and Billy Joel, to benefit victims of the Ethiopian famine.

May 13, 1985 Springsteen weds Julianne Phillips in Lake Oswego, Oregon.

November 10, 1986 *Bruce Springsteen & the E Street Band Live/1975–85* is released; becomes first boxed set to debut at No. 1.

1987 Springsteen and the E Street Band part ways.

April 1987 Springsteen and Phillips separate.

October 6, 1987 *Tunnel of Love* is released.

August 30, 1988 Phillips files for divorce, alleging irreconcilable differences. It becomes finalized the following year.

September 2–October 15, 1988 Springsteen headlines the six-week Amnesty International Human Rights Now! tour, along with Sting, Peter Gabriel, Tracy Chapman, and Youssou N'Dour. He also releases *Chimes of Freedom,* a four-song EP.

October 1989 Springsteen officially disbands the E Street Band.

April 1990 Springsteen purchases a four-and-a-half acre $14 million estate in Beverly Hills.

July 25, 1990 Evan James Springsteen is born to Springsteen and Patti Scialfa.

June 8, 1991 Springsteen and Patti Scialfa marry.

December 30, 1991 Jessica Ray Springsteen is born.

March 31, 1992 *Human Touch* and *Lucky Town* are released simultaneously but quickly fall off the charts, prompting *Entertainment Weekly* to ask, "Whatever Happened to Bruce?"

May 1992 Springsteen makes his television debut on *Saturday Night Live.*

1994 "Streets of Philadelphia" becomes Springsteen's first top-ten single since "Tunnel of Love."

January 5, 1994 Sam Ryan Springsteen is born.

January 1995 Springsteen and the E Street Band reunite in the studio and cut three new songs for Springsteen's *Greatest Hits* package: "Secret Garden," "Blood Brothers," and "This Hard Land."

March 1995 "Streets of Philadelphia" wins an Academy Award for Best Song of 1994, the first time a rock song wins in that category; it also wins four Grammys.

March 1995 *Greatest Hits* is released.

November 21, 1995 *The Ghost of Tom Joad* is released.

1996 *The Ghost of Tom Joad* wins the Grammy for best contemporary folk album.

March 25, 1996 Springsteen sings "Dead Man Walking" from the film of the same name at the Academy Awards; the song, however, does not win the coveted "Best Song" award.

October 26, 1996 Springsteen is given the John Steinbeck Award, "in the souls of the people," after performing a three-hour benefit concert for the Steinbeck Research Center at San Jose State University in San Jose, California.

November 28, 1997 Springsteen attends his thirtieth high school reunion at the Holiday Inn in Tinton Falls, New Jersey.

April 26, 1998 Douglas Springsteen dies at age 73.

November 10, 1998 *Tracks* is released.

1999 Patrolmen's Benevolent Association of New York City calls for a boycott of Springsteen's New York City performances because of "American Skin (41 Shots)," the singer's controversial song about the fatal shooting of an unarmed African immigrant by NYC police officers.

March 15, 1999 Springsteen is inducted into the Rock and Roll Hall of Fame. Bono introduces him at induction ceremonies in New York City.

2000 Bruce Springsteen and the E Street Band reunion tour begins.

December 8, 2001 The Bruce Springsteen Special Collection is donated to the Asbury Park Public Library by the editors of the Springsteen fanzine *Backstreets*.

March 27, 2001 *Bruce Springsteen & the E Street Band/Live in New York City* is released.

September 21, 2001 Springsteen performs "My City of Ruins" live for the

America: A Tribute to Heroes telethon, honoring those who perished in the events of 9/11.

May 2002 An activist group, Independence for New Jersey, launches a drive to place Springsteen's name on the general election ballot as a possible candidate for the U.S. Senate. "If Bruce Springsteen threw his hat in the ring and made a real serious run at this, I think you'd see thousands of volunteers coming out from all over the place," said Doug Friedline, the group's spokesman and a former campaign adviser to ex–Minnesota governor Jesse Ventura. Springsteen rejects the offer. In a prepared statement, he notes, "If nominated, I will not run. If elected, I will not serve."

May 18, 2002 Vinyard Park in Freehold, New Jersey, is named in honor of Gordon "Tex" and Marion Vinyard. The couple was responsible for nurturing Springsteen early in his career. Springsteen speaks at the tribute.

July 30, 2002 *The Rising,* the first all-new studio recording with the E Street Band since 1984, is released.

September 22, 2002 "Springsteen: Troubadour of the Highway," a touring exhibition organized by the Frederick R. Weisman Art Museum in Minneapolis, opens.

February 2003 Springsteen wins three Grammys, for Best Male Rock Performance ("The Rising"), Best Rock Song ("The Rising"), and Best Rock Album (*The Rising*).

September 2003 *Born to Run* ranks No. 1 on the most popular albums list in Zagat's first music guide. *Darkness on the Edge of Town* also makes the top ten.

October 1, 3–4, 2003 Springsteen and the E Street Band play the grand finale of the 2002–2003 *The Rising* world tour at New York's Shea Stadium. Guest artists include Joe Ely in Austin, Texas, ex-Steel Mill vocalist-guitarist; Robbin Thompson and Bruce Hornsby in Richmond, Virginia; Joe Grushecky in Pittsburgh; and Bob Dylan in New York.

November 11, 2003 *The Essential Bruce Springsteen* is released.

Newark by the Sea

Gene Lazo

Jersey boys looking for Jersey girls
in juke joint bars and Tilt-a-Whirls
Summer nights dripped with passion sweat
Shiver now in winter's neglect
Like a rusting GTO
that was born to run again
The boardwalk waits
'neath a neon Cheshire grin
Madam Marie, oh Madam Marie
the cops are asking
what do you see?
Madam Marie, oh Madam Marie
is the moon waxing
over Newark by the sea?

RACING IN THE STREET

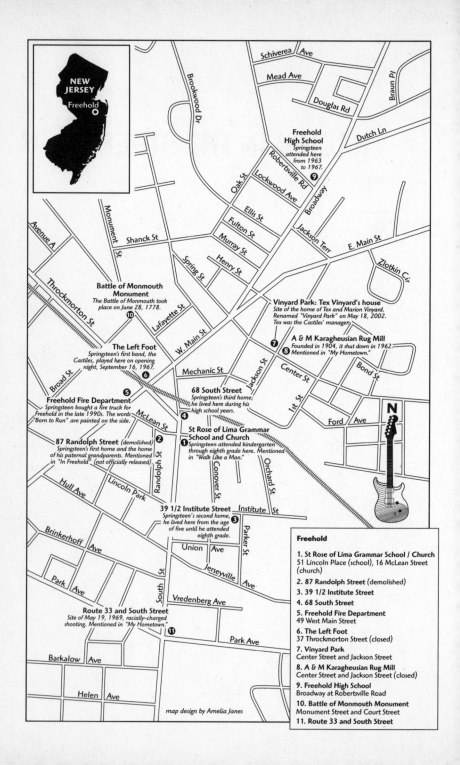

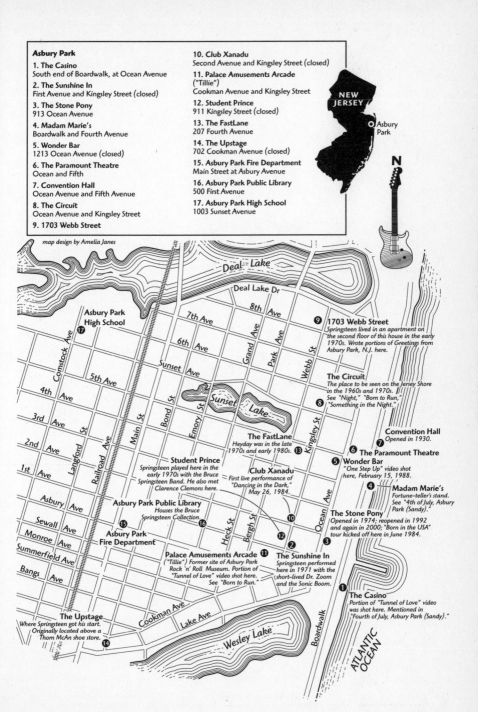

Asbury Park

1. The Casino
South end of Boardwalk, at Ocean Avenue

2. The Sunshine In
First Avenue and Kingsley Street (closed)

3. The Stone Pony
913 Ocean Avenue

4. Madam Marie's
Boardwalk and Fourth Avenue

5. Wonder Bar
1213 Ocean Avenue (closed)

6. The Paramount Theatre
Ocean and Fifth

7. Convention Hall
Ocean Avenue and Fifth Avenue

8. The Circuit
Ocean Avenue and Kingsley Street

9. 1703 Webb Street

10. Club Xanadu
Second Avenue and Kingsley Street (closed)

11. Palace Amusements Arcade
("Tillie")
Cookman Avenue and Kingsley Street

12. Student Prince
911 Kingsley Street (closed)

13. The FastLane
207 Fourth Avenue

14. The Upstage
702 Cookman Avenue (closed)

15. Asbury Park Fire Department
Main Street at Asbury Avenue

16. Asbury Park Public Library
500 First Avenue

17. Asbury Park High School
1003 Sunset Avenue

map design by Amelia Janes

NEW JERSEY

Asbury Park

N

1703 Webb Street
Springsteen lived in an apartment on the second floor of this house in the early 1970s. Wrote portions of Greetings from Asbury Park, N.J. here.

The Circuit
The place to be seen on the Jersey Shore in the 1960s and 1970s. See "Night," "Born to Run," "Something in the Night."

Convention Hall
Opened in 1930.

The Paramount Theatre

Wonder Bar
"One Step Up" video shot here, February 15, 1988.

Madam Marie's
Fortune-teller's stand. See "4th of July, Asbury Park (Sandy)."

The Stone Pony
Opened in 1974; reopened in 1992 and again in 2000; "Born in the USA" tour kicked off here in June 1984.

The FastLane
Heyday was in the late 1970s and early 1980s.

Student Prince
Springsteen played here in the early 1970s with the Bruce Springsteen Band. He also met Clarence Clemons here.

Club Xanadu
First live performance of "Dancing in the Dark," May 26, 1984.

Asbury Park Public Library
Houses the Bruce Springsteen Collection.

Asbury Park Fire Department

Palace Amusements Arcade
("Tillie") Former site of Asbury Park Rock 'n' Roll Museum. Portion of "Tunnel of Love" video shot here. See "Born to Run."

The Sunshine In
Springsteen performed here in 1971 with the short-lived Dr. Zoom and the Sonic Boom.

The Casino
Portion of "Tunnel of Love" video was shot here. Mentioned in "Fourth of July, Asbury Park (Sandy)."

The Upstage
Where Springsteen got his start. Originally located above a Thom McAn shoe store.

Deal Lake

Deal Lake Dr

Asbury Park High School

7th Ave

8th Ave

6th Ave

Sunset Ave

Grand Ave

Park Ave

Webb St

Comstock Ave

5th Ave

4th Ave

Sunset Lake

Bond St

Emory St

Kingsley St

3rd Ave

2nd Ave

Main St

1st Ave

Railroad Ave

Langford St

Asbury Ave

Sewall Ave

Ocean Ave

Monroe Ave

Summerfield Ave

Heck St

Bergh St

Bangs Ave

Cookman Ave

Lake Ave

Wesley Lake

Boardwalk

ATLANTIC OCEAN

Introduction

■

*I painted houses. If you want your house green, I paint it green.
But when I walk out onstage, I do what I want to do.*
                                        —Bruce Springsteen, 1975[1]

"Well I Got This Guitar . . ."

Of all the figures to perform in the rock and roll arena, few have had as remarkable, or as paradoxical, a career as Bruce Springsteen. He is many things to many people. Iconic rocker. Archetypal American. Working-class hero. All-American sex symbol. Introspective lyricist *and* goofy showman. Compassionate chronicler of misfits, losers, and loners—hard people living hard lives—but also a bastion of hope, faith, and glory. The man who carries the mantle of Chuck Berry, Elvis, Woody Guthrie, *and* Bob Dylan on his shoulders. Unlike the Beatles or Dylan, however, he is not an innovator and never made any such claims. Rather, he considers himself a traditionalist—a synthesist—more a throwback to rock and roll glory than a harbinger of rock and roll future. "I like the whole idea of a rock and roll lineage. . . . I wasn't interested in immediate success or how much each particular record sold. I was interested in becoming part of people's lives and, hopefully, growing up with them—growing up together," he told Neil Strauss in 1995.[2]

What is even more impressive is the breadth of Springsteen's decades-spanning career and his extraordinary facility for growth. The person who created the dazzling wordplay of *Greetings from Asbury Park, N.J.* differs greatly from the person who, years later, penned the largely somber songs of *The Rising*—separated by time, certainly, but also by vast degrees of maturity and worldly experience. We have watched him change over the years, just as we ourselves have changed.

Springsteen invests meaning in a musical form not generally known for its propensity for introspection. He does this not by preaching but by sharing stories, his own and others. Like Dylan, he is a great storyteller. Unlike the bard from Hibbing, Minnesota, however, he exudes sincerity, not cynicism. Never before has the artificial barrier between performer and audience been so transparent. To Springsteen, the audience has always been a key part of the equation. He writes for them, *to* them. They are, in essence, his mirror, personifying mutual trust. "Springsteen has always remained committed to his high standard of artistic integrity, sung about what he knew and what he strove to comprehend, and he has always asked more of his audience than most, if not all, other rock musicians," writes Michael Newall.[3]

Springsteen pursued his rock and roll dream relentlessly, with a fury seldom seen. With the exception of a few weeks in 1968, when he toiled as a gardener, Springsteen, the great working-class icon of America, has never held a regular job. Rather, writes Josh Tyrangiel in *Time*, "His great gift—the one that makes him the best rock and roll singer of his era—is empathy."[4] To Bono, that other great contemporary rock and roller, Springsteen created an alternative mythology, "one where ordinary lives became extraordinary and heroic."[5] And Springsteen himself told Bill Flanagan, "I always felt the song was my fundamental means of communication."[6]

■ A JERSEY STATE OF MIND ■

Born of mixed Italian, Irish, and Dutch ancestry on September 23, 1949, in Long Branch, New Jersey, Bruce Frederick Springsteen was the firstborn child of Douglas and Adele Springsteen. He spent the first eighteen years of his life in the working-class and highly segregated town of Freehold, living in a lower-middle-class neighborhood called Texas because of the large number of Southerners who had settled there. "Texas," wrote Springsteen biographer Dave Marsh, "was on the wrong side of the railroad tracks; it bordered the town's black ghetto."[7]

The local economy centered around a 3M factory, a rug mill, a Nescafé plant, and other small manufacturing companies. Douglas Springsteen, a taciturn loner, struggled to find his own place in his own hometown. He worked at various jobs: taxi driver, rug mill worker, bus driver, prison guard. Years later, at the Rock and Roll Hall of Fame induction ceremony, his now-famous son admitted that donning work clothes was a way to honor the memory of his father. "My parents' experiences forged my own," he said. "They shaped my politics. . . ."[8]

The modest house at 87 Randolph Street that Bruce called home—it has since been demolished—was located near the center of town and had been in the family of his paternal grandparents for generations. When Bruce was six, the Springsteens moved to a two-bedroom cold-water duplex on nearby Institute Street. And when economic conditions forced his father's parents to live with them—they previously had lived together at the Randolph Street address—they were once again on the move, this time to a house on South Street. Bruce lived here during his high school years. In his high school yearbook, Springsteen described himself as "quiet and shy," someone who "liked to putter with cars."

The moment that transformed the young boy's life occurred on a Sunday night in the 1950s when he watched Elvis Presley perform on *The Ed Sullivan Show*. His mother bought him a guitar and arranged for lessons. But his hands were too small to maneuver around the frets. His obsession faded somewhat until the Beatles arrived. By then nothing could stop him. He went to the local pawn shop and bought a guitar for $18. That simple gesture could be construed as the start of something big. His cousin taught him his first few rudimentary chords. Late at night, with his radio stashed under his pillow, he would listen to Roy Orbison, the Drifters, and Smokey Robinson. The songs that he heard during those days and nights stayed with him. In their innocence and joyful release as well as their coded paeans to rebellion and forbidden passion, they seemed to promise a better life than the one that he understood. Every Wednesday night he would "religiously" write down the Top 20, and he would practice on his guitar incessantly—up to eight hours a day. Daydreamer and loner and the object of much derision at school, Springsteen soon learned that rock could save lives. He started with his own.

Springsteen joined his first band, the Castiles, when he was a teenager, playing at dances, junior highs and high schools, roller rinks, country clubs, local drive-ins, any place where he and the boys could get a gig. Other bands followed: the short-lived heavy-metal power-trio sound of Earth; the heavy-metal blues of Child, which later changed its name to Steel Mill and which enhanced Springsteen's musical reputation considerably; the tongue-in-cheek, everything-but-the-kitchen-sink approach of Dr. Zoom and the Sonic Boom; and the ten-piece R&B of the Bruce Springsteen Band, complete with horns and female backup singers. It was from these close friendships and collegial associations that emerged the members of the E Street Band (David Sancious, the band's original keyboard player, lived on E Street in Belmar, New Jersey). In addition to Sancious (later replaced by Roy Bittan), the core members of the band included saxophonist Clarence Clemons, bassist Garry Tallent, drummer Vini "Mad Dog" Lopez (replaced by Max Weinberg), organist Danny Federici, and, most crucially perhaps, guitarist Steve Van Zandt.

A favorite Jersey Shore hangout at the time was the Upstage, run by a local by the name of Tom Potter. It stayed open later than the other clubs along the Shore and, best yet, it allowed a semblance of creative freedom—you could play whatever you wanted—into the wee hours of the morning, usually from one to five. The musicians who formed part of this unique scene never amounted to much outside their small circle of friends and acquaintances, but to Springsteen they were local heroes "because they were each in their own way a living spirit of what, to me, rock and roll is all about," he wrote in the liner notes to Southside Johnny and the Asbury Jukes's *I Don't Want to Go Home*. "It was music as survival and they lived it down in their souls, night after night."[9]

By 1972, Springsteen began writing long, stream-of-consciousness songs. A wider world now beckoned.

■ IT'S HARD TO BE A SAINT IN THE CITY ■

With the formidable assistance of his aggressive manager, Mike Appel, Springsteen walked into the New York City offices of John Hammond, the legendary Columbia Records executive who had "discovered" Billie Holiday, Pete Seeger, and Bob Dylan, among others. It was a spring day in early May 1972. It was also a day that Springsteen would never forget.

"It was a big, big day for me . . . ," Springsteen admitted many years later in an interview with Mark Hagen of *MOJO*. "I was twenty-two and come up on the bus with an acoustic guitar with no case which I'd borrowed from the drummer from the Castiles. I was embarrassed carrying it around the city." He remembers that the engineers at Columbia were "very old fashioned: everybody in ties and shirts. I felt I'd written some good songs and this was my shot. I had nothing to lose and it was like the beginning of something."[10]

Despite the offensive behavior of Appel ("For God's sake, just stop it!" an exasperated Hammond bellowed at one point. "You're going to make me hate you."), Hammond was very encouraging toward the young singer. "[S]imply being in that room with him at the board," said Springsteen, "was one of my greatest recording experiences."

Springsteen was signed, although both Hammond and Appel initially saw him as more a folk than rock act. In truth, Springsteen possessed too complex an image for anyone to get a full handle on. But the record company needed a peg that was simple and direct—an easy hook. Hence, Columbia's promotional department came up with the disastrous "new Dylan" tag.

Springsteen now began writing music that required attention from the audience—in other words, music that didn't go over too well in a noisy club or bar. "[I] felt if I was going to take a real shot at it, I was going to have to do something very distinctive and original," he told Hagen. "I wanted the independence, the individuality of a solo career, and that's when I began to write some of the initial songs for *Greetings from Asbury Park*."[11]

He did most of his writing in the back of a beauty salon beneath his Asbury Park apartment, "amidst the old hair dryers and washing sinks. . . . I had an Aeolian spinet piano my aunt had given me . . . ," he recalled in *Songs*.[12] *Greetings* was the only album for which Springsteen wrote the lyrics first and then set them to music. Most of the songs, he says, were "twisted autobiographies. . . . I wrote impressionistically. . . ." He told Hagen, "Basically, it was street music,"[13] populated by the types of characters he knew from days and nights at the Shore.

Greetings from Asbury Park, N.J. (1973) was recorded in just three weeks. An extended adolescent fantasy consisting of the street, the beach, and the boardwalk, it contained such now-classic Springsteen songs as "Spirit in the Night," "Growin' Up," "For You," "It's Hard to Be a Saint in the City," and "Lost in the Flood." The influences were impressive: critics heard Van Morrison, Bob Dylan, the Band, as well as the Stax/Volt sound set against an R&B rhythm.

The songs from *Greetings* were written, according to Springsteen, "in a style that had developed out of my earlier acoustic writing. From the late '60s on, I always had a notebook full of acoustic songs. I'd do the occasional coffeehouse, but mostly that material went unused." Significantly, he would later remark that he "never wrote in that style again. . . . Your early songs come out of a moment when you're writing with no sure prospect of ever being heard. Up until then, it's just you and your music. That only happens once."[14]

The reviews were mostly excellent. Lester Bangs, in *Rolling Stone*, called Springsteen "a bold new talent with more than a mouthful to say. . . ."[15]

Springsteen may have considered the songs and the sound his own, but the record company and aspects of the media continued to think otherwise, branding him with the dreaded "new Dylan" curse that seemed to plague every singer/songwriter with a thought in his head and a guitar in his hand. Nor did it help that, with his dark curly hair, scraggly beard, and thin-as-a-rake frame, he was a dead ringer for Dylan. It was a label that would take considerable effort, and years, to shake.

Later, though, he turned away from the florid type of writing that characterized the early albums, paring down the imagery and adopting a more straightforward, storytelling approach. Truth be told, the Dylan comparisons stung. "If you go back and listen, it's really not like Dylan at all," he told Hagen, "but at the time I was very sensitive about creating my own identity. . . . It still comes up in 'Born to Run' and 'Jungleland' and a few other places, but by the time you get to 'Darkness' it's just about gone."[16]

Later that same year, in July, Springsteen went back into the studio to record his second album, *The Wild, the Innocent & the E Street Shuffle*. Like *Greetings*, it also was made on the quick: recorded in less than two months on a slight budget. This time, though, he seemed to have a better idea of what he wanted the album to sound like (Springsteen's inexperience in the recording studio showed on *Greetings*). Some still consider *Wild* his best album, as he portrays a particular place (life as lived on the Jersey Shore) at a particular time (the early 1970s) and the fleeting end of adolescence and the summer romances that permeate it. At that time, blues, R&B, and soul were still heard up and down the Shore. Crowds along the boardwalk were dwindling though—Asbury Park had suffered the economic and social consequences of the race riots that plagued the town in the late '60s and early '70s—and, according to Springsteen, "[m]any of the usual summer vacationers were now passing Asbury Park by for less troubled locations farther south along the coast."[17]

Wild was a buoyantly exuberant album, at turns folksy and bluesy— an acoustic record with a particularly strong rhythm section that added to its overall festive carnival sound. Once again, it received mostly positive reviews but, as with *Greetings*, sales were disappointing.

Enter Jon Landau, not quite twenty-seven, an influential critic and record review editor for *Rolling Stone* as well as columnist for Boston's respected alternative weekly, *The Real Paper*. He had already written a positive review of *The Wild, the Innocent & the E Street Shuffle* that had appeared in the paper, but he had not yet seen Springsteen perform live.

On May 9, 1974, Springsteen played a full set as the opening act for Bonnie Raitt at the Harvard Square Theatre in Cambridge. Fate was about to intervene.

"Last Thursday, at the Harvard Square theatre, I saw my rock 'n' roll past flash before my eyes," Landau wrote in the quote that made rock and roll history. "And I saw something else: I saw rock and roll future and its name is Bruce Springsteen. And on a night when I needed to feel young, he made me feel like I was hearing music for the very first time."

He continued.

"When his two-hour set ended I could only think, can anyone really be this good; can anyone say this much to me; can rock 'n' roll still speak with this kind of power and glory? And then I felt the sores on my thighs where I had been pounding my hands for the entire concert and knew that the answer was yes."

Springsteen, in Landau's estimation, was the complete rock and roller: "He is a rock 'n' roll punk, a Latin street poet, a ballet dancer, an actor, a joker, bar band leader, hot-shit rhythm guitar player, extraordinary singer, and a truly great rock 'n' roll composer. He leads a band like he has been doing it forever. I racked my brains but simply can't think of a white artist who does so many things so superbly."

And then he describes Springsteen's distinctive *appearance*: "Bruce Springsteen is a wonder to look at. Skinny, dressed like a reject from Sha Na Na, he parades in front of his all-star rhythm band like a cross between Chuck Berry, early Bob Dylan, and Marlon Brando."[18]

■ FOLLOW THAT DREAM ■

By this time in his fledgling career, Springsteen felt he was ready to make a great rock album, that he was on the verge of something big—that is, if only he could capture the mesmerizing power of his live shows. It was now or never. The album that was swirling in his fervent imagination would combine Phil Spector's wall of sound, the intelligence of Dylan's lyrics, and the twangy guitars of Duane Eddy. Emotionally, it would be for anyone who ever had a dream, who ever yearned for something that seemed perennially out of reach.

Born to Run was written in the summer of 1974 but recorded over an interminable period of time—from June 1974 to July 1975. Although he shared coproducing credits with both Springsteen and Mike Appel, Jon Landau also played a pivotal role in bringing the project to completion. The *Born to Run* sessions were a far cry from the muddled proceedings that dominated Springsteen's two previous albums. The many layers of guitars and strings, the dense, complex sound, and the anthemic songwriting all came together. Although there was a point at which the perfectionist in Springsteen, still not satisfied after many months of recording, felt tempted to scrap it altogether and start over, cooler heads prevailed.

"The orchestral sound of *Born to Run* came from most of the songs being written on piano," Springsteen would later recall. "It was on the keyboard that I could find the arrangements needed to accompany the stories I was writing."[19] Springsteen later recalled the pressure associated with recording *Born to Run* as "the most horrible period of my life. . . ."[20]

Born to Run sold 700,000 copies in its first two months. And, in a remarkable feat, the Jersey rocker appeared on the covers of both *Time* and *Newsweek* during the same week, an achievement usually reserved for heads of state and other such luminaries (Appel, the ever-diligent bulldog, had orchestrated a "no cover, no interview" strategy). The *Newsweek* piece by staffer Maureen Orth emphasized the hype more than the artist, while Jay Cocks of *Time* filed a more flattering straightahead portrait. Both articles appear in this volume.

The critics wasted no time in voicing their opinions. Greil Marcus called *Born to Run* "exhilarating." Admitting that the stories Springsteen told treaded familiar terrain—the thrill of the night, the romance of the open road, "one thousand and one American nights, one long night of fear and love"—he nonetheless proclaimed that the songs rang true. "What is new," he wrote, "is the majesty Springsteen and his band have brought to this story. . . . For all it owes to Phil Spector, it can be compared only to the music that Bob Dylan and the Hawks made onstage in 1965 and '66. With that sound, Springsteen has achieved something very special. He has touched his world with glory, without glorifying anything. . . ."[21]

Eric Alterman agreed that although *Born to Run* could not be considered innovative or groundbreaking like *Sergeant Pepper*, "It was—and remains—perhaps the most powerful explication of the pure spirit of rock 'n' roll that any artist has been able to capture since the night in July 1954 at the Sun Records studio in Memphis, when an unknown nineteen-year-old-kid with the unlikely name of Elvis Presley let loose on Arthur 'Big Boy' Crudup's 'That's All Right.'"[22]

And what about the hype? Perhaps Paul Nelson said it best, and prophetically so, in *The Real Paper:* "What most people don't realize is that Springsteen is here to stay—all that publicity doesn't make him a one-shot artist."[23]

Unfortunately, legal issues with Mike Appel delayed the release of Springsteen's next album, as the two filed countersuits against each other. Appel stated that, under the terms of his contract, Springsteen could not record with Landau.[24] At the height of his popularity, Springsteen was prevented from recording for ten long months. In the meantime, he and the band continued to barnstorm across the country. In May 1977, after much emotional hand-wringing, the lawsuit was settled. By this time, Springsteen's sound was changing as well as his writing style. He began composing shorter, more tightly constructed songs. His mood had altered, too. Darkness, alienation, isolation, and a healthy dose of cynicism—but always leavened with a smidgen of hope—were prominently featured.

"After *Born to Run* I wanted to write about life in the close confines of the small towns I grew up in. . . . I felt a sense of accountability to the people I'd grown up alongside of . . . ," he recalled. "I began to listen seriously to country music. . . . I discovered Hank Williams. I liked the fact that country dealt with adult topics, and I wanted to write songs that would resonate down the road. . . . After *Born to Run,* I wanted to ensure that my music continued to have value and a sense of place."[25]

He also began reading about the life and music of Woody Guthrie and discovered the type of writing that he felt most comfortable with. Maintaining "a loose continuity from record to record," he told Mark Hagen, became increasingly important to him.[26] He admired too the colloquial writing style of Robbie Robertson. "It sounded like people telling stories and talking about themselves, as if you were sitting on the couch."[27]

But now too the stakes were raised. His fans and especially the record company demanded more from him. Whether he liked it or not, he was a commodity, and a hot one at that. "All of a sudden you're being watched a lot more closely; all of a sudden your actions have implications. I began to think about who I was and where I came from," he told Hagen.[28]

Feeling invisible as a child, he had picked up the guitar in order to be heard. But now that he had an audience—a huge audience—who wanted to listen, he felt at his most vulnerable, at his most isolated.

"How you handle it from that point on has a lot to do with the course your music takes. . . . It was a central moment when my writing took a fundamental turn—which has continued for the rest of my work."[29]

Darkness on the Edge of Town (1978) was a continuation of the characters from *Born to Run* but several years further down the road, and not necessarily wiser either. Essentially, they were the people left behind. Some 20 years after the fact, Joyce Millman could look back and describe the songs on *Darkness* as "urban folk music that quotes rock and roll the way Jimmie Rodgers and Hank Williams quoted black and Appalachian spirituals."[30]

The River, released in August 1980, revealed the thirty-year-old Springsteen's paradoxical and ambivalent attitude toward life, which was amply reflected by the eclecticism of the music. A double album, *The River* was full of darkly romantic fatalism as well as traditional '60s-style love songs. Like life itself, it reflected different moods: at times somber and exuberant, at other times deadly serious and hysterically funny. To Stephen Holden, it conjured up a strictly American world, a provincial universe, "of a guy, a girl, and a car hurtling into the night, fleeing time itself."[31] During the period Springsteen wrote *The River* he was living on a farm in rural Holmdel, New Jersey, watching old John Ford films and listening to the music of Hank Williams, Roy Acuff, and Johnny Cash. "*The River*," writes Holden, "makes emotional sense: the spirits of James Dean and Elvis merge in the body of a warmhearted hood from a backwater seashore town."[32]

The River also spawned Springsteen's first top-five single, "Hungry Heart."

■ A RESTLESS YEARNING ■

But Springsteen was still not satisfied with his own life or the direction that the country seemed to be headed. In early 1982, he was living alone in a rented house in Colts Neck, New Jersey, when he asked one of his assistants for equipment that would allow for cheap and easy home recording. In the isolation of his New Jersey home, and using a four-track Teac tape machine—"a little tape player about three or four times the size of a book" is how Springsteen described it[33]—he recorded the follow-up to *The River*. After completing the demo tape, he tried to convert the songs into rock settings. But it didn't work—it seemed strained and unnatural.

Springsteen had also picked up additional literary and musical influences. He read the short stories of Flannery O'Connor, fascinated by the Southern writer's dark spirituality and grotesque characters; listened intently to the eerie ballads and laments that so dominated Harry Smith's seminal *Anthology of American Folk Music;* and identified with the unbearable sadness of the darkest of the blues.

"The songs [in *Nebraska*] had religious and political overtones. . . . I thought of John Lee Hooker and Robert Johnson—records that sounded so good with the lights out," he wrote. "I wanted to let the listener hear the characters think, to get inside their heads, so you could hear and feel their thoughts, their choices. . . . If there's a theme that runs through the record, it's the thin line between stability and that moment when time stops and everything goes to black, when the things that connect you to your world—your job, your family, your faith, the love and grace in your heart—fail you. I wanted the music to feel like a waking dream and the record to move like poetry. I wanted the blood on it to feel destined and fateful."[34]

Springsteen has often called *Nebraska* his most personal record, as he dug deeply into recollections of his childhood and the house in Freehold where he grew up. In various interviews, he said he felt disconnected at the time. "I just wasn't any good, right at the moment that record occurred. . . . There are things that make sense of life for people: their friends, the work they do, your community, your relationship with your partner. What if you lose those things," he asked, "then what are you left with?"[35]

In a word, *Nebraska.*

Seven years earlier, in 1992, Springsteen told James Henke, "I tend to be an isolationist by nature. And it's not about money or where you live or how you live. It's about psychology. My dad was certainly the same way. You don't need a ton of dough and walls around your house to be isolated. I know plenty of people who are isolated with a six-pack of beer and a television set."[36]

He said much the same thing to Dave Marsh when he discussed the dangerous consequences of living a life in isolation and what he perceived to be the loss of community in the United States. "*Nebraska* was about that American isolation: what happens to people when they're alienated from their friends and their community and their government and their job. Because those are the things that keep you sane, that give meaning to life in some fashion. And if they slip away, and you start to exist in some void where the basic constraints of society are a joke, then life becomes kind of a joke. And anything can happen."[37]

Mikal Gilmore in the *Los Angeles Herald Examiner* called *Nebraska* "the most successful attempt at making a sizable statement about American life that popular music has yet produced."[38] To Steve Pond of *Rolling Stone* it was "a violent, acid-etched portrait of a wounded America . . ." and ". . . a vocabulary derived from the plain-spoken folk music of Woody Guthrie and the dark hillbilly laments of Hank Williams."[39]

■ A WIDE-OPEN COUNTRY ■

Springsteen's biggest heroes—from Sinatra to Elvis to Dylan—connected with huge audiences during their respective careers. Reaching a mass community of like-minded souls meant something to him. It was, he thought, a worthwhile and worthy goal.

Springsteen had savored his first real taste of mainstream success with *Born to Run,* of course. *Born in the U.S.A.* (1984), though, was something altogether different. But he was ready for it.

Born in the U.S.A. stayed on the *Billboard* charts for a mesmerizing two years and spawned seven top-ten singles. In short, it captured the imagination of America as well as much of the Western world, with its irresistible combination of rousing rockers, catchy pop melodies, and heart-on-the-sleeve romanticism. It became Columbia's biggest-selling record ever up to that point.

Despite its mass appeal, *Born in the U.S.A.* was also about the people left behind by Reaganomics. The record, wrote Stephen Holden in the *New York Times,* had "transfused rock and roll and social realism into one another. . . ." Holden cited Springsteen as "one of a very small number of rock performers who uses rock to express an ongoing epic vision of this country, individual social roots and the possibility of heroic self-creation."[40]

■ HEART SONGS ■

The mid-'80s was a tumultuous time for Springsteen on the domestic front. The elusive wanderer settled down to presumably married bliss in May 1985, only to separate less than two years later, finally divorcing in 1989.

As always, he turned to music to reconcile the roiling emotions of a failed relationship. *Tunnel of Love* (1987) is about love gone wrong. But these were fully developed songs—full of considerable weight and insight—that explored the complexity of lives intertwined, of trust compromised, of struggles confronted.

Some consider *Tunnel of Love,* recorded in three weeks at his makeshift home studio in Rumson, New Jersey, his most perceptive album, certainly his most mature. To Eric Alterman, *Tunnel* consists of "a series of quickly sketched short stories—reminiscent of the works of Raymond Carver in their deceptive simplicity—about people struggling to find themselves a physical, emotional, and spiritual place in the world. The theme of emotional and spiritual—as opposed to physical—searching is what permeates all these stories."[41] The *Seattle Times* called the record "as genuine a statement as any rocker has ever made and one of the most truthful LPs in rock history. . . ."[42]

Springsteen continued plumbing domesticity with two albums released simultaneously in 1992: *Human Touch* and *Lucky Town.* "*Human Touch* began as an exercise to get myself back into writing and recording," he recalled. "I wrote a variety of music in genres that I had always liked: soul, rock, pop, R&B. The record, once again, took awhile because I was finding my way to the songs. I also worked for the first time with musicians other than the E Street Band. I felt I needed to see what other people brought with them into the studio and how my music would be affected by collaborating with different talents and personalities."[43]

To these ears, though, *Human Touch* is his weakest effort, an uneven collection, with the exception of the title track, of mediocre rockers and lackluster ballads. Thematically, the two records act as bookends. The songs on *Human Touch* reflect a fall from grace and subsequently the courage to face rejection and betrayal, while the vastly superior *Lucky Town* represents redemption, a form of spiritual rebirth. It's one of his most joyful and optimistic recordings, full of such first-rate songs as "Living Proof," "If I Should Fall Behind," "Book of Dreams," and "My Beautiful Reward."

■ THE CIRCLE IS UNBROKEN ■

With *The Ghost of Tom Joad* (1995), Springsteen returned to the social realism that so imbued *Darkness on the Edge of Town, Nebraska,* and portions of *The River* and *Born in the U.S.A.* The primary difference was not the themes but the faces and ethnicity of the down-on-their-luck characters that Springsteen portrayed: bewildered members of the new underclass as well as Mexican and Asian immigrants lost in George H. W. Bush's "new world order." The music was stark, at times the melodies barely discernible. The plain and austere rhythms, according to Springsteen, "defined who these characters were and how they expressed themselves. . . . [The] songs completed a circle, bringing me back to 1978 and the inspiration I'd gotten from Steinbeck's *The Grapes of Wrath*. Their skin was darker and their language had changed, but these were people trapped by the same brutal circumstances."[44] Many critics consider *Joad* his boldest work to date.

It would be seven years before Springsteen made a record of entirely new material. In between, he released the four-CD set *Tracks* (1998), sixty-six cuts that span twenty-five years, augmented by *18 Tracks* in 1999, and *Bruce Springsteen & the E Street Band Live in New York City* in 2001.

The Rising (2002), written in the aftermath of 9/11, is about many things: faith, duty, love, death, survival, loss, decency, resurrection, redemption, suffering, hope—the litanies and incantations that comprise the whole. On many levels, *The Rising* exemplifies what sets Springsteen apart from the rock and roll pack. It captures the heart and soul of his music. He writes about the essentials, the fundamentals, what is worth preserving in a society. Ultimately, his best songs are about finding meaning in one's personal life, in one's community, and in the larger world.

Drive All Night

"An American changes his residence ceaselessly."

Few people would argue with that statement. It was written, though, by Alexis de Tocqueville in 1835. The more things change, the more they remain the same.

"[I]solation is a big part of the American character," Springsteen told interviewer Mark Hagen. "Everyone wakes up on one of those mornings when you just feel like you want to walk away and start brand new."[45] In other words, to move and keep on moving.

The cult of the new, the need to forget the past and begin again, to reinvent oneself, is of course a common theme that runs throughout much of American literature. To William Leach it is the restless urge to "be free to imagine,"[46] while Lewis Lapham refers to "the invention of self." "Who else," he asks, "is the American hero if not a wandering pilgrim who goes forth on a perpetual quest?"[47]

Springsteen belongs to this class of edgy wanderers and free spirits who traverse the nation's highways, a company of like-minded souls that ranges from Walt Whitman to Jack London, Mark Twain to Jack Kerouac, Woody Guthrie to Bob Dylan.

Given Springsteen's strong sense of place, it is ironic that so many of his characters long for roots and yet feel essentially rootless. They remain most at home on the open road and attempt to postpone the responsibilities of adulthood as long as possible. He understands that impulse well. "I was trying to avoid responsibility, that was why I became a musician," he tells Hagen.[48] The romantic escape is fully on display in "4th of July, Asbury Park (Sandy)," "Rosalita," "Born to Run," and so many other songs in the Springsteen canon. But where does the road to nowhere lead? At its most fundamental level, Springsteen's work embodies the quintessentially American paradox of forgetting the past while ignoring the future. Springsteen knows better than most that you pay a price for living exclusively in the moment.

Dreaming with Eyes Open

Springsteen has always been the most cinematic—and literary—of rock composers. In songs such as "Meeting Across the River," "Born to Run," "Stolen Car," "Johnny 99," "State Trooper," "Highway 29," and "Straight Time," he creates strong characters and vividly rendered scenes in a matter of minutes. Notes the independent film director John Sayles, "'Jungleland' and 'Meeting Across the River' pack as much punch in a few minutes as I got into *City of Hope*, which is a whole movie."[49] Springsteen himself has acknowledged the influence of the cinema in general and film noir (*Out of the Past*), B pictures (*Gun Crazy*), and John Ford westerns (*The Searchers*) in particular on his songwriting. What's more, entire albums have a strong cinematic quality about them, especially *Nebraska,* with its attention to narrative detail and intricate pacing.

The cinema is important to Springsteen in other ways, too. His songs appear on the sound tracks of numerous movies (see the Discography for a selected list), and he has written songs directly for the screen, including the title track for Paul Schrader's *Light of Day*, "Streets of Philadelphia" for Jonathan Demme's *Philadelphia*, and the title track for Tim Robbins's *Dead Man Walking*. One song, "Highway Patrolman," was adapted in 1991 into a film called *The Indian Runner*, written and directed by Sean Penn.

The title track from *Nebraska* was inspired by the deadly escapades of Charles Starkweather and Caril Ann Fugate, although they remain unnamed in the song itself. Springsteen had read a book about Fugate, *Caril*, which led him to write the song "Nebraska." Indeed, "Nebraska" is Springsteen's musical equivalent of Terence Malick's 1973 film classic *Badlands*, which starred Martin Sheen and Sissy Spacek, and is in turn a fictionalized account of the couple's 1958 killing spree that stretched from Lincoln, Nebraska, to eastern Wyoming, leaving ten people dead in eight days. Extending the connection further, Springsteen opens the song with an image taken directly from the film ("I saw her standin' on her front lawn just twirlin' her baton").

As he would in *The Ghost of Tom Joad* and again in *The Rising*, Springsteen did his own research to flesh out the story, even going so far as to contact Ninette Beaver, one of the authors of *Caril*. By that time, some twenty-five years after the crimes had taken place, she was an assignment editor at KMTV in Omaha. They reportedly talked for about a half hour, and when Springsteen played Lincoln in 1984, he invited her to the show as his guest and dedicated "Nebraska" to her.[50]

"There's was something about that song that was the center of the record," he told Mark Hagen, "but I couldn't say specifically what it was, outside of the fact that I'd read something that moved me. I think in my own life I had reached where it felt like I was teetering on this void. I felt a deep sense of isolation, and that led me to those characters and to those stories—people I remembered growing up, my father's side of the family, a certain way they spoke, a certain way they approached life, and that resonated through that music."[51]

A few years later, in 1987's *Tunnel of Love*, Springsteen turned to Charles Laughton's *Night of the Hunter* (1955) for inspiration for the cut "Cautious Man." Like the Robert Mitchum character in the film, the song's troubled protagonist, Bill Horton, the "cautious man" of the title, has the word "love" tattooed on his right hand and "fear" on his left hand. And as Springsteen has made clear numerous times, *The Ghost of Tom Joad* was inspired mostly by John Ford's film adaptation rather than Steinbeck's classic book.

Long-Distance Salvation

Springsteen fans are among the most loyal in the fickle world of rock and roll. Not surprisingly, then, a Springsteen concert has often been compared to a revival meeting of kindred souls. In *Bob Dylan, Bruce Springsteen, and American Song*, a fascinating analysis of the work of the two artists, Larry David Smith describes Springsteen's early shows as a "blend of spirituality, theatricality, and musicality" that "was a direct extension of the Southern black church and its long, joyous, liberating communal rituals."[52]

He goes on: "Springsteen-the-preacher uses working-class stories that are articulated through a working-class vernacular that probes his emotional autobiography in an attempt to invoke universal principles of use to his constituency."[53] Springsteen himself has admitted that the spiritual intensity of his shows had their origins in soul music, ". . . the idea of going for both your spirit and your gut. . . . My idea was the show should be part circus, part political rally, part spiritual meeting, part dance party. . . ."[54] In his most fervent songs, he pays witness, cajoles, pleads, and implores for salvation or at least some form of transformation. The "ministry of rock 'n' roll" makes anything possible. And by extension, members of his own band celebrate the universal concept of community, in a sense, acting as the embodiment of the democratic ideal.

Some find Springsteen's music to be identifiably moral, ". . . not because it does anything as simplistic as espouse a particular ethic . . . but because it creates a form of address . . . whose greatest concern and sympathy have to do with consequences: What happens when we act out of passion or cowardice, weakness or strength, love or hate, the crazed desire for redemption and transcendence? How do we deal with guilt? And what happens when all these things flow into one another, when they become part of what Springsteen calls . . . the Big Muddy? Rock 'n' roll isn't supposed to be about consequences, but Springsteen has turned it to moral account in a way which forces its Dionysian passion to face the disasters that often follow in its wake."[55]

Springsteen is both seeker and skeptic. Like a good Catholic boy, he creates concerts that are one prolonged ritual in search of a transcendent moment, but more than this, Springsteen seems to be trying to create a transcendent—albeit a necessarily temporary—community. Dave Marsh offers some food for thought. "In the Pentecostal churches whose gospel music spawned so much of rock and roll," he writes, "the purpose of music is to enhance interaction between congregation and performers. What Springsteen idealized in early rock and roll music were attempts to achieve something similar. . . . Springsteen seemed a throwback because it was his intention to regain that dialogue with the audience. It was as if he couldn't rest until the distance between artist and onlooker was obliterated."[56]

Steve Pond finds *Tunnel of Love* to be a particularly Catholic record and one that best sheds light on Springsteen's Catholic upbringing, as "lovers pray for deliverance, romance is depicted as a manifestation of God's grace, and love brings with it doubt and guilt."[57] (For a more detailed examination of Springsteen's "Catholic imagination," see the Andrew Greeley essay in this volume.) Indeed, the language on *Tunnel* is in sharp contrast to the petulant rantings and ravings that sprinkle Springsteen's early work (who can forget the striking image of "nuns" running "bald through Vatican halls pregnant, pleadin' Immaculate Conception" or the "fire alley virgins on a midnight vamp"?). The harsh criticism of the past—the Church's rigid rules that he rebelled against—has been replaced by the more generous attitudes of compassion and forgiveness, of a human being humbled by the unknown and in the thralls of a great mystery. Like the human race itself, Springsteen seems to be saying the universe is essentially an inscrutable place.

"I'm now a believer in all the rituals and things. I think they're really valuable . . . ," he told James Henke in 1992. "I don't buy into all the dogmatic aspects, but I like the idea of people coming together for some sort of spiritual enrichment or enlightenment or even just to say hi once a week."[58]

It is no secret that Springsteen takes rock and roll and its majestic power seriously; that he firmly believes it can—and does—save lives, including his own; that it is truly redemptive and can lead to salvation. He uses a Christian idiom in a rock setting, of camaraderie and people coming together, while working the crowd like a possessed gospel singer or a Pentecostal preacher waiting for the sky to fall in on him. The church of rock and roll (what Larry David Smith calls Springsteen's "Rock Church" and what Eric Alterman calls Springsteen's "invisible church") is, after all, a very public ideal of community stoked by the rock and roll beat. In Springsteen's world, rock and roll and community go hand in hand, along with faith in himself, faith in his music, faith in his audience, and ultimately faith in the community he has created. But it's a two-way street. As Springsteen has shouted in concert at the top of his lungs, "I want you to go with me because I need to go with you—that's why I'm here."

In an article that ran in *Time,* Springsteen tells Josh Tyrangiel that he sometimes feels like a rock and roll preacher when he's onstage, complete with the fire-and-brimstone sermon and call-and-response monologue. "It was one of those things that was joking but serious at the same time. I think it fits in with the concept of our band as a group of witnesses. That's one of our functions."[59]

If Springsteen is, as he has insisted scores of times during his concerts, "just a prisoner of rock and roll," then his fans are willing companions on the journey. While the frenzy that is so common at Springsteen concerts should not be confused with religion itself, it does involve the same kind of unexpressed urges and needs—a sense of belonging, shared values, a form of devotion (albeit secular), and, most important, a way of creating meaning in everyday life. Music, especially rock, writes Jefferson Cowie, can offer a "collective salvation from the isolation and loneliness of our seemingly individual struggles."[60]

Born to Run is often interpreted as a tale of desperate characters trying to escape from their desperate surroundings. But it is also a search for answers and the struggle to maintain an element of faith and hope in an increasingly angry world. Springsteen once described the album as "religiously based, in a funny kind of way. Not like orthodox religion, but it's about basic things, you know? That searchin', and faith, and the idea of hope . . . people tryin' to find some sort of consolation, some sort of comfort in each other."[61] More recently, he referred to the verses of the songs on *The Rising* as "the blues, the chorus is the gospel."[62]

There have been countless references to fans whose lives were "saved" by Springsteen and his music. "He had been a source of hope and inspiration, of friendship and . . . exhilaration," writes Eric Alterman in *It Ain't No Sin to Be Glad You're Alive.* After attending a Springsteen concert at Madison Square Garden, he admits, "This was not just music anymore. It was something bigger, more powerful, more . . . like religion."[63]

Cowie, though, sees something else going on. "There is," he writes, "a solidarity in the individual," and in Springsteen's lyrics a "perhaps uniquely American struggle to make one's way in an often mean world. It is an odd solidarity in that one is not alone: that when the house lights go up, there are thousands of others singing the same lyrics and asking the same questions.

"The travails of Springsteen's characters may not offer any real solutions to concrete problems of working people, but they paint a portrait of alienation and a sensitivity to class not seen in popular culture since the passing of the elder Hank Williams."[64]

And yet, in 1988, Springsteen came to a personal and professional fork in the proverbial road when he realized that music wasn't enough anymore. "I guess I used to think that rock could save you. . . . I don't believe it can anymore. It can do a lot. It's certainly done a lot for me—gave me focus and direction and energy and purpose. . . . But as you get older, you realize that it is not enough. Music alone—you can take some shelter there, and you can find some comfort and happiness . . . but you can't hide in it. . . . You can use all your powers to isolate yourself, to surround yourself with luxury, to intoxicate yourself in any particular fashion that you so desire. But it just starts eating away inside, because there is something you get from engagement with people, from a connection with a person, that you cannot get anyplace else."[65]

Brother Bruce's expansive universe is big enough to hold anyone who wants to join him: white and black, male and female, young and old, employer and employee, the rich and the poor, the native and the immigrant, saints and sinners. In his lyrics, in his music, in his world, we are all somehow connected—if only by the link of our common humanity. And to Springsteen, that is apparently enough.

The Working Life

Springsteen, the lapsed Catholic, has taken the Protestant work ethic to dizzying heights. He has frequently referred to what he does as a job. He puts on his work clothes—faded jeans, flannel shirt, cowboy boots—and he goes to work. His songs are steeped in class-consciousness. But even from the Dylanesque beginnings, they had powerful political undercurrents. The runaway American dream of *Born to Run* often led to the soured American dreams of later albums.

"Without question," write Michael R. Hemphill and Larry David Smith, "Springsteen's version of the American Dream was distinct from that of most middle-class Americans. These characters never envisioned a college diploma that would lead to a job in corporate America."[66]

And yet Springsteen suggested that all was not lost. Even when he was surrounded by utter darkness and despair, his songs offered hope.

A large part of that hope, that self-effacing groundedness, came no doubt from his humble background. To most eyes, he seemed a solid figure, without pretenses. "Springsteen's appeal," writes Kevin Coyne, Freehold's town historian, "has always rested on his Everyman qualities. . . . Springsteen seemed . . . to rise up from among us, a concentrated, pluperfect, ideal version of ourselves."[67]

"I always saw myself as a nuts-and-bolts kind of person," he told Mikal Gilmore. "I felt what I was going to accomplish I would accomplish over a long period of time. . . . To keep an even perspective on it all, I looked at it *like* a job—something that you do every day and over a long period of time. . . . My idea was that when I went on a stage, I wanted to deliver my best to pull out the best in *you*, whatever that may be."[68]

During a monologue in Stockholm in 1981, Springsteen recalled growing up in Freehold: "I grew up in this little town," he told the crowd. "As I got older, I started looking around me, and it didn't seem there was any way I was going to get out of there. I looked back at my father, and the only time he got out of that town was to go to World War II. When he came out of the Army, he got married, settled down, and went to work in a plastics factory. And his father had done the same thing. It seemed that the one thing we had in common was that we didn't have enough information; we didn't have enough knowledge about the forces that were controlling our lives. I watched my old man end up a victim, and he didn't even know it. . . ."[69]

For the last thirty or so years, Springsteen, the community college dropout, has been on the lookout for fresh ideas, for new twists to old theories. He finds transcendence in mundane, everyday events. Jim Cullen has called him "a direct inheritor" of the republican artistic tradition, whose visionary forebears included Walt Whitman and Ralph Waldo Emerson—admittedly heady company—and further back to Stephen Foster, "whose songs about everyday life won him enormous popularity in the years preceding and following the Civil War."[70]

Springsteen has always been interested in continuity and about connecting at some fundamentally profound level with an imagined community—the community that comprises his audience. But more than this, he wanted to create music—a body of work—that would last. He told a *Minneapolis Star-Tribune* reporter, "When I started, I wanted to document what it felt like to grow up in America during the time that I was growing up in. And I wanted to follow those characters, not just when they were teenagers or in their twenties, but into the middle parts of their lives, into their forties and on. The idea was to draw my own map and maybe help other people draw their maps."[71]

At the end of the day, what is left behind is important to Springsteen.

"It's about work—the work, working, *working,*" he told Ken Tucker. "Write that next song and put that next record out; speak to my audience and continue to have that conversation that's been going on for so long."[72]

The Promise

I think people listen to my music to find out about themselves.
—Bruce Springsteen, November 1992

Fame and the trappings of celebrity have dogged Springsteen for decades. Unlike others before and since, Springsteen has seemed to be able to take it all in stride. Poet David Wojahn has called rock "an allegory for the consequences of fame and power, stories for which there are very few happy endings."[73] By all accounts, Springsteen has proven to be the exception. Another poet, Peter Balakian, comments, "In its totality, American rock might be viewed as one long, never-to-be-finished American epic poem."[74] In a very real sense, Springsteen's body of work can also be viewed that way, as an ongoing exploration, via popular song, of the very heart of the American psyche.

Rock and roll gave Springsteen a purpose. "It really gave me a sense of myself, and it allowed me to become useful, which I think most people want to be."[75] It was a pathway to respect, a defiant retort to the oblivion of anonymity. Ironically, it was Springsteen's way of *fitting in.* For him, rock offered the best of both worlds. Naturally reserved (at least offstage), he could maintain the image of the loner, the outsider, and still connect. Onstage, with a guitar in his hands, he had everything. He was somebody.

Or, as a former high school classmate once remarked, "If he hadn't turned out to be Bruce Springsteen, would I remember him? I can't think of why I would. You have to remember, without a guitar in his hands, he had absolutely nothing to say."[76]

Things have changed considerably since then. He has not only forever altered the lives of countless people throughout the world, he has offered hope, inspiration, and more than a little magic in the rock and roll night. He has been called the last of rock's great innocents. Probably so. He is also the rock star with the undeniably human touch.

Notes

1. Quoted in John Rockwell, "New Dylan from New Jersey?," *Rolling Stone*, October 9, 1975.
2. Neil Strauss, "The Springsteen Interview," *Guitar World*, October 1995.
3. Michael Newall, "Between What's Flesh and What's Fantasy," *Backstreets*, Summer 2000.
4. Josh Tyrangiel, "Bruce Rising: An Intimate Look at How Springsteen Turned 9/11 into a Message of Hope," *Time*, August 5, 2002.
5. Bono, induction dinner, Rock and Roll Hall of Fame, Waldorf-Astoria Hotel, New York City, March 15, 1999.
6. Bill Flanagan, "Ambition, Lies, and the Beautiful Reward: Bruce Springsteen's Family Values," *Musician*, November 1992.
7. Dave Marsh, *Glory Days: Bruce Springsteen in the 1980s* (New York: Pantheon, 1987), pp. 30–31.
8. Bruce Springsteen, induction dinner, Rock and Roll Hall of Fame, Waldorf-Astoria Hotel, New York City, March 15, 1999.
9. Quoted in Dave Marsh, *Born to Run: The Bruce Springsteen Story* (New York: Dell, 1981), p. 29.
10. Mark Hagen, "Interview," *MOJO*, January 1999.
11. Ibid.
12. Bruce Springsteen, *Songs* (New York: Avon, 1998), p. 6.
13. Hagen, "Interview."
14. Springsteen, *Songs*, p. 7.
15. Lester Bangs, "'Greetings from Asbury Park, N.J.' Album Review," in *Bruce Springsteen: The Rolling Stone Files: The Ultimate Compendium of Interviews, Articles, Facts and Opinions from the Files of Rolling Stone*. Edited by Parke Puterbaugh (New York: Hyperion, 1996), p. 33.
16. Hagen, "Interview."
17. Springsteen, *Songs*, p. 25.
18. Jon Landau, "Growing Young with Rock and Roll," *The Real Paper*, May 22, 1974. According to Christopher Sandford, English rock critic Richard Williams penned a rave review of *Greetings* in *Melody Maker* a year or so before Landau's more famous review. He even referred to Springsteen as the "future of rock and roll." See Christopher Sandford, *Springsteen: Point Blank* (New York: Da Capo Press, 1999), pp. 66, 85.
19. Springsteen, *Songs*, p. 46.
20. Robert Duncan, "Bruce Springsteen Is Not God (and Doesn't Want to Be)," *CREEM*, January 1976.
21. Greil Marcus, "Springsteen's Thousand and One American Nights," *Rolling Stone*, October 9, 1975.

22. Eric Alterman, *It Ain't No Sin to Be Glad You're Alive: The Promise of Bruce Springsteen* (Boston: Little, Brown, 1999), p. 74.

23. Paul Nelson, "The Year's Ten Best Albums," *The Real Paper*, December 17, 1975. See also Nelson's "Is Springsteen Worth the Hype?," *Village Voice*, August 25, 1975.

24. For Mike Appel's side of the story, see the lengthy piece published in *Backstreets* in November 1990, "Mike Appel: Interview by Charles R. Cross." In *Backstreets: Springsteen—The Man and His Music*, by Charles R. Cross and the editors of *Backstreets* magazine (New York: Crown, 1992).

25. Springsteen, *Songs*, p. 66.

26. Hagen, "Interview."

27. Flanagan, "Ambition, Lies."

28. Hagen, "Interview."

29. Ibid.

30. Quoted in Alterman, *It Ain't No Sin*, p. 101.

31. Stephen Holden, "Springsteen Scans the American Dream," *New York Times*, May 27, 1984.

32. Ibid.

33. Hagan, "Interview."

34. Springsteen, *Songs*, pp. 138–39.

35. Hagen, "Interview."

36. James Henke, "Bruce Springsteen: The Rolling Stone Interview," *Rolling Stone*, August 6, 1992.

37. Marsh, *Glory Days*, p. 102.

38. Quoted in Alterman, *It Ain't No Sin*, p. 138.

39. Steve Pond, "*Nebraska* Album Review: Springsteen Delivers His Bravest Record Yet," *Rolling Stone*, October 28, 1982.

40. Quoted in Alterman, *It Ain't No Sin*, p. 150.

41. Ibid., p. 185.

42. Quoted in Larry David Smith, *Bob Dylan, Bruce Springsteen, and American Song* (Westport, Conn.: Praeger, 2002), p. 181.

43. Springsteen, *Songs*, p. 216.

44. Ibid., p. 276.

45. Hagen, "Interview."

46. William Leach, *Country of Exiles: The Destruction of Place in American Life* (New York: Vintage Books/Random House, 1999), p. 13.

47. Lewis Lapham, "Who and What Is an American?," *Harper's*, January 1992.

48. Hagen, "Interview."

49. Quoted in Alterman, *It Ain't No Sin*, p. 176.

50. Marsh, *Glory Days*, p. 98. *Caril* was cowritten by Ninette Beaver, B. K. Ripley, and Patrick Trese (New York: Lippincott, 1974). There have been other books written on the subject. See also William Allen, *Starkweather: The Story of a Mass Murderer* (Boston: Houghton Mifflin, 1976). Charles Starkweather was executed in 1959; Caril Fugate served an eighteen-year prison sentence and was paroled in 1976.

51. Hagen, "Interview."
52. Smith, *Bob Dylan, Bruce Springsteen,* p. 217.
53. Ibid., p. 218.
54. Ibid., p. 145.
55. Cornel Bonca, "Save Me Somebody: Bruce Springsteen's Rock 'n' Roll Covenant." KillingtheBuddha.com, 2001.
56. Marsh, *Glory Days,* p. 17.
57. Steve Pond, "*Tunnel of Love* Album Review: Bruce's Hard Look at Love," *Rolling Stone,* December 3, 1987.
58. Henke, "The Rolling Stone Interview."
59. Tyrangiel, "Bruce Rising."
60. Jefferson Cowie, "Fandom, Faith, and Bruce Springsteen," *Dissent,* Winter 2001.
61. Quoted in Smith, *Bob Dylan, Bruce Springsteen,* p. 149.
62. Jon Pareles, "His Kind of Heroes, His Kind of Songs," *New York Times,* July 14, 2002.
63. Alterman, *It Ain't No Sin,* p. 4.
64. Cowie, *"Fandom, Faith."*
65. Quoted in Smith, *Bob Dylan, Bruce Springstein,* p. 151.
66. Michael R. Hemphill and Larry David Smith, "The Working American's Elegy: The Rhetoric of Bruce Springsteen," in *Politics in Familiar Contexts.* Edited by Robert L. Savage and Dan Nimmo (Norwood, N.J.: Ablex, 1990).
67. Kevin Coyne, "The Faulkner of Freehold," *Asbury Park Press/Home News Tribune,* March 14, 1999.
68. Mikal Gilmore, "Twentieth Anniversary Special: Bruce Springsteen Q&A," *Rolling Stone,* November 5–December 10, 1987.
69. Smith, *Bob Dylan, Bruce Springsteen,* pp. 135–36.
70. Jim Cullen, *Born in the U.S.A.: Bruce Springsteen and the American Tradition* (New York: HarperCollins, 1996), p. 30.
71. Quoted in Smith, *Bob Dylan, Bruce Springsteen,* p. 148.
72. Ken Tucker, "Springsteen: The Interview," *Entertainment Weekly,* February 28, 2003.
73. Quoted in Jim Elledge, ed., *Sweet Nothings: An Anthology of Rock and Roll in American Poetry* (Bloomington, Ind.: Indiana University Press, 1994), p. 267.
74. In Elledge, *Sweet Nothings,* p. 235.
75. Marsh, *Glory Days,* p. 90.
76. Alterman, *It Ain't No Sin,* p. 16.

Part One

■

GROWIN' UP

Bruce Springsteen arrived on the musical scene like a cyclone on the Jersey Shore. Touted as a latter-day Bob Dylan, he somehow managed to live up to the hype. After all, it's not every twenty-something rocker who graces the covers of both Newsweek and Time in the same week. But it didn't take terribly long for jaded music critics and hopeful rock fans alike to realize that they had come across the real thing.

This section begins with Peter Knobler and Greg Mitchell's "Who Is Bruce Springsteen and Why Are We Saying All These Wonderful Things About Him?," which ran in the March 1973 issue of Crawdaddy! and is considered the first major article written about the Jersey rocker. Here too are classic pieces by Dave Marsh, John Rockwell, and Lester Bangs.

Genuine superstar or throwaway hipster for the disposable generation? Legendary producer John Hammond, who is credited with "discovering" Springsteen, originally thought of him as more along the lines of a folk singer—as it turns out, a perceptive and prophetic assessment. But even in the early days of his fledgling career, Springsteen wore many faces: both cocky rocker and sensitive street poet, rock and roll messiah and throwback to an earlier, presumably more innocent, musical era, the outsider who roamed the city streets and back roads of America at night and the quintessential romantic in search of someone to call his own. He was tough and sweet, articulate and tongue-tied, defiant and confused.

By the end of the 1970s, Springsteen had already proven that he was here to stay.

Peter Knobler,
with Greg Mitchell

■

Crawdaddy!, the first music fanzine and the first rock magazine in the United States, was founded in 1966 by Paul Williams at Swarthmore College, and named in honor of the Crawdaddy Club in London, an early hangout of the Yardbirds and the Rolling Stones. Peter Knobler and Greg Mitchell served as editors from 1971 to 1979. In *Very Seventies: A Cultural History of the 1970s,* from which the following article is taken, Knobler and Mitchell contend that they transformed *Crawdaddy!* from "a hippie-style . . . biweekly tabloid" to a "general-interest, generational magazine, with rock and roll still at its core." The Springsteen piece that appears here originally ran in the March 1973 issue of the magazine and is reportedly the first major article written about the Jersey rocker. Although Springsteen was still an unknown commodity at the time, Knobler and Mitchell chose to devote ten pages of the magazine to him and his performance at Kenny's Castaways in New York City, "despite the fact that no one ever heard of him." As we soon learn, barely thirty people were in the audience that night, but they were in for an unexpected treat. Springsteen, then twenty-three, comes across as intense, passionate, and likable, who comes fully alive only when a guitar is strapped to his shoulder. He also can't believe his good luck.

Who Is Bruce Springsteen and Why Are We Saying All These Wonderful Things about Him?

Crawdaddy!

We first heard Springsteen in Sing Sing prison. It was in late 1972. Bruce had recorded his first album but it hadn't yet been released, and his manager saw a gig at Sing Sing as a great publicity gimmick. He said this kid was a combination of Bob Dylan, Chuck Berry, and Shakespeare, so we figured, hey, what's to lose? (We were always suckers for a "new Dylan" and the riot at Attica[1] was fresh in the mind.) Turns out we were the only editors in New York who bit. Bruce and the band played in the prison chapel. The sound system stunk. In the middle of an R&B song, a short, squat, bald black guy with bunched muscles came rumbling down the aisle like the law was still after him. He got past the guard, hit the stage at a gallop, reached into his shirt, and pulled out . . . an alto sax! And he was great! There was a roar that could start engines and bend steel. Then, silence. Like the oxygen was cut off. Like cyanide. The inmate finished the number and returned to his seat. A few guys patted him on the ass. Bruce approached the mike and said, "When this is over you can all go home!" What follows is the first article ever written about the future Boss.

■TWO MONTHS AGO I was living under a sorry illusion. Jaded, sick to death of imitations and nostalgia, I figured rock and roll had priced itself out of its own salvation. Artists & Repertoire men were combing the coffeehouses and cellars of the country like major league scouts, offering bonus baby bribes to anyone within four octaves of the big time. No one, my reasoning went, could possibly mature *before* being discovered and *absolutely* no one could ignore his own hype and do it afterwards. There were no transcendent phenoms coming out of hideaway woodsheds.

It turns out I was wrong.

Bruce Springsteen (double *e*; it's originally a Dutch name) has been hiding in New Jersey writing these incredible songs. He's twenty-three, has spent the last eight or nine years playing in rock and roll bands, and sings with a freshness and urgency I haven't heard since I was rocked by "Like a Rolling Stone." His phrasing is as weird, laconic, and twisted as his words, borrowing liberally from acknowledged masters Dylan, Van Morrison, and The Band. He wears his influences on his sleeve—he can be easily dismissed as "just another Dylan rip-off" if you're not really listening—but increasingly, as he begins a road he knows has done in fellow travelers, he is his own man.

Springsteen tosses words around like marrow in a meat shop, and if that weren't enough he presides over a band that jolts out his music like anti-aircraft. Let me explain:

It was just a normal Friday night December crowd at New York's Kenny's Castaways. There was no air of great tension, no scent of earth-shaking significance about to be loosed. In fact, there were only about thirty people there to see the first show and most of them only came for the atmosphere. Bruce Springsteen was headlining and there weren't a dozen people inside who knew who he was. Outside, on the hand-drawn marquee, they'd misspelled his name.

He arrived onstage in jeans and a beat-up hooded sweatshirt, adjusted the mike to his acoustic guitar, dropped a flat pick, bent to retrieve it, stood up, strummed a bit, and asked out over the audience's head to one friend at the back, "How long have I been up here?" Hardly an auspicious opening.

But when he began to sing it was like the ocean had calmed out and you knew a storm was brewing by the way it prickled your skin.

"Circus boy dances like a monkey on barbed wire," he sang. *"The barker romances with a junkie, she's got a flat tire."*

His voice growled lines after they'd been sung, making them sinister, mysterious, and somehow necessary. . . .

Phrases, images, and sounds flew by. Lines were fleeting; you got glimpses of them where full stares, gapes were required. They passed once—these were completely new songs—and left their mark.

His eyebrows rose and shifted like waves with each line. His hair, cut short, curled vaguely and his beard was hardly filled in. No doubt about it, he looked like Dylan. If the passion hadn't been so genuine, this might have been a problem. He moved from a howl to a whisper in an instant and caught the crowd unawares. His voice made words into sounds, and then reconverted sounds to sense. He gulped and spat syllables, and the song ended like a tide receding, the applause chasing after like beach rain.

Bruce Springsteen's songs offer that wonderfully bewildering problem of how to keep up. Words tumble over one another, phrases mysteriously *feel* right and then disappear. There was no way, sitting there without warning in the middle of the wash, that I could even begin to define what his power was. This was an entirely new perspective offered, like nothing I'd heard before. There was no given, no center I knew all these spokes were connected to. I was once again on my own with new eyes, and it was exhilarating!

A song ended, but not for Springsteen. The stage was cluttered with equipment, and while Bruce switched the guitar mike to the piano stand he absently hummed a verse he had just sung, like a carpenter amusing himself while sawing. The tune had not finished its moment with him and he just kept humming.

When he's playing alone, Springsteen carries himself onstage with a rather humorous reserve. He'll say what he's thinking ("Got to get these wires out off the keyboard," or "How do those words go?") and talk to the crowd like acquaintances. Not quite friends, but beyond strangers.

He is easily amused, listens to his own words, and even laughs or smiles at a good line. His material was, and continues to be, so new that he seemed to be hearing much of it for the first time. I'd never seen a performer more in touch with his songs.

> *"In how many wasted have I seen the sign*
> *'Hollywood or Bust'*
> *Or, left to ride those ever-ghostly Arizona gusts . . ."*

He had stilled the place.
"All right, let's bring up the band!"
Stepping out of the calm, he clapped his hands together and rubbed his palms like a greedy coach at game time. Out of the crowd stepped four guys, and as they took the half-step onto the stage, he took attendance, strapped on a wood Fender cutaway, and diddled some impatient, cut-crystal blues riffs.

The band consisted of bass, drums, organ, and sax, and as they casually tuned there was a different air to Springsteen's presence. Where he had bent over his acoustic guitar he leaned back from his electric. It was slung low and hung from his shoulder as from a gunslinger's hip. There was a measure of comfort, almost a psychic opulence, to the way he found his form. He was digging it, and he got cockier for its power.

The band slammed into the song like downfield blockers and what had seemed at first a "folk" night burst into flaming rock and roll.

> *"Madman drummers bummers and Indians in the summer*
> *with a teenage diplomat . . ."*

Springsteen's eyebrows arched again, this time from force as he leaned up and into the microphone, placed only a little too high. A shoulder up to the band and another to the audience, Springsteen tipped the music toward the crowd and it poured in a torrent. It was hard to believe he was that good; but that, it turned out, was just for starters.

His voice flew between Van Morrison and Dylan, but imitation was out of the question. There was influence all right—undenied and rather unconcealed—but the tone was coming out Springsteen.

The song built, words thick and fast but now even more difficult to pin down above the roar of the electricity. It was catch as catch can, and the odd catch was a prize. I hadn't felt this kind of intelligent/lunatic intensity since *Blonde on Blonde.* The thought immediately made me self-conscious, but the more I thought about it the more I liked it. Then I started to grin. I went home beaming.

I woke up the next morning and snatches of song hung from me as if by static electricity. I hummed phrases I didn't know I knew, riffs that seemed like they'd always been there. You know the kid is good when you wake up and you're singing his songs—and you've only heard them once!

Where did he come from? Where has he been?

He was signed to Columbia Records by John Hammond Sr., noted for a similar decision ten years ago; Columbia president Clive Davis called to wish him a Merry Christmas; he hasn't got a decent record player; and he is still flattered that people like his stuff.

Bruce Springsteen was brought up Catholic in Freehold, New Jersey. (His songs show the influence of parochial school and a sinner's familiarity with the Church.) He first picked up the guitar at age nine. "I saw Elvis Presley on TV and knew that that, for me, was where it was at. I went down, got a guitar, started taking guitar lessons. But my hand was too small to get into it. Plus, guitar lessons at that time were like a coma, buzzing on the B string. I *knew* that wasn't the way Elvis Presley did it."

We sat in Bruce's newly rented apartment ("the first one of my own") in Bradley Beach, New Jersey. The place had the disheveled lived-in look of a million off-campus spots, but it was home and, for Bruce, almost the first luxury. His phonograph was a Longines Symphonette, the kind you get free from record clubs.

"Nothing hit me until I was about fourteen," Bruce said. "And when it did, it hit me completely, took over my whole life. Everything from then on revolved around music. Everything."

From the time he learned to play, Bruce has been in one band or another. At sixteen he was commuting to Greenwich Village nightly to play guitar at the Cafe Wha? "I was *ready,*" he laughed. "It's like when you're a kid. . . ." He stopped and added, "Well, I'm still a kid, but when you're younger, you know, you've got this incredible idealistic enthusiasm. And I was always popular in my little area, and at the time it was something I needed very badly, because I didn't have anything else. So I wanted to be as big as you could make it—the Beatles, Rolling Stones. I went to New York and I learned earlier than most people you had to write your own material."

With a six-month background in folk music and an overriding interest in R&B, he spent most of the next eight years putting bands together. He fronted a group called Steel Mill ("a Humble Pie–type band") and got fairly popular for a while, and fairly well paid. He has clippings of him with shoulder-length hair screaming like a maniac on a rave-up.

Steel Mill lasted a couple of years, "when I was eighteen–nineteen. Then came Dr. Zoom and the Sonic Boom where we had everybody I knew that could play an instrument . . . and some that couldn't!" The sax player, for instance, served essentially as a percussionist, and they set up a Monopoly board on a table in the middle of the stage for no apparent reason.

"That lasted two or three gigs. Then there was the big band, which was my band," the first he alone put together. He speaks of it rather proudly, if incredulously. "I gave it my name. A ten-piece band when I was around twenty." Vini Lopez and Danny Federici, who now play drums and organ respectively for him, were also in the ten-piece. "That one lasted for about two years, then it slowly dwindled from ten to seven to five. Then, about a year ago, I started to play by myself." He was pretty well broke. His parents had moved to the West Coast when he was seventeen, and he'd been evicted from the house he'd grown up in a month later. Living in a surfboard factory, he got good and depressed and "just started writing lyrics, which I never did before. I would just get a good riff, and as long as it wasn't too obtuse I'd sing it. So I started to go by myself and started to write those songs."

A friend introduced Bruce to Mike Appel and Jim Cretecos, whose claim to fame to that point had been responsibility for writing the Partridge Family's million-seller, "Doesn't Somebody Want to Be Wanted," among others. Appel and Cretecos were astounded, and encouraged Springsteen to write more. He did. Sometimes he finished three songs a week.

"Last winter I wrote like a madman. Put it out. Had no money, nowhere to go, nothing to do. Didn't know too many people. It was cold and I wrote a lot. And I got to feeling very guilty if I didn't," he explained. "Terrible guilt feelings. Like it was masturbation." He laughed a liberated Catholic school laugh. "That bad!"

Appel and Cretecos gave him New York transfusions of encouragement and it worked. Three weeks after he signed to be managed by them he was in John Hammond's office.

Mike Appel is what you might call a fast talker. In one breath he can and has compared Bruce Springsteen to Wordsworth, Dylan, Keats, Byron, and Shakespeare. On the other hand, he knows how to get through doors.

John Hammond's office is a five-by-ten-foot cubicle on the eleventh floor of the CBS building. It is cluttered and jumbled and as good as you can do to unconsciously disrupt the well-documented aridity of a corporate spread. A stand-up piano is tucked into one corner, a tape deck in another.

Hammond himself is a friendly man with an enthusiasm for Springsteen that, when I entered, was both unleashed and infectious.

"He walked into my office," he recalled. "He was *led* into my office! My secretary made the appointment. She said, 'I think you might do this—he came on very strong.' Mike Appel, the note said; I said okay, I have fifteen minutes.

"Bruce, who looked marvelously beat, was sitting over there." Hammond gestured to a chair tucked away in the far corner. "And so Mike started yakking. He said, 'I want you to know that we're just, you know, being nice to you because you're the guy who discovered Dylan and we just wanted to find out if that was luck or whether you really have ears.'

"So I said, 'Stop, you're making me hate you!'" He laughed incredulously. "Bruce was very quiet, sort of grinning over there in the corner. He told me he played both guitar and piano, and I said, well, you want to get your guitar out? He said, sure. And he started. I think the first song he played was 'Saint in the City.' And I. . . ." He recreated his wonder. "You know, I couldn't believe it!

"So then I started to talk. I said to him, have you ever worked as a single? He said no. Well, two hours later, by this time it was a little after one, I had set up a performance for him at the Gaslight. By this time he'd played some more songs, and I was just convinced that he really *was*. . . . Just 'cause he was so unassuming and so right. Everything he did.

"I ran and got some other people down the hall here and they all kinda liked him. The initial reaction was, well he looks so much like Dylan, he's a copy of him. But he's not. I mean not even remotely. You see, when Bobby came to me, he was Bobby Zimmerman. He said he was Bob Dylan; he had created all this mystique. Bruce is Bruce Springsteen. And he's much further along, much more developed than Bobby was when he came to me.

"So I went straight to Clive on this. You know, I've brought in a few stiffs as well as some good people to Columbia. Well, Clive just had to check around a bit," he chuckled, remembering the scene, "but Clive loved what he heard on the tape. He said, 'You know, John, he's very amusing, isn't he?' 'Yeah,' I said. 'He's more than that, Clive,' I said. 'He's fantastic!'"

Bruce Springsteen's record is *Greetings from Asbury Park,* and it's a delight. Completed last September, it offers a picture of the performer/ creator as he was stepping out of one sense into another.

"It's definitely a first album," says Bruce. "And it shows how the band came into being; there's some by myself, then there's some with a small band, and there's some which is pretty much where the band is now, which is 'Spirit in the Night' and 'Blinded by the Light.'"

The album takes its toll on your time. One day one song reigns, demanding attention like the brightest kid in class; the next day, another. There hasn't been an album like this in ages, where there are words to play with, to riff off yourself, to pull out of the air and slap down with a gleam on the shiny counter of your conversation. There are individual lines worth entire records. The record rocks, then glides, then rocks again. There is the combined sensibility of the chaser and the chaste, the street punk and the bookworm.

It is not perfect, of course. Springsteen was originally signed as an acoustic act, a folksinger ("I told them I'd been playing in bands for eight years and by myself for two–three months. They forgot about the eight years and went with the two months.") The album, as a result, was originally planned as basically acoustic. Bruce plays excellent electric guitar, but nobody knew that until the sessions were almost complete, and the record loses some power for it. Bruce's vocals are quirkier now too, as his style has developed. The production is a bit muddy and leaves something to be desired, and by the time the sessions were almost finished Bruce had written a dozen new songs and grown beyond some of the old ones.

The band is plenty turned up now. Garry Tallent was added on bass and Clarence Clemons on sax, and the group fairly steams with fresh energy. They are tight and growing tighter.

At Kenny's Castaways, at The Main Point coffeehouse near Philadelphia, in rehearsal in an old, unheated garage, we heard Bruce play more than two dozen songs, only six of which were on his album (the record has nine in all). The *next* album should be unbelievable! "That's why I like the band," Bruce said with pleasure. "We get into those great funky riffs, that Gary U.S. Bonds stuff that is lost forever in the annals of time." He snickered at his radio diction. "You can get into that groove, get it *there,* and sing weird words to it too!"

Bruce Springsteen laughs easily. He's like the new boy in town and seems genuinely unaware of the temptation to treat him like a Man of Importance, perhaps because that's not the way he sees himself. He's writing continuously. Two days before I visited a rehearsal, he'd cooked up "Kitty's Back," a song with claws. He finished an epic South of the Border number *between sets* at a club one night. He is like a man undimmed: prolific and unpolluted. At twenty-three he stands perceptively between childhood and worldly wisdom. "This is the songwriter-poet as innocent," he announced before one song; "And now the songwriterpoet as pervert" before another. Both times it got a laugh.

"I'm at a place now where I'm flattered." The kitchen table had been cleared after dinner and he sat picking his new guitar (one of the few uses to which he's put his advance money). "I'm flattered and I'm happy that people would take an interest, you know? You have to watch out, though. You don't want to get too self-centered. It's easy to do, you know, because people are always shovin' *you* in your face."

But it's only just begun for him. He'd never been interviewed before, the openness a delight.

"My songs are very mysterious to me, in a way. It's good if I can look back on a song and be excited by it, then I know it's good. You know when you've written a good song, too, because it's there in your room, before you even go into the living room and sing it there. Right there when you finish it, you know, then it's a good song, then it excites you.

"Like that line in 'Spirit of the Night'. . . ." He skimmed verbally through the tune as if scanning it looking for a spot. "'. . . take you all out to gypsy angel row. . . . They're built like light.' It's like that, you know. 'They're built like light and dance like spirits in the night.' That's what it is to me, that's the essence of all the songs to me. Built like light, to be run through. . . ."

He had stopped picking, and he looked up and smiled. "It's exciting to me! It's very weird, you know. I'm happy and the music is exciting to me." He looked for an explanation, his eyes glazing over for a moment. "It's like I'll write a song and I'll think back on some of the lines, and they get me off!" He was so pleased a grin almost shone. "As an observer, you know.

"'Cause in my mind, my mind was thinking, 'Hmmm, need something to rhyme with night, need something to rhyme with . . . all night.' And it works like that; it focuses it in. 'Well, you got the universe to think about but you need something that rhymes with night!'" We exploded with laughter and he chortled, "So that narrows it down a bit, and out it'll come. And that's how I write!"

"You're going to get confronted with the Dylan image sooner or later," I said. "How can you deal with that?"

"I don't know," he answered. He's already been tagged a "new Dylan" and it's an uncomfortable harness. "I don't like it and it's hard to live with," he said. "I mean, I resent it when *I* hear it about anyone.

"I love Dylan!" he laughed. "What can you say? I think Dylan is great. I listen to all his records.[2] It's *the* greatest music ever written, to me. The man says it all, exactly the right way. Incredibly powerful. You don't get no more intense. Such a great instrumental sound. And he was . . .." He searched for an exact description. "He was Bob Dylan, you know?

"But it's like a map. You gotta read a map. You just can't go off in the middle of the woods and go off in the right direction. You don't, so you've gotta look. You've gotta say, I dig the way this cat's doing it; I want to do it like that, but . . ." He glided his hand on an arc to the left, ". . . like this.

"I go onstage and feel myself. And I'm not worrying about, 'Oh, man, that note sounds like this dude. Hey man, I heard that word off of "Subterranean Homesick Blues"!'" He laughed and shook his head. "At one time it worried me but it doesn't anymore, because when I get onstage finally I feel myself. That's who I am."

"Your vocal style changes from acoustic to electric sets," I mentioned. In fact, when he's alone with his guitar he is at once supple and bristly. It has the effect of soothing by scraping, leaving a rough edge smoothed.

"I got a thing which is like percussion-on-voice." He punctuated the words and we laughed at the demonstration. "It's a different style of singing than with the band; it's based on little voice cracks and little, like, percussion things. For instance:

> *"Oh, when the night grew fear*
> *and the jungle grew near*
> *It was so dark I couldn't talk at all . . ."*

He laughed at the phrasing. "It's an Adam's apple trip," he chuckled.

Bruce Springsteen doesn't know how good he is. People are only just now beginning to tell him. Clive Davis called to wish him a Merry Christmas and he didn't know that was unheard of. People continue to be floored when they see him play and he still says "Really?" That can't last. But he's writing prolifically, as if there's no other way. It's an exciting thing to see happen. Even his mother is having a hard time believing it.

"I called her and told her, 'Hey I signed a record contract!'

"'Oh yeah?' she said. 'What did you change your name to?'"

Notes

1. The Attica prison riot began on September 9, 1971, at the Attica Correctional Facility in upstate New York. When it ended four days later, eleven correctional officers and thirty-two inmates were dead. With the exception of Officer William Quinn, who died from injuries inflicted by the inmates, all fatalities resulted when nearly two hundred New York State police officers stormed the prison.
2. On January 20, 1988, in New York City, Springsteen introduced Bob Dylan when Dylan was inducted into the Rock and Roll Hall of Fame. He recalled, "The first time I heard Bob Dylan, I was in the car with my mother listening to WMCA and on came that snare shot that sounded like somebody'd kicked open the door to your mind: 'Like a rolling stone.' My mother—she was no stiff with rock 'n' roll, she liked the music—sat there for a minute, then looked at me and said, 'That guy can't sing.' But I knew she was wrong. . . ." He continued, "When I was a kid, Bob's voice somehow thrilled and scared me, it made me feel kind of irresponsibly innocent—it still does—when it reached down and touched what little worldliness a fifteen-year-old high-school kid in New Jersey had in him at the time. Dylan was a revolutionary. Bob freed your mind the way Elvis freed your body. He showed us that just because the music was innately physical did not mean that it was anti-intellectual. He had the vision and the talent to make a pop song that contained the whole world. He invented a new way a pop singer could sound, broke through the limitations of what a recording artist could achieve and changed the face of rock 'n' roll forever." Quoted in *The Dylan Companion,* edited by Elizabeth Thomson and David Gutman (New York: Da Capo Press, 2001), pp. 286, 287.

Paul Williams

■

The following interview by Paul Williams, the founder of *Crawdaddy!,* took place in October 1974, at Springsteen's apartment in Long Branch, New Jersey. *Crawdaddy!* was an early supporter of the then unknown Jersey rocker and some say, without its ongoing encouragement, the Boss's career would not have taken off the way it did. At the time of the interview, Springsteen was writing the lyrics to the songs that would appear on *Born to Run,* his breakthrough album.

Lost in the Flood

PAUL WILLIAMS: What Dylan influenced you musically?

BRUCE SPRINGSTEEN: In 1968 I was into *John Wesley Harding.* I never listened to anything after *John Wesley Harding.* I listened to *Bringing It All Back Home, Highway 61, Blonde on Blonde.* That's it. I never had his early albums and to this day I don't have them, and I never had his later albums. I might have heard them once, though. There was only a short period of time when I related, there was only that period when he was important to me, you know, where he was giving me what I needed. That was it.

PW: That was really true for a lot of people.

BS: Yeah, it was the big three. I never was really into him until I heard "Like a Rolling Stone" on the radio, because it was a hit. FM radio at the time was just beginning, but even if there was no FM at the time, I never had an FM radio. In 1965 I was like 15 and there were no kids 15 who were into folk music. There had been a folk boom, but it was generally a college thing. There was really no way of knowing because AM radio was really an incredible must in those days. The one thing I dug about those albums was—I dug the sound. Before I listened to what was happening in the song, you had the chorus and you had the band and it had incredible sound and that was what got me.

PW: What about the Stones?

BS: Yeah, I was into the Stones. I dug the first few Stones albums, the first three or four maybe. After that I haven't heard any of it lately except the singles, "Tumbling Dice" and stuff like that—it was great. There was *December's Children* and *Aftermath* . . .

PW: And *Between the Buttons* and . . .

BS: *Between the Buttons* was when I started to lose contact with the Stones. It was right around there.

PW: What came after *Between the Buttons*?

BS: First *Their Satanic Majesties*, then *Let It Bleed* . . . See, I never had a record player for years and years. It was a space from when my parents moved out west and I started to live by myself, from when I was 17 until I was 24, and I never had a record player. So it was like I never heard any albums that came out after, like '67. (*Laughs.*) And I was never a social person who went over to other people's houses and got loaded and listened to records—I never did that. And I didn't have an FM radio, so I never heard anything. From that time on, from around '67, until just recently when I got a record player. I lived with Diane [Rosito] and she had an old beat-up one that only old records sounded good on. So that's all I played. Those old Fats Domino records, they sounded great on it. If they were trashed, they sounded terrific. A lot of those acts lost what was important after they could really be heard—it just didn't hold. They didn't seem to be able to go further and further. They made their statement. They'd make the same statement every record, basically, without elaborating that much on it.

PW: How about the Yardbirds? Did you listen to them?

BS: Oh yeah. I listened to the Yardbirds' first two albums. And the Zombies, all those groups. And Them.

PW: That's funny for the people who talk about your Van Morrison influence, that it really came from the Them records.

BS: Yeah, that was the stuff I liked. There's some great stuff on those records. When he was doing stuff like "Out-a-Sight James Brown."

PW: But mostly your contact has been through jukeboxes and AM radio?

BS: I guess, yeah. I stopped listening to AM radio, too, because it got really trashy and I didn't have a car. I got a classic example right here (*reaches down and picks up a record*). You've got your Andy Kim records.

PW: And you've got stuff like "The Night Chicago Died." Those are the same guys who wrote "Billy, Don't Be a Hero."

BS: Oh God. If somebody shot those guys, there's not a jury in the land, there's not a jury in the land that would find them guilty. (*Laughs.*)

PW: But it was like that in the sixties prior to the Beach Boys.

BS: Yeah, a wasteland.

PW: Yeah, "Poetry in Motion." But maybe there's hope. It's all cyclical. I sometimes wonder, though, if what the record business is like these days could stop things from happening. I mean at least on the radio.

BS: Only to a certain degree. I don't want to get into specifics because I know some things that have been done to me. I don't want to sound like—I don't want to whine—but at least to a degree they can't stop you from going out there and playing every night. They can't stop you from being good if you've got it. They *can* keep it off the radio. They *can* make sure it gets little airplay, or no airplay, which, really, it hurts you.

Like look at us: we've been going for two years and the second record is at 70,000. That's nothing. That really is nothing. That's zero. It depends on who they're dealing with, who they're messing with. It depends on the person. It's like anything—some people can be stopped and other people can't be stopped. It's just like me—I can't stop. It's like once you stop, that's it—I don't know what I'd do. But it's like that, though—if you're dealing with people who say, "Ah hell, I gotta go back to hanging wallpaper," or who say, "Ah, I'm gonna go back to college and forget this stuff"—that's what people always say—"I don't know if I want to play or if I want to get married." If you have to decide, then the answer is don't do it. If you have a choice, then the answer is no. I like to use the term "the record company" because they always get painted as the bad guys. But the pressures of the business are powerless in the face of what is real.

PW: It's like what happens when they push you to make a hit single. Then you get a hit and they push you to go on the road because now you can make $10,000 a night and you might only be able to make $10 a night five years from now. It happens to a lot of people, most people. Then you get out on the road and you can't write anymore and then you can't figure out what the hell else is happening besides.

BS: What happens is there are certain realities that force you into things right now. We got a band; we got a blue bus; we got a sound man; we got an office in New York. Those are the sort of things that influence my decisions. We have to play, because if we don't, everything falls apart. We don't make any money off records. We have to go out and play every week, as much as we can. If not, nobody gets paid. In order to maintain and raise the quality of what we're doing, we gotta play all the time.

PW: At this point you're on salary?

BS: Yeah.

PW: And is that it? Does everything else go back into it?

BS: Everything else pays for the blue bus and everything else.

PW: And you got debts, I bet?

BS: Oh, we owe like a mint.

PW: Some people don't realize that the economic remuneration at this point is like working in an office.

BS: At best. Diane came in and said, "Oh, this is terrific. I just got a raise working at my newspaper job in Boston." She said, "Now I'll be getting this much." And I realized that was how much I was making. There's no money saved at all. You can't sell 80,000 records and have any money saved. Unless you're totally by yourself and you're your own manager. Then you can make a thousand dollars and stick it all in your own pocket and go home and put some in the bank. But when you're trying to do what we're trying to do, there's no way.

PW: The thing that bothers me, that you seem to have gotten around, is that there seems to be nowhere to play except big arenas, new acts or old acts.

BS: What you gotta do is, like . . . I did the Chicago tour. I did that tour because I had never played big places. And I said, "I ain't gonna say no because I don't know what they're like." So we went and played it, about 14 nights in a row. I went crazy—I went insane during that tour. It was the worst state of mind I've ever been in, I think, and just because of the playing conditions for our band. The best part of the tour was the guys in Chicago—they are great guys. They are really, really real. But I couldn't play those big places. It had nothing to do with anything, but I couldn't do it. It had nothing to do with anything that had anything to do with me, those big arenas. So I won't go to those places again. That was it. Usually we won't play anyplace over 3,000—that's the highest we want to do. We don't want to get any bigger. And that's even too big.

PW: The challenge comes when you get more popular, which is inevitable.

BS: But there's no way. I'm always disappointed in acts that go out and play those places. I don't know how the band can go out and play like that. I don't know how Joni Mitchell can do it. You can't. You can't effectively do it.

PW: But then there's the Who. They announce they're playing Madison Square Garden and it sells out in an hour. So I'd guess they'd have to book a week, a whole week.

BS: You gotta do that. And if you get that big, you gotta realize that some people who want to see you ain't gonna see you. I'm not in that position and I don't know if I'll ever be in that position. All I know is that those big coliseums ain't where it's supposed to be. There's always something else going on all over the room. You go to the back row, you can't see the stage, talk about what's on it. You see a blot of light. You better bring your binocs.

PW: I guess people go for the event.

BS: What happens is you go to those places and it turns into something else that it ain't. It becomes an event. It's hard to play. That's where everybody is playing, though. I don't know how they do it. I don't know what people expect you to do in a place like that. Especially our band— it would be impossible to reach out there the way we try to do. Forget it!

PW: Listen, I got the word from somebody in New York that you're a real sex star now.

BS: Who?

PW: Well, a girl who works at the newspaper. She's 26. I guess 26-year-old women haven't found anything for years that they could get off on.

BS: That's interesting.

PW: And like, pow, they went to your show at the Bottom Line and Schaffer and it's natural because it's all part of the thing. It was a big thrill for them.

BS: Well, we do some pretty heavy things onstage sometimes. There's lots of different currents, lots of different types of energy going on in each song, and that current is very strong. But that's interesting.

PW: I tried to get her to describe why. I made notes as she was talking over the phone. She said it's like "he knows that you know that he knows what he's doing." She said certain circles are really aware of what a joke it is because it's done really totally seriously. But she also says she'll sit there and laugh her ass off.

BS: There's so many different conflicts and tensions going on in each tune. It can affect people in totally different ways. That's what a lot of the act is based on—it's setting up certain conflicts and tensions. We're going for the moment and then, there'll be no . . . release.

PW: And you'll say, "We'll be back next time."

BS: Really. And that's the way this life is. Next, next, next, next. No matter how heavy one thing hits you, no matter how intense any experience is, there's always, like, next. And that's the way some things we do are structured, for there never to be any resolve, for there never to be any way out, or an answer, or a way in, anything! It's like a constant motion in a circle.

PW: And the two-hour sets are a manifestation of that, needing room to build?

BS: That's a lot. Right now that's the utmost amount we could ever do. It could work better than it's been. It's just a question of finding the right spot for everything, where things make more sense than other things, what's just the right place. When we were playing the Bottom Line we'd do an hour and a half. And those were long. We'd do an oldie, we'd do "Saint in the City," we'd do "Jungleland," we'd do "Kitty's Back," we'd do "New York City," we'd do "Rosalita" sometimes. We'd do like ten things. Now we're doing like . . . one . . . two . . . we're doing "Lost in the Flood," we haven't been doing that . . . we're doing that new song "She's the One" and a few other things. We're going about two hours. I think the longest we did was Avery Fisher, which was about two-twenty.

PW: Most acts will do that with an intermission.

BS: An intermission might be a smart idea just because it will set up a reference point where people can collect their thoughts. At clubs I never expect people to order alcohol because they're too tired. I know I'm pooped, I figure they're dead. There's outlets for a lot of different things in our shows, a lot of different emotions. It runs the gamut, from violence to anything. It runs through a lot of different outlets. We try to make people as close to it as they want to get.

PW: There are a couple of songs on the first album, "Growin' Up" and "For You," that are more personal.

BS: Well, we were doing "For You" for a while with the new band a few weeks ago, but there's just no time. You gotta realize there's just no time.

PW: Also, I feel the new songs have been more towards archetypes and away from . . .

BS: Yeah, to a degree. I think what happened is I'm using a slightly different language to express the same thing. The songs haven't gotten any less personal—probably just more and more.

PW: They're not as first-personal. On those songs on the first record, you identified with the singer.

BS: I find that if it gets too personal, people get too high. So you've got to use this second person. I tend to be more direct, I'm just getting down there, you know. I think it gets harder to do if you want to continue reaching out there, if you don't want to fall back and play it safe.

PW: I like "Jungleland" a lot.

BS: That's been coming along. There's a verse that's not really finished. It goes . . . there's a chorus that goes . . ."The street's alive with tough kid jets in nova light machines."

PW: "Tough kids in nova light machines"?

BS: "Boys flash guitars like bayonets, and rip holes in their jeans. The hungry and the hunted explode into rock 'n' roll bands that face off against each other in the street, down in Jungleland."

Then the band plays. And what goes next . . . uh . . . I think the next part is the slow part. It goes "beneath the city, two hearts beat, soul engines warm and tender, in a bedroom locked, silent whispers soft refusal and then surrender. In the tunnel machine, the rat chases his dreams on a forever lasting night. Till the barefoot girl brings him to bed, shakes her head and with a sigh turns out the light."

PW: Tunnel machines?

BS: Yeah. (*Sings/talks.*) "Outside the street's on fire in a real death waltz, between what's flesh and what's fantasy. The poets down here don't write nothing at all, they just sit back and let it be. In the quick of the night, they reach for their moment and try to make an honest stand. But they wind up wounded and not even dead. Tonight in Jungleland." Those are some of the words. There's a new verse and some that's not done, but that's the slow part.

PW: "In the quick of the night, they reach for their moment."

BS: Yeah, it resolves.

PW: You could call the whole album that because it fits all your songs.

BS: I thought of that. I'm thinking of titles for the next album, that was my initial thought. That's one of them.

PW: It fits. It makes sense.

BS: Yeah, but I usually change them. I work a lot on the lyrics before we record a song. I get self-conscious about them. So I change them. It's the same with a lot of the old songs. I notice them so even on some of the old songs I add new bits. There's a bit on "E Street" and that one on "New York City." It's done differently.

PW: And I like the violin.

BS: Yeah, it's great.

PW: Well, I better call a taxi.

BS: Yeah, what time is it?

John Rockwell

■

From 1974 to 1980, John Rockwell was the chief rock critic for the *New York Times.* He is also the author of two books, *All American Music: Composition in the Late Twentieth Century* (1983) and *Sinatra: An American Classic* (1984). In the following piece, which ran in the *New York Times* on August 29, 1975, Rockwell contrasts Springsteen's recording career with his live performances, and finds the former lacking, until, that is, the release of *Born to Run.* In a longer article that Rockwell wrote a month or so later in *Rolling Stone,* "New Dylan from New Jersey? It Might as Well Be Springsteen," he describes the "astonishing" way Springsteen recycles musical bits and pieces from America's musical past: "from Elvis to Dylan to the Drifters to Van Morrison to Leonard Bernstein and his *West Side Story.*"[1]

Springsteen's Rock Poetry at Its Best

New York Times

■BRUCE SPRINGSTEEN'S THIRD ALBUM, *Born to Run,* should be in the record stores about now, and it should be all he needs to push him over the top.

The trouble with Mr. Springsteen's career, as anyone who has followed rock music at all recently already knows, is that his records haven't matched the astonishing impact of his live performances.

The first record, which came out in late 1972, was called *Greetings from Asbury Park, N.J.* It's an inconsistent disk, which Mr. Springsteen attributes to the fact that Columbia Records thought of him as a conventional singer-songwriter and thus blunted the rock impact of his style. Even so, with memories of his live performances fresh in one's ears, the best songs ("Growin' Up" and "Spirit in the Night," for instance) work wonderfully well.

The second album came out a year later and was entitled *The Wild, the Innocent and the E Street Shuffle.* This is really a great record already, but it's not quite as consistently fine or as consistently rock-oriented as the third. However winning the songs sound, they really function as rough models for the fully formed versions one hears live.

❊   ❊   ❊

Born to Run gets us closer still to what Bruce Springsteen is all about. The range is as wide as either of the earlier albums, from poignancy to street-strutting cockiness to punk poetry to quasi-Broadway to surging rock anthems. But all of it (except "Meeting Across the River," which works superbly on its own terms) is solidly rock 'n' roll.

Mr. Springsteen's gifts are so powerful and so diverse that it's difficult even to try to describe them in a short space. Sometimes his lyrics still lapse too close to self-conscious mythmaking but generally they epitomize urban folk poetry at its best—overflowing with pungent detail and evocative metaphors, but never tied to their sources in a way that is binding. This is poetry that attains universality through the very sureness of its concrete imagery. And Mr. Springsteen's themes perfectly summarize the rock experience, full of cars and love, street macho and desperate aspiration. Hearing these songs is like hearing your own life in music, even if you never lived in New Jersey or made love under the boardwalk in Asbury Park.

In the first album the music seemed secondary to the words, but in retrospect that seems largely a matter of production. Mr. Springsteen's music is both a compendium of rock influences and absolutely personal. He uses lots of inexorably building repetition, and that was what sounded a little bland on the first album. But properly mixed, as the second and third albums have been, the repetition becomes overwhelming.

And the tunes, the hoarse, fervent singing, the arrangements and their instrumental execution and above all the sheer feeling for what rock is about simply pour out of the speakers. Mr. Springsteen's music is astonishing for many things, perhaps most immediately for its exultant rhythmic energy. In live performance especially, however, he constructs symphonic set pieces out of his songs, knitting together dramatic and musical ideas that amount to a tapestry of American imagery and popular music.

At any given moment the sound stays true to its essential simplicity and directness, even if the textures can approach almost orchestral richness. But the real diversity lies in the different sorts of popular music that he and his wonderful E Street Band can do so well.

The only nagging question is how this new record is going to sound out in the heartland, where people may have never heard of Bruce Springsteen, or, worse, may think of him as some overhyped Easterner.

All this observer can say is that on repeated hearings and after seeing him perform again this summer, *Born to Run* seems one of the great records of recent years.[2] If Mr. Springsteen has to perform more to get his message across, let him perform away—he seems to enjoy it enough. We're still waiting for the live (double?) album from him that should justify the whole notion of live albums. No doubt he will make still greater studio albums than this someday. But in the meantime, you owe it to yourself to buy this record.

Notes

1. See John Rockwell, "New Dylan from New Jersey? It Might as Well Be Springsteen." In *Bruce Springsteen: The* Rolling Stone *Files* (New York: Hyperion, 1996), p. 42.
2. Greil Marcus called the opening guitar riff on *Born to Run* "the finest compression of the rock & roll thrill since the opening riffs of 'Layla.'" See Greil Marcus, "Born to Run," *Rolling Stone*, October 9, 1975.

Dave Marsh

■

Dave Marsh has often been called America's best rock critic as well as the closest thing to Springsteen's biographer as we are likely to get. He is the author of *Born to Run: The Bruce Springsteen Story* (1979) and *Glory Days: Bruce Springsteen in the 1980s* (1987) as well as the author and editor of numerous other music-related books, including *Before I Get Old: The Story of the Who* (1983); *Fortunate Son: The Best of Dave Marsh* (1985), a collection of his criticism and essays; *Trapped: Michael Jackson and the Crossover Dream* (1985); and *Louie Louie: The History and Mythology of the World's Most Famous Rock 'n' Roll Song* (1993), among many others. *Bruce Springsteen: Two Hearts, the Story,* which brings the Springsteen saga up to date, was published in late 2003. This review of Springsteen's ten sold-out Bottom Line shows in Greenwich Village appeared in the September 25, 1975, issue of *Rolling Stone.*

Bruce Springsteen: A Rock "Star Is Born"

Rolling Stone

Bruce Springsteen and the E Street Band
The Bottom Line/New York City
August 13th–17th, 1975

■NOT SINCE ELTON JOHN'S initial Troubadour appearances has an artist leapt so visibly and rapidly from cult fanaticism to mass acceptance as at Bruce Springsteen's ten Bottom Line shows.[1] Hundred of fans lined the Village streets outside the 450-seat club each night, hoping for a shot at 50 standing-room seats. It was a time to hail from New Jersey with pride.

Springsteen is everything that has been claimed for him—a magical guitarist, singer, writer, rock & roll rejuvenator—but the E Street Band has nearly been lost in the shuffle. Which is ridiculous because this group may very well be the great American rock & roll band.

Like Springsteen, the E Street Band could cite a plethora of influences: Spector, Orbison, the Who, Van Morrison, Dylan and the Hawks, Booker T. & the M.G.s, any number of more obscure R&B and Sixties rock acts. The interpreted material describes the scope: "It's Gonna Work Out Fine," "Out of Limits," "When You Walk in the Room," the Crystals' "Then He Kissed Me." "Kitty's Back" is the best blues-based instrumental since the Butterfield Blues Band of *East-West* days.

The songs invariably build from a whisper to a scream, not only because Springsteen's composing focuses so often on dynamics, but also vocally and emotionally. When Springsteen slips into one of his sly tales of life in the Jersey bar bands all of them matured in, drummer Mighty Max Weinberg and bassist Garry Tallent key their comping to his every expression and gesture; it sounds natural but it's about as spontaneous as Pearl Harbor. Saxman Clarence Clemons and guitarist Miami Steve Van Zandt are perfect foils for these stories, the ominous cool of Clemons playing off the stranger, hipster frenzy of Van Zandt while Springsteen races back and forth like an unleashed puppy. They look tough and live up to their looks.

The recent addition of Miami Steve is the difference. Previously, when Springsteen had dropped his guitar to simply sing, the band was left with its focus on the keyboards. No great help since pianist Roy Bittan is inclined to overembellish everything and organist Danny Federici is too reticent to lead. Van Zandt plays perfect Steve Cropper soul licks and great rock leads; his slide playing on "The E Street Shuffle" had changed that song from an ordinary soul number to the focus of the show.

None of this is to obscure Springsteen's importance. Like only the greatest rock singers and writers and musicians, he has created a world of his own. Like Dylan and the Who's Peter Townshend, he has a galaxy of fully formed characters to work with. But while he is comparable to all of the greats, that may only be because he is the living culmination of 20 years of rock & roll tradition. His show is thematically organized but it's hard to pin down the theme: *American Quadrophenia,* perhaps. But Springsteen doesn't write rock opera; he lives it. And, as all those teenage tramps in skin-tight pants out there know, it's the only way to live.

Note

1. In September 2003, New York University, the Bottom Line's landlord, filed an eviction notice, claiming that the venerable Village club owed $185,000 in back rent.

Springsteen and others, including Mel Karmazin, president of Viacom, pledged several hundred thousand dollars to be used for the preservation and renovation of the club. In a prepared statment, Springsteen wrote, "Over the last 20 years, the Bottom Line has made itself a central part of New York City culture. When I think of the most memorable nights in my own career, few match the week of shows we did there in 1975. As a musician, as a citizen, and as one who loves New York City, I truly hope that a solution can be found that allows the Bottom Line and Allan [Pepper] and Stanley [Snadowsky] to continue their important, valuable work for many years to come."

Maureen Orth, Janet Huck, and Peter S. Greenberg

■

After *Born to Run* was released in late summer 1975, Bruce Springsteen was on an emotional and career high. He embarked on his first national tour to wildly enthusiastic audiences. Virtually every newspaper in the country devoted some space to the Springsteen phenomenon. Media response was almost uniformly excellent, especially reviews of his live shows. Demand for interviews was so high that Springsteen's manager at the time, Mike Appel, agreed to grant access only to those publications that would promise a cover story. *Newsweek* thought the Springsteen "hype" offered the perfect opportunity to publish a piece on the "making of a rock star." Staffer Maureen Orth, who had written only sporadically about rock, was given the assignment along with additional research by Janet Huck and Peter S. Greenberg. Rock critic Dave Marsh perhaps rather cruelly declared that her writing style was "as compatible with rock as cannibalism is with missionary work."[1] Not to be outdone, *Time* also ran a cover story—during the same week: October 27, 1975. (It is reprinted in this volume.)

Making of a Rock Star

Newsweek

■THE MOVIE MARQUEE in Red Bank, N.J., simply said "HOMECOMING" because everyone knew who was home. Out in the audience was Cousin Frankie, who taught him his first guitar chords. So were the guys from Freehold High who played in his early rock 'n' roll bands. They did not have to be hyped on Bruce Springsteen. This was the scruffy kid they had seen for years in the bars and byways of coastal Jersey. But Bruce was suddenly big time. The rock critics, the media, the music-industry heavies all said so. And in Red Bank, Bruce showed them just how far he had come. With Elvis shimmies and Elton leaps, Springsteen re-created his own electric brand of '50s rock 'n' roll magic. He clowned with saxophonist Clarence Clemons, hustled and bumped his way around the stage and gave a high-voltage performance that lasted more than two hours. When he leaned into the microphone, ripped off his black leather jacket and blasted, "Tramps like us, baby, we were born to run," the Jersey teeny-boppers went wild. After four footstomping encores they were ready to crown Bruce Springsteen the great white hope of rock 'n' roll.

The official investiture took place last week in Los Angeles at Springsteen's carefully staged West Coast debut, at the Roxy Night Club on Sunset Strip. At the kind of opening-night event that defines hip status for at least six months, new Hollywood and rock royalty[2] embraced Bruce Springsteen as one of their own. In a rare ovation that lasted a full four minutes, Jack Nicholson, Ryan and daughter Tatum O'Neal, Wolfman Jack and Neil Diamond seconded Cousin Frankie and the boys from Freehold High in Red Bank. Bruce Springsteen was a superstar.

Bruce who? He is still not exactly a household name across America. In San Mateo, Calif., last week, his 13-year-old sister Pam said, "Only one girl at school has his record." The bus driver's son—who bears a striking resemblance to Dylan, sports black leather jackets like Brando in *The Wild One* and wears a gold hoop earring—was known to only a small coterie of East Coast devotees a year ago. But since the release last August of his highly professional third album, *Born to Run,* which rocketed to a million-dollar gold album in six weeks, 26-year-old Bruce Springsteen has exploded into a genuine pop-music phenomenon. He has already been compared to all the great performers—Elvis, Dylan and Mick Jagger. And rock critic Robert Hilburn of *The Los Angeles Times* called him "the purest glimpse of the passion and power of rock 'n' roll in nearly a decade." Springsteen's own insistence on performing in small halls and clubs has created a kind of cult hysteria and his emergence as one of the most exciting live acts in rock today has only added to the mystique. Springsteen buttons, T shirts, decals, key chains and three different kinds of wall posters are currently the hot rock paraphernalia. In fact, Bruce Springsteen has been so heavily praised in the press and so tirelessly promoted by his record company, Columbia, that the publicity about his publicity is now a dominant issue in his career. And some people are asking whether Bruce Springsteen will be the biggest superstar or the biggest hype of the '70s.

In a $2 billion industry that thrives on smash hits, the artist who grabs the public's emotions the way Elvis or the Beatles once did is the fantasy of rock critics and record-industry pros alike. Springsteen's punk image, his husky, wailing voice, his hard-driving blues-based music and his passionate, convoluted lyrics of city lowlife, fast cars and greaser rebellion recall the dreams of the great rock 'n' roll rage of the 1950s:

> *. . . All the redemption I can offer, girl*
> *Is beneath this dirty hood*

But he also injects the images with a new sophistication:

> *The highway's jammed with broken heroes*
> *On a last-chance power drive*
> *Everybody's out on the run tonight . . .*

Some critics, however, find Springsteen's music one-dimensional, recycled teen dreams. "Springsteen's lyrics are an effusive jumble," music critic Henry Edwards wrote in *The New York Times,* "his melodies either second-hand or undistinguished and his performance tedious. Given such flaws there has to be another important ingredient to the success of Bruce Springsteen: namely, vigorous promotion."[3] Even some of his champions, like disk jockey Denny Sanders of WMMS in Cleveland, agree on that point. "Columbia is going overboard on Springsteen," he says. "He is the only unique artist to come out of the '70s, but because the rock 'n' roll well is really dry, they are going crazy for Springsteen."

As the real world has caught up with the record world, the penny-pinched economy has begun to erode the record industry. Album sales are down (Warner Brothers, for one, is off by nearly 20 percent), the albums going to the top of the charts are getting there on fewer sales while advertising budgets are being drastically slashed. "Unless an act has a great potential for sales," says one record-company executive, "the companies won't spend the big dollars."

Too often, the companies have gotten burned when they spent their money on the sizzle and forgot the steak. Bell Records dished out more than $100,000 last year in parties to promote an act nobody ever heard of—Gary Glitter—and people are still asking who he is. Atlantic bankrolled the rock group Barnaby Bye for an estimated $200,000 but failed to turn up any album sales. MGM decided to promote a singer-songwriter named Judi Pulver. They sent her to a Beverly Hills diet doctor, created a Charles Schulz "Peanuts" ad campaign, rented a Boeing 727 to fly journalists to her opening in San Francisco and even got astronaut Edgar

Mitchell to go along for the ride. When the evening was over, the inevitable truth set in. Judi Pulver just couldn't carry the hype. MGM's
$100,000 experiment bombed.

Everyone in the industry is aware of the pitfalls of The Hype and in-
siders think that the current Springsteen mania might inflict damage on
his career. "All the attention Bruce is getting now might hurt him later
on," says Hilburn. "What I'm afraid of is that while Springsteen has all the
potential everyone says he has, it's still chiefly potential. I just hope he's
strong enough to stand up under the pressure." Warner Brothers Records
president Joe Smith appreciates the "tumult" Bruce is creating for the
industry but is dubious about the extent of his ultimate influence on the
development of music. "He's a hot new artist now," says Smith, "but he's
not the new messiah and I question whether he will establish an international mania. He's got a very long way to go before he does what Elton
has done, or Rod Stewart or The Rolling Stones or Led Zeppelin."

Bruce himself is concerned about the effect the publicity campaign
will have on his creative equilibrium. "What phenomenon? What phenomenon?" Springsteen asked in exasperation last week while driving up
from Jersey to New York. "We're driving around, and we ain't no phenomenon. The hype just gets in the way. People have gone nuts. It's
weird. All the stuff you dream about is there, but it gets diluted by all the
other stuff that jumped on you by surprise."

Springsteen is experiencing superstar culture shock. He has never
strayed far from his best friends like Miami Steve Van Zandt and Garry
Tallent, who are in his E Street Band. He has spent hours hanging out
on the boardwalk at Asbury Park, N.J., and listening to the barkers tell
their tales. For gigs, he used to hitchhike to New York to play his guitar
in Greenwich Village. In both places, he found the cast of characters who
people his lyrics—Spanish Johnny, the Magic Rat, Little Angel, Puerto
Rican Jane. They inspired him but they didn't corrupt him. Springsteen
rarely drinks, does not smoke, doesn't touch dope and never swears in
front of women.

"I'm a person—people tend to forget that kind of thing," he says. "I
got a rock 'n' roll band I think is one of the best ones. I write about things
I believe that are still fun for me. I love drivin' around in my car when
I'm 26 and I'll still love drivin' around in my car when I'm 36. Those
aren't irrelevant feelings for me." The feelings usually find their way to
vinyl. "The record is my life," says Springsteen. "The band is my life.
Rock 'n' roll has been everything to me. The first day I can remember

lookin' in the mirror and standin' what I was seein' was the day I had a guitar in my hand."

Throughout his unconventional career, Springsteen has found people who felt he was born to star. From the moment he and his abrasive new manager, Mike Appel, walked into Columbia Records in 1972 to audition for the legendary John Hammond—discoverer of Billie Holiday, Aretha Franklin and Bob Dylan—Springsteen was the object of high-pressure salesmanship. "I went into a state of shock as soon as I walked in," says Springsteen. "Before I ever played a note Mike starts screamin' and yellin' 'bout me. I'm shrivelin' up and thinkin', 'Please, Mike, give me a break. Let me play a damn song.' So, dig this, before I ever played a note the hype began."

"The kid absolutely knocked me out," Hammond recalls. "I only hear somebody really good once every ten years, and not only was Bruce the best, he was a lot better than Dylan when I first heard him." Within a week, Springsteen was signed to Columbia and although he and Appel had little previous recording experience, they insisted on producing their own album—the uneven *Greetings from Asbury Park, N.J.,* released in January 1973. At the time Bruce had no band; he sang alone with an acoustic guitar. And because of the originality of his lyrics—and perhaps the familiarity of their cadence—he was compared to Dylan.

> *Oh, some hazard from Harvard*
> *Was skunked on beer playin' Backyard bombardier . . .*

The comparison was so tantalizingly close that Columbia promoted the first album with ads announcing they had the new Bob Dylan. The cover letter on the records Columbia sent to the DJ's flatly stated the same thing. But the hard sell backfired. "The Dylan hype from Columbia was a turnoff," said Dave Herman, the early-morning DJ for WNEW-FM, the trend-setting pop station in New York. "I didn't even bother to listen to it. I didn't want Columbia to think they got me."

Without radio airplay—the single most important ingredient in any hit—a record dies. Though the Springsteen campaign was a special project of then–Columbia president Clive Davis, who personally read Springsteen's lyrics on a promotional film, and even though Bruce got good notices from important rock publications like *Crawdaddy,* only a handful of the 100 or so major FM stations across the country played him. The record sold less than 50,000 copies. "He was just another media hype that failed," said Herman. "He was already a dead artist who bombed out on his first album."

Springsteen's personal appearance at the Columbia Records convention in the summer of 1973 was his biggest bomb. "It was during a period when he physically looked like Dylan," says Hammond. "He came on with a chip on his shoulder and played too long. People came to me and said, 'He really can't be that bad, can he, John?'"

That fall, Springsteen's second album, *The Wild, The Innocent and the E Street Shuffle,* was released. Again it got some terrific reviews—*Rolling Stone* later named it one of the best albums of 1974—but it sold even less than his first LP. This time, accompanying a stack of favorable reviews, the DJ's got a letter from Springsteen's manager Appel saying, "What the hell does it take to get airplay?" Meanwhile, Springsteen had a disastrous experience playing as the opening act for the supergroup Chicago on tour, and he refused to do what most new rock acts must do to get exposure—play short, 45-minute sets in huge halls before the main act goes on.

Columbia began to ignore Springsteen because he couldn't make a best-selling album or hit single. But Springsteen was getting better in his live performances and was starting to build followings in towns like Austin and Philadelphia, Phoenix and Cleveland. "The key to Bruce's success was to get people to see him," says Ron Oberman, a Columbia staffer who pushed hard for Springsteen's first album within the company. After a concert in Cleveland, says local DJ Sanders, "Springsteen was a smash, and requests zoomed up. We had played him before but now the requests stayed on."

In April 1974, Jon Landau, the highly respected record editor of *Rolling Stone,* caught Bruce's act in Boston, went home and wrote an emotional piece for the *Real Paper* stating, "I saw rock and roll future and its name is Bruce Springsteen." Landau's review was the turning point in Springsteen's faltering career—for the artist as well as the company. "At the time," says Springsteen, "Landau's quote helped reaffirm a belief in myself. The band and I were making $50 a week. It helped me go on. I realized I was gettin' through to somebody." Columbia cannily used the blurb in marketing Springsteen's second album and other critics began to take notice. It was the first time a record label used the prestige of a rock critic to push an artist so hard.

"His first two albums' not selling was the best possible thing for Bruce," says the 28-year-old Landau. "It gave him time to develop a strong identity without anyone pushing him prematurely. For twelve years he has had time to learn how to play every kind of rock 'n' roll. He has far more depth than most artists because he really has roots in a place—coastal Jersey, where no record company scouts ever visit."

One month after the Landau review, Springsteen, alone with Mike Appel in a sparsely equipped studio in upstate New York, began to record his third album—his last chance to make it. It took three months to record the title song, "Born to Run," and Columbia immediately sent it out to some key people to review for singles potential. The word came back: It's not top 40, forget it, it's too long. Then the ever-assertive Appel released a rough mix of the song to a handful of stations that had played Springsteen.

The response was overwhelmingly positive. The stations wanted the record. But the potential superstar was in the studio for the next six months unable to finish his masterpiece. "He told me he was having trouble getting the sound he heard in his head on record," says Landau. In April 1975, a year after his review, Landau became an adviser on the album and quit his job at *Rolling Stone* to become co-producer. He moved them into a better studio, and helped shape the album into a heavily produced wall of pulsating sound.

Last June, a group of Columbia executives heard a rough cut of the album and decided to launch an unprecedented campaign. Building on the Landau quote and $40,000 worth of radio spots on FM stations in twelve major markets, they promoted the first two dud albums, mentioning a third was on the way. It worked. Sales for the first two LP's climbed back on the charts, more than doubling their original sales.

Columbia knew it had a winner; the question was how to showcase the act. Appel, without consulting Springsteen, thought big. He asked a booking agent to get 20,000-seat Madison Square Garden for an artist who had never sold more than 150,000 records. He finally settled on the 400-seat Bottom Line club in Greenwich Village for the week before the release of the third album last August. The tickets sold out in three and a half days, with Columbia picking up 980 of the 4,000 tickets for the media "tastemakers." "Columbia put it on the line," said DJ Richard Neer of WNEW-FM. "They said, 'Go see him. If you don't like him, don't play him—don't write about him.'" With the tickets so limited in number, the ensuing hysteria created more press coverage and critical acclaim for Springsteen—who delivered topnotch shows—than any recent event of its kind. "It was a very intelligent use of an event," says Stan

Snadowsky, co-owner of the Bottom Line. "Columbia got all the right people down there." DJ Dave Herman, who refused to even play Springsteen's first album because of the hype, was completely won over. The next day he apologized on the air. "I saw Springsteen for the first time last night," he told his audience. "It's the most exciting rock 'n' roll show I've ever seen."

Orders for the new album, which had been given an initial press ordering of 175,000, came in at 350,000. The LP has sold 600,000 so far, and Columbia has spent $200,000 promoting it. By the end of the year they will spend an additional $50,000 for TV spots on the album. "These are very large expenditures for a record company; we depend on airplay, which cannot be bought," says Bruce Lundvall, Columbia Records' vice president. "What the public does not understand is that when you spend $100,000 on an album for a major artist, your investment is not so much on media as on the number of people you have out there pushing the artist for airplay." Now, for the first time, a Springsteen single, "Born to Run," has broken through many major AM stations, where the mass audience listens.

The stakes are enormous, since a hot album can earn up to several million dollars for the record company in a matter of a few weeks. Today Bruce Springsteen is still a promising rookie. Nobody knows whether he can sell like Elton John or even lesser publicized groups like Earth, Wind & Fire—a group that will ship more than 750,000 initial orders with the release of its new LP. Because of his enormous build-up, Springsteen now has the awesome task of fulfilling everyone's fantasy of what a new rock hero should be. And most of the country—which isn't even aware of Springsteen yet—may or may not agree that he is born to succeed. "Bruce is undergoing a backlash right now," says Irwin B. Segelstein, president of Columbia Records, "but even his critics are treating him importantly."

Springsteen himself has not yet seen any big bucks. He keeps 22 people on his payroll. He maintains sophisticated sound and lighting equipment for his shows and has a video crew following him everywhere. He only plays small halls where he can barely cover his expenses, but that hasn't put a crimp in his style. He has just moved into his first home, a sparsely furnished cottage overlooking the ocean—about a 10-minute drive from the Asbury Park boardwalk. His girlfriend, 20-year-old Karen Darbin,[4] a Springsteen fan from Texas, lives across the Hudson River in Manhattan. In Bruce's garage stands his prized possession—a '57 yellow Chevy convertible customized with orange flames, the same color as his first guitar.

On the eve of his West Coast debut last week, Springsteen seemed to be down. "People keep telling me I ought to be enjoying all this but it's sort of depressing to me." He riffled through his beloved '50s records— Elvis and Dion—from stacks of albums on the floor, which also included Gregorian chants, David Bowie and Marvin Gaye. "Now this," Bruce announces in a faintly Jimmy Durante delivery, "is the sound of universes colliding." The room fills with Phil Spector's classic production of the Ronettes' "Baby I Love You." Springsteen swoons. "Come on, do the greaser two-step," he says, beginning to dance.

Although Springsteen is a German[5] name, Bruce is mostly Italian, and he inherited his storytelling ability from his Neapolitan grandfather Zirili.[6] "In the third grade a nun stuffed me into a garbage can under her desk because she told me that's where I belonged," he relates. "I also had the distinction of being the only altar boy knocked down by a priest on the steps of the altar during Mass. The old priest got mad. My Mom wanted me to learn how to serve Mass but I didn't know what I was doin' so I was tryin' to fake it."

He finally saved $18 to buy his first guitar—"one of the most beautiful sights I have ever seen in my life"—and at age 14, Springsteen joined his first band. He was originally a Rolling Stones fanatic but gradually worked back to early rock. "We used to play the Elks Club, the Rollerdrome and the local insane asylum," he says. "We were always terrified at the asylum. One time this guy in a suit got up and introduced us for twenty minutes sayin' we were greater than the Beatles. Then the doctors came up and took him away."

Springsteen's parents moved to California when he was 16, but he stayed behind scuffling in local bands. A year later he drove across country—someone else had to shift because Bruce did not know how to drive—to play a New Year's Eve gig at the Esalen Institute. "I've never been outta Jersey in my life and suddenly I get to Esalen and see all these people walkin' around in sheets," he says. "I see someone playing bongos in the woods and it turns out to be this guy who grew up around the corner from me." "Everybody expected Bruce to come back from California a star," says his old friend "Southside Johnny" Lyon who used to play with Bruce at the Stone Pony bar in Asbury Park. But according to Bruce, "Nobody wanted to listen to a guy with a guitar."

They do today. Onstage Springsteen projects the same kind of high school macho and innocence that many young male fans, for whom glitter is dull, strongly identify with. Women think he's sexy and it's likely he'll end up with a movie contract. "He's able to say what we can't about growing up," said John Bordonaro, 23, a telephone dispatcher from the Bronx who traveled to Red Bank to see Bruce in concert. "He's talking about hanging around in cars in front of the Exxon sign. He's talking about getting your hands on your very first convertible. He's telling us it's our last chance to pull something off, and he's doing it for us." "The peace and love movement is gone," chimed in his friend, Chris Williams. "We have to make a shot now or settle into the masses."

The question is will Bruce Springsteen be able to reach the masses? "Let's face it," says Joe Smith of Warner Brothers Records. "He's a kid with a beard in his 20s from New Jersey who happens to sing songs. He's not going to jump around any more than Elton. His voice won't be any sweeter than James Taylor's and his lyrics won't be any heavier than Dylan's."

Springsteen's promoters would disagree, but they don't think it matters. "The industry is at the bottom of the barrel," declares Springsteen's manager Mike Appel, 32, as he paces around the Manhattan office once occupied by Dylan's manager, Albert Grossman. "We've got people scratching around for new talent. There's an amazing paucity of talent because there hasn't been anyone isolated enough to create a distinctive point of view." He whispers dramatically, "What I'm waiting for, what Bruce Springsteen is waiting for, and we're all waiting for is something that makes you want to dance!" He shouts, "Something we haven't had for seven or eight years! Today anything remotely bizarre is gobbled up as the next thing. What you've got to do is get the universal factors, to get people to move in the same three or four chords. It's the real thing! Look up America! Look up America!" Appel sat down. Hypes are as American as Coca-Cola so perhaps—in one way or another—Bruce Springsteen *is* the Real Thing.

Notes

1. See Dave Marsh, *Born to Run: The Bruce Springsteen Story* (New York: Doubleday, 1979), p. 119.
2. According to Greil Marcus, "Glenn Frey and Eagles manager Irving Azoff stalked out after the fourth song; Jackson Browne ended the night standing on a table, screaming." Marcus, "Live at the Roxy," *New West*, July 2, 1979. See *In the Fascist*

Bathroom: Punk in Pop Music, 1977–1992 (Cambridge, Mass.: Harvard University Press), p. 47.

3. Henry Edwards, "If There Hadn't Been a Bruce Springsteen, Then the Critics Would Have Made Him Up," *New York Times,* October 5, 1975.
4. The correct spelling of the last name is Darvin.
5. The name is Dutch in origin, not German.
6. Adele Springsteen's maiden name is spelled Zerilli.

Jay Cocks

∎

Best known as a screenwriter (*Gangs of New York, The Age of Innocence*), Jay Cocks was, in 1975, *Time*'s film critic. A few years later, he became the magazine's rock critic. Like Maureen Orth's profile in *Newsweek,* which is also reprinted in this volume, Cocks's addressed the issue of "hype," but seemed to take Springsteen more seriously as a genuine artist. The fallout was predictably corrosive as the media—especially the print media—issued volley after volley of disparaging remarks about the simultaneous covers, which, in Dave Marsh's opinion, reflected "the national news media's antagonism toward rock and roll, or toward any other expression of non-Milquetoast culture."[1] But Cocks already had a head start. A year earlier, in the April 1, 1974, issue of *Time,* he described Springsteen's musical style: "Like rock musicians of the '60s, Springsteen dips back to the '50s for the blazing chord colors and nagging syncopations inside his walls of throbbing sound. . . . Bursting with words, images rush along in cinematic streams of consciousness." Cocks would go on to write additional pieces on Springsteen for *Time,* including "Against the American Grain" (November 15, 1982), "Round the World: A Boss Boom" (August 26, 1985), and "There's Magic in the Night" (November 10, 1986).

Rock's New Sensation: The Backstreet Phantom of Rock

Time

∎THE ROCK-'N'-ROLL GENERATION: everybody grows up by staying young.

Bruce Springsteen is onto this. In fact, he has written a song about it:

> . . . *I hid in the clouded warmth of the crowd,*
> *But when they said "Come down" I threw up.*
> *Ooh . . . growin' up.*

He has been called the "last innocent in rock," which is at best partly true, but that is how he appears to audiences who are exhausted and on fire at the end of a concert. Springsteen is not a golden California boy or a glitter queen from Britain. Dressed usually in leather jacket and shredded undershirt, he is a glorified gutter rat from a dying New Jersey resort town who walks with an easy swagger that is part residual stage presence, part boardwalk braggadocio. He nurtures the look of a lowlife romantic even though he does not smoke, scarcely drinks and disdains every kind of drug.

In all other ways, however, he is the dead-on image of a rock musician: street-smart but sentimental, a little enigmatic, articulate mostly through his music. For 26 years Springsteen has known nothing but poverty and debt until, just in the past few weeks, the rock dream came true for him. ("Man, when I was nine I couldn't imagine anyone not wanting to be Elvis Presley.") But he is neither sentimental nor superficial. His music is primal, directly in touch with all the impulses of wild humor and glancing melancholy, street tragedy and punk anarchy that have made rock the distinctive voice of a generation.

Springsteen's songs are full of echoes—of Sam Cooke and Elvis Presley, of Chuck Berry, Roy Orbison and Buddy Holly. You can also hear Bob Dylan, Van Morrison and the Band weaving among Springsteen's elaborate fantasias. The music is a synthesis, some Latin and soul, and some good jazz riffs too. The tunes are full of precipitate breaks and shifting harmonies, the lyrics often abstract, bizarre, wholly personal.

Springsteen makes demands. He figures that when he sings

> *"Baby this town rips the bones from your back*
> *It's a death trap, it's a suicide rap*
> *We gotta get out while we're young . . ."*

everybody is going to know where he's coming from and just where he's heading.

Springsteen first appeared in the mid-'60s for a handful of loyal fans from the scuzzy Jersey shore. Then two record albums of wired brilliance (*Greetings from Asbury Park, N.J.,* and *The Wild, the Innocent, and the E Street Shuffle*) enlarged his audience to a cult. The albums had ecstatic reviews—there was continuing and growing talk of "a new Dylan"—but slim sales. Springsteen spent nearly two years working on his third album, *Born to Run,* and Columbia Records has already invested $150,000 in ensuring that this time around, everyone gets the message. The album has made it to No. 1, the title track is a hit single, and even the first two albums are snugly on the charts. Concerts have sold out hours after they were announced. Last Thursday Springsteen brought his distinctively big-city, rubbed-raw sensibility to a skeptical Los Angeles, not only a major market but the bastion of a wholly different rock style. It remained to be seen how Springsteen would go down in a scene whose characteristic pop music is softer, easier, pitched to life on the beaches and in the canyons, hardly in tune with his sort of dead-end carnival. Springsteen's four-day stand at a Sunset Strip theater called the Roxy was a massive dose of culture shock that booted everyone back to the roots, shook 'em up good and got 'em all on their feet dancing.

Even the most laid-back easy rocker would find it tough to resist his live performance. Small, tightly muscled, the voice a chopped-and-channeled rasp, Springsteen has the wild onstage energy of a pinball rebounding off invisible flippers, caroming down the alley past traps and penalties, dead center for extra points and the top score.

Expecting a monochromatic street punk, the L.A. crowd got a dervish leaping on the tables, all arms and flailing dance steps, and a rock poet as well. In over ten years of playing tanktown dates and rundown discos, Springsteen has mastered the true stage secret of the rock pro: he seems to be letting go totally and fearlessly, yet the performance remains perfectly orchestrated. With his E Street Band, especially Clarence Clemons' smartly lowdown saxophone, Springsteen can caper and promenade, boogie out into the audience, recite a rambling, funny monologue about girl-watching back in Asbury Park or switch moods in the middle of songs.

He expects his musicians to follow him along. Many of the changes are totally spur of the moment, and the band is tight enough to take them in stride. "You hook on to Bruce on that stage and you go wherever he takes you," says Clarence Clemons. "It's like total surrender to him." A Springsteen set is raucous, poignant, brazen. It is clear that he gets off on the show as much as the audience, which is one reason why a typical gig lasts over two hours. The joy is infectious and self-fulfilling. "This music is forever for me," Springsteen says. "It's the stage thing, that rush moment that you live for. It never lasts, but that's what you live for."

He once cautioned in a song that you can "waste your summer prayin' in vain for a savior to rise from these streets," but right now Springsteen represents a regeneration, a renewal of rock. He has gone back to the sources, rediscovered the wild excitement that rock has lost over the past few years. Things had settled down in the '70s: with a few exceptions, like Paul Simon, Jackson Browne and Linda Ronstadt, there was an excess of showmanship, too much din substituting for true power, repetition—as in this past summer's Rolling Stones tour—for lack of any new directions. Springsteen has taken rock forward by taking it back, keeping it young. He uses and embellishes the myths of the '50s pop culture: his songs are populated by bad-ass loners, wiped-out heroes, bikers, hot-rodders, women of soulful mystery. Springsteen conjures up a whole half-world of shattered sunlight and fractured neon, where his characters re-enact little pageants of challenge and desperation.

The *Born to Run* album is so powerful, and Springsteen's presence so prevalent at the moment, that before the phenomenon has had a chance to settle, a reaction is already setting in. He is being typed as a '50s hood in the James Dean mold, defused for being a hype, put down as a product of the Columbia promo "fog machine," condemned for slicking up and recycling a few old rock-'n'-roll riffs. Even Springsteen remains healthily skeptical. "I don't understand what all the commotion is about," he told *Time* correspondent James Willwerth. "I feel like I'm on the outside of all this, even though I know I'm on the inside. It's like you want attention, but sometimes you can't relate to it."

Springsteen defies classification. This is one reason recognition was so long in coming. There is nothing simple to hold on to. He was discovered by Columbia Records Vice President of Talent Acquisition John Hammond, who also found Billie Holiday, Benny Goodman and Bob Dylan, among others. Hammond knew "at once that Bruce would last a generation" but thought of him first as a folk musician.

Casting Springsteen as a rebel in a motorcycle jacket is easy enough—it makes a neat fit for the character he adopted in "Born to Run"—but it ignores a whole other side of his importance and of his music.

Born to Run is a bridge between Springsteen the raffish rocker and the more ragged, introverted street poet of the first two albums. Although he maintains that he "hit the right spot" on *Born to Run*, it is the second album, *The Wild, the Innocent, and the E Street Shuffle*, that seems to go deepest. A sort of free-association autobiography, it comes closest to the wild fun-house refractions of Springsteen's imagination. In "Wild Billy's Circus Song," when he sings, "He's gonna miss his fall, oh God save the human cannonball," Springsteen could be anticipating and describing his own current, perhaps perilous trajectory. In case of danger, however, Springsteen will be rescued by the music itself, just as he has always been. "Music saved me," he says. "From the beginning, my guitar was something I could go to. If I hadn't found music, I don't know what I would have done."

He was born poor in Freehold, N.J.,[2] a working-class town near the shore. His mother, Adele ("Just like Superwoman, she did everything, everywhere, all the time"), worked through his childhood as a secretary. His father, Douglas Springsteen (the name is Dutch), was "a sure-money man" at the pool tables who drifted from job to job, stalked by undetermined demons.

"My Daddy was a driver," Springsteen remembers. "He liked to get in the car and just drive. He got everybody else in the car too, and he made us drive. He made us all drive." These two-lane odysseys without destination only reinforced Springsteen's already flourishing sense of displacement. "I lived half of my first 13 years in a trance or something," he says now. "People thought I was weird because I always went around with this look on my face. I was thinking of things, but I was always on the outside, looking in."

The parents pulled up stakes and moved to California when Bruce was still in his teens. Bruce stayed behind, with some bad memories of hassles with nuns in parochial school, an $18 guitar and random dreams of a phantom father for company. By the time he was 18, he had some perspective on his father. "I figured out we were pretty much alike," Springsteen says, by which he means more than a shared cool skill at the pool table and a taste for long car rides. "My father never has much to say to me, but I know he thinks about a lot of things. I know he's driving himself almost crazy thinking about these things . . . and yet he sure ain't got much to say when we sit down to talk." The elder Springsteen currently drives a bus in San Mateo, a suburb south of San Francisco. Neither he nor his wife made it to Los Angeles for their son's big show.

Bruce bunked in with friends back in Jersey and tried to make it through public high school. He took off on weekend forays into Manhattan for his first strong taste of big-city street life and began making music. He started writing his own because he could not figure out how to tune his guitar to play anyone else's material accurately. "Music was my way of keeping people from looking through and around me. I wanted the heavies to know I was around."

In 1965, while he was still finishing high school, Springsteen began forming bands like the Castiles, which did gigs for short money in a

Greenwich Village spot called the Cafe Wha? He met up with Miami Steve Van Zandt, current lead guitarist of the E Street Band, around that time. "We were all playing anything we could to be part of the scene," Van Zandt recalls. "West Coast stuff, the English thing, R&B and blues. Bruce was writing five or ten songs a week. He would say, 'I'm gonna go home tonight and write a great song,' and he did. He was the Boss then, and he's the Boss now."

Still, the Boss was sufficiently uncertain of his musical future to quit school altogether. He enrolled in Ocean County College, showed up in what is still his standard costume—Fruit of the Loom undershirt, tight jeans, sneakers and leather jacket—and was soon invited round for a chat by one of the guidance staff. As Springsteen tells it, the counselor dropped the big question on him immediately.

"You've got trouble at home, right?"

"Look, things are great, I feel fine," Springsteen replied warily.

"Then why do you look like that?"

"What are you talking about?"

"There are some students who have . . . complained about you."

"Well, that's their problem, you know?" said Springsteen, ending the conversation and his formal education.

Instead, he took his music anywhere they would listen. His bands changed names (the Rogues, the Steel Mill, Dr. Zoom and the Sonic Boom) as frequently as personnel. "I've gone through a million crazy bands with crazy people who did crazy things," Springsteen remembers. They played not only clubs and private parties but firemen's balls, a state mental hospital and Sing Sing prison, a couple of trailer parks, a roller-drome, the parking lot of a Shop-Rite and under the screen during intermission at a drive-in. A favorite spot for making music, and for hanging out, was Asbury Park.

"Those were wonderful days," says Springsteen's buddy, Southside Johnny Lyon. "We were all young and crazy." Bustling with music and the fever of young musicians, bands swapping songs and members, new jobs and old girls, Asbury Park sounds, if only in memory, like Liverpool before it brought forth the Beatles. Springsteen lived in a surfboard factory run by a displaced Californian named Carl Virgil ("Tinker") West III, who became, for a time, his manager.

Everybody had a band; not only Springsteen and Southside, but also Miami Steve, Vini ("Mad Dog") Lopez (who played drums on Bruce's first two albums) and Garry Tallent (now bass guitarist for the E Street Band). They all would appear at a dive called the Upstage Club for $15 a night, work from 8 P.M. to 5 A.M., then party together, play records and adjourn till the next afternoon, when they would meet on the boardwalk to check the action and talk music. For sport everyone played Monopoly, adding a few refinements that made the game more like the Jersey boardwalk they knew. There were two special cards: a Chief McCarthy card (named in honor of a local cop who rousted musicians indiscriminately) and a Riot card. The McCarthy card allowed the bearer to send any opponent to jail without reason; whoever drew the Riot card could firebomb any opponent's real estate.

Springsteen was a demon player and won frequently, according to Southside, because "he had no scruples." Nicknamed "the Gut Bomb King" because of his passion for junk food, he would show up for a Monopoly tourney with armfuls of Pepsis and Drake's cakes. Whenever anyone would get hungry and ask for a snack, Springsteen was ready with a deal: one Pepsi, one hotel.

Nobody was getting rich outside of Monopoly. In 1970 Asbury Park was the scene of a bad race riot. And the tourists stayed away. "The place went down to the ground, and we rode right down with it," says Miami Steve. There were jobs to be had in a few of the bars, playing easy-listening rock, but Springsteen and his pals disdained them because, as he says simply, "We hated the music. We had no idea how to hustle either. We weren't big door knockers, so we didn't go to New York or Philly." Adds Van Zandt, who lived on a dollar a day: "We were all reading in the papers how much fun rock 'n' roll was—it seemed like another world. We didn't take drugs. We couldn't afford any bad habits."

A lot of the life Springsteen saw then and lived through found its way into his songs, but indirectly. Filtered through an imagination that discovered a crazy romanticism in the ragtag boardwalk life.

> *She worked that joint under the boardwalk,*
> *She was always the girl you saw boppin' down the beach with*
>   *the radio,*
> *Kids say last night she was dressed like a star. . . .*

Tinker, the surfboard manufacturer and manager, called Mike Appel on Springsteen's behalf. Appel, whose major claim to fame until then was the co-authorship of a Partridge Family hit called "Doesn't Somebody Want to Be Wanted," was smart enough to see Springsteen's talent and brash enough to spirit him away from Tinker. Appel got Springsteen to work up a clutch of new songs by simply calling him frequently and asking him to come into New York. Springsteen would jump on the bus and have a new tune ready by the time he crossed the Hudson.

Appel also called John Hammond at Columbia. The call was Springsteen's idea, but the come-on was all Appel. He told Hammond he wanted him to listen to his new boy because Hammond had discovered Bob Dylan, and "we wanna see if that was just a fluke, or if you really have ears." Hammond reacted to Springsteen "with a force I'd felt maybe three times in my life." Less than 24 hours after the first meeting, contracts were signed.

Even before Springsteen's first album was released in 1973, Appel was already on the move. He offered the NBC producer of the Super Bowl the services of his client to sing "The Star-Spangled Banner." Informed that Andy Williams had already been recruited, with Blood, Sweat & Tears to perform during halftime, he cried, "They're losers and you're a loser too. Some day I'm going to give you a call and remind you of this. Then I'm going to make another call and you'll be out of a job." Says Hammond: "Appel is as offensive as any man I've ever met, but he's utterly selfless in his devotion to Bruce."

Appel and Springsteen understood each other. They agreed that Bruce and the band should play second fiddle to nobody. After a quick but disastrous experience as an opening act for Chicago, Springsteen appeared only as a headline attraction. That meant fewer bookings. There was also little to be done about the narrowing future of Bruce's recording career. Regarded as a pet of banished Columbia Records President Clive Davis, Springsteen was ignored by the executives who took over from Davis. *The Wild, the Innocent, and the E Street Shuffle* was not so much distributed as dumped.

For two years Springsteen crisscrossed the country, enlarging his following with galvanic concerts. Early last year, playing a small bar called Charley's in Cambridge, Mass., he picked up an important new fan. Jon Landau, a *Rolling Stone* editor, had reviewed Bruce's second album favorably for a local paper, and Charley's put the notice in the window. Landau remembers arriving at the club and seeing Springsteen hugging himself in the cold and reading the review. A few weeks later, Landau wrote, "I saw the rock and roll future and its name is Springsteen."[3]

Some loyalists at Columbia persuaded the company to cough up $50,000 to publicize the quote. Columbia's sudden recommitment caught Springsteen in a creative crisis. He and Appel had spent nine months in the studio and produced only one cut, "Born to Run." The disparity between the wild reaction to his live performances and the more subdued, respectful reception of his records had to be cleared up. Landau soon signed on as co-producer of the new album and began to find out about some of the problems firsthand.

"Bruce works instinctively," Landau observes. "He is incredibly intense, and he concentrates deeply. Underneath his shyness is the strongest will I've ever encountered. If there's something he doesn't want to do, he won't." Springsteen would work most days from 3 P.M. to 6 A.M. and sometimes as long as 24 hours, without stopping. Only occasionally did things go quickly. For a smoky midnight song, called "Meeting Across the River," Springsteen just announced, "O.K., I hear a string bass, and I hear a trumpet," and, according to Landau, "that was it." Finally the album came together as real roadhouse rock, made proudly in that tradition. The sound is layered over with the kind of driving instrumental cushioning that characterized the sides Phil Spector produced in the late '50s and '60s. The lyrics burst with nighthawk poetry.

> *The screen door slams*
> *Mary's dress waves*
> *Like a vision she dances across the porch . . .*

If all this effort has suddenly paid off grandly, and madly, Springsteen remains obdurately unchanged. He continues to hassle with Appel over playing large halls, and just last month refused to show up for a Maryland concert Appel had booked into a 10,000-seat auditorium. The money is starting to flow in now: Springsteen takes home $350 a week, the same as Appel and the band members. There are years of debt and back road fees to repay. Besides, Springsteen is not greatly concerned about matters of finance. Says John Hammond: "In all my years in this business, he is the only person I've met who cares absolutely nothing about money."

Springsteen lives sometimes with his girlfriend Karen Darvin, 20, a freckled, leggy model from Texas, in a small apartment on Manhattan's East Side. More frequently he is down on the Jersey shore, where he has just moved into more comfortable—but not lavish—quarters, and bought his first decent hi-fi rig. He remains adamantly indifferent to clothing and personal adornment, although he wears a small gold cross around his neck—a vestigial remnant of Catholicism—and, probably to challenge it, a small gold ring in his left ear, which gives him a little gypsy flash.

When he is not working, Springsteen takes life easy and does not worry about it. "I'm not a planning-type guy," he says. "You can't count on nothing in this life. I never have expectations when I get involved in things. That way, I never have disappointments." His songs, which he characterizes as being mostly about "survival, how to make it through the next day," are written in bursts. "I ain't one of those guys who feels guilty if he didn't write something today," he boasts. "That's all jive. If I didn't do nothing all day, I feel great." Under all circumstances, he spins fiction in his lyrics and is careful to avoid writing directly about daily experience. "You do that," he cautions, "and this is what happens. First you write about struggling along. Then you write about making it professionally. Then somebody's nice to you. You write about that. It's a beautiful day, you write about that. That's about 20 songs in all. Then you're out. You got nothing to write."

Some things, however, must change. Southside Johnny recalls that after *Born to Run* was released, "We had a party at one of the band members' houses. It was like old times. We drank and listened to old Sam and Dave albums. Then someone said my car had a flat tire. I went outside to check, and sitting in the street were all these people waiting to get a glimpse of Brucie, just sitting under the streetlights, not saying anything. I got nervous and went back inside."

These lamppost vigilantes, silent and deferential, were not teenyboppers eager to squeal or fans looking for a fast autograph. As much as anything, they were all unofficial delegates of a generation acting on the truth of Springsteen's line from "Thunder Road": "Show a little faith, there's magic in the night." Just at that doorstep, they found it. Growin' up.

Notes

1. Dave Marsh, *Born to Run: The Bruce Springsteen Story* (Garden City, N.Y.: Doubleday, 1979), p. 119.
2. Springsteen was born at Monmouth Memorial Hospital in Long Branch, New Jersey, although he grew up in Freehold.
3. The actual quote is: "I saw rock and roll future and its name is Bruce Springsteen." Jon Landau, "Growing Young with Rock and Roll," *Real Paper,* May 22, 1974.

Lester Bangs

■

Lester Bangs (1949–1982), considered by many to be the most influential rock critic of his generation, has been described as part Hunter S. Thompson, part Charles Bukowski, and part Jack Kerouac—all rolled into one very combustible frame. He was an editor at *CREEM* for five years and also wrote for *Rolling Stone* and the *Village Voice*. His books include *Blondie* (1980); *Psychotic Reactions and Carburetor Dung* (1987), a collection of his essays; and *Elvis Presley: The Rebel Years* (1997). In 2000, *Chicago Sun-Times* rock critic Jim DeRogatis wrote a biography of Bangs, *Let It Blurt: The Life and Times of Lester Bangs, America's Greatest Rock Critic* (2000), which attempted to capture his raucous, living-on-the-edge lifestyle and his insatiable love of the music. In 2003, Anchor Books published *Main Lines, Blood Feasts, and Bad Taste: A Lester Bangs Reader,* a companion volume to *Psychotic Reactions* and edited by fellow rock critic John Morthland. The following piece, which ran in the November 1975 issue of *CREEM,* is full of superlatives. But when Bangs felt strongly about something or someone, he pulled no punches.

Hot Rod Rumble in the Promised Land

CREEM

And in his excited way of speaking I heard again the voices of old companions and brothers under the bridge, among the motorcycles, along the wash-lined neighborhood and drowsy doorsteps of afternoon where boys played guitars while their older brothers worked in the mills. All my other current friends were "intellectuals."... But Dean's intelligence was every bit as formal and shining and complete.... And his "criminality" was not something that sulked and sneered; it was a wild yea-saying overburst of American joy... long prophesied, long a-coming (he only stole cars for joy rides).

—Jack Kerouac, of Neal Cassady

■ BRUCE SPRINGSTEEN REACHES his stride at a time when the listening audience is not only desperate for a new idol but unprecedentedly suspicious of all pretenders to the throne. We have no idea what the Next Big Thing will be, but we're pretty certain what it isn't—and one thing it certainly isn't is Another Bob Dylan. So here's this kid Spring-steen, coming on like a customized wordslinger in a black leather jacket, his mother's own favorite François Villon. And as if we weren't suspi-cious enough already of all run-on rhapsodic juvenile delinquents, we have another cabal of rock critics (including one who later went on to be-come his producer)[1] making extravagant claims for him, backed up by one of the biggest hypes in recent memory. Out here in the Midwest, where at this writing Springsteen has not even toured yet, you can smell the backlash crisp as burnt rubber in the air.

Springsteen can withstand the reactionaries, though, because once they hear this album even they are gonna be ready to ride out all cyni-cism with him. Because, street-punk image, bardic posture and all, Bruce Springsteen is an American archetype, and *Born to Run* will prob-ably be the finest record released this year.

Springsteen is not an innovator—his outlook is rooted in the Fifties; his music comes out of folk-rock and early rock 'n' roll, his lyrics from 1950s teenage rebellion movies and beat poetry as filtered through Six-ties songs rather than read. Springsteen's gifts lie in the way he has rethought traditional sounds and stances, coming up with a synthesis fresh enough to constitute a minor renaissance. After all, what's more old-fashioned than the avant-garde?

When his first album was released, many of us dismissed it: he wrote like Bob Dylan and Van Morrison, sang like Van Morrison and Robbie Robertson, and led a band that sounded like Van Morrison's. We were too hasty, of course, but I still don't think Springsteen's true voice began to emerge until this album, and a friend's criticisms still nag: "When I lis-ten to Bruce Springsteen, I hear a romanticization of New York. When I listen to Lou Reed, I hear New York."

Maybe so, but maybe that's precisely the point. Springsteen's land-scapes of urban desolation are all heightened, on fire, alive. His charac-ters act in symbolic gestures, bigger than life. Furthermore, there's absolutely nothing in his music that's null, detached, or perverse and even his occasional world-weariness carries a redemptive sense of lost battles passionately fought. Boredom appears to be a foreign concept to him—he reminds us what it's like to love rock 'n' roll like you just dis-covered it, and then seize it and make it your own with certainty and precision.

If I seem to OD on superlatives, it's only because *Born to Run* demands them; the music races in a flurry of Dylan and Morrison and Phil Spector and a little of both Lou Reed and Roy Orbison, luxuriating in them and an American moment caught at last, again, and bursting with pride.

If Springsteen's music is calculated, it's to extract the most emotional mileage out of relatively spare instrumentation—rich without being messy, the solos are succinct, built for speed, providing a perfect counterpoint to the headlong surge of the lyrics. Particularly intelligent use is made of keyboards and instruments like the glockenspiel which contribute mightily to the Spectorish feel. And Clarence Clemons' sax solos, like Andy Mackay's in Roxy Music, demonstrate that in terms of sheer galloping exuberance, Johnny and the Hurricanes are just as valid an influence as John Coltrane.

The playing is clean but the mix is keyed to a slightly distorted throb in which Springsteen's voice is almost buried. When you do get to the words, you discover that they have been tightened up from his first two albums; no longer cramming as many syllables as possible into every line, he is sometimes almost economical, and the album resonates with breathtaking flashes like this:

> *The amusement park rises bold and stark*
> *Kids are huddled on the beach in the mist*
> *I wanna die with you Wendy on the streets tonight . . .*

It could almost be a concept album, from the opening "Thunder Road," where Springsteen grabs his girl and hits the highway in his car, "riding out tonight to case the promised land," to the melded metaphors of "Jungleland":

> *Kids flash guitars just like switchblades*
> *Hustling for the record machine*
> *The hungry and the hunted . . .*

Through all of these songs Springsteen's characters "sweat it out in the streets of a runaway American dream," skating for a longshot in automobiles and beds with the omnipresent roar of the radio driving them on to connect anew, as even in the failure of their striving they are redeemed by Springsteen's vision: "Tramps like us—baby, we were born to run."

In a time of squalor and belittled desire, Springsteen's music is majestic and passionate with no apologies. He is so romantic, in fact, that he might do well to watch himself as he comes off this crest and settles into success—his imagery is already ripe, and if he succumbs to sentiment or sheer grandiosity it could well go rotten. For now, though, we can soar with him, enjoying the heady rush of another gifted urchin cruising at the peak of his powers and feeling his oats as he gets it right, that chord, and the last word ever on a hoodlum's nirvana.

Note
1. Jon Landau.

Ariel Swartley

∎

The following long essay on the various pleasures of listening to Springsteen's second album, *The Wild, the Innocent & the E Street Shuffle* (1973) was written specifically for *Stranded: Rock and Roll for a Desert Island* (1979), edited by Greil Marcus. Swartley is, she says, "a sucker for someone who takes rock and roll as a religion. . . ." In Springsteen, she sees many things: a romantic at heart, a mythmaker, a rock and roll storyteller, and a street poet with a bit of James Joyce and the Dovells in his corner boy swagger, as well as touches of Bob Dylan and Van Morrison.

The Wild, the Innocent and the E Street Shuffle
Bruce Springsteen (Columbia 32432) 1974

from *Stranded: Rock and Roll for a Desert Island*

The band's playing and the singer's singing something about going home.

—"Incident on 57th Street"

∎IT MUST HAVE BEEN the summer of '65 when Sandy's, our late night rendezvous, closed down and the action moved across the street. The Cave & Pit was in tune with the times—two entrances and a wall down the middle that divided more than the bar and burger halves of the establishment. You didn't just go in one door or the other; you picked a side and made a stand: dope or booze, freak or straight, FM or AM, dove or hawk. Lines were drawn down the middle of everything, including old friendships. But down in back where the jukeboxes were, there was a connecting door that was always open. And standing in that doorway you were on the firing line in the loudest confrontation of them all—the battle of the bands. Nightly the Kingsmen fought it out with Dylan, party boys against the prophet, Louie knocking at the gates of Eden. Usually I knew which side of the wall I belonged on (and where I couldn't get served). But back between the Wurlitzers I was caught out on the fence, wanting both: the visions and the dumb exuberance, a prophet and a party, rock and rock and roll.

It still seems like the perfect combination. A kind of ethical hedonism, an enlightened savagery, a wise naiveté. An American dream out of Fenimore Cooper or Mark Twain—but I don't want to talk about history. All I want is for a voice to come out of the wilderness and the stereo to crackle in flames like the burning bush. I don't want to have to ask, "Are you talking to me?" I want to know. And then I want to dance. In other words, I'm going to be a sucker for someone who takes rock and roll as a religion, and romanticizes the hell out of mundane details. For someone who says, "Sparks fly on E Street when the boy prophets walk it handsome and hot." Bruce Springsteen wins my heart with the first line of *The Wild, the Innocent and the E Street Shuffle,* wins it over and over again. Used to be only rock critics took lyrics that seriously and turned the romance of the streets so explicitly into myth. But while Springsteen's making his pronouncements the horns are waggling their hips and sassing him. And just when you think the song's going to collapse under the weight of its verses, the party-time chorus shouts the immortal instruction: "Everybody form a line." Then the only thing left on anybody's mind is the latest step—the E Street Shuffle or the Bristol Stomp. James Joyce meets the Dovells? Creation myths from The Land of a Thousand Dances? Yes, I say. Yes. Yes.

With its mumbled lyrics, its street slang, nicknames, and local references, the song, "The E Street Shuffle," seems as deliberately insular as the kids it's describing. But then dance songs have always flaunted their authenticity and traded on an exclusivity that's an open invitation: learn the steps, join the crowd, they're doing it in Philly, instructions included. Springsteen's insularity is just as artificial and provocative a barrier. The narrator doesn't figure you know the neighborhood—he points out the spots of interest—but he assumes you're on his side. It's an assumption that's hard to resist, as rock and roll has always understood. From the start its appeal has been partisan (call it anti-intellectual, anti-establishment, provincial, chauvinistic, ageist, sexist, all or none of the above—doesn't matter). All you have to do to join is want to. Having gotten you to buy into the rock and roll myth, Springsteen invites you to examine it. He plays with associations the way he plays with overtones on the guitar: picking at them while he's playing a line and just letting them ring.

Nice word, "shuffle." It applies so well: to the motion of the corner-boys, their heel-and-toe strut before the girls, their ironic and provocative defiance of authority. And to the wild cards and jokers who fan out when the cops come, only to rearrange themselves at another hangout. It's all a dance—Little Angel changing partners, the dos-si-dos with the riot squad, the poses and the posturing and the attitudes. The cosmic E Street Shuffle. Even Leonard Bernstein saw the light: put the corner kids on the stage, wrapped them up in literary allusions, and orchestrated the thing. But Springsteen leaves the dance on the street where it lives. He is a participant as well as an observer, and he takes the details as seriously as their metaphoric possibilities. The song's final scene has the hypernaturalism of a closing shot in a grade B western: "He slips on his jeans and they move on out down to the scene—all the kids are there." That string of adverbs is as deliberate as a walk into the sunset. It's a hero's exit, except the boy-prophet's on his way to the hop. For if it's all a dance, it's also *just* a dance, and that's enough. Springsteen's laughing like the party's starting and all his oldest friends have just walked in the door and he picks up a guitar and twangs out lines the Ventures would have killed for.

Smack dab in the visionary tradition of Dylan and Van Morrison, Springsteen's got the former's faith that words, stretched and piled on fast enough, are music; the latter's feel for the grinning warmth and greased motions of R&B. Listen to Springsteen and you know he's listened to them both, and also to garage bands, Little Eva, one-shot singles, late-night TV giveaway deals. He hasn't only learned from masters. But it's not the knee-jerk nostalgia of teen-scene verité he's after in his authentic dialogue and his blasts from a past that never seems so bright except in retrospect. He treats rock and roll history as our common language, our shared mythology, and thereby reinforces rock and roll's promise of community. Spectoral echo, (James) Brownian motion, Dion-ysian brawl—he triggers memories like you were a jukebox and he was the man with all the quarters; plays it like a slot machine and wins. Hell yes, he exploits rock and roll's past, just like he exploits the language itself—turning it inside out, digging for the metaphors under the surface of conversation.

The Wild, the Innocent and the E Street Shuffle is Springsteen's most extravagant and most easygoing album. He insists you can have rock and roll both ways—even the title makes it clear. Two value judgments and a dance step—what's going on here is synthesis. But Springsteen's double vision doesn't have an ironist's cruel double edge. Sure, characters in his dramatic monologues reveal themselves. The narrator of "Sandy" is an adolescent loser, the kid whose shirt gets stuck in the fun-fair ride, leaving him stranded and looking like a fool. You'd think he was ruining his chances with the girl: he can't stop telling her about his humiliations, about the girls who led him on, about the waitress that got tired of him. He can't even hand her a line without blowing it: "I promise I'll love you—forever?" Springsteen's voice squeaks incredulously. Oh, there'll always be another girl; adolescence is something you grow out of. But that's cold comfort and Springsteen's offering something warmer and more immediate: the moon is rising, the organ notes twinkle like stars, the "sha la las" are triumphant and irresistible. The chorus promises romance despite the odds.

"New York City Serenade" opens with a piano riff as night dark and extravagant as the song's title, as glitteringly arrogant as the city itself. A marching band tootles at the beginning of "The E Street Shuffle," fat and self-important. Springsteen doesn't just establish a mood or a groove; his songs begin with gaudy overtures—instrumental trailers for the story that's to follow. The piano in "New York" is stilled by a single acoustic guitar note coming soft and startling like an unexpected kiss; the marching band is taunted by a cheeky guitar and an electric piano line that sprints away before they can retort. The action begins before Springsteen sings a word. When his voice finally comes, it seems to be fighting its way through the elaborate arrangements, the flood of words, determined to get to you, to grab you, to convince you. Intimate against the grand scale of the songs, compelling in its compulsion to be heard, Springsteen's voice is that of a man possessed. His techniques are those of a master storyteller: the whispers to get your attention, the shouts to bring you to your feet, the teasing expectations. He builds songs into an ache of tensions, laying on strings like whips, applying pressure with drawn-out horn notes; dissolves the tensions in chants as rowdy as a Bronx cheer. But release is only temporary: he pulls the next phrases taut, the percussion threatens, the horns renew their urgency. Springsteen's timing reels you in through the artifice and sentimentality in "Wild Bill's [*sic*] Circus Story." The verses, spun out wide-eyed, filmed in ever slower motion, lead you on, "past the kids, past the sailors, to his dimly lit trailer / And the ferris wheel turns and turns like it's never going to stop." He delays the punch line till the last possible second, then spits it out in a rattle of phlegm and tobacco juice: "Hey sonny, wanna try the big top?" Who wouldn't be a fool for a tall tale? Springsteen's one himself. Sprawling, methodical, impassioned, and manipulative, *The Wild, the Innocent and the E Street Shuffle* teeters on the edge of melodrama and slips into rapture. "Ooh, ooh, ooh, it's all right"; "Good night, it's all tight, Jane." Springsteen's final choruses are incantations. Benedictions. Acts of surrender. He's caught up in his own spells.

If Springsteen is a storyteller, so are his characters. In some sense hustlers, both he and they live by their lines, by their powers of persuasion (and self-persuasion), by their ability to transform prosaic material into something shining. His stories are set in a self-absorbed, circumscribed world of adolescents, small towns, closed communities, where appearances count and reputations are as unshakable as a nickname. No one travels Springsteen's streets incognito. He identifies them all: Spanish Johnny, Lover Boy, Jazz Man. Even nouns. They aren't modified, they're christened: fire trails, rude boys, bruised arms, blond girls. More than descriptions, the adjectives, like nicknames, have the force of characterizations. Say "the girls were blond" and you're talking about the color of their hair. Say "blond girls" and they're something special, blond all through, a race apart. It's the old rosy-fingered dawn trick: the epic-maker's device for turning ordinary words symbolic and loading details down with implication. But it's not like the songs lay out in neatly knitted metaphors (or plots)—one tug and they're unraveled. They come at a rush and you grab what you can. Still, the implications are felt. The omnipresent compounds in "The E Street Shuffle"—double-shot, sweet-sixteen—drag at the verses like heels scuffing the pavement. Each stretched-out line ambles on, coolly oblivious to the insistent jab of the horns, the frenetic blather of wah-wah and percussion: "But the boys are still on the corner loose doin' that lazy E-Street shuffle." The rhythm of the words is as nonchalant as the boys, and it's only when Springsteen finishes "shuffle" with a wheeze and a gasp for breath, that there's any suggestion that that cool costs an effort to maintain. Sometimes the implications are felt in the sheer weight of words: "with bruised arms and broken rhythm and a beat-up old Buick—" ("Incident on 57th Street"). They beat upon the line till it's punch-drunk, so that the phrase that steps out clear when the dust settles seems all the more defiant "—but dressed just like dynamite."

Spanish Johnny's clothes and cornerboy's shuffle are gestures falling somewhere between courage and bravado, between a hustle and a good story. Johnny plays the gallant promising Janey he'll take her away from the battles on the street, but she's got his number: "Those romantic young boys / All they ever want to do is fight." She knows they're not going anywhere. The corner is "The E Street Shuffle," the boardwalk in "Sandy," the hometown alleys of "Kitty's Back," even the traveling midway of "Wild Bill's [*sic*] Circus Story," the tenement neighborhood of "Incident on 57th Street," the back roads and parent-and-school dominated world of "Rosalita"—Springsteen's settings are territories in limbo. Satellites of the metropolis, overshadowed, robbed and ruined; resort towns begging to be invaded, dependent on other people's leisure and mobility; home turf staked out and fought for but never owned. And adolescence itself. Like the "man-child" or the "boy-prophet," neither one thing or the other. All of Springsteen's characters live on islands close enough to shore to see the mainland, too far away to make the crossing light or easy.

But isolation is chosen as well as imposed. Caught in the middle, challenged from the outside, each community is self-protective, fiercely partisan. When Kitty comes back, it's almost too good to be true, for her departure was a double betrayal, forsaking the hometown and the kids in the alley for marriage and the big city, power, prestige, and opportunity. Her return not only vindicates her small-town admirer, but all of those who've never left. And their victory is as sweet and keen-edged as the notes of Springsteen's guitar. Yet her defection raised doubts and questions that still hang like the sax's final whistling high note. As envied and disdained as a resort visitor, as threatening and tempting as the city, adulthood glimmers just over the horizon too. And like the Corner or the Street, it has to be claimed. The final song on the album confronts growing up and the metropolis head-on: "New York City Serenade" is a rite of passage. Enticing with its jazz and drugs and promises of plunder, dangerous—"a mad-dog's promenade"—the city is a domineering mistress, sneering like Fishlady that cornerboys are too easy, grinding supplicants in their own insignificance. In her hostile, garishly-lit embrace, manhood becomes a matter of self-assertion—"I'm a young man walking real proud for you"—and self-respect: "Sometimes you just have to walk on."

But then, he doesn't sing the line quite straight; there's a gulp in his voice, an exaggeration to his drawl. Dangers over the horizon, oppression at home—what's a poor boy to do? One solution is obvious, and Springsteen concedes the point so fast you trip over it in the album's most explicitly autobiographical cut. In "Rosalita" he's no street fighting man, and no more under the thumb of circumstances, adults, and authorities than any other kid. When he comes to the door he may be a truant, a hot-rodder, and what your mother would call a bad influence, but rock and roll is his guarantee of respectability. Hell, that record company advance is probably a lot bigger than Rosie's father's salary. There's an edge of mockery that keeps Springsteen's heroism honest. He's found the perfect escape: work that's fun, rebellion that's legitimate, eternal youth, a name that's known not just on the corner but on the global street, all that stuff. But however much he romanticizes rock and roll as an ideal of a code, he only plays the star in fun. Sometimes it seems like he's deliberately burying his voice in the mix, as if to deny that he's anything but another member of the band. Sometimes it seems like he and the other guys have never left the corner at all.

Certainly the songs seem like they were filmed on location, or maybe it's just that the settings feel like characters themselves. Springsteen is a compulsive recorder of detail—the sheets "damp with sweat," the girl "bopping down the beach with a radio." But it's not like you'd call him a realist. Sometimes it seems as though he's looking back at the corner through a rearview mirror—the streets turned shimmery and the action blurred by the speed at which he's traveling. It's not just that the language slips out of the colloquial into the high-flown. It's as though he's caught up in the rhythm and led by his own words to more and more audacious leaps. From neat tricks like putting hard girls on easy street, to metaphors that are high wire acts: "Let the black boys in to light the soul flame." (I mean, I always figured that phrase had to do with turning the radio to an R&B station. But?) And finally he skips beyond probability and any tidy interpretation to visions: Of "golden-heeled fairies" fighting with .38s (and it's anybody's guess what kind of fairies). Of "barefoot street boys" throwing down their switchblades and kissing each other goodbye. Visions of the natural order he's been at pains to record turned on its head. But then, calling the kids on E Street "boy-prophets" was a leap as well. Springsteen's double vision, seeing the what-is beside, on top of, through the what-could-be, is consistent enough to take on a moral force. Like a hardboiled detective, he observes as though his life depended on it, on recognizing the shift in stance that tells you the other guy's about to go for his gun. And like the detective, once he's established the facts, they're not enough. His characters aren't presented as free agents: they're shown, if not as victims, at least as products of an environment. And still, they're held accountable for their actions. They can walk on or not. The choice may be only a gesture, but the space between courage and bravado, between a hustle and a good story, is also the place where appearances become truth. Where Fishlady's gibe is picked up and worn as a badge of honor: "Hey babe, I'm easy, won't you take my arm?" Where the only names that matter are the names you give or call yourself.

Knowing the score is how you survive; knowing, for instance, that midnight in Manhattan is not the time to get cute. Faith, on the other hand, is how you manage—well—whatever it is that's more than survival. Yeah, it sounds hokey, but faith in these songs isn't just some smarmy, self-help estuary. It's nothing more or less than an act of imagination (like the songs themselves). Envisioning a junkman dressed in satin is as absurd as falling in love. The facts don't justify the faith; no loved one ever lives up to a lover's dream; still, no love ever survived on facts alone. So buy the vision. Believe the lady's sawed in half. Be willing to be made a fool. Listen to the junkman. If only every act of faith were just as easy.

Still, held in any kind of limbo, trapped in stupid circumstances, it's nice to hear him singing. Singing something about the towns I grew up in and the boys I loved. And why I left and why I care about them still. But I didn't grow up in towns much like the ones he describes. Or something about the songs I listened to and the beat I danced and turned around. Something then, about growing up. But I'm already grown. Aah, it doesn't matter. The band's playing and the singer's singing something about a prophet, something about a party. And rock and roll's going to take me home.

Dave Marsh

∎

Dave Marsh, a founding editor of *CREEM,* has written extensively about Springsteen, both in his own books as well as in the pages of *Rolling Stone,* the *Village Voice,* and *CREEM.* The following excerpt from *Born to Run* (1979) examines the album's impact and makes a strong case for its status as an instantaneous classic. He also touches on such subjects as rock and roll and the American Dream, Elvis Presley, Jimi Hendrix, and Springsteen's undying commitment to rock as a legitimate musical form.

Thunder Road

from *Born to Run:*
The Bruce Springsteen Story

∎ *BORN TO RUN* was an instant classic. Anyone who loves rock and roll must respond to its catalogue of styles, the rough and tough music, the lyrics that sum up the brightest hopes—and some of the darkest aspects—of the rock and roll dream. The album may have been a monster in the making, but it was also, as Greil Marcus has said, "like a '57 Chevy running on melted-down Crystals records. And it shuts down every claim that has been made for him."

Born to Run makes no stylistic breakthroughs, as the fundamental Elvis Presley and Beatles recordings had done. But it does represent the culmination of twenty years of rock and roll, and when it was released in October 1975, it was the strongest possible testimony to the continued vitality of that tradition.[1] Springsteen had synthesized his music largely from secondary sources. Rather than delving directly into blues or gospel or even early rock, he went for what he recalled of the forgotten, sometimes-junky hit singles he and his friends had loved when they were kids.

There is something about a one-shot hitmaker, like Little Eva, or an underrated one, like Roy Orbison, that is more fascinating than the big league musicians who have been prominent for years. Springsteen's record recalled, and in a sense redeemed, this important part of rock and roll. Part of the appeal of these brief successes is what they tell the fans about themselves, people who love the music as a secret world not easily discovered, and whose place in the music is confirmed through a memory that is more than nostalgic.

Another part of the magic of one-shot hits lies in what they tell about the transience of success and failure. Rock and roll, in this sense, typifies the American dream: The star on the wane, like the one-shot hit, reminds us that everyone has a shot at the top. And *Born to Run* takes us out there among those whose shot has arched off into the distance, beyond the possibility of recovery. It is a record that explores the horizon and examines people whose horizons are closing in. "My early albums were about being someplace and what it was like there," says Bruce. "*Born to Run* is about being nowhere at all."

But Nowhere is not Anywhere. *Born to Run* is as locked into an America of screen doors, fast cars and casual violence as the Beatles' "Penny Lane" is locked into the English everyday. To miss the point is to miss the reason why Bruce Springsteen is such a powerful influence on his fans. As the American Incarnate, he has become the first American hard rock hero since . . . well, I'll argue, since Elvis himself.

With one exception, the figures who unified the Sixties rock scene were British. And that exception, Bob Dylan, lacked a commitment to rock as music; his rock period was, in fact, brief—lasting only from *Bringing It All Back Home* (1965) through *Blonde On Blonde* (1966) and *The Basement Tapes* (recorded 1967, released 1977). Before and after, Dylan played music that could be identified as rock only through its association with a similar audience.

In fact, some of the American groups of the Sixties had the sort of commitment to rock and roll as a form that the Who, the Rolling Stones and (at their best) the Beatles brought to it. The Beach Boys diddled with dreary, if complex, pop forms after 1966. The folk rock bands—the Lovin' Spoonful, the Byrds, Buffalo Springfield—were too concerned with their own cool. So were the acid rock bands of the San Francisco sound; their LSD experimentation may have been chic, but that sort of music never had much connection with rhythm and blues or the Elvis Presley/Buddy Holly rockabilly school. It was, instead, a mélange of effects pilfered from West Coast jazz, from the cool school, from campus folk music, from country and western—from almost anything but rock and soul themselves.

In any event, none of these groups had a figure of sufficient charisma to challenge British rockers like Keith Richard, Keith Moon, John Lennon or Pete Townshend. Only three American stars of the Sixties had the commitment and personal magnetism to challenge the English rock hegemony. Of them, the Berkeley-based John Fogerty was dishonored in his own backyard, as a result of which he denied his natural instinct in vain attempts to make Creedence Clearwater Revival conform to the artificial aesthetic of the "album rock" groups across San Francisco Bay. Nevertheless, Fogerty's great series of CCR hits is the closest thing to rockabilly since the Fifties.

Sly Stone was an inspirational figure in his own right, but he rarely turned his considerable imagination to rock itself, preferring instead to demolish the conventions of soul music and afterward to march to his own distinctive beat. (In the Seventies, Sly's rhythm inventions would be codified and repackaged as disco music—a form which has more merit than the white rock audience is willing to grant it, but which has yet to move beyond Sly's original concept.)

After Presley's decline in Hollywood, the closest we came to an American rock hero was Jimi Hendrix. Not only was Hendrix black, which presented problems of perception (rock racism did not *start* with the anti-disco movement), but he had to escape to England to live out his fantasy that a black man could do what Dylan and Presley had done. Hendrix was great at everything he set his hand to, but even today his immeasurable influence is underacknowledged. And in the Sixties the rock audience in America was already too far gone on its pretentious path to see Jimi for what he was: The One.

Everybody else was either a hippie or an entertainer. Left without an American rock star, the underclass rebels who formed rock and roll's natural constituency drifted away from music, toward motorcycles and petty crime. The few who stuck with the music listened more often to black music than to white sounds, which left an enormous vacuum. Bruce Springsteen was the first American rock performer in nearly a decade—since Jimi's death—to attempt to fill that space. And his emergence would create, in surprising ways, a flood of followers and would reopen issues many had thought closed. If the meaning of "punk" has changed drastically since 1975, *Born to Run* must be counted as the record that set the stage for its re-emergence at all. It was a record that took the music from the hands of craftsmen and profiteers and gave it back to the sort of people who loved it because they lived it.

But *Born to Run* is much more than a resurrection of the punk esthetic. It is also the story of where such people had been since the rocker became an *artiste*: truly Nowhere. *Born to Run* is a record for everyone who grew up during the heyday of Woodstock and peace and love and couldn't embrace such foppish trappings. Everyone in America with a chip on his shoulder can accept these stories. In fact, the little stories add up to one big story, one that simply follows a boy and his girlfriend through a long, tragicomic day, a bit like *American Graffiti* without the saccharine. In some ways, though, it is more like *Mean Streets:* There is a sense that every life we encounter has a half-realized potential not just for violence but for catastrophe.

Note
1. The actual release date was August 25, 1975.

Part Two

∎

GLORY DAYS

In the 1980s Springsteen was riding high on a wave of patriotic fervor, even if his lyrics were often misunderstood by the very people and institutions he railed against. The decade began with an ambitious double recording, The River, which brought together both sides of the singer: the rocker who loved nothing better than to party all night and the loner who feared that the little that he had was about to be taken away from him. In many ways, The River indicated the direction that Springsteen's career would take two years later with the release of the solemn Nebraska.

By 1984, though, Springsteen had become the most recognized rock performer in the world. Born in the U.S.A. proved to be the career-defining turning point, transforming the charismatic rocker to megastar status. In a way, it was the beginning of the end, for Springsteen would never quite reach those heights again—at least on such a massive scale. But during the summer of 1984, his music seemed to be everywhere: blasting from the radio, in the columns of political pundits such as George F. Will, and even gracing the pages of Bobbie Ann Mason's bittersweet Vietnam novel In Country.

As the decade progressed, Springsteen's often densely compact lyrics were subjected to intense academic scrutiny and pensive reflection. He became the role model for the perfect rock star: sexy, caring, intelligent, and committed to the most noble of causes. These were glory days, indeed.

Robert Hilburn

∎

Longtime *Los Angeles Times* pop music critic and author of the best-selling *Springsteen* (1985), Robert Hilburn has been a Springsteen admirer almost from the beginning.

Out in the Streets

Los Angeles Times

ROBERT HILBURN: What about the destructiveness? All the deaths, including now Led Zeppelin's John Bonham,[1] must make you worry at times about the demands on you.

BRUCE SPRINGSTEEN: Rock has never been a destructive thing for me. In fact, it was the first thing that gave me self-respect and strength. But I totally understand how it can be destructive to people. There was a point when I felt very low after *Born to Run.* I felt bad for two, three, maybe four months. Before that, it had been me and the band and we'd go out and play. We'd sleep where we could and drive to the next show. All of a sudden I became a person who could make money for other people, and that brings new forces and distractions into your life.

RH: What does that do to you?

BS: Two things happen. Either you are seduced by the distractions of success and fame and money or you're not. Look at all the examples of people in rock and what happened to them—people who once played great but don't play great anymore, people who once wrote great songs but don't write great songs anymore. It's like they got distracted by *things.* You can get hooked on things as much as you can on drugs.

RH: What led to your confusion?

BS: I felt like I had lost a certain control of myself. There was all the publicity and all the backlash. I felt the thing I wanted most in my life— my music—being swept away and I didn't know if I could do anything about it. I remember during that period someone wrote, "If Bruce Springsteen didn't exist, rock critics would invent him."[2] That bothered me a lot, being perceived as an invention, a ship passing by. I'd been playing for ten years. I knew where I came from, every inch of the way. I knew what I believed and what I wanted.

RH: What was the low point?

BS: One night in Detroit, I didn't want to go onstage. That was the only time in my life—that period—that happened. At that moment I could see how people get into drinking or into drugs, because the one thing you want at a time like that is to be distracted—in a big way. I was lucky. I had my band, which was people I had grown up with. No matter where we went, they were always there for support.

RH: Don't the pressures continue when you get more successful? Do they ever stop?

BS: Yes, it keeps coming, more so. But I'm a different person now. When you're young and vulnerable, you listen to people whose ideas and direction may not be what you want. But you don't know that. You just stepped off the street and walked into the studio. On the first album there's almost no electric guitar. If anyone ever told me I was going to make a record without guitars, I would have flipped out. I would not have believed him. But I did make an album like that.

RH: Why do you still work so hard on the stage? Don't most performers tend to ease up as time goes by?

BS: I don't know how people do that—if that's what they do. To me, you do that when you're dead. You don't live anymore. You don't exist. That's what "Point Blank" on the new album is a little about.

RH: There's a lot of idealism and inspiration in your work. What were the things that inspired you?

BS: When you listen to those early rock records or any great rock 'n' roll, or see a great movie, there are human values that are presented. They're important things. I got inspired mainly, I guess, by the records, a certain purity in them.

I just know that when I started to play, it was like a gift. I started to feel alive. It was like some guy stumbling down a street and finding a key. Rock 'n' roll was the only thing I ever liked about myself.

On the new album I wrote this song called "Out on the Street." I wasn't gonna put it on the album because it's all idealism. It's about people being together and sharing a certain feeling of joy. I know it's real, but it's hard to see sometimes. You go out in the street and there's a chance you get hit over the head or mugged. The song's not realistic in a way, but there's something very real at the heart of it.

RH: But there's also a lot of struggle in your music.

BS: Life is a struggle. That's basically what the songs are about. It's the fight everyone goes through every day. Some people have more success with it than others. I'm a romantic. To me, the idea of a romantic is someone who sees the reality, lives the reality every day, but knows about the possibilities too. You can't lose sight of the dreams.

That's what great rock is about to me, it makes the dream seem possible. It's like I felt more dead than alive before I started music. I said that before, but it's true. I go to places and see people all the time, and what they're doing ain't at all livin'. They're dyin'. They're just taking a real long time about it.

I found something in rock that says it doesn't have to be that way. We try to say that to people in the songs, and they say it back to you with their reaction. The greatest part of the show is that they will sing the words back.

I came out the first night of the tour in Ann Arbor to do "Born to Run" and I forgot the words. I knew it was gonna happen. I listened to the song ten times just before the show, but when I walked up to the microphone my mind was blank. I went back to the drums and all of a sudden I heard the words faintly in the back of my mind and I realized the audience was singing. That was a real thrill. It was like a special bond. They weren't just sitting out there; they were really involved.

I started sensing that bond during the last tour. It's more than just that you're successful or a big rock star. There's something else happening. I meet kids in the street and there's something we have in common—something they know and I know, even if we don't talk about it.

RH: On the new album, there's more of a balance between the idealism and the realism than before.

BS: Rock 'n' roll has always been this joy, this certain happiness that is, in its way, the most beautiful thing in life. But rock also is about hardness and coldness and being alone. With "Darkness" it was hard for me to make those things coexist. How could a happy song like "Sherry Darling" coexist with "Point Blank" or "Darkness on the Edge of Town"? I could not face that.

I wasn't ready for some reason within myself to feel those things. It was too confusing, too paradoxical. But I finally got to the place where I realized life had paradoxes, a lot of them, and you've got to live with them.

RH: You talk a lot on the album about dreams, losing them and regaining them.

BS: That's one of the things that happens in life. The great possibilities you have in your twenties. When you're in your thirties or late thirties, the world is different. At least it looks different. You may not have the same expectations. You're not as open to options. You may have a wife and a kid and a job. It's all you can do to keep those things straight. You let the possibilities go. What happens to most people is when their first dreams get killed off nothing ever takes its place. The important thing is to keep holding out for possibilities, even if no one really ever makes it. There was a Norman Mailer article that said the one freedom that people want most is the one they can't have: the freedom from dread. That idea is somewhere at the heart of the new album. I know it is.

RH: A lot of the songs on the album talk about marriage, but many are yearning for it and others are racing away from it.

BS: One of the ideas this time was to touch on the feelings that everyone has. People want to be part of a group, yet they also want to disassociate themselves. People go through these conflicts every day in little ways. Do you wanna go to the movies tonight with your friends, or stay home? I wanted to get part of that on the record—the need for community, which is what "Out on the Street" is about. Songs like "Ties That Bind" and "Two Hearts" deal with that too. But there's also the other side, the need to be alone.

RH: You used to say that it was harder to write songs because they got more personal.

BS: That's what writing and growth are all about, I guess. I had an album of 13 songs finished a year ago September, but I didn't put the record out because it wasn't personal enough. This album seems much more personal to me.

RH: In many of your songs you deal with the same images: streets and cars. One of the critical complaints about you is that they become almost clichés.

BS: The songs are always different to me. I became fascinated with John Ford movies in the fact that they were all Westerns. I watched the early ones and the late ones. It was fascinating to me how he'd film the same scene—a dance scene or a confrontation—and make it different in every picture. There was a lot of continuity in his work. I liked that.

RH: Why?

BS: You go back to the previous movie and have a clearer understanding of where he was coming from. What he was saying in this film was changing the shape of what he said in another one.

RH: Why cars and streets?

BS: I always liked those images. That's American, in some ways. If you're outside of the big cities, there's people and there's cars—there's transition. That's why people are moving so much in my songs. They're always going from one place to another, and it seemed the natural place for them. Besides, I love the road. I like to get on the bus after the show and ride all night.

RH: Do you like to leave a town after the show?

BS: Yes, I'd rather go on the bus to another city than stay in a hotel. I don't like *staying*. It's funny. It makes me feel uncomfortable.

RH: Why so much night imagery?

BS: I don't know. I think there seems to be more possibilities at night. You look up ahead and you can't see nothin'. You don't know what's there until you get there. And I've been playing in bars since I was 15. I live by night. I was never up during the day. People are alive at night.

RH: Looking ahead, what do you see for yourself over the next five years?

BS: I don't do that. Now is now. Tonight you can do something. I don't count on my tomorrows. I don't like to let myself think about the next night. If you do that, you begin to plan too much and begin rationing yourself.

RH: What do you mean by "rationing"?

BS: There may be no tomorrow, there may be no next record. If you start rationing, you're living life bit by bit when you can live it all at once. I like the latter. That's what I get the most satisfaction out of: to know that tonight when I go to bed I did my best. It's corny, I guess, but isn't that what living is all about? If you go to the show, the kid has a ticket for tonight. He's got no ticket for the show in L.A. or New York. He doesn't have a ticket for Detroit. He only has a ticket for Cleveland. You can't live on what you did yesterday or plan on what's gonna happen tomorrow. So if you fall into that trap, you don't belong onstage. That's what rock 'n' roll is: a promise, an oath. It's about being as true as you can be at any particular moment.

Notes

1. John Bonham, Led Zeppelin's thunderous drummer, died on September 25, 1980. He choked on his own vomit after an all-night drinking binge.

2. Henry Edwards charged that ". . . the very derivativeness of Springsteen's music, and the throwback quality of his punkish persona, have an irresistible appeal—both for younger rock music fans who were discovering their own new stars for the first time as well as older nostalgists hankering for the return of the days when rock music was considered a 'challenge to the establishment' and rock performers were looked upon as symbolic rebels." See Henry Edwards, "If There Hadn't Been a Bruce Springsteen, Then the Critics Would Have Made Him Up," *New York Times*, October 5, 1975.

Don McLeese

■

At the time of the following concert review in the October 24, 1980, issue of the *Chicago Reader,* Don McLeese was the popular music critic of the *Chicago Sun-Times.* Since then, he has moved on to the *Austin American-Statesman* and, most recently, has become the associate editor of *Midwest Living.* McLeese has always been one of the more reflective and thoughtful of music journalists. Here he argues that treating our musicians as icons only dehumanizes both them and us. Springsteen has echoed that very sentiment in various interviews. He told *Rolling Stone*'s Kurt Loder once, "I believe that the life of a rock & roll band will last as long as you look down into the audience and can see yourself, and your audience looks up at you and can see themselves—and as long as those reflections are human, realistic ones. The biggest gift that your fans can give you is just treatin' you like a human being, because anything else dehumanizes you."[1]

Abdicating the Rock 'n' Roll Pedestal:
Bruce Springsteen Gets Down
Chicago Reader

■A PEDESTAL IS no place for rock 'n' roll. As Bruce Springsteen understands, something vital is sacrificed when we turn our rockers into icons. It's tough to let loose in a shrine.

Despite Springsteen's antihero assertion, however, the weeks of hoopla surrounding his Chicago appearances have made it obvious that rock 'n' roll idolatry remains very much with us. Although those who stood in line for three days or paid some outrageous sum to a scalper for the chance to "BROOCE" at Springsteen probably consider themselves among the most ardent true believers around, it seems to me that such adulation subverts the spirit of rock 'n' roll. By elevating our rockers into larger-than-life stature, we make it difficult for anything truly human to sneak through.

There's something of a paradox involved here: treating a Springsteen as something special, we threaten to undermine so much of what made him special in the first place. At the beginning, Springsteen and his

E Street Band presented themselves as a glorified bar band, a band that had absorbed everything great it had ever heard from 20 years of rock 'n' roll and lived for the chance to prove it all night, night after night. As a reaction against pampered, postured superstars who had totally lost touch with their audiences, Springsteen brought a street-level grit and grandeur back to the music, wrenching some hope for redemption—or at least escape—out of everyday experience.

A star through sheer force of passion, Springsteen reaffirmed that whatever is magic about rock 'n' roll is gut-level; that it exists within us rather than outside us; that it is something we create ourselves rather than waiting for some artiste to bestow it upon us. He showed that rock 'n' roll is a process, an interaction, not an artifact. He showed that the sparks truly fly, on E Street or anywhere else, when band and audience meet each other on equal terms, spurring each other on, pushing a little harder/faster/further than either thought possible.

If a surge of self-determination provided Springsteen's music with its heart, the idolization that followed has been dishearteningly passive. We look toward the stage for "a savior" to provide the sort of significance, or at least excitement, that we are unwilling or unable to struggle toward in our own lives. We shower Springsteen with the same sort of mindless adulation—the bovine "BROOCE"-ing, the knee-jerk "Boss"-ing—that his music represented such a refreshing reaction against. Trying to make rock more than it is, we make it something less than it could be. Deifying Springsteen, we diminish ourselves.

And we haven't done Springsteen much good either. For a while there, I feared that he was in danger of becoming paralyzed by the burdens of devotion. Ever since his ascendancy, there's been little room to breathe in his music. As he has strained toward the momentousness that so many ascribed to him, what had once rung instinctively true began slipping dangerously close to melodramatic self-parody. Who would have thought that all the crazy, risk-filled exhilaration of *The Wild, the Innocent and the E Street Shuffle* would lead to the numbingly ponderous clichés of "Racing in the Street"? That the anything-goes electricity of his live performances would rigidify itself into the set-piece predictability of those extended monologues? That a guy whose sensibility was shaped by the first-take vitality of Mitch Ryder and Gary "U.S." Bonds would find it necessary to spend a couple years polishing his own releases? For those of us who would rather listen to men than myths, Springsteen seemed in danger of becoming terminally Springsteenesque.

As it turns out, perhaps no one understood all this better than Bruce himself. A couple of weeks ago, before I'd been able to get a hold of his new *The River* album, I was driving around when a song called "I'm a Rocker" came on the radio—a tough, take-no-prisoners little battery-burner that practically blasted through my windshield. It sounded a little like Springsteen, or somebody obviously influenced by him. But it was both blunter and freer than anything I thought we'd ever hear from him again. And a lot more playful as well—references to 007 and "Secret Agent Man," a fade out lifted from "California Sun." Instinctive stuff, no overwrought social significance whatsoever. This is the kind of stuff he *should* be doing, I thought to myself.

Then I heard the show and got the album and I found out that this is the kind of stuff he *is* doing—and not just "I'm a Rocker" as a roots-homage change of pace either. There's a feeling of spontaneous combustion about songs such as "Cadillac Ranch," "Ramrod," and "You Can Look (But You Better Not Touch)," sparks of influence from countless one-shot supernovas from our collective subconscious. Less Kierkegaard, lots more Kingsmen and Bobby Fuller Four.

From the album credits, it seems that the stylistic shift is a recent one. The straightforward stuff is all copyright 1980. The material on *The River* that aims at some sort of mythic resonance—"Point Blank," "Stolen Car," the title cut—is all earlier, either material left off *Darkness* or written shortly afterward. Since the production never attempts the studied grandiosity of *Born to Run* or the epic heavy-handedness of *Darkness*, themes that might previously have been overladen with bombast are rendered more powerful through understatement. While I haven't spent enough time with *The River* to judge it Springsteen's best, it certainly is far more encouraging than the long delay had left any reason to hope.

His performances are benefiting from the looser approach as well. Although I wasn't able to stay for an entire Uptown show, what I did hear was a no-nonsense band in peak form, giving its all before an audience that would have been satisfied with far less. No heightened dramatics or overblown soliloquies. Just one hour after another of feverish performances—ballads and blowouts alike—that seemed to synthesize, summarize, and revitalize the ongoing rock 'n' roll heritage. At his effortless best, the music doesn't seem to flow from Springsteen so much as through him.

While the show left me feeling good about Springsteen, it left me feeling even better about rock 'n' roll as a whole. It left me feeling that the fire that burned inside Springsteen in the Asbury Park bars still burns inside him today, and still burns wherever there's a great bar band with the determination to pour it all out, to risk it all, knowing there's really nothing to lose. It didn't make me want to wait a month or a year for Springsteen to return; it made me want to go out and hear Desmond or B. B. Spin[2] and stomp all night. As Springsteen himself understands, there's no need to wait for some "savior" to provide that rock 'n' roll jolt.

Rock 'n' roll is what you make it. "Show me a little faith, there's magic in the night." Be your own Boss.

Notes

1. See Kurt Loder, "Bruce!," *Rolling Stone,* February 28, 1985.
2. Desmond and B. B. Spin were rock bands popular in Chicago at the time of the article.

Greil Marcus

■

If the history of rock and roll has proven anything, it is that we have agreed
to disagree. This was true on December 22, 1980—when the following article was published—and it is especially true today, as rock has splintered off
into smaller and smaller fragments of the vast musical melting pot. If one believes, as posited by Lester Bangs and seconded by Greil Marcus, that "We
will never again agree on anything as we agreed on Elvis," then Springsteen's
status as the heir of a legitimate musical tradition is all the more important.

The Next President of the United States

New West

■IN OCTOBER BRUCE SPRINGSTEEN released *The River,* which
went swiftly to number one, and began a tour that before it ends, sometime in the summer of 1981, will take him and the E Street Band across
the length and breadth of the United States, into Canada, to Great
Britain, to Europe, to Japan and Australia. As interesting as this event is
its context.

Rock 'n' roll is, today, too big for any center. It is so big, in fact, that no
single event—be it Springsteen's tour, Sid Vicious's overdose, or John
Lennon's first album in five years—can be much more than peripheral.
Writing in August 1977, Lester Bangs may have gotten it right: "We will
never again agree on anything as we agreed on Elvis."

Rock 'n' roll now has less an audience than a series of increasingly dis-
crete audiences, and those various audiences ignore each other. With the
exceptions of disco in the U.S. and reggae in the U.K., blacks and whites
have not had so little to do with each other musically since the early
fifties, when rock 'n' roll began—and those exceptions are linked to the
emergence of hip racism in the U.S. (many discos that play black music
"discourage" the patronage of blacks) and of organized racism among
white youth in the U.K. The audience that has gathered around punk
and postpunk groups may have a grip on the formal history of the music—the account, as written by white critics, of the music's pursuit of

new forms and new ideas—but that pursuit has never had so little to do with what most rock consumers actually hear or, for that matter, what they've heard of.

In one sense, this is salutary and inevitable. The lack of a center means the lack of a conventional definition of what rock 'n' roll is, and that fosters novelty. Rules about what can go into a performance and, ultimately, about how and what it can communicate are not only unenforced, they're often invisible, both to performer and audience. That rock 'n' roll has persisted for so long, and spread to such diverse places, precludes its possession by any single generation or society—and this leads not only to fragmentation but to a vital, renewing clash of values. We agreed on Elvis, after all, because he was the founder, because he represented the thing itself; if we will never agree on anyone as we agreed on Elvis, it's equally true that Americans have never agreed on anyone as they agreed on George Washington. But this state of affairs is also debilitating and dispiriting. The fact that the most adventurous music of the day seems to have taken up residence in the darker corners of the marketplace contradicts rock 'n' roll as aggressively popular culture that tears up boundaries of race, class, geography and (oh yes) music; the belief that the mass audience can be reached and changed has been the deepest source of the music's magic and power. The music does not now provide much evidence that this belief is based on anything like reality, and on a day to day basis this means there is no longer common ground for good rock 'n' roll conversation. To find an analogy one must imagine that many Americans who care passionately about baseball would be unfamiliar with Reggie Jackson. Bands with very broad—or at least very big—audiences continue to exist, of course, but they don't destroy boundaries; they disguise them, purveying music characterized principally by emotional vapidity and social vagueness. No doubt the Doobie Brothers have their fans among the Moral Majority as among the ACLU, but that doesn't mean the Doobie Brothers have given such people anything to talk about.

A concert by Bruce Springsteen offers many thrills, and one is that he performs as if none of the above is true. The implicit promise of a Bruce Springsteen concert is that This Is What It's All About—This Is the Rock. Whether the promise is more than a night's happy illusion is, at the time, less important than whether Springsteen can live up to it.

As songwriter, singer, guitarist, and bandleader, he appears at once as the anointed successor to Elvis Presley and as an imposter who expects to be asked for his stage pass; his show is, among other things, an argument about the nature of rock 'n' roll after twenty-five years. The argument is that rock 'n' roll is a means to fun that can acknowledge the most bitter defeats, that it has a coherent tradition which, when performed, will reveal possibilities of rock 'n' roll the tradition did not previously contain.

Having posited a tradition, Springsteen performs as if every bit of it is backing him up—rooting for him. This allows him to hit the boards as if his status as a rock 'n' roll star is both privileged and ordinary, and the result onstage is a unique combination of authority and prank. It means that at his finest, Springsteen can get away with almost anything, stuff that coming from anyone else would seem hopelessly corny and contrived—and that he can come up with stuff to get away with that most rockers since Little Richard would be embarrassed even to have thought of. Such as, in Portland, under the brooding eye of Mt. St. Helens, singing "On Top of Old Smokey."

Two nights later, on October 27 in Oakland, the best seat in the house—front row on the center aisle—was the prize of a small blond woman, a thirty-three-year-old attorney from San Francisco named Louisa Jaskulski. She spent the first hour and a half of the concert dancing in front of her chair—nothing fancy, just the sweetest, most private sort of movements, the kind of dance one might do in front of a mirror. She was so expressive she seemed to add a dimension to every song, and early into the second half of the concert Springsteen responded in kind. He leaped from the stage and, with a gesture of gleeful courtliness, offered Jaskulski his arm, whereupon the two cakewalked up the aisle to the astonishment of everyone in the arena. This wasn't Elvis bestowing a kiss on a lucky female, who then, according to the inescapable script, collapsed in tears like a successful supplicant at Lourdes; prancing down that aisle, Springsteen was not a star and Jaskulski was not a fan. They were a couple. He'd picked up a hint, asked for a dance, and she had said yes.

An hour later Springsteen almost topped that moment. Introducing the band just before heading into "Rosalita," he added a touch to his usual obeisance to Clarence Clemons, the enormous, splendidly decked-out black saxophone player: "King of the World . . . Master of the Universe . . . and . . . the Next President of the United States!" In two seconds it seemed like an obvious thing to do; one second before that it had been a shock so delicious it almost justified the campaign. Then, hard into "Rosalita," Springsteen and the band reached that point when the song hangs in the air—when the pace is most fierce and the question of whether our hero will get the girl most in doubt. At the precise moment when the tension almost cracks the song in half, Springsteen turned to Clemons and kissed him square on the lips.

On Halloween night in Los Angeles, fog covered the stage. Six crew members, dressed as ghouls, brought out a coffin. Springsteen emerged and sang "Haunted House," a 1964 hit by a deservedly obscure rockabilly singer called Jumpin' Gene Simmons. Don't cringe—he could just as well have sung "Ding Dong the Witch Is Dead," a 1939 hit by the Munchkins.

Five days after that, in Phoenix, Springsteen did not introduce Clarence Clemons as the next president of the United States. Instead, he walked onstage and said, "I don't know what you thought about what happened last night. I think it's terrifying."[1] Then he sang "Badlands," the most appropriate song he had to offer—for the time being.

As Jon Landau, now Springsteen's manager, wrote in 1968, an awareness of the Vietnam War could be felt all through Bob Dylan's *John Wesley Harding;* it is an almost certain bet that the songs Springsteen will now be writing will have something to do with the events of November 4. Those songs likely will not comment on those events; they will, I think, reflect those events back to us, fixing moods and telling stories that are, at present, out of reach. Not many rock 'n' rollers can be expected to react on this level. If Springsteen is able to do so, it will be at least in part because of his evident conviction that whether or not rock 'n' roll has a center, someone must act as if it does.

Note
1. Ronald Reagan was elected president on November 4, 1980.

George F. Will

■

Conservative columnist and commentator George F. Will attended a Springsteen concert at the Capitol Center in Landover, Maryland, in late August 1984, donning his typical uniform of bow tie and suit. On September 13, his column on Springsteen was syndicated nationwide. Will, like many others in the media at the time, misinterpreted Springsteen's message, believing Bruce was saying, in effect, if you work hard and long enough you too will also be able to live the vaunted American Dream, no matter what your socioeconomic circumstances. The column also appears in *The Morning After: American Successes and Excesses, 1981–1986* (1986), a collection of Will's commentary.

Bruuuuuce

■WHAT I DID on my summer vacation:

My friend Bruce Springsteen . . .

Okay, he's only my acquaintance, but my children now think I am a serious person. I met him because his colleague Max Weinberg and Max's wife, Rebecca, invited me to enjoy Max's work, which I did. He plays drums for Springsteen, who plays rock and roll for purists, of whom there are lots. For ten shows in New Jersey, he recently sold 16,000 $16 tickets in the first hour, all 202,000 in a day. His albums can sell one million copies on the first day of release.

There is a smidgen of androgyny in Springsteen who, rocketing around the stage in a T-shirt and headband, resembles Robert DeNiro in the combat scenes of *The Deerhunter*. This is rock for the United Steelworkers, accompanied by the opening barrage of the battle of the Somme. The saintly Rebecca met me with a small pouch of cotton—for my ears, she explained. She thinks I am a poor specimen, I thought. I made it three beats into the first number before packing my ears.

I may be the only 43-year-old American so out of the swim that I do not even know what marijuana smoke smells like. Perhaps at the concert I was surrounded by controlled substances. Certainly I was surrounded by orderly young adults earnestly—and correctly—insisting that Springsteen is a wholesome cultural portent.

For the uninitiated, the sensory blitzkrieg of a Springsteen concert is stunning. For the initiated, which included most of the 20,000 the night I experienced him, the lyrics, believe it or not, are most important. Today, "values" are all the rage, with political candidates claiming to have backpacks stuffed full of them. Springsteen's fans say his message affirms the right values. Certainly his manner does.

Many of his fans regarded me as exotic fauna at the concert (a bow tie and double-breasted blazer is not the dress code) and undertook to instruct me. A typical tutorial went like this:

Me: "What do you like about him?"

Male fan: "He sings about faith and traditional values."

Male fan's female friend, dryly: "And cars and girls."

Male fan: "No, no, it's about community and roots and perseverance and family."

She: "And cars and girls."

Let's not quibble. Cars and girls are American values, and this lyric surely expresses some elemental American sentiment: "Now mister the day my number comes in / I ain't never gonna ride / in no used car again."

Springsteen, a product of industrial New Jersey, is called the "blue-collar troubadour." But if this is the class struggle, its anthem—its "Internationale"—is the song that provides the title for his 18-month, worldwide tour: "Born in the U.S.A."

I have not got a clue about Springsteen's politics, if any, but flags get waved at his concerts while he sings songs about hard times. He is no whiner, and the recitation of closed factories and other problems always seems punctuated by a grand, cheerful affirmation: "Born in the U.S.A.!"

His songs, and the engaging homilies with which he introduces them, tell listeners to "downsize" their expectations—his phrase, borrowed from the auto industry, naturally. It is music for saying good-bye to Peter Pan: Life is real, life is earnest, life is a lot of work, but . . .

"Friday night's pay night, guys fresh out of work / Talking about the weekend, scrubbing off the dirt . . . Someday, mister, I'm gonna lead a better life than this."

An evening with Springsteen—an evening tends to wash over into the A.M., the concerts lasting four hours—is vivid proof that the work ethic is alive and well. Backstage there hovers the odor of Ben-Gay: Springsteen is an athlete draining himself for every audience.

But, then, consider Max Weinberg's bandaged fingers. The rigors of drumming have led to five tendonitis operations. He soaks his hands in hot water before a concert, in ice afterward, and sleeps with tight gloves on. Yes, of course, the whole E Street Band is making enough money to ease the pain. But they are not charging as much as they could, and the customers are happy. How many American businesses can say that?

If all Americans—in labor and management, who make steel or cars or shoes or textiles—made their products with as much energy and confidence as Springsteen and his merry band make music, there would be no need for Congress to be thinking about protectionism. No "domestic content" legislation is needed in the music industry. The British and other invasions have been met and matched.

In an age of lackadaisical effort and slipshod products, anyone who does anything—anything legal—conspicuously well and with zest is a national asset. Springsteen's tour is hard, honest work and evidence of the astonishing vitality of America's regions and generations. They produce distinctive tones of voice that other regions and generations embrace. There still is nothing quite like being born in the U.S.A.

T. Coraghessan Boyle

■

Although the story of "Greasy Lake" is inspired by Springsteen's "Spirit in the Night"—the epigraph is from the song—the characters come completely from the imagination of T. C. Boyle. Written in 1981, it appears in *Greasy Lake & Other Stories* (1985). Says Boyle, who was raised in the Hudson River Valley town of Peekskill, New York, "I see 'Greasy Lake' as a kind of riff on the song, a free take on its glorious spirit." A member of the English Department at the University of Southern California since 1978, Boyle is the author of many novels and short story collections, including *Descent of Man* (1979), *Water Music* (1982), *World's End* (1987), *If the River Was Whiskey* (1989), *East Is East* (1990), *The Road to Wellville* (1993), *Riven Rock* (1998), *T. C. Boyle Stories* (1999), *A Friend of the Earth* (2000), *After the Plague* (2001), and, most recently, *Drop City* (2003). A rock and blues fan, he has called rock "the most informative music of my life" (one of his short stories, "Stones in My Passway, Hellhound on My Trail," offers his typically idiosyncratic take on the death of the legendary bluesman Robert Johnson). Boyle once told *Rolling Stone* writer Anthony DeCurtis that he has been a Springsteen fan "from the beginning. I really love the early albums a lot, really related to them. Particularly this 'greasy lake' kind of notion. I get the impression," he adds, "that Asbury Park and Peekskill were similar in a lot of ways. So that song was the departure point for the story."[1]

Greasy Lake

from *Greasy Lake & Other Stories*

It's about a mile down on the dark side of Route 88.
—Bruce Springsteen

■THERE WAS A TIME when courtesy and winning ways went out of style, when it was good to be bad, when you cultivated decadence like a taste. We were all dangerous characters then. We wore torn-up leather jackets, slouched around with toothpicks in our mouths, sniffed glue and ether and what somebody claimed was cocaine. When we wheeled our parents' whining station wagons out into the street we left a patch of rubber half a block long. We drank gin and grape juice. Tango, Thunderbird, and Bali Hai. We were nineteen. We were bad. We read Andre Gide and struck elaborate poses to show that we didn't give a shit about anything. At night, we went up to Greasy Lake.

Through the center of town, up the strip, past the housing developments and shopping malls, street lights giving way to the thin streaming illumination of the headlights, trees crowding the asphalt in a black unbroken wall: that was the way out to Greasy Lake. The Indians had called it Wakan, a reference to the clarity of its waters. Now it was fetid and murky, the mud banks glittering with broken glass and strewn with beer cans and the charred remains of bonfires. There was a single ravaged island a hundred yards from shore, so stripped of vegetation it looked as if the air force had strafed it. We went up to the lake because everyone went there, because we wanted to snuff the rich scent of possibility on the breeze, watch a girl take off her clothes and plunge into the festering murk, drink beer, smoke pot, howl at the stars, savor the incongruous full-throated roar of rock and roll against the primeval susurrus of frogs and crickets. This was nature.

I was there one night, late, in the company of two dangerous characters. Digby wore a gold star in his right ear and allowed his father to pay his tuition at Cornell; Jeff was thinking of quitting school to become a painter/musician/head-shop proprietor. They were both expert in the social graces, quick with a sneer, able to manage a Ford with lousy shocks over a rutted and gutted blacktop road at eighty-five while rolling a joint as compact as a Tootsie Roll Pop stick. They could lounge against a bank of booming speakers and trade "man"s with the best of them or roll out across the dance floor as if their joints worked on bearings. They were slick and quick and they wore their mirror shades at breakfast and dinner, in the shower, in closets and caves. In short, they were bad.

I drove. Digby pounded the dashboard and shouted along with Toots & the Maytals while Jeff hung his head out the window and streaked the side of my mother's Bel Air with vomit. It was early June, the air soft as a hand on your cheek, the third night of summer vacation. The first two nights we'd been out till dawn, looking for something we never found. On this, the third night, we'd cruised the strip sixty-seven times, been in and out of every bar and club we could think of in a twenty-mile radius, stopped twice for bucket chicken and forty-cent hamburgers, debated going to a party at the house of a girl Jeff's sister knew, and chucked two dozen raw eggs at mailboxes and hitchhikers. It was 2:00 A.M.; the bars were closing. There was nothing to do but take a bottle of lemon-flavored gin up to Greasy Lake.

The taillights of a single car winked at us as we swung into the dirt lot with its tufts of weed and washboard corrugations; '57 Chevy, mint, metallic blue. On the far side of the lot, like the exoskeleton of some gaunt chrome insect, a chopper leaned against its kickstand. And that was it for excitement: some junkie half-wit biker and a car freak pumping his girlfriend. Whatever it was we were looking for, we weren't about to find it at Greasy Lake. Not that night.

But then all of a sudden Digby was fighting for the wheel. "Hey, that's Tony Lovett's car! Hey!" he shouted, while I stabbed at the brake pedal and the Bel Air nosed up to the gleaming bumper of the parked Chevy. Digby leaned on the horn, laughing, and instructed me to put my brights on. I flicked on the brights. This was hilarious. A joke. Tony would experience premature withdrawal and expect to be confronted by grim-looking state troopers with flashlights. We hit the horn, strobed the lights, and then jumped out of the car to press our witty faces to Tony's windows; for all we knew we might even catch a glimpse of some little fox's tit, and then we could slap backs with red-faced Tony, roughhouse a little, and go on to new heights of adventure and daring.

The first mistake, the one that opened the whole floodgate, was losing my grip on the keys. In the excitement, leaping from the car with the gin in one hand and a roach clip in the other, I spilled them in the grass—in the dark, rank, mysterious nighttime grass of Greasy Lake. This was a tactical error, as damaging and irreversible in its way as Westmoreland's decision to dig in at Khe Sanh.[2] I felt it like a jab of intuition, and I stopped there by the open door, peering vaguely into the night that puddled up round my feet.

The second mistake—and this was inextricably bound up with the first—was identifying the car as Tony Lovett's. Even before the very bad character in greasy jeans and engineer boots ripped out of the driver's door, I began to realize that this chrome blue was much lighter than the robin's-egg of Tony's car, and that Tony's car didn't have rear-mounted speakers. Judging from their expressions, Digby and Jeff were privately groping toward the same inevitable and unsettling conclusion as I was.

In any case, there was no reasoning with this bad greasy character— clearly he was a man of action. The first lusty Rockette kick of his steel-toed boot caught me under the chin, chipped my favorite tooth, and left me sprawled in the dirt. Like a fool, I'd gone down on one knee to comb the stiff hacked grass for the keys, my mind making connections in the most dragged-out, testudineous way, knowing that things had gone wrong, that I was in a lot of trouble, and that the lost ignition key was my grail and my salvation. The three or four succeeding blows were mainly absorbed by my right buttock and the tough piece of bone at the base of my spine.

Meanwhile, Digby vaulted the kissing bumpers and delivered a savage kung-fu blow to the greasy character's collarbone. Digby had just finished a course in martial arts for phys-ed credit and had spent the better part of the past two nights telling us apocryphal tales of Bruce Lee types and of the raw power invested in lightning blows shot from coiled wrists, ankles, and elbows. The greasy character was unimpressed. He merely backed off a step, his face like a Toltec mask, and laid Digby out with a single whistling roundhouse blow . . . but by now Jeff had got into the act, and I was beginning to extricate myself from the dirt, a tinny compound of shock, rage, and impotence wadded in my throat.

Jeff was on the guy's back, biting at his ear. Digby was on the ground, cursing. I went for the tire iron I kept under the driver's seat. I kept it there because bad characters always keep tire irons under the driver's seat, for just such an occasion as this. Never mind that I hadn't been involved in a fight since sixth grade, when a kid with a sleepy eye and two streams of mucus depending from his nostrils hit me in the knee with a Louisville slugger; never mind that I'd touched the tire iron exactly twice before, to change tires: it was there. And I went for it.

I was terrified. Blood was beating in my ears, my hands were shaking, my heart turning over like a dirt bike in the wrong gear. My antagonist was shirtless, and a single cord of muscle flashed across his chest as he bent forward to peel Jeff from his back like a wet overcoat. "Motherfucker," he spat, over and over, and I was aware in that instant that all four of us—Digby, Jeff, and myself included—were chanting "motherfucker, motherfucker," as if it were a battle cry. (What happened next? the detective asks the murderer from beneath the turned-down brim of his porkpie hat. I don't know, the murderer says, something came over me. Exactly.)

Digby poked the flat of his hand in the bad character's face and I came at him like a kamikaze, mindless, raging, stung with humiliation— the whole thing, from the initial boot in the chin to this murderous primal instant involving no more than sixty hyperventilating, gland-flooding seconds—I came at him and brought the tire iron down across his ear.

The effect was instantaneous, astonishing. He was a stunt man and this was Hollywood, he was a big grimacing toothy balloon and I was a man with a straight pin. He collapsed. Wet his pants. Went loose in his boots.

A single second, big as a zeppelin, floated by. We were standing over him in a circle, gritting our teeth, jerking our necks, our limbs and hands and feet twitching with glandular discharges. No one said anything. We just stared down at the guy, the car freak, the lover, the bad greasy character laid low. Digby looked at me; so did Jeff. I was still holding the tire iron, a tuft of hair clinging to the crook like dandelion fluff, like down. Rattled, I dropped it in the dirt, already envisioning the headlines, the pitted faces of the police inquisitors, the gleam of handcuffs, clank of bars, the big black shadows rising from the back of the cell . . . when suddenly a raw torn shriek cut through me like all the juice in all the electric chairs in the country.

It was the fox. She was short, barefoot, dressed in panties and a man's shirt. "Animals!" she screamed, running at us with her fists clenched and wisps of blow-dried hair in her face. There was a silver chain round her ankle, and her toenails flashed in the glare of the headlights. I think it was the toenails that did it. Sure, the gin and the cannabis and even the Kentucky Fried may have had a hand in it, but it was the sight of those flaming toes that set us off—the toad emerging from the loaf in *Virgin Spring,* lipstick smeared on a child: she was already tainted. We were on her like Bergman's deranged brothers—see no evil, hear none, speak none—panting, wheezing, tearing at her clothes, grabbing for flesh. We were bad characters, and we were scared and hot and three steps over the line—anything could have happened.

It didn't.

Before we could pin her to the hood of the car, our eyes masked with lust and greed and the purest primal badness, a pair of headlights swung into the lot. There we were, dirty, bloody, guilty, dissociated from humanity and civilization, the first of the Ur-crimes behind us, the second in progress, shreds of nylon panty and spandex brassiere dangling from our fingers, our flies open, lips licked—there we were, caught in the spotlight. Nailed.

We bolted. First for the car, and then, realizing we had no way of starting it, for the woods. I thought nothing. I thought escape. The headlights came at me like accusing fingers. I was gone.

Ram-bam-bam, across the parking lot, past the chopper and into the feculent undergrowth at the lake's edge, insects flying up in my face, weeds whipping, frogs and snakes and red-eyed turtles splashing off into the night: I was already ankle-deep in muck and tepid water and still going strong. Behind me, the girl's screams rose in intensity, disconsolate, incriminating, the screams of the Sabine women, the Christian martyrs, Anne Frank dragged from the garret. I kept going, pursued by those cries, imagining cops and bloodhounds. The water was up to my knees when I realized what I was doing: I was going to swim for it. Swim the breadth of Greasy Lake and hide myself in the thick clot of woods on the far side. They'd never find me there.

I was breathing in sobs, in gasps. The water lapped at my waist as I looked out over the moon-burnished ripples, the mats of algae that clung to the surface like scabs. Digby and Jeff had vanished. I paused. Listened. The girl was quieter now, screams tapering to sobs, but there were male voices, angry, excited, and the high-pitched ticking of the second car's engine. I waded deeper, stealthy, hunted, the ooze sucking at my sneakers. As I was about to take the plunge—at the very instant I dropped my shoulder for the first slashing stroke—I blundered into something. Something unspeakable, obscene, something soft, wet, moss-grown. A patch of weed? A log? When I reached out to touch it, it gave like a rubber duck, it gave like flesh.

In one of those nasty little epiphanies for which we are prepared by films and TV and childhood visits to the funeral home to ponder the shrunken painted forms of dead grandparents, I understood what it was that bobbed there so inadmissibly in the dark. Understood, and stumbled back in horror and revulsion, my mind yanked in six different directions (I was nineteen, a mere child, an infant, and here in the space of five minutes I'd struck down one greasy character and blundered into the waterlogged carcass of a second), thinking, the keys, the keys, why did I have to go and lose the keys? I stumbled back, but the muck took hold of my feet—a sneaker snagged, balance lost—and suddenly I was pitching face forward into the buoyant black mass, throwing out my hands in desperation while simultaneously conjuring the image of reeking frogs and muskrats revolving in slicks of their own deliquescing juices. AAAAArrrgh! I shot from the water like a torpedo, the dead man rotating to expose a mossy beard and eyes cold as the moon. I must have shouted out, thrashing around in the weeds, because the voices behind me suddenly became animated.

"What was that?"

"It's them, it's them: they tried to, tried to . . . *rape* me!" Sobs.

A man's voice, flat Midwestern accent. "You sons a bitches, we'll kill you!"

Frogs, crickets.

Then another voice, harsh, *r*-less, Lower East Side: "Motherfucker!" I recognized the verbal virtuosity of the bad greasy character in the engineer boots. Tooth chipped, sneakers gone, coated in mud and slime and worse, crouching breathless in the weeds waiting to have my ass thoroughly and definitively kicked and fresh from the hideous stinking embrace of a three-days-dead-corpse, I suddenly felt a rush of joy and vindication: the son of a bitch was alive! Just as quickly, my bowels turned to ice. "Come on out of there, you pansy motherfuckers!" the bad greasy character was screaming. He shouted curses till he was out of breath.

The crickets started up again, then the frogs. I held my breath. All at once there was a sound in the reeds, a swishing, a splash: thunk-a-thunk. They were throwing rocks. The frogs fell silent. I cradled my head. Swish, swish, thunk-a-thunk. A wedge of feldspar the size of a cue ball glanced off my knee. I bit my finger.

It was then that they turned to the car. I heard a door slam, a curse, and then the sound of the headlights shattering—almost a good-natured sound, celebratory, like corks popping from the necks of bottles. This was succeeded by the dull booming of the fenders, metal on metal, and then the icy crash of the windshield. I inched forward, elbows and knees, my belly pressed to the muck, thinking of guerrillas and commandos and *The Naked and the Dead.* I parted the weeds and squinted the length of the parking lot.

The second car—it was a Trans-Am—was still running, its high beams washing the scene in a lurid stagy light. Tire iron flailing, the greasy bad character was laying into the side of my mother's Bel Air like an avenging demon, his shadow riding up the trunks of the trees. Whomp. Whomp. Whomp-whomp. The other two guys—blond types, in fraternity jackets—were helping out with tree branches and skull-sized boulders. One of them was gathering up bottles, rocks, muck, candy wrappers, used condoms, pop-tops, and other refuse and pitching it through the window on the driver's side. I could see the fox, a white bulb behind the windshield of the '57 Chevy. "Bobbie," she whined over the thumping, "come *on.*" The greasy character paused a moment, took one good swipe at the left taillight, and then heaved the tire iron halfway across the lake. Then he fired up the '57 and was gone.

Blond head nodded at blond head. One said something to the other, too low for me to catch. They were no doubt thinking that in helping to annihilate my mother's car they'd committed a fairly rash act, and thinking too that there were three bad characters connected with that very car watching them from the woods. Perhaps other possibilities occurred to them as well—police, jail cells, justices of the peace, reparations, lawyers, irate parents, fraternal censure. Whatever they were thinking, they suddenly dropped branches, bottles, and rocks and sprang for their car in unison, as if they'd choreographed it. Five seconds. That's all it took. The engine shrieked, the tires squealed, a cloud of dust rose from the rutted lot and then settled back on darkness.

I don't know how long I lay there, the bad breath of decay all around me, my jacket heavy as a bear, the primordial ooze subtly reconstituting itself to accommodate my upper thighs and testicles. My jaws ached, my knee throbbed, my coccyx was on fire. I contemplated suicide, wondered if I'd need bridgework, scraped the recesses of my brain for some sort of excuse to give my parents—a tree had fallen on the car, I was blindsided by a bread truck, hit and run, vandals had got to it while we were playing chess at Digby's. Then I thought of the dead man. He was probably the only person on the planet worse off than I was. I thought about him, fog on the lake, insects chirring eerily, and felt the tug of fear, felt the darkness opening up inside me like a set of jaws. Who was he, I wondered, this victim of time and circumstance bobbing sorrowfully in the lake at my back. The owner of the chopper, no doubt, a bad older character come to this. Shot during a murky drug deal, drowned while drunkenly frolicking in the lake. Another headline. My car was wrecked; he was dead.

When the eastern half of the sky went from black to cobalt and the trees began to separate themselves from the shadows, I pushed myself up from the mud and stepped out into the open. By now the birds had begun to take over for the crickets, and dew lay slick on the leaves. There was a smell in the air, raw and sweet at the same time, the smell of the sun firing buds and opening blossoms. I contemplated the car. It lay there like a wreck along the highway, like a steel sculpture left over from a vanished civilization. Everything was still. This was nature.

I was circling the car, as dazed and bedraggled as the sole survivor of an air blitz, when Digby and Jeff emerged from the trees behind me.

Digby's face was crosshatched with smears of dirt; Jeff's jacket was gone and his shirt was torn across the shoulder. They slouched across the lot, looking sheepish, and silently came up beside me to gape at the ravaged automobile. No one said a word. After a while Jeff swung open the driver's door and began to scoop the broken glass and garbage off the seat. I looked at Digby. He shrugged. "At least they didn't slash the tires," he said.

It was true: the tires were intact. There was no windshield, the headlights were staved in, and the body looked as if it had been sledgehammered for a quarter a shot at the county fair, but the tires were inflated to regulation pressure. The car was drivable. In silence, all three of us bent to scrape the mud and shattered glass from the interior. I said nothing about the biker. When we were finished, I reached in my pocket for the keys, experienced a nasty stab of recollection, cursed myself, and turned to search the grass. I spotted them almost immediately, no more than five feet from the open door, glinting like jewels in the first tapering shaft of sunlight. There was no reason to get philosophical about it: I eased into the seat and turned the engine over.

It was at that precise moment that the silver Mustang with the flame decals rumbled into the lot. All three of us froze; then Digby and Jeff slid into the car and slammed the door. We watched as the Mustang rocked and bobbed across the ruts and finally jerked to a halt beside the forlorn chopper at the far end of the lot. "Let's go," Digby said. I hesitated, the Bel Air wheezing beneath me.

Two girls emerged from the Mustang. Tight jeans, stiletto heels, hair like frozen fur. They bent over the motorcycle, paced back and forth aimlessly, glanced once or twice at us, and then ambled over to where the reeds sprang up in a green fence round the perimeter of the lake. One of them cupped her hands to her mouth. "Al," she called. "Hey, Al!"

"Come on," Digby hissed. "Let's get out of here."

But it was too late. The second girl was picking her way across the lot, unsteady on her heels, looking up at us and then away. She was older—twenty-five or -six—and as she came closer we could see there was something wrong with her: she was stoned or drunk, lurching now and waving her arms for balance. I gripped the steering wheel as if it were the ejection lever of a flaming jet, and Digby spat out my name, twice, terse and impatient.

"Hi," the girl said.

We looked at her like zombies, like war veterans, like deaf-and-dumb pencil peddlers.

She smiled, her lips cracked and dry. "Listen," she said, bending from the waist to look in the window, "you guys seen Al?" Her pupils were pinpoints, her eyes glass. She jerked her neck. "That's his bike over there—Al's. You seen him?"

Al. I didn't know what to say. I wanted to get out of the car and retch, I wanted to go home to my parents' house and crawl into bed. Digby poked me in the ribs. "We haven't seen anybody," I said.

The girl seemed to consider this, reaching out a slim veiny arm to brace herself against the car. "No matter," she said, slurring the *t*'s, "he'll turn up." And then, as if she'd just taken stock of the whole scene—the ravaged car and our battered faces, the desolation of the place—she said: "Hey, you guys look like some pretty bad characters—been fightin', huh?" We stared straight ahead, rigid as catatonics. She was fumbling in her pocket and muttering something. Finally she held out a handful of tablets in glassine wrappers: "Hey, you want to party, you want to do some of these with me and Sarah?"

I just looked at her. I thought I was going to cry. Digby broke the silence. "No, thanks," he said, leaning over me. "Some other time."

I put the car in gear and it inched forward with a groan, shaking off pellets of glass like an old dog shedding water after a bath, heaving over the ruts on its worn springs, creeping toward the highway. There was a sheen of sun on the lake. I looked back. The girl was still standing there, watching us, her shoulders slumped, hand outstretched.

Notes

1. Quoted in Anthony DeCurtis, "A Punk's Past Recaptured," *Rocking My Life Away: Writing About Music and Other Matters* (Durham, N.C.: Duke University Press, 1998), p. 306.
2. The siege of Khe Sanh began on January 21, 1968, when the North Vietnamese launched a full-scale attack on American forces; 205 Marines lost their lives. Considered a major tactical error, the siege distracted General William Westmoreland's attention while the Viet Cong planned bigger and deadlier assaults. Springsteen refers to Khe Sanh in "Born in the U.S.A." ("He had a brother at Khe Sahn [sic] fighting off the Viet Cong. / They're still there, he's all gone).

Bobbie Ann Mason

■

Bobbie Ann Mason writes primarily about working-class characters from western Kentucky; consequently, a sense of place is an important theme throughout her work. Her novels and short stories include *Shiloh and Other Stories* (1982), *In Country* (1985), *Spence + Lila* (1988), *Feather Crowns* (1993), and *Zigzagging Down a Wild Trail: Stories* (2001). She has also written nonfiction: *Clear Springs* (1999) is her memoir about a bookish girl growing up in the rural South; *Elvis Presley: A Penguin Life* (2003) is a brief biography of the seminal rock and roller in the Penguin Lives series. Rock and roll is featured quite prominently in *In Country*. It is her first novel and still, perhaps, her best known (it was adapted into a movie starring Bruce Willis and Emily Lloyd). It tells the story of the rather awkward relationship between Vietnam War veteran Emmett and his niece Sam (Samantha) Hughes, whose father died in the war. Mason has said, "In Sam's quest to learn about her father, she develops a crush on Tom, another Vietnam veteran, and she looks also upon the persona of Bruce Springsteen in *Born in the U.S.A.* as a father figure. Springsteen's album seems to bridge the gap between Sam's father's generation and her own, and it looks to the future." Mason once told Cara Feinberg, of *The Atlantic*'s online journal (Atlantic Unbound, September 19, 2001), that "*Born in the U.S.A.* is sort of a soundtrack to the whole book. The story takes place in the summer of 1984, and that was the album that was at the top of the charts; it just seemed to fall into place." The following excerpts include several passages in which Springsteen—and his larger-than-life persona—appear in the book.

from *In Country*

■It was the summer of the Michael Jackson *Victory* tour and the Bruce Springsteen *Born in the U.S.A.* tour, neither of which Sam got to go to. At her graduation, the commencement speaker, a Methodist minister, had preached about keeping the country strong, stressing sacrifice. He made Sam nervous. She started thinking about war, and it stayed in her mind all summer.

Emmett came back from Vietnam, but Sam's father did not. After his discharge, Emmett stayed with his parents two weeks, then left. He couldn't adjust. Several months later, he returned, and Sam's mother let him live with them, in the house she had bought with her husband's life insurance policy. Emmett stayed, helping out around the house. People said Irene babied him. She treated him like someone disabled, and she never expected him to get a job. She always said the war "messed him up." She had worked as a receptionist for a dentist, and she received compensation payments from the government. In retrospect, Sam realized how strange those early years were. When Emmett moved in, he brought some friends with him—hippies. Hopewell didn't have any hippies, or war protesters, and when Emmett showed up with three scruffy guys in ponytails and beads, they created a sensation. The friends came from places out west—Albuquerque, Eugene, Santa Cruz. Boys in Hopewell didn't even wear long hair until the seventies, when it finally became fashionable. Sam had a strong memory of Emmett in his Army jacket and black boots, with a purple headband running through his wild hair. She remembered his friends piling out of a psychedelic van, but she remembered little else about them. People in town still talked about the time Emmett and the hippies flew a Vietcong flag from the courthouse tower. The county circuit court clerk saw them head up the stairs and said later she knew something was about to happen. They fastened the flag to the side of the tower with masking tape, covering part of the clock face. Merchants around the square got nervous and had them arrested for disturbing the peace. The funny part, Emmett always said, was that nobody had even recognized that it was a Vietcong flag. He had had it made by a tailor in Pleiku, the way one might order a wedding suit. Soon after the flag incident, when burglars broke into a building supply company on Main Street, using a concrete block to smash a window, people were suspicious of Emmett's crowd, but no one ever proved anything.

The friends went away eventually, and Emmett calmed down. For a couple of years, he attended Murray State, but then he dropped out. He did odd jobs—mowing yards, repairing small appliances—and got by. Now and then a rumor would surface. At one time, neighbors had the idea that Patty Hearst was hiding out with Emmett and Irene. For a week, Sam had been too embarrassed to go to school, but later she was proud of Emmett. He was like a brother. She and Emmett were still pals, and he didn't try to boss her around. They liked the same music— mostly golden oldies. Emmett's favorite current groups were the Cars and the Talking Heads.

❁ ❁ ❁

"Which do you think would be worse—to die from a brain tumor or be killed in a war?"

Dawn kept scrubbing the skillet, in thought. "I don't know. Sometimes I think it must be better to die all of a sudden. My mom just lingered on, and they said it was awful. I was too little to remember."

When she finished the skillet, Dawn took a quart of Coke from the refrigerator and got out some ice. Dawn's refrigerator was small and old-fashioned, with one of those freezers that didn't have a separate door. In the living room, they drank the Cokes, and Sam flipped through some old records Dawn's brothers had left—Willie Nelson, Christopher Cross, Elton John, singers Sam hated.

"I wish I could buy that new Springsteen album," Sam said. "But I have to save all my money for a car."

"I hear that on the radio all the time at the Burger Boy."

"Did you know the title song's about a vet?"

"'Born in the U.S.A.'?"

"Yeah. In the song, his brother gets killed over there, and then the guy gets in a lot of trouble when he gets back home. He can't get a job, and he ends up in jail. It's a great song."

"I like the song about the car wash—where it rains all the time and he lost his job and his girlfriend. That's the saddest song. That song really scares me." Dawn shuddered and rattled ice in her glass. "My brother took all my records," she said. "He stole the stereo I had in my room, and my radio blew up."

"I've been listening to my mother's old records," said Sam. "She's off in Lexington having a good time, and she doesn't seem worried about Emmett. That really gripes my soul."

Hopewell did not have a mall, but it had a small shopping center, a dozen stores between Penney's and the K Mart. Sam met Dawn at the shopping center that afternoon. On the telephone, Dawn had said it was urgent. Over Cokes in a booth at the K Mart, Dawn told Sam she might be pregnant. Sam had been dying to tell Dawn about riding around with Tom, but now her news seemed inappropriate and trivial. This was unreal, like a scene in a movie.

"Have you told Ken?" Sam asked anxiously, her insides stirring.

"Not yet."

"Will your daddy kill you if you have to get married?"

"Oh, he just doesn't want to lose his housekeeper. He can find some woman. Then he won't have to pretend he's working late." Dawn laughed. "He tries to set such a good example, but if it wasn't for me, he'd just go wild."

Sam tried to cheer Dawn up by telling her about Tom and the VW. He hadn't let her drive the car, because it didn't have insurance. They had gone as far as the Holiday Inn and turned around, and he had dropped her off at home.

"He's really sexy," Sam said. "Come to think of it, he looks sort of like Bruce Springsteen, but he got wounded in Vietnam and his back is stiff. He moves kind of jerky."

"How old is he?"

"About thirty-four."

"Wow! That's old." Dawn drank from her Coke and squirmed in the booth, her tanned legs sucking the orange vinyl. Her earrings had purple feathers on them. "Come to the drugstore with me," she said. "They've got a good jewelry counter there."

At the drugstore, Dawn whispered, "I want to buy one of those kits to test for pregnancy."

Bruce Springsteen's new performance video, *Dancing in the Dark,* was on TV. His jeans were as tight as rubber gloves, and he danced like a revved-up sports car about to take off.

"He's awful good," said Emmett.

"He turns me on high," said Sam, mesmerized.

"What do you mean?"

"It's something about the way his jeans fit," Sam said. "You wouldn't understand."

It made her sad. She kept thinking about what it would be like to dance with Tom. He had said she was cute. But he could never move with Bruce Springsteen's exuberant energy. She recalled Frankenstein and his monster dancing to "Puttin' on the Ritz" in an old Gene Wilder movie. The monster wore clubfoot shoes and clomped. It was pathetically funny. She hoped the veteran's dance wouldn't be like that. It would be too depressing.

"They call Bruce 'the Boss,'" Emmett said idly. Bruce was still dancing in the dark. Sam loved the part where he picked a girl in the audience to dance with. The girl was in shock that he chose her.

"Man, he can boss me around any old time he wants to," Sam said.

❋   ❋   ❋

As she spotted the Golden Arches, she thought of Emmett. And then it occurred to her that Emmett might have the same problem as Tom. It seemed so obvious now. That was why he didn't have any girlfriends. Maybe Emmett even had an actual wound, nerve damage of some kind. Tom said he didn't have a wound, but maybe he did. Emmett didn't want a job because men had jobs to support families, and if they couldn't have families, then why bother? It seemed a simple explanation. Women wanted jobs to prove a point, but men had jobs because of women.

Tom *had* to get one of those pumps, she thought. And maybe Emmett needed one too. She wondered what had happened between him and Anita last night. She'd had a pleasant picture in her mind of them together, in Anita's apartment. But now she wasn't sure.

She realized a song was playing in her head.

> *You can't start a fire without a spark*
> *This gun's for hire*
> *Even if we're just dancing in the dark*

She turned the radio on, hoping to hear Bruce Springsteen. Somehow there was a secret knowledge in his songs, as though he knew exactly what she was feeling. Some dumb song by the Thompson Twins was playing. . . .

She switched on MTV. Cyndi Lauper and her fat face. On Channel 7, *The Dogs of War* was ending. It occurred to Sam that being a mercenary soldier in Africa would be more exciting than anything she could think of doing around Hopewell. She switched back to MTV, hoping the Springsteen video would come on. Tom's smile was like Bruce's. Tom was the only exciting thing in Hopewell. The only reason to stay there was so she could work at the Burger Boy and wait on Tom if he came in. The sadness of his affliction hit her then like a truck. She thought of all the lives wasted by the war. She wanted to cry, but then she wanted to yell and scream and kick. She could imagine fighting, but only against war. All the boys getting killed, on both sides. And boys getting muti-lated. And then not being allowed to grow up. That was it—they didn't get to grow up and become regular people. They had to stand outside, playing games, fooling around, acting like kids who couldn't get girl-friends. It was absurd. She thought she was crashing.

They are in Maryland. Sam is at the shopping mall down the road from the Holiday Inn. The transmission has been repaired—for $258.69—and Emmett and Mamaw are waiting for her at the motel. At the record store, she flips through the Beatles albums: the *White Album, Sgt. Pepper's Lonely Hearts Club Band, Abbey Road, Meet the Beatles, Magical Mystery Tour, Let It Be.* No new album. There's nothing in the 45s either. The new song must be a bootleg tape, the chatty, rotund clerk suggests. But he hasn't heard of it. Sam's gaze lingers on the *Born in the U.S.A.* album, displayed near the counter. On the cover, Bruce Springsteen is facing the flag, as though studying it, trying to figure out its meaning. It is such a big flag the stars don't even show in the picture—just red-and-white stripes. Her mother's credit card could buy that album. Impulsively, Sam buys it, realizing too late that the vinyl will probably melt in the hot car.

James Wolcott

■

One of the criticisms leveled at Springsteen over the years is that he comes, in the words of James Wolcott circa the December 1985 issue of *Vanity Fair*, "built to rock-critic specifications" (earlier, in October 1980, Springsteen countered: "That bothered me a lot, being perceived as an invention, a ship passing by. I'd been playing for ten years. I knew where I came from. . . . I knew what I believed and what I wanted." See "Out in the Streets" by Robert Hilburn in this volume).[1] Wolcott also critically addresses several other issues, including the passing of the rock and roll crown from Elvis to Springsteen, the increasingly religious fervor associated with Springsteen's live performances, and the singer's essentially cheerful and optimistic nature.

The Hagiography of Bruce Springsteen
Vanity Fair

■BRUCE SPRINGSTEEN HAS turned the deindustrialization of America into a poetic dirge, a bitter hymn to polluted waters and hulks of rust. Silent factories are to him what church ruins were to the English Romantics, crumbling theaters of decay which serve as houses of lost faith. With his guitar slung over his shoulder like an assault rifle, Springsteen has staked out the high ground in rock.

It would be a fib to say that I'm a big fan of Springsteen's: I'm not. His is not a voice that speaks to me in the night. I would rather listen to Elvis Costello pour his blue moods into a shot glass or John "Rotten" Lydon caw like a raven across a field of electronic static than accompany Bruce Springsteen once again down that long, lonesome highway. He's just too cornball sincere for my corrupt taste. But what makes me feel like a killjoy regarding the Springsteen craze has less to do with Springsteen himself than with the elephant caravan of blather that now attends his every move. Piety has begun to collect around Springsteen's curly head like mist around a mountaintop. The mountain can't be blamed for the mist, but still—the reverence is getting awfully thick. It's beginning to obscure the view.

Springsteen has long been a darling of the city-slick Establishment.

Time and *Newsweek* splashed him on their covers when he was barely a rumor beyond the Eastern Seaboard, and the New York *Times* loves bouncing him on its bony knee. (During Springsteen's '85 mega-tour, John Rockwell, Jon Pareles, and Robert Palmer of the *Times* shuffled behind the Boss bearing gold, frankincense, and myrrh.) Indeed, one of the early criticisms of Springsteen was that he might have been built to rock-critic specifications, so perfectly choice were his moving parts. I mean, here he was, a raw diamond from New Jersey who could rock it simple like Buddy Holly, rhyme it complex like Bob Dylan, rasp it from the gut like Gary U.S. Bonds, and comb mystery from the ether like Van Morrison. No wonder cynics (like me) thought he was a slice of Wonder Bread in funky wrapping, blandly wholesome, vitamin-enriched, and doomed to stale. But this great white hope was no Gerry Cooney, making a quick flurry for a fat paycheck. Springsteen's staying power has proved the cynics wrong.

Over the years, Springsteen's mandate has changed. In the beginning his mission was to restore muscular faith in rock during a time of narcissism, power chords, and dazed androids wandering the world in Supp-Hose. (The release of Springsteen's first two albums coincided with David Bowie's *Ziggy Stardust–Aladdin Sane* mutant phase.) Let others play stinky pinky: Springsteen would rule the scene with a righteous raised fist. And as Springsteen became a fixture in the lives of his fans, they began to fashion a larger role for him. This becomes evident with a peek into the devotional pages of Robert Hilburn's recent book on the Boss, *Springsteen.*[2] A coffee-table clunker that consists mostly of photographs of its subject striking hallelujah poses, *Springsteen* has a sliver of text in which Hilburn fits his hero for a crown. Whose crown? Three guesses, and the first two don't count. "I never thought we'd see another figure in American rock as embracing as Elvis, but Springsteen has become that figure," he declares.

We know what happened to Elvis, of course—bloat, a talent prostituted to kitsch, nights of drug-zombie isolation in an enormous bed. So to the shining eyes of the faithful, Springsteen's task is to redeem the promise that Elvis fumbled. Where Elvis became a pearl-encrusted whale, Springsteen has kept weight-lifter fit; where Elvis doled out Cadillacs to his friends and embodied a honcho individualism, Springsteen donates money to food banks and unions under siege; where Elvis made dinky movies, featuring speedboats, padded bikinis, and such immortal ditties as "Do the Clam," Springsteen makes homey videos, in which he plays baseball and his wife waves hi.

To the more political of Springsteen's admirers, Elvis is an iffy role model—after all, he shook hands with Nixon, who made him an honorary narc, complete with crime fighter's badge. The journalist Jack Newfield, a Machiavelli in search of a prince, finds in Springsteen the "existential growth" of a Robert Kennedy and the populist values of a Jack Newfield. "The values he extols are the best old American values—work, family, hometown roots, loyalty, idealism despite bad times," wrote Newfield in the *Village Voice*. "They are certainly my values." Oh, Jack, you're such a slut. In the populist dream scenario, Springsteen emerges as the Woody Guthrie of America's tent cities and cheese lines. And of course Springsteen has helped cradle such dreams by incorporating Guthrie's "This Land Is Your Land" into his live show, blowing the dust off that hokey anthem. What will he do as a follow-up? Carry the entire Joad family on his back in a remake of *The Grapes of Wrath*?[3]

A sacred-heart-of-Jesus note is creeping into the more idolatrous writing on Springsteen. Hilburn speaks of the "prayerful edge" Springsteen gives to the words of "Follow That Dream," and Chet Flippo in *People* refers to Springsteen's "psalms" and "rock theology."[4] Concert reports on Springsteen have tended to paint him as a gentle shepherd quieting his flock with stories about baseball, his folks, and credit unions. One amusing thing that's happened since Springsteen started playing big outdoor stadia is that the natives have gotten a little restless during these parables ("not as attentively listened to as they once were," noted *Rolling Stone*), which has put critics and old-time Springsteen fans in a huff. Critics have also fretted over the fact that audiences react to "Born in the U.S.A." as a rouser rather than take heed of its whipped-dog lyrics.

It seems to me that the fans have the saner response. The thunderboom beat of "Born in the U.S.A." is more compelling than its case history about a small-town loser being sent to 'Nam to "kill the yellow man," just as the saloon esprit of "Glory Days" carries more conviction than its ironic message. Similarly, fans recognize that Springsteen's soul-baring raps are simply something he has to dislodge from his craw, like *Nebraska*. Besides, not everybody wants to be evangelized.

Where I part company from the fans is in their hostility to Springsteen's new wife, Julianne Phillips. (In concert, they boo the mention of her name.) Apparently, people wish Bruce had married a woman of "substance" rather than a swimsuit model and movie-of-the-week actress. But if Springsteen is going to be coached by stone faces like Jack Newfield as to his social responsibilities, he's going to need every light moment he can hoard. One of my favorite characters is the old college chum of Dr. Johnson's who remarked that he tried to be a philosopher but somehow cheerfulness kept breaking in. That's Bruce Springsteen's saving grace, too. He tries to be a prophet but cheerfulness keeps breaking in. After the car-stereo bombast of *Born in the U.S.A.* (album and tour), Bruce Springsteen certainly needs to undo his bandanna and let his mighty brow cool. Marriage may be the place where he recharges his cheerfulness between heavy clanks of toil. Virtue, it's a wearisome thing.

Notes

1. As recently as August 2002, Mark Gauvreau Judge decried what he considered the idolatry of Bruce Springsteen—that is, the public's attempt, in effect, to turn him into a secular saint. See "The Cult of Bruce," *Wall Street Journal,* August 23, 2002. In a blistering article in *Esquire,* John Lombardi said much the same thing, but years earlier. See "The Sanctification of Bruce Springsteen and the Rise of Mass Hip," *Esquire,* December 1988.
2. Robert Hilburn, *Springsteen* (New York: Rolling Stone Press, 1985).
3. The spirit of Woody Guthrie did indeed live on. Ten years later, in 1995, Springsteen released *The Ghost of Tom Joad,* which was inspired by John Steinbeck's *The Grapes of Wrath* and, especially, John Ford's film adaptation.
4. Chet Flippo, "Blue Collar Troubadour," *People,* September 3, 1984.

Simon Frith

■

English rock critic Simon Frith has written extensively on music and culture for the *Village Voice* and other publications. He has taught sociology at the University of Warwick and is director of the John Logie Baird Centre for Research in Film, Television, and Music at the University of Strathclyde in Glasgow. The following essay, written in 1987, is from *Music for Pleasure: Essays in the Sociology of Pop* (1988). Its overriding theme is the perception of authenticity. Frith offers a distinctly European perspective on the Springsteen phenomenon. Thus, Springsteen, in his dual roles of rock and roll icon and bard of the common man and common woman, represents "an authentic popular tradition."

The Real Thing— Bruce Springsteen

from *Music for Pleasure*

Introduction

■ MY GUESS IS that by Christmas 1986 Bruce Springsteen was making more money per day than any other pop star—more than Madonna, more than Phil Collins or Mark Knopfler, more than Paul McCartney even; *Time* calculated that he had earned $7.5 million in the first *week* of his *Live* LP release. This five-record boxed set went straight to the top of the American LP sales charts (it reputedly sold a million copies on its first day, grossing $50 million "out of the gate") and stayed there throughout the Christmas season. It was the nation's best-seller in November and December, when more records are sold than in all the other months of the year put together. Even in Britain, where the winter charts are dominated by TV-advertised anthologies, the Springsteen set at £25 brought in more money than the tight-margin single-album compilations. (And CBS reckon they get 42% of their annual sales at Christmas time.) Walking through London from Tottenham Court Road down Oxford Street to Piccadilly in early December, passing the three symbols of corporate rock—the Virgin, HMV and Tower superstores—each claiming to be the biggest record shop in the world, I could only see Springsteen boxes, piled high by the cash desks, the *safest* stock of the season.

Sales success at this level—those boxes were piled up in Sydney and Toronto too, in shop aisles in Sweden and Denmark, West Germany, Holland and Japan—has a disruptive effect on the rest of the rock process. American television news showed trucks arriving at New York's record stores from the CBS warehouses—they were immediately surrounded by queues too, and so, in the USA, Springsteen was sold off the back of vans, frantically, like a sudden supply of Levi's in the USSR. Within hours of its release, the Springsteen box was jamming up CBS's works. In America the company announced that nothing from its back catalogue would be available for four months, because all spare capacity had been commandeered for Springsteen (and even then the compact disc version of the box was soon sold out—not enough, only 300,000, had been manufactured). In Europe the company devoted one of its three pressing plants exclusively to the box. Springsteen dominated the market by being the only CBS product readily available.

Whatever the final sales figures turn out to be (and after Christmas the returns of the boxes from the retailers to CBS were as startling as the original sales), it is already obvious that *Bruce Springsteen and the E Street Band Live* is a phenomenal record, a money-making achievement to be discussed on the same scale as *Saturday Night Fever* or Michael Jackson's *Thriller*. Remember, too, that a live record is cheaper to produce than a new studio sound (and Springsteen has already been well rewarded for these songs from the sales of previous discs and the proceeds of sell-out tours). Nor did CBS need the expensive trappings or promo videos and press and TV advertising to make this record sell. Because the Springsteen box was an event in itself (the only pop precedent I can think of is the Beatles' 1968 *White Album*), it generated its own publicity as "news"—radio stations competed to play the most tracks for the longest times, shops competed to give Bruce the most window space, newspapers competed in speculations about how much money he was really making. The Springsteen box became, in other words, that ultimate object of capitalist fantasy, a commodity which sold more and more because it had sold so well already, a product which had to be *owned* (rather than necessarily used).

In the end, though, what is peculiar about the Springsteen story is not its marks of a brilliant commercial campaign, but their invisibility. Other superstars put out live sets for Christmas (Queen, for example) and the critics sneer at their opportunism; other stars resell their old hits (Bryan Ferry, for example) and their fans worry about their lack of current inspiration. And in these sorry tales of greed and pride it is Bruce Springsteen more often than not who is the measure of musical integrity, the model of a rock performer who cannot be discussed in terms of financial calculation. In short, the most successful pop commodity of the moment, the *Springsteen Live* set, stands for the principle that music should not be a commodity; it is his very disdain for success that makes Springsteen so successful. It is as if his presence on every fashionable turntable, tape deck and disc machine, his box on every up-market living-room floor, are what enables an aging, affluent rock generation to feel in touch with its "roots." And what matters in this post-modern era is not whether Bruce Springsteen *is* the real thing, but how he sustains the belief that there are somehow, somewhere, real things to be.

False

Consider the following:

Bruce Springsteen is a millionaire who dresses as a worker. Worn jeans, singlets, a head band to keep his hair from his eyes—these are working clothes and it is an important part of Springsteen's appeal that we do see him, as an entertainer, working for his living. His popularity is based on his live shows and, more particularly, on their spectacular energy: Springsteen works *hard,* and his exhaustion—on our behalf—is visible. He makes music physically, as a *manual* worker. His clothes are straightforwardly practical, sensible (like sports people's clothes)—comfortable jeans (worn in) for easy movement, a singlet to let the sweat flow free, the mechanic's cloth to wipe his brow.

But there is more to these clothes than this. *Springsteen wears work clothes even when he is not working.* His off-stage image, his LP sleeves and interview poses, even the candid "off duty" paparazzi shots, involve the same down-to-earth practicality (the only time Springsteen was seen to dress up "in private" was for his wedding). Springsteen doesn't wear the clothes appropriate to his real economic status and resources (as compared with other pop stars), but neither does he dress up for special occasions like real workers do—he's never seen flashily attired for a sharp night out. It's as if he can't be seen to be excessive or indulgent except on our behalf, as a performer for an audience. For him there is no division between work and play, between the ordinary and the extraordinary. Because the constructed "Springsteen," the star, is presented plain, there can never be a suggestion that this is just an act (as Elvis was an act, as Madonna is). There are no other Springsteens, whether more real or more artificial, to be seen.

Springsteen is employer-as-employee. It has always surprised me that he should be nicknamed "The Boss," but the implication is that this is an affectionate label, a brotherly way in which the E Street Band honour his sheer drive. In fact "boss" is an accurate description of their economic relationship—Springsteen *employs* his band; he has the recording contracts, controls the LP and concert material, writes the songs and chooses the oldies. And whatever his musicians' contributions to his success (fulsomely recognized), he gets the composing/performing royalties, could, in principle, sack people, and, like any other good employer, rewards his team with generous bonuses after each sell-out show or disc. And, of course, he employs a stage crew too, and a manager, a publicist, a secretary/assistant; he has an annual turnover now of millions. He may express the feelings of "little" men and women buffeted by distant company boards but he is himself a corporation.

Springsteen is a 37-year-old teenager. He is 20 years into a hugely successful career, he's a professional, a married man old enough to be the father of adolescent children of his own, but he still presents himself as a young man, waiting to see what life will bring, made tense by clashes with adult authority. He introduces his songs with memories—his life as a boy, arguments with his father (his mother is rarely mentioned)[1]— but as a performer he is clearly *present* in these emotions. Springsteen doesn't regret or vilify his past; as a grown man he's still living it.

Springsteen is a shy exhibitionist. He is, indeed, one of the sexiest performers rock and roll has ever had—there's a good part of his concert audience who simply fancy him, can't take their eyes off his body, and he's mesmerising on stage because of the confidence with which he displays himself. But, for all this, his persona is still that of a nervy, gauche youth on an early date.

*   *   *

Springsteen is superstar-as-friend. He comes into our lives as a recording star, a radio sound, a video presence and, these days, as an item of magazine gossip. Even in his live shows he seems more accessible in the close-ups on the mammoth screens around the stage than as the "real" dim figure in the distance. And yet he is still the rock performer whose act most convincingly creates (and depends on) a sense of community.

Springsteen's most successful "record" is "live." What the boxed set is meant to do is reproduce a concert, an *event,* and if for other artists five records would be excessive, for Springsteen it is a further sign of his album's truth-to-life—it lasts about the same length of time as a show. There's an interesting question of trust raised here. I don't doubt that these performances were once live, that the applause did happen, but this is nevertheless a false event, a concert put together from different shows (and alternative mixes), edited and balanced to sound like a live LP (which has quite different aural conventions than an actual show). Springsteen fans know that, of course. The pleasure of this set is not that it takes us back to somewhere we've been, but that it lays out something ideal. It describes what we *mean* by "Springsteen live," and what makes him "real" in this context is not his transparency, the idea that he is who he pretends to be, but his art, his ability to articulate the right *idea* of reality.

True

The recurring term used in discussions of Springsteen, by fans, by critics, by fans-as-critics is "authenticity." What is meant by this is not that Springsteen is authentic in a direct way—is simply expressing himself—but that he represents "authenticity." This is why he has become so important: he stands for the core values of rock and roll even as those values become harder and harder to sustain. At a time when rock is the soundtrack for TV commercials, when tours depend on sponsorship deals, when video promotion has blurred the line between music-making and music-selling, Springsteen suggests that, despite everything, it still gives people a way to define themselves against corporate logic, a language in which everyday hopes and fears can be expressed.

If Bruce Springsteen didn't exist, American rock critics would have had to invent him. In a sense, they did, whether directly (Jon Landau,

Rolling Stone's most significant critical theorist in the late sixties, is now his manager) or indirectly (Dave Marsh, Springsteen's official biographer, is the most passionate and widely read rock critic of the eighties). There are, indeed, few American rock critics who haven't celebrated Springsteen, but their task has been less to explain him to his potential fans, to sustain the momentum that carried him from cult to mass stardom, than to explain him to himself. They've placed him, that is, in a particular reading of rock history, not as the "new Dylan" (his original sales label) but as the "voice of the people." His task is to carry the baton passed on from Woody Guthrie, and the purpose of his carefully placed oldies (Guthrie's "This Land Is Your Land," Presley and Berry hits, British beat classics, Edwin Starr's "War") isn't just to situate him as a fellow fan but also to identify him with a particular musical project. Springsteen himself claims on stage to represent an authentic popular tradition (as against the spurious commercial sentiments of an Irving Berlin).

To be so "authentic" involves a number of moves. Firstly, authenticity must be defined against artifice; the terms only make sense in opposition to each other. This is the importance of Springsteen's image—to represent the "raw" as against the "cooked." His plain stage appearance, his dressing down, has to be understood with reference to showbiz dressing up, to the elaborate spectacle of cabaret pop and soul (and routine stadium rock and roll)—Springsteen is real *by contrast.* In lyrical terms too he is plain-speaking; his songwriting craft is marked not by "poetic" or obscure or personal language, as in the singer/songwriter tradition following Dylan, folk-rock (and his own early material), but by the vivid images and metaphors he builds from common words.

What's at stake here is not authenticity of experience, but authenticity of feeling; what matters is not whether Springsteen has been through these things himself (boredom, aggression, ecstasy, despair) but that he knows how they work. The point of his autobiographical anecdotes is not to reveal himself but to root his music in material conditions. Like artists in other media (fiction, film) Springsteen is concerned to give emotions (the essential data of rock and roll) a narrative setting, to situate them in time and place, to relate them to the situations they explain or confuse. He's not interested in abstract emotions, in vague sensation or even in moralizing. He is, to put it simply, a story-teller, and in straining to make his stories credible he uses classic techniques. Reality is registered by conventions first formulated by the nineteenth-century naturalists—a

refusal to sentimentalize social conditions, a compulsion to sentimentalize human nature. Springsteen's songs (like Zola's fictions) are almost exclusively concerned with the working-class, with the effects of poverty
and uncertainty, the consequences of weakness and crime; they trawl
through the murky reality of the American dream; they contrast Utopian
impulses with people's lack of opportunity to do much more than get by;
they find in sex the only opportunity for passion (and betrayal). Springsteen's protagonists, victims and criminals, defeated and enraged, are
treated tenderly, their hopes honoured, their failure determined by circumstance.

It is his realism that makes Springsteen's populism politically ambiguous. His message is certainly anti-capitalist, or, at least, critical of the effects
of capitalism—as both citizen and star Springsteen has refused to sub-
mit to market forces, has shown consistent and generous support for the
system's losers, for striking trade unionists and the unemployed, for battered wives and children. But, at the same time, his focus on individuals'
fate, the very power with which he describes the dreams they can't realize (but which he has) offers an opening for his appropriation, appropriation not just by politicians like Reagan but, more importantly, by hucksters
and advertisers, who use him to sell their goods as some sort of *solution*
to the problem he outlines. This is the paradox of mass-marketed populism: Springsteen's songs suggest there is something missing in our lives,
the CBS message is that we can fill the gap *with a Bruce Springsteen
record.* And for all Springsteen's support of current causes, what comes
from his music is a whiff of nostalgia and an air of fatalism. His stories
describe hopes-about-to-be-dashed, convey a sense of time passing beyond our control, suggest that our dreams can only be dreams. The formal conservatism of the music reinforces the emotional conservation
[*sic*] of the lyrics. This is the way the world is, he sings, and nothing really
changes.

But there's another way of describing Springsteen's realism. It means
celebrating the ordinary not the special. Again the point is not that
Springsteen is ordinary or even pretends to be, but that he honours or-
dinariness, making something intense out of experiences that are usually
seen as mundane. It has always been pop's function to transform the ba-
nal, but this purpose was to some extent undermined by the rise of rock
in the sixties, with its claims to art and poetry, its cult-building, its heavy
metal mysticism. Springsteen himself started out with a couple of wordy,
worthy LPs, but since then he has been in important ways committed to

common sense. Springsteen's greatest skill is his ability to dramatize everyday events—even his stage act is a pub rock show writ large. The E Street Band, high-class professionals, play with a sort of amateurish enthusiasm, an affection for each other which is in sharp contrast to the bohemian contempt for their work (and their audience) which has been a strand of "arty" rock shows since the Rolling Stones and the Doors. Springsteen's musicians stand for every bar and garage group that ever got together in fond hope of stardom.

His sense of the commonplace also explains Springsteen's physical appeal. His sexuality is not displayed as something remarkable, a kind of power, but is coded into his "natural" movements, determined by what he has to do to sing and play. His body becomes "sexy"—a source of excitement and anxiety—in its routine activity; his appeal is not defined in terms of glamour or fantasy. The basic sign of Springsteen's authenticity, to put it another way, is his sweat, his display of *energy*. His body is not posed, an object of consumption, but active, an object of exhaustion. When the E Street Band gather at the end of a show for the final bow, arms around each other's shoulders, drained and relieved, the sporting analogy is clear: this is a team which has won its latest bout. What matters is that every such bout is seen to be real, that there are no backing tapes, no "fake" instruments, that the musicians really have played until they can play no more. There is a moment in every Springsteen show I've seen when Clarence Clemons takes centre-stage. For that moment he is the real star—he's bigger than Springsteen, louder, more richly dressed. And he's the saxophonist, giving us the clearest account all evening of the relationship between human effort and human music.

To be authentic and to sound authentic is in the rock context the same thing. Music cannot *be* true or false, it can only refer to *conventions* of truth and falsity. Consider the following.

Thundering drums in Springsteen's songs give his stories their sense of unstoppable momentum, they map out the spaces within which things happen. This equation of time and space is the secret of great rock and roll and Springsteen uses other classic devices to achieve it—a piano/organ combination, for example (as used by The Band and many soul groups), so that melodic-descriptive and rhythmic-atmospheric sounds are continually swapped about.

The E Street Band makes music as a group, but a group in which we can hear every instrumentalist. Our attention is drawn, that is, not to a finished sound but to music-in-the-making. This is partly done by the refusal to make any instrument the "lead" (which is why Nils Lofgren, a "lead" guitarist, sounded out of place in the last E Street touring band). And partly by a specific musical busy-ness—the group is "tight," everyone is aiming for the same rhythmic end, but "loose," each player makes their own decision as to how to get there (which is one reason why electronic instruments would not fit—they're too smooth, too determined). All Springsteen's musicians, even the added back-up singers and percussionists, have individual voices; it would be unthinkable for him to appear with, say, an anonymous string section.

The textures and, more significantly, the melodic structures of Springsteen's music make self-conscious reference to rock and roll itself, to its conventional line-up, its clichéd chord changes, its time-honoured ways of registering joys and sadness. Springsteen himself is a rock and roll star, not a crooner or singer/songwriter. His voice *strains* to be heard, he has to shout against the instruments that both support and compete with him. However many times he's rehearsed his lines they always sound as if they're being forged on the spot.

Many of Springsteen's most anthemic songs have no addresses (no "you") but (like many Beatles songs) concern a third person (tales told about someone else) or involve brooding aloud, explaining his situation impersonally, in a kind of individualised epic. Listening to such epics is a public activity (rather than a private fantasy), which is why Springsteen concerts still feel like collective occasions.

Conclusion

In one of his monologues Springsteen remembers that his parents were never very keen on his musical ambitions—they wanted him to train for something safe, like law or accountancy: "They wanted me to get a little something for myself; what they did not understand was that I wanted *everything!*"

This is a line that could only be delivered by an American, and to explain Springsteen's importance and success we have to go back to the problem he is really facing: the fate of the individual artist under capitalism. In Europe, the artistic critique of the commercialization of everything has generally been conducted in terms of Romanticism, in a state of bohemian disgust with the masses and the bourgeoisie alike, in the name of the superiority of the *avant-garde*. In the USA there's a populist anti-capitalism available, a tradition of the artist as the common man (rarely woman), pitching rural truth against urban deceit, pioneer values against bureaucratic routines. This tradition (Mark Twain to Woody Guthrie, Kerouac to Creedence Clearwater Revival) lies behind Springsteen's message and his image. It's this tradition that enables him to take such well-worn iconography as the road, the river, rock and roll itself, as a mark of sincerity. No British musician, not even someone with such a profound love of American musical forms as Elvis Costello, could deal with these themes without some sense of irony.

Still, Springsteen's populism can appeal to everyone's experience of capitalism. He makes music out of desire aroused and desire thwarted, he offers a sense of personal worth that is not determined by either market forces (and wealth) or aesthetic standards (and cultural capital). It is the USA's particular account of equality that allows him to transcend the differences in class and status which remain ingrained in European culture. The problem is that the line between democratic populism (the argument that all people's experiences and emotions are equally important, equally worthy to be dramatized and made into art) and market populism (the argument that the consumer is always right, that the market defines cultural value) is very thin. Those piles of Bruce Springsteen boxes in European department stores seem less a tribute to rock authenticity than to corporate might.

"We are the world!" sang USA for Africa, and what was intended as a statement of global community came across as a threat of global domination. "Born in the U.S.A.!" sang Bruce Springsteen on his last great tour, with the Stars and Stripes fluttering over the stage, and what was meant as an opposition anthem to the Reaganite colonization of the American dream was taken by large sections of his American audiences as pat patriotism (in Europe the flag had to come down). Springsteen is, whether he or we like it or not, an American artist—his "community" will always have the Stars and Stripes fluttering over it. But then rock and roll is American music, and Springsteen's *Live—1975–1985* is a monument. Like all monuments it celebrates (and mourns) the dead, in this case the idea of authenticity itself.

Note
1. "The Wish" is Springsteen's heartfelt love letter to his mother. It appears on *Tracks* (1998).

Kevin Major

■

Kevin Major is a native of Newfoundland, and much of his work (*Dorylands*, an anthology of Newfoundland writing; *Blood Red Ochre; No Man's Land; Diana: My Autobiography; Gaffer*) centers around the history and rich culture of that distinctly unique Canadian province. *Dear Bruce Springsteen* (1988), then, may appear to be a bit of a departure. Touching and funny, it is written in the form of letters from a young man—fourteen-year-old Terry Blanchard—to the rock star as the likable but confused Blanchard confides to "the Boss" about his troubled family life and the sudden departure of his "old man." Major understands the inner turmoil and shaky identity of the still developing teenage mind. "Springsteen seems to me a very decent human being," Major told me, "with a social conscience, someone who cares more about human relationships than the trappings of celebrity. I had written a few young adult novels prior to this, all in some way personal explorations. I was fascinated by how young people look to rock musicians for guidance in their lives. To me, there could be no better choice than Springsteen."[1]

from *Dear Bruce Springsteen*

APRIL 5

Dear Bruce Springsteen,

This letter might never get to you. If it does, it might take years before you get around to reading it because you must get tons of mail. I'm going to write it anyway.

You see, I just want to say how much I like your music and to tell you a bit about myself. I don't want to take up much of your time. You probably got millions of things on your mind, but I figure if you ever had a few spare minutes you wouldn't mind listening. That's the kind of person I figure you are.

My name is Terry Blanchard. The story goes that my father named me after a buddy of his from high school who was killed in a motorcycle accident. I heard someone say once that the old man was going to go riding with him that day but changed his mind at the last minute. It's just what I've heard. He never really talked about it.

Hey, know what I just figured out? That you're old enough to be my father. In fact, my old man and you must be about the same age. Weird, right? You're not that much alike though.

I'm getting off track. I'm fourteen. I'm in the ninth grade at school. I got a sister who's ten. The place where I live is not very big, fifteen thousand people maybe. Big enough to have a McDonald's and a few other things, if that means anything. There are a lot of worse places to live, I guess. It used to be better, when the mill wasn't getting rid of people.

Bored yet? Guess I shouldn't be taking up your time.

Anyway, I just want to say that I really get off on your music and that my biggest dream is to see you in concert someday. Man, from the clips I've seen on TV, the concerts must be wicked.

> Yours truly,
> *Terry*

APRIL 21

Dear Bruce Springsteen,

I never got an answer to either one of my letters, so I guess that means you don't mind me writing.

That's a little joke. I heard you're on tour in Japan. My letters are probably at the bottom of a sack of fan mail in your record company's basement somewhere.

I can handle that. I'm writing to you anyway because I like doing it, that's all. Even if they're not getting to you, yet.

Today in school Jerkins was on my back again. Man, if he don't quit picking on me, one of these days he's going to get more than he bargained for. I was tapping my fingers on the desk to some music that was running around in my head. First he used his regular put-down: "Empty vessels make the most noise." I don't know where the hell he got that from. He uses it so often, you'd think he'd get sick of it. I sure am. Then he said, "Blanchard, smarten up. We all know how easy it is for you to make a fool of yourself. You don't have to keep proving it."

I never said nothing back to him. Not that I didn't have a few things in my mind. What I thought about doing was roping him to his chair, then plunking a ghetto blaster on the desk in front of him and vibrating his eardrums with one of your songs, one of the real rockers like "Cadillac Ranch" or "Ramrod." Just to teach him a few things about what's noise and what's not. You picture that? I could, for the whole rest of math class. My imagination I figure is what gets me through the day half the time.

It's got to be great to let loose like you do onstage. To rip into a song with all you got and have everything what's inside you come out. And not have to answer to anybody for it. The most I do is slam a few doors. That really don't do the job.

A few times when there's been nobody in the house, only me, I've cranked up one of your songs on eight or nine and made out I was singing it, with a flashlight or something for a mike. Once, Mrs. MacKinnon from next door showed up in the apartment and caught me. Man, talk about turn red. I probably glowed. She had no reason to be nosing around. She said the music was so loud, she thought something was wrong. Likely story. Of course she had to tell my mother, although Mom never said much. Now I use headphones, but it's not the same. You can't really cut loose.

I got my eyes on a poster of you in concert right now. Man, the sweat is just pourin' off you, but it looks like you're having a wicked time. That's the only poster I got on my bedroom wall anymore. My kid sister's got some pictures of you on her wall that she cut from some of those stupid magazines she buys. It looks dumb because she's got you next to this bunch of wimps dressed in sparkly clothes. She don't know any better. Man, she don't know you're The Boss. When she starts talking about you I got to leave the room. It's so dumb, it's embarrassing. She's dumb about a lot of things, if you really want to know.

It's about midnight, and everyone's gone to bed long ago. I better turn off the light and try to get some sleep. Can't wait for tomorrow. Another wonderful week of school. Thank God there's only two months left before the summer break.

> Cutting loose,
> *Terry (Blanchard)*

MAY 4

Dear Bruce Springsteen,

I know I got no real right to dump all this personal stuff on you. I thought about it yesterday after I sent the last letter. Here I am, probably making a fool of myself, going on and on about my life to someone I never even met.

Then when I thought about it some more, I felt like I almost know you. I've read everything I can lay my hands on that's been written about you. I've gone to the library and dug out old copies of *Rolling Stone* from six and seven years ago. I've read three full-length books on you, three times each. I play your music all the time. (Man, my ghetto blaster practically spits back any tape that's not yours.)

And in a way you're sort of a connection between me and my father. For my fourteenth birthday he gave me one of your tapes. Then a week after that he was gone.

It was the first time he ever went out of his way to give me a present himself. Usually it was something from the both of them. I can hear him now when he handed it to me: "It's about time you got over that heavy-metal crap. Listen to something decent for a change." He gave me the tape, and he never said nothing else about it.

I knew he was into your music a lot. He never listened to it much in the house, mostly when he was driving the old van we used to have. Mostly then by himself. The four of us were in the van once and he put on *Nebraska*. Mom made him take it off because, she said, it sounded too depressing. He sort of grunted something about she didn't know what good music was and popped out the tape. She said if you're going to spend money we can't afford on music, then you might as well spend it on something that'll cheer you up. He ignored her.

After that he never played your music much when Mom was around. But I know the tapes must have been used a lot. He had a special place in the van where he kept them. Once when it was just the two of us driving someplace to pick up some secondhand furniture, he put on *The River*. The only song of yours I knew from that tape was "Hungry Heart." Everything was sort of quiet between us, so I said to him that I liked that song. He said he liked it, too, he liked the words.

I never thought about it much till after he left. Then I bought the tape and started paying attention to the words. The old man's got a hungry heart.

So now you know some of the reasons why I'm writing these crazy letters. There's more to it than that. I got dreams about things I want to do when I get older.

Dream on, right?
Terry

OCTOBER 30

Dear Bruce Springsteen,

It's been a long time since I wrote you. I've thought about it a lot, and I think maybe I'll make this the last one.

When I started all this I really needed someone I could talk to. (Lucky you, right?) Now I'm going to give you a break and shut up.

The past few months have been a bit crazy. The letters that I wrote to you are the one thing that tied it all together.

Sometimes I wonder if you ever read any of the letters. Maybe now that your tour is over, you might get around to it. Like I said before, it wouldn't really bother me if I knew you didn't. I kind of like to think you did, but I know you still got a lot of things to be doing. Maybe someday I'll hear from you. Who knows?

I read once that after a concert some guy you never met before started talking to you and asked you to his house for a meal with his family. And you said yes. Man, that offer goes for me, too. Mom could cook up her famous spaghetti. Of course I'd have to call up the old man and get him to make a special trip here. We'd have a lot to talk about. That's an open invitation, if you're ever in this part of the country.

Maybe you'll come closer to where I live on your next tour. You've got a lot of fans around here. If you do, I'll be the first one to buy tickets.

But no matter if you come near here or not, I'll still be going to see you. That's the one promise I made to myself—to see you in concert the next time you're on tour. I'll be the one in the front row looking like he's in heaven.

My time for writing letters will be taken up with writing to the old man, I hope. I owe him one now. It's me that's being the slacker this time.

Well, I guess this is the end of the line, Bruce Springsteen, man. (I was going to call you just Bruce for once, but I couldn't bring myself to do it.) Anyway, this is about it.

Remember—take it easy. Take a break, you've been touring for a long time. Enjoy your life, man, and remember, if you ever have kids, spend lots of time with them.

And keep the music coming. I'll be watching out for a new album.

Yours truly, man,
Terry Blanchard

Note

1. E-mail correspondence with the author, April 12, 2003. When asked, Are you a big Springsteen fan? Major answered, "Yes, I was a big fan of Springsteen, and now my own son is an even bigger fan."

Jefferson Morley

■

In this article, which ran in the March 23, 1987, issue of the *New Republic*, Jefferson Morley examines the careers of two cultural icons, Bruce Springsteen and Ronald Reagan, and finds they have much in common—to a point.

Darkness on the Edge of the Shining City: Bruce Springsteen and the End of Reaganism

New Republic

■ON NOVEMBER 10 Bruce Springsteen fans began lining up outside record stores to buy the first copies of a boxed five-record set called *Bruce Springsteen and the E Street Band Live 1975–1985*. Three days later President Reagan first acknowledged reports that his administration had sold weapons to the government of the Ayatollah Khomeini in Iran.

If scandal and album are a cultural coincidence, so too are the careers of Reagan and Springsteen. Both have become cultural icons by giving the American people a reflection, a vision, of themselves. Both deftly use the mass media to define what is American, to present a seemingly natural but carefully molded persona with which their audience can identify: Reagan as genial patriarch of "traditional" middle-class values; Springsteen as exuberant yet sensitive son of the working class. Columnist George Will,[1] recognizing their similarities as pop culture figures during the 1984 presidential campaign, suggested that Springsteen and Reagan stood for the same thing: that "America is back."

Will's attempt to conscript the rock star into the Reagan crusade, though scorned, was not entirely misguided. Springsteen is conservative, both temperamentally and musically (though not politically; he gives to left-liberal causes such as unions and food banks, and recently appeared in an anti-apartheid rock video). Will's mistake was to portray Springsteen as an ornament on Reaganism, to view Springsteen's short hair, heterosexual demeanor, and fondness for the American flag as right-wing credentials. Springsteen's rock critic friends on the left are less superficial than Will when they cast Springsteen as leftist savior, but they are also succumbing to the old temptation of using a rock star for wish fulfillment. Such fans were impatient with Springsteen's mild response to the Reaganites' effort to co-opt him. Springsteen declined to appear in public with the president during the 1984 campaign, and, except for a few good-natured remarks in his concerts, left it at that.

Springsteen and Reagan confound sympathizers and critics alike by moving from one pop culture role to the next. The president can be the spokesman for a shimmering future or the abashed father explaining away some family embarrassment—like the killing of 241 Marines in Lebanon or the Challenger disaster—or the gruff sheriff enforcing (or breaking) international law. Springsteen moves with equal ease from greaser in a leather jacket to scraggly hippie in denim to all-American boy rocking and rolling in your average football stadium. They both stay credible regardless of what role they take up because their performances embody the values that their audiences want to believe in.

They also reverse the expected generational roles. The older man sounds young and the younger man sounds old. Reagan is the hedonist. He revels in the tumult of capitalism with little regard for its consequences; in happy dreams of consumption with little regard for their unreality; in the righteousness of "traditional" values without ever having bothered to live them. Springsteen, while optimistic, is more cautious; this is his conservatism. He sings about failed factories and failed parents and about the difficulties of finding, as the title of one of his songs puts it, "Reason to Believe."

Nowhere is this paradox more evident than in the way each recalls the past in order to define the future. Springsteen is obsessed with confronting his own painful memories, with (in a recurring phrase in his songs) "the price you pay." Reagan, by contrast, is utopian. He sees the past as literally priceless—valuable beyond measure, yet costing nothing today. He relies on this mythology of the past in much the way a radical relies on ideology, as the blueprint for a glorious epoch in the making. The future is the Puritans' "shining city on a hill."

The '60s are the most important period of the past for both men. Springsteen, born in 1949, is a typical member of the baby boom generation. Reagan first won office in California in 1966 on the strength of his opposition to the emerging student movement. Springsteen's music and his memories are rooted in the period between the debut of Elvis Presley and the release of the Beatles' *White Album*. Reagan's politics are defined in opposition to the same period. His foreign policy defines itself as the rejection of the anti-war movement. His "supply-side" economic policies are promoted as the corrective to the "tax and spend" economic policies of the Great Society. His espousal of "traditional values" is a rhetorical rejection of cultural innovation since the '60s.

Scandal and album are occasions for taking stock of the '60s. The scandal is Reagan's refusal to explain or even to acknowledge his actions in the Iran-*contra* affair. Underlying all of Reagan's actions was the illusion that suffered most in the '60s: that America's good intentions enabled and entitled it to do anything. If we are confused and astounded by each new round of revelations, it is only an indication of how successful Reagan was at sustaining that illusion.

The live album is Springsteen's effort to make sense out of where he and his audience have come from in the last ten years. Springsteen's career is the funny and sad story of growing up after the '60s, of coming of age in what he called, in the title of his 1978 album, the *Darkness on the Edge of Town.*

In September 1974 a little-known rock musician named Bruce Springsteen was featured on the cover of *Time* and *Newsweek* in the same week.[2] This remarkable burst of hype, long since forgotten, says less about Springsteen's mass popularity than it does about his appeal to an elite of rock critics and corporate executives at three of the country's largest media corporations. (Springsteen's first two albums, released by CBS Records, were both commercial duds.) Time Inc., Washington Post–Newsweek, CBS Records, and the critics understood that Springsteen was a figure who could help sell their products to the generation emerging out of the '60s.

Similarly, General Electric employed Reagan as a corporate spokesman from 1954 to 1962 because the affable matinee star who never outshone anyone seemed to them to be the embodiment of white middle-class conformity—what we might now call pre-'60s American values. Reagan's purpose wasn't simply to sell GE products any more than Springsteen's is simply to sell CBS records. They were hired because GE and CBS Records had identified cultural tastes and needed public figures to appeal to those tastes and shape them. The culture of capitalism discovered both Springsteen and Reagan; their status as cultural icons is not an accident.

Springsteen emerged from the heart of the post-'60s generation, from

"Middle America," with the emphasis on the middle. He didn't belong to the relatively small counterculture that dominated elite college campuses and mass media coverage—though he was influenced by it. He was into cars, not acid or the Viet Cong. Yet in 1967, when he graduated from high school, he had long hair and didn't want to go to Vietnam. Nor did he belong to the "Silent Majority," that substantial but usually exaggerated part of the American public that wasn't young or black, that wasn't protesting, that wasn't rejecting traditional values, and that resented the "anything goes" attitude of many who were. Springsteen was, as he sings in one of his songs, "caught in a crossfire I don't understand."

CBS Records was similarly situated between mainstream and counterculture. Between 1964 and 1969, CBS Records went from doing 15 percent of its business in rock to 60 percent; its sales rose 15 to 20 percent annually. Perhaps foremost among record companies, CBS relied on advertising in the radical, sexually explicit, anarchistic underground press to reach its young customers. CBS had long since recognized the profits in transmitting the counterculture to the mainstream.

Mainstream culture and counterculture were feeding off of each other. As rock critic Jon Landau asked in *Rolling Stone* in 1971, "We say we are a counterculture, yet are we really so different from the culture against which we rebel?" Maybe not. Springsteen had signed with CBS in 1972, right at the point when, for better and worse, counterculture was becoming the new mainstream of American society. (Landau would go on to become Springsteen's manager and an important influence on his career.)

Springsteen begins his retrospective album in 1975, the year he assembled the E Street Band and figured out his rock 'n' roll ambitions.[3] Most importantly, the '60s were unambiguously over: the Vietnam War had been lost, the oil embargo had brought a deep recession, and his own crazy-kid spirit had begun to fade.

The songs, though not organized in the order they were released, are arranged thematically to reflect the progress of Springsteen's career. In his first song Springsteen reminds his fans that the journey of the last ten years began in fear. "So you're scared and you're thinking / That maybe we ain't that young anymore," he sings plaintively in "Thunder Road." Well, Bruce tells his girl, he's not a hero and he doesn't have anything to offer, just a ride in his car out on a highway toward some lost sense of freedom. Unlike Jack Kerouac in the '50s or the easy riders of the '60s,

Springsteen isn't seeking the freedom of "anything goes." Through the first third of the album he is an ordinary teenager—a silly romantic, a pseudo-poet, and all-around wise guy—who nevertheless wants something more.

By the middle third of the album, the false bravado is gone, and with it Springsteen's penchant for histrionics. These songs, drawn from all phases of his career, are fiercer and more desperate. They combine catchier melodies with harsher stories and a hard rock edge. The music is at once tougher and more lyrical, reflecting the tension within Springsteen himself. In songs like "Badlands," he is fighting off a vague sense of hopelessness with the conviction that "it ain't no sin to be glad you're alive."

Springsteen doesn't rig his emotional gambles. Sometimes he wins and sometimes he loses. What makes his downbeat songs such as "Darkness on the Edge of Town" and "Backstreets" inspiring is the faith that he musters even while imagining himself with the losers on the edge of society. But after giving a proud version of Woody Guthrie's populist national anthem "This Land Is Your Land," Springsteen tests his own compassion and that of his fans by singing about "Johnny 99," a man who kills a night clerk in a stickup. He does not patronize the killer as "a victim of society." Although Johnny has been stripped of his dignity by an economy that won't give him a job, Johnny himself tells the judge that it was more than his debts that put the gun in his hand. People like Johnny, Springsteen says, are responsible for succumbing to "the meanness in this world." That weakness though is what makes him human. Johnny too was "Born in the U.S.A."—and the ringing introductory chords of that song are the next thing you hear on the album.

Which explains another intriguing cultural coincidence. The album *Born in the U.S.A.*, which elevated Springsteen from rock star to cultural icon, was released in June 1984. President Reagan, in what history is sure to see as the high tide of Reaganism, ran for re-election that fall on the slogan "It's Morning in America." Perhaps more than anything else, the album cover, which features Springsteen thrashing his guitar in front of an immense red, white, and blue flag, has linked him in the public mind with Reagan. Yet the patriotisms of the two men could not be more different.

In *Born in the U.S.A.* Springsteen turned to the theme of national birth because he believed that our common identity, forged in the pain of the past, could sustain Americans in the face of the "meanness in this world." Reagan turned to the idea of national rebirth in order to celebrate the promised restoration of a glorious and pain-free past. If Springsteen seemed to embody a mood of "America is back," it was because he had captured people's desire to come to grips with the legacy of the '60s. Reagan appealed to the desire to mythologize the '60s, especially the Vietnam War.

Reagan's mythology of the past succeeded with the public, not because it was right-wing, but because it tapped the myths of the '60s shared by left and right alike. The indignant claim that the anti-war movement was the real "noble cause" only helped Reagan. Whether rejected as a period of youthful stupidity or sentimentalized as a bygone period of unmatched idealism, the '60s were painless, and painlessness was what Reagan was offering in 1984.

Reagan had outflanked liberals on both the left and the right by adapting the myths of the '60s for his own purposes. His ideal social type, the entrepreneur, resembled no one so much as the hippie of the '60s. For both, freedom and self-fulfillment were identical; for both, the credo "Do your own thing" promised a better world. Like '60s radicals, Reagan envisioned the world politics as a duel between good and evil in which a group of Americans (radicals or Reaganites) appointed themselves as the good. "Amerika" the imperialist demon in the banners of '60s radicals became "Amerika" the besieged innocent in the 1987 miniseries. Both '60s radicals and '80s Reaganites believed that the virtue of their ends justified almost any means. Both viewed the niceties of democratic procedure as a sham that slowed them on their appointed rounds of historic duty. For '60s radicals, there was the infatuation with revolutionary violence and contempt for those foolish enough to disagree. For the infinitely more powerful Reaganites it was "anything goes" in Iran, in the National Security Council, in Nicaragua, and only God (and the special prosecutor) knows where else.

The past has now caught up with both Springsteen and Reagan. Springsteen tells his audience, in two between-song monologues, what he thinks are the most important lessons of the '60s. With a churchlike organ playing softly in the background, he recounts how his father used to taunt him: "I can't wait until the army gets you, because they'll make a man out of you." He tells about getting his draft notice and how scared he was when he went to take his physical. When he got home his father asked him what happened; Bruce said he had failed the physical. His father just said, "That's good." The crowd roars at Douglas Springsteen's admission that he didn't want the army and the traditional values it stood for to capture his son after all. One lesson is that the "Silent Majority" had to acknowledge the wisdom of its children.

Springsteen brings us back to the future with "Seeds," a populist blues-rock screed about a homeless family living in their car outside Houston. He doesn't want to revive the '60s protest as much as show that it is now a part of the American mainstream. Then he plays uncle to the teenagers in the crowd, telling them about growing up in the '60s "with war on TV every night." He warns them that "the next time they're going to be coming after you," and grimly concludes that "in 1985 blind faith in your leaders or in anything will get you killed."[4] To clinch the importance of remembering the anti-war movement, he and the band rip into "War," a Motown protest song from 1970 that opens with a mighty shout: "War / What is it good for? / Absolutely nothing." He wants to remind his fans that the rebellious ways of the '60s have been vindicated.

Springsteen, though, is bound to disappoint those who expect him to lead their political crusades. When he warns his fans against having blind faith in their leaders, he does not exclude himself. He does not reject his own message any more than he abandons his past. In the final third of the album, he returns to cruising down the highway toward "The Promised Land" or cutting up with a buddy in "Darlington County" or braving the terrors of New York City and the "Tenth Avenue Freeze-Out." He has reached maturity, but that hardly means he must become a political activist and abandon what he has always loved the most.

Springsteen, in fact, sounds just like he does at the beginning, like he's scared that maybe he isn't that young anymore. In the second song on the album, "Adam Raised a Cain," Springsteen sang about his painful relationship with his father: "Daddy worked his whole life for nothing but the pain / Now he walks these empty rooms looking for something to blame / You inherit the sins, you inherit the flames." By the end of the album, Springsteen has taken up the role of the father himself. In "My Hometown" a man drives down Main Street with his young son. As he sees the whitewashed store windows on Main Street, he remembers how his father had taken him for the same ride and how the town has declined. "Son, take a good look around," he tells the boy. "This is your hometown."

This is the end of the ride that began in 1975. Springsteen proclaims that he is still "Born to Run," but he sounds rueful about his youthful pledge of "No Surrender." He closes with "Jersey Girl," a sentimental lullaby for his true love (no doubt his wife, whom he married in 1985) and a gentle kiss-off to his huge audience. As with millions of his fans, Springsteen's new family marks the end of his coming of age.

Springsteen, though, would never pretend that we can escape inheriting the sins and the flames of the past. Reaganism is an essential part of the decade that Springsteen has covered in his retrospective album. In his melancholy ballad "The River," Springsteen asks himself the question that he says haunts him like a curse: "Is a dream a lie if it don't come true / Or is it something worse?" While Springsteen's own dreams seem to have come true, Reagan's dream has gone bad and become frightening. The homeless in Houston and the crooks on Wall Street and the Fifth Amendment patriots in Washington are proof that Reaganism has failed. Maybe it was a lie. Or maybe, Springsteen suggests, it was something worse.

Notes

1. See "Bruuuuuce" by George F. Will in this volume.
2. The actual date of the dueling covers was October 27, 1975.
3. The chronology of the E Street Band is, at times, confusing. As with many rock bands, the line-up has changed over the years, although the core members have remained remarkably consistent. The first E Street Band was formed in 1972. See the Appendix for additional information.
4. On July 15, 2003, toward the end of the Rising tour, Springsteen commented on the Iraq war: "People come to my shows with many different kinds of political beliefs; I like that, we welcome all. There have been a lot of questions raised recently about the forthrightness of our government. . . . The question of whether we were misled into the war in Iraq isn't a liberal or conservative or Republican or Democratic question, it's an American one. Protecting the democracy that we ask our sons and daughters to die for is our responsibility and our trust. Demanding accountability from our leaders is our job as citizens. It's the American way. So may the truth will out." See www.backstreets.com.

Jack Ridl

■

"Video Mama" by poet Jack Ridl, an English professor at Hope College in Holland, Michigan, appears in *Sweet Nothings: An Anthology of Rock and Roll in American Poetry* (1994) edited by Jim Elledge. Ridl's poems have appeared in the *Denver Quarterly, Yarrow,* and *Poetry.* In the contributor notes, Ridl remarks, "My mother stormed the stage at a Frank Sinatra concert when she was a teenager. She made sure we saw the Beatles. And in her late sixties she became a Springsteen fan. She has gone to his concerts, sitting in the tenth row, has everything by him and about him and wears a black Springsteen T-shirt."

Video Mama

My mother watches videos,
tapes them on the VCR, keeps
a list of her top twenty.
In the next room, her grandchildren
play, pretending they are rabbits.
On the wall, behind the TV,
she's hung family photographs:
her father, mother, mother's father,
aunts and uncles, cousins, two
great-grandfathers, and her children
and their children and her wedding
picture. Next to Cousin Dot,
is an autographed picture
of The Boss, Bruce Springsteen,
bare-shouldered, sweating.
Guitar slung across his thighs,
he watches her all day long.

Andrew M. Greeley

■

Iconoclastic priest, historian, sociologist, and novelist, the always prolific Andrew Greeley is a literary force all his own. He has written best-selling novels (too many to list); social history—*That Most Distressful Nation: The Taming of the American Irish* (1972), *The Irish Americans: The Rise to Money and Power* (1981); numerous studies on Catholicism—*The Catholic Myth* (1990), *The Catholic Imagination* (2000), *The Great Mysteries: Experiencing Catholic Faith from the Inside Out* (2003); and memoir—*Confessions of a Parish Priest: An Autobiography* (1988). In the following essay from the February 6, 1988, issue of *America,* the Catholic weekly, Father Greeley looks at the remnants of Catholicism—film critic Richard A. Blake uses the word "afterimage" to describe the phenomenon[1]—that linger in the music of Bruce Springsteen, especially in *Tunnel of Love.*

The Catholic Imagination
of Bruce Springsteen

America

■THE IMAGINATION is religious. Religion is imaginative. The origins and the power of both are in the playful, creative, dancing self. Once influenced by Catholic imagery, that self is forever Catholic. Hence, the popular rock star Bruce Springsteen, perhaps without knowing or understanding it, is a Catholic meistersinger.

This essay is the third and final installment of an investigation I began last summer of the relationship between religious imagination and the persistent loyalty of American Catholics.

In the first essay, "Why Catholics Stay in the Church" (*America,* 8/8/87), I argued that a sociological analysis reveals that Catholics remain in the church because their faith provides them with identity, community and sacramentality—the last of which constitutes, at the deep levels of the personality, paradigmatic symbols that become templates for living and life. One clings to Catholic images and stories because of the richness of meaning they provide—a meaning that is frequently implicit. (Theologically, lest I be accused again of denying the work of God, these phenomena might be conceived as the secondary causes through which, in Catholic theology, God normally works.)

In the second essay, "Empirical Liturgy: The Search for Grace" (*America,* 11/21/87), I suggested that the Sacraments correlate the experience of self-communication of God in secular life with the narratives that constitute the overarching Catholic heritage. It is precisely in this exercise of correlation, I now add, that the church's Sacraments and liturgy create the identity, the community and the personal set of metaphorical life-templates for the lives of individual Catholics. Liturgy as correlation (even if unintentionally and ineptly so) is the answer to the question of why Catholics stay in the church: The rich narrative symbols that give (perhaps implicit) direction and purpose for life are communicated by liturgy as the bridge between personal experience of grace and the heritage's experiences of grace.

In this final essay, I want to complete the cycle by suggesting that there is a powerful link between religious imagery, which is created by the Sacraments, and works of artistic and literary creativity. I will do so by analyzing the most recent work of the Catholic minstrel Bruce Springsteen and argue that (a) his work is profoundly Catholic, and (b) it is so because his creative imagination is permeated by Catholic symbolism he absorbed, almost necessarily, from the Sacraments.

Springsteen is a liturgist, I propose, because he correlates the self-communication of God in secular life with the overarching symbol/narratives of his/our tradition. Moreover, I also propose that he engages in this "minstrel ministry" without ever being explicit about it, or even necessarily aware of it, precisely because his imagination was shaped as Catholic in the early years of life. He is both a liturgist, then, and a superb example of why Catholics cannot leave the church.

These two phenomena are not logically connected. There is no a priori philosophical reason why religion and creativity are so essentially linked.

The connection is rather existential, based on the way we humans know reality. Our species has been designed so that creativity and religious experience take place in the same dimension of the self. Our "way of knowing" involves a contact with the world beyond the self that bridges the gap between sense and spirit. Herein is to be found what I would like to call the dancing self, the playful, creative, frolicsome modality of our being.

❋ ❋ ❋

The ancients thought of it as a Muse, so fiercely independent is it of propositional reasoning and ordinary consciousness. In the movie *8½* Federico Fellini uses the same metaphor—a beautiful, illusive, gentle, demanding, fascinating woman (Claudia Cardinale). An image of her comes to my mind whenever I think of the human preconscious—which is what a good metaphor is supposed to do.

Various names are used for this aspect of the self: preconscious, creative intuition, poetic imagination, even (*pace* Aristotle and Jacques Maritain) agent intellect—the "active" intellect that rushes out and grabs images. This dimension of the self may be pictured as the scanner that collects images from the outside world and juxtaposes them with images in our memories so as to provide raw material for reflection and abstraction. The preconscious (the agent intellect) is a metaphor maker. It is a phase of our knowing process (our giving of meaning to the phenomena of our life) in which the self spontaneously decides that A is like B and like thousands of other images too. We begin to know by creating metaphors.

During the time of the year when I am writing this draft (Christmas), my agent intellect scans the warmth and light of the fire and transiently juxtaposes it with the image of the sun. My cognitive self may then take over and say that both are forms of light. Then my agent self returns and juxtaposes the image that corresponds to the word "light" with the image of "light of the world." A child wondering what "life" means, juxtaposes "life" with "mother and a baby in a crib," and the first religious metaphor (or sacrament) begins to exist. In this perspective, then, religion is simply the specialized metaphor (or the metaphor system) that provides the raw material for knowing what life ultimately means by explaining it.

Other species may not need to be poetic before they are prosaic, or to make metaphors before they make propositions. Angels, if they are pure spirits, perhaps have no need of metaphors. If, on the other hand, one holds with the pre-Thomistic fathers that angels have bodies—albeit "ethereal" ones—then perhaps they too must go through the agony and the ecstasy of making metaphors.

The preconscious is the ceaselessly active, nonrational, childlike, playful dynamic of the self that we observe knowing the altered states of consciousness between sleeping and waking, between dreaming and "full" consciousness. It is the leading edge of the self, the fine point of the organism reaching out for union with the rest of reality.

It is, I think, the aspect of the self St. Paul had in mind when he said that the Spirit speaks to our spirit—the self insofar as it is charmed and fascinated by the Ultimate as mediated by the good, the true and the beautiful of creation. It is where the Spirit encounters our spirit, seduces it, invites it to dance all night long, and then endeavors to hold it in thrall for ever and ever. Amen.

Ordinarily, these are the dynamics of our grace, hope, renewal experiences—processes in which God works through the secondary causes of the regular processes of experiencing and of giving name and meaning to the phenomena of life. I do not exclude the possibility of other models in which the Spirit whispers directly in our ear, models fondly loved by pious letter writers and by cardinals coming out of conclave. I merely assert with the Catholic tradition that ordinarily the Spirit enters the dance with our spirit through secondary causes and not through special direct intervention.

It is hard to describe this aspect of the self in a way that does not make it sound like a "part" of the self, a mental counterpart of an arm or a leg. But while the right hemisphere of the brain might be the locale of its activity, the dancing self is not a "faculty" of the self so much as it is a modality of the self—or more likely a collection of modalities, of "altered states," of different but related ways of knowing.

Religion—at the pre-reflective level—is, then, closely correlated with creativity because both are metaphor-making, meaning-bestowing processes—the former a highly specialized manifestation of the latter. Catholicism is a religion rich with metaphor systems (and a Metaphor system in the Sacraments). It inundates the preconscious of its members very early in life with intense, powerful, pervasive and durable images that shape the activity of the agent intellect for the rest of life—images that shape the self for dancing the waltz of life. The preconscious is certainly Catholic by the time one is six and, arguably, after one's first conscious Christmas experience.

This is true even if the transmission of Catholic metaphors is ineptly accomplished and if the reflective interpretation of these metaphors in various forms of Catholic education is barren or even oppressive. Obviously, the metaphors are even more effective if the church's representatives administer them with skill and understanding.

A word about the Catholic imagination: Unlike the other religions of Yahweh, Catholicism has always stood for the accessibility of God in the world. God is more like the world than unlike it. Hence Catholicism, unlike Protestantism, Judaism and Islam, permits angels and saints, shrines and statues, stained glass and incense and the continuation of pagan customs—most notably for our purposes here, holy water and blessed candles.

The point is not that the Catholic sensibility is better or worse than other religious sensibilities, but different. Nor is the point that any of the sensibilities can survive provided they are integrated with the others. Finally, the point is not that Catholicism has any monopoly on light and water symbolism, but rather it emphasizes them more strongly than other traditions. No one else has holy water or blessed candles.

Why did James Joyce use such rich Catholic imagery in his work (in, for example, the encounter with the girl on the beach at Clontarf), when he rejected the Catholic religion he learned in school and the Catholic Church he thought was destroying his Irish heritage? The answer is that he had absorbed much earlier in life a more primary, a more pristine and, yes, a more powerful and more benign version of Catholicism.

In the context of religion (in its origins) as an exercise of the metaphor-making dynamisms, Bruce Springsteen's album *Tunnel of Love* may be a more important Catholic event in this country than the visit of Pope John Paul II. The Pope spoke of moral debates using the language of doctrinal propositions that appeal to (or repel) the mind. Springsteen sings of religious realities—sin, temptation, forgiveness, life, death, hope—in images that come (implicitly perhaps) from his Catholic childhood, images that appeal to the whole person, not just the head, and that will be absorbed by far more Americans than those who listened to the Pope.

I intend no disrespect to the Pope or to the importance of his trip. I merely assert the obvious: Troubadours always have more impact than the theologians or bishops, storytellers more influence than homilists.

Some rock critics contend that Springsteen has turned away from the "positive" music of *Born in the U.S.A.* to return to the grimmer and more pessimistic mood of *Nebraska* or *The River.* It might be debated how optimistic *U.S.A.* really was. But, while there is tragedy in *Tunnel of Love,* there is also hope. The water of the river still flows, but now it stands, not for death, but for rebirth. Light and water, the Easter and baptismal symbols of the Catholic liturgy, the combination of the male and female fertility principles, create life in *Tunnel of Love.*

Religion is more explicitly expressed in *Tunnel of Love* than in any previous Springsteen album. Prayer, heaven and God are invoked naturally and unself-consciously, as though they are an ordinary part of the singer's life and vocabulary (and the singer is the narrator of the story told in the song, not necessarily Springsteen). Moreover, religion is invoked to deal precisely with those human (as opposed to doctrinal) problems—love, sin, death, rebirth—that humankind in its long history has always considered religious.

On the subject of human sinfulness, Springsteen sounds like St. Paul, who lamented that "the good which I would do, I do not do; and the evil which I would not do, that I do."

In "Two Faces" the singer complains that he is two men, one good, one evil; one sunny, one dark; one that says "hello" and one that says "goodbye." He tells us that at night he gets down on his knees and prays that "love will make that other man go away," but admits that the other will never leave. For nearly 2,000 years in Western culture that experience has been called Original Sin—the only Christian doctrine, as the Lutheran church historian Martin Marty has remarked, for which there is empirical evidence.

Springsteen returns to this theme in "One Step Up." The singer and his wife are alienated. She is no longer the girl in white outside the church, and the church bells are not ringing any more. The singer does not know who is to blame, but he is caught in his own guilt. He is not the man he wanted to be; somehow he has slipped off the track. He is trapped, "movin' one step up and two steps back."

In "Cautious Man" the singer (Billy) has tattooed the word "love" on one of his hands, and "fear" on the other. In autumn he marries his spring lover because he always "wanted to do what was right." But, "alone on his knees in the darkness for steadiness he'd pray / for he knew in a restless heart the seed of betrayal lay."

One night, the fear tattoo got the better of him and he stole away from his marriage bed and strode down the highway. The road, in the symbolism of earlier Springsteen lyrics, is always the way to freedom. Now, when he gets there, "he didn't find nothing but road."

And in the title song of the album, the singer realizes how difficult married love is: It ought to be easy when a woman and a man fall in love, but they live in a haunted house and their ride in the tunnel of love is rough, rough, rough.

In all these songs the singer discovers the tragedy of life in the conflict between the two men that St. Paul described 1,900 years ago. Tragedy, however, is not pessimism, not despair. It is still possible to fight back.

Possible, but not easy. Love dies. "When it goes, it's gone gone." And "when you're alone, you ain't nothing but alone."

Despite his "Brilliant Disguise" the singer knows in the wee hours that he is not the good husband he swore to be at the altar, but a harsh doubter whose bed is cold. He invokes God's mercy "on the man who doubts what he's sure of." And he knows he is a fool. He may have all the riches in the world but he lacks his beloved: he "Ain't Got You."

If Springsteen left us there, the charge of despair might be appropriate. Theologically he might well be characterized as a Manichee, one who believes that human love is perverse and evil. But he does not stop at either sin or the difficulty of fighting sin. He sings of renewal, each time using the Easter/baptismal renewal symbols of light or flowing water—usually both of them.

In the song "Spare Parts," Janey, a young mother deserted on her wedding day by her child's father, bemoans her fate: She is young and misses the party lights. She hears of a woman who has put her baby in the river "and let the river roll on." She is tempted to do the same, she kneels before his crib and "cried till she prayed."

Then, despite her prayer, Janey brings her son to the river. As in every case where he sings of hope, Springsteen becomes poetic: Waist deep in the running water, with the sun shining brightly above her, she lifts her son up to the sky and then carries him home. She lays him in his bed, takes her wedding dress and ring to the pawnshop and returns home with good cold cash.

The story of the young mother, holding her son in the waters of the river under the bright sun, then lifting him up and carrying him home, now sanctified for life, is surely a baptismal image. How could it be anything else? Could someone not raised in the traditions of blessed light and holy water, not exposed as a child to the light and water of Easter, have produced such a scene?

Sure.

But the point here is that Bruce Springsteen did acquire this imagery in his Catholic childhood. Even if he is not aware of the Catholic symbolism of light and water (and I suspect that he may know what he is doing, but not quite know that he knows), he is using in Catholic fashion these profoundly Catholic symbols of his youth: He is using light and water as symbols of rebirth.

Billy does not desert his wife. Knowing that he will always be caught between fear and love, he returns to his marriage bed and brushes the hair from his sleeping wife's face, which the moon has turned to white. Her glowing face fills the room with the beauty of God's fallen light. The light now becomes quite explicitly God's light—it is a sacrament, a hint of a power that, together with his wife's beauty, enables him to fight his fear. And the singer, who knows that he has two faces, will not give up his woman. He defies the evil man he would not be. He will not deprive the singer of his love. Let him go ahead and try!

Why such confidence? The most "liturgical" of all the songs in *Tunnel of Love* invokes a saint in the song "Valentine's Day"—the Catholic feast (abandoned by our own prudish liturgical priests) of the renewal of romantic love.

The singer is driving home, pondering the truth that in independence there is freedom and reveling in the excitement of the road. Yet he has just spoken to a friend who has become a father. The friend's voice sounds like the light of the skies and the rivers and the timberwolf in the pines. Maybe, the singer admits, he travels fastest who travels alone; but tonight, as his big car rushes down the highway, he misses his girl and he misses his home. Now that might not be quite your man Seamus Heaney, but it's not bad poetry either. And it also has light and flowing waters.

In the final verses of the song—and of the album—Springsteen closes the circle of sacramentality: Light (God's light again) and the river and the bride and God become one, an irresistible symbol and story of the rebirth and renewal of life and love. He wakes up from a nightmare and finds "God's light came shinin' on through." He is scared and terrified and also born anew. The water rushing over him is not the cold river bottom, the wind rushing through his arms is not the bitterness of a dream that did not come true. No, the wind and the water and the light is his wife. So he quietly asks her to be his Valentine.

If that's despair, I'm the Dalai Lama. Rather, it is Catholicism, pure and simple.

Are these songs the story of Springsteen's marriage? Such a question is none of our business. An artist creates out of his experiences and does not necessarily describe them autobiographically. Surely the new maturity, the new sense of tragedy and the new feeling of light, water, rebirth and hope in human love must come out of his experience of marriage, encoded in the fictional narratives of his lyrics. To leave no doubt, the last words on the record jacket are: "Thanks, Juli."

Rock critic Steve Perry notes that throughout his career Springsteen has been obsessed with the themes of community (which is what one would expect from a person steeped in the Catholic imagination). On the one hand, he laments the death of his communities of origin; and on the other, he strains for the freedom of the river and the road. The advantage of such a position is that one can combine nostalgia with freedom from intimacy. Now in marriage he finds that he has created a new community of his own with its demands, frustrations and disappointments. He can still escape from it to the road. He can still flee from complexity and intimacy and human frailty to the power of the high-speed car.

Only mostly he does not want to, not for long, because it is at home with the beloved that one finds healing water and God's holy light. And the Valentine.

The cover of *Tunnel* portrays the singer leaning, rather ruefully, against the Big White Car. It is not as much fun as it used to be. A car is an easier and a less demanding joy than a woman. But not nearly so rewarding.

Is Juli the Valentine? Again that is none of our business. But if she is, she has much to be proud of.

The piety of these songs—and I challenge you to find a better word—is sentient without being sentimental, an Italian-American male piety not unlike that found in some of the films of Martin Scorsese (especially *Mean Streets*). It is, perhaps, not Sunday Mass piety, but it is, if anything, much richer and deeper and more powerful. It is the piety of symbol rather than doctrine. (Most of the rock critics, by the way, agree that in terms of lyrics, music and singing technique, *Tunnel* is the most important artistic stride in Springsteen's life.)

I have no desire to claim Springsteen as Catholic in the way we used to claim movie actors and sports heroes. I merely observe that this is (not utterly unique) Catholic imagery on the lips of a troubadour whose origins and present identification are Catholic. I also observe that the Catholic origin of the imagery serves to explain them. I finally observe that the critics seem to pay no attention to the images, perhaps because without a Catholic perspective one has a hard time understanding where they come from and what they mean.

So if the troubadour's symbols are only implicitly Catholic (and perhaps not altogether consciously so) and if many folks will not understand them or perceive their origins, what good are they to the Catholic Church? Surely they will not increase Sunday collections or win converts or improve the church's public image. Or win consent to the pastoral letter on economics.

But those are only issues if you assume that people exist to serve the church. If, on the other hand, you assume that the church exists to serve people by bringing a message of hope and renewal, of light and water and rebirth, to a world steeped in tragedy and sin, you rejoice that such a troubadour sings stories that maybe even he does not know are Catholic.

Whenever I propose this analysis, I am assailed by charges that Springsteen is motivated by the desire to make money, that he is not a nice man, that his marriage is in trouble, etc. This is celebrity talk, magazine drivel, which is both utterly irrelevant to the work of the man and a perverse violation of Christian charity. It is much easier, it would seem, for many Catholic teachers and liturgists than the hard work of searching for grace.

From my analysis in this article I draw the following conclusions:

1. Grace is to be found in popular culture (but not in all forms of popular culture) if one is willing to look for it. In some cases, one need not look very hard.

2. The failure of the church to understand Springsteen's importance and to embrace him (even, indeed, to provide him with the religious support to which he has a right) shows how profound is the alienation of the church from the fine and lively arts, most of which it created and nurtured for a thousand years. There was a time when we really appreciated a meistersinger.

3. Those Catholics who speak to the meaning of life out of the (perhaps) unself-conscious images of their Catholic heritage have a more profound claim to be liturgists than diocesan liturgical directors, for example, who gather to devise ways to use the liturgy to brainwash the laity into accepting the social action views of those who draft pastorals. (I do not know whether the assumption that this can be done is more hilarious than the attempt to do so is obscene.) The Catholic minstrels, such as these may be, are the true sacrament-makers because they revive and renew the fundamental religious metaphors. We must treasure them rather than ignore or denounce them. Or impugn their motives.

4. If religion, in its raw and primal origins and power, is imaginative, and especially if it is the ultimate-meaning metaphors we absorb early in life, and finally if it is these meaningful metaphors that hold Catholics (like Springsteen himself) in the church, then the personages of the institutional church (bishops, priests, theologians, teachers, etc.) ought to be much more concerned about the imagination than they are.

I finish this series with a sense of frustration. I deduce from the reactions and nonreactions, the anger and the defensiveness, from the misunderstanding and the ridicule (especially the ridicule), not that the argument is too intricate to be followed, but rather that it is too strange to be taken seriously. Metaphor, religious imagination, secular grace, correlation, Valentine's Day, Springsteen, Madonna, the sacramentality of erotic love, the playful and creative dancing self—these categories do not fit the paradigms of either the Catholic left or the Catholic right, of either the theologians or the parish clergy in its various ministerial forms.

That is a shame. Unless and until the institutional church is willing to examine this approach to religion (not necessarily in the form I have presented it), it will not understand either its own people or its own immense resources. Rabbi Jacob Neusner has written of this tradition: "We are Jews by reason of imagination." Cannot our various leaders perceive that, for Catholics, such a statement is equally true, if not even more strongly true?

Why don't they understand that we are Catholic, first of all, by reason of imagination?

Note

1. Writes Father Blake, "In psychological terms, 'afterimage' is not a self-conscious or voluntary phenomenon. It is merely 'the image that remains after a stimulus ceases or is removed.' It is that continuation of a powerful stimulus that lingers in the eyes for an instant. It can be uncomfortable, but it is there. Everyone has experienced this when the photographer at a wedding gets too close with a flash camera. The sensation of the blast of light remains even after the eyelid closes and the bulb is dark. . . . That stimulus . . . is so strong that like the flashbulb it leaves an afterimage on the artistic imagination long after it has been removed, or in many cases, after the artists have removed themselves from the stimulus." See Richard A. Blake, *Afterimage: The Indelible Catholic Imagination of Six American Filmmakers* (Chicago: Loyola Press, 2000), pp. xiv–xv.

Robert Santelli

■

Robert Santelli, a product of the Jersey Shore, has written extensively about Springsteen, blues, and rock. In January 1994 he joined the staff of the Rock and Roll Hall of Fame and Museum in Cleveland as assistant curator. Since 2000 Santelli has been the deputy director of public programs for Experience Music Project in Seattle. He is the executive editor of the American Music Masters series, published by Wesleyan University Press; the coeditor of *Hard Travelin': The Life and Legacy of Woody Guthrie* (1999); *American Roots Music* (2001); *Martin Scorsese Presents the Blues: A Musical Journey* (2003), *The Appalachians: America's First and Last Frontier* (2004); and the author of *The Best of the Blues: The 101 Essential Albums* (1997), *The Big Book of Blues: A Biographical Encyclopedia* (2001), and *Guide to the Jersey Shore* (2003, 6th ed.). He also wrote the liner notes to *Badlands: A Tribute to Bruce Springsteen's Nebraska* (2000) and edited *Songs*, the complete collection of Springsteen's recorded album lyrics (1998; 2003). He has written for *Rolling Stone*, the *New York Times*, *CD Review, Downbeat, Backstreets, Asbury Park Press*, and *New Jersey Monthly*. The following selection is from *Backstreets: Springsteen—The Man and His Music* (1989; 1992).

Twenty Years Burning Down the Road: The Complete History of Jersey Shore Rock 'n' Roll

from *Backstreets: Springsteen—The Man and His Music*

■MENTION THE ENGLISH CITY of Liverpool to the average soul on the street, and chances are the first vision that will pass through his or her mind is that of four mop-topped lads called the Beatles. Try it sometime. Ask your mom or dad, or your boss. Ask the postperson, or the middle-aged woman in the supermarket.

Liverpool isn't known or remembered as an important prewar seaport, which it was, or for its soccer team. It's known to the world as the city where the Beatles originated. It's practically impossible to separate this glum, working-class city from the legacy of the Beatles, and vice versa.

Mention Asbury Park, New Jersey, to that same person, and it's a good bet that they'll say something like "Asbury Park? Yeah, that's the place where Bruce Springsteen comes from." Granted, that's not entirely accurate, because Springsteen was, of course, born and raised in nearby Freehold (although at times in the late sixties and early seventies, he did reside in Asbury Park, and he certainly spent much time playing the city's clubs and bars).[1]

Nonetheless, because of Bruce Springsteen, Asbury Park has earned a secure place in rock history books. The city's rich past as a prewar seaside resort, with once-beautiful beaches and a bustling boardwalk, and the nationally reported race riots that tore through the city and devastated its downtown shopping district in 1970 are both, historically speaking, secondary to the city's relationship to the man they call the Boss. The fact is, Asbury Park is inextricably linked with Bruce Springsteen, and vice versa.

There are other similarities that, in a way, make Liverpool and Asbury Park sister cities. Each is a city whose past is brighter than its present. In each, unemployment remains high, decay is dominant, and the landscape can best be painted in shades of gray. True, there is much talk about a renaissance or rebirth of Asbury Park. And over the past couple of years the city has striven hard to initiate a massive facelift and implement a more positive image. Yet, sadly, Asbury Park largely remains the same Asbury Park that Bruce Springsteen pinpointed so forcefully in his early music.

Interestingly, ever since Springsteen came to prominence, the media have possessed a somewhat morbid fascination with Asbury Park. To many journalists, photographers, TV reporters and filmmakers, Asbury Park has routinely symbolized a particular slice of America's underbelly, a place just brimming with the kinds of stark, gloomy images from which great works of art, literature—and music—originate.

The idea was always that if you could understand the environment (Asbury Park and the rest of the Jersey Shore) of the artist (Springsteen)—namely, the seaside bars and blue-collar beer joints, the boardwalk amusements and pizza parlors, the lonely streets and broken dreams—then you'd appreciate more fully the artist's art (Springsteen's songs). To a large degree, this is true. Few American songwriters have been able to take such detailed images of the American Dream, as well as the tales of hardship and disappointment that accompany them, and imbue them with the universality that Bruce Springsteen has. Springsteen took from all around him. He transformed the characters that hung out in Asbury Park's bars and boardwalk into song personalities that symbolized life's struggle. He worked his impressions of Asbury Park and the rest of the Jersey Shore into his lyrics in such a way that the songs weren't about Asbury or Jersey, but about America and about you and me.

"It was natural right from the beginning that when people wanted to learn more about Bruce, that they came to Asbury," said one local. "It's not much to look at, I know, but for rock 'n' roll it's a great place. It's a rock 'n' roll town if there ever was one. And it's really pretty spiritual. I mean, you don't go visiting the town where Jackson Browne came from, do you?"

Actually, the media fascination with Asbury Park began more than a decade ago—in 1975, to be precise. And it started with the biggest of bangs. What longtime Springsteen fan can ever forget that amazing week in October when the covers of both *Time* and *Newsweek* were graced with the face of Bruce Springsteen? Before that came the cover story on Bruce in the now defunct but at the time critically praised magazine *Crawdaddy*.[2] And there were others. It was part hype and part intrigue, but all of a sudden Asbury Park was being touted the same way Liverpool was some ten years earlier.

"It was really weird," said Southside Johnny in an interview a few years ago. "You had photographers and reporters poking their heads into clubs and looking for God knows what. Nobody ever paid attention to Asbury Park or the musicians who played there and lived there before. Some people never got the hang of it."

The world found out about Bruce Springsteen's roots and about Asbury Park. And in the process, some of the more astute observers discovered a music scene that was vibrant and rich with bands. There was Southside Johnny and the Asbury Jukes. There was Cahoots. There were Lord Gunner, the Shakes, and Cold, Blast, and Steel.[3] They were the local stars in the local clubs. Few of them had ever ventured beyond the Jersey Shore with their guitars and amps. It was strictly a homegrown rock scene. While popular music in the mid-seventies began flirting with disco, and rock was caught with a bad case of the blahs, the music heard in Asbury Park clubs—like the Stone Pony—revolved around rhythm and blues and sixties soul. Outside the scene, such influences were considered dated and passé. But in Asbury Park, R&B-based rock was hot and sassy.

Also, blues was big, especially in the late sixties, just as it was in San Francisco and England. It was an easily adaptable style of music, and it lent itself to jamming. Jamming was what Asbury Park's legendary club, the Upstage, was all about. In fact, if any one element was (and still is) most representative of the Jersey Shore music scene in general and Asbury Park's in particular, it was the concept of late-night jams and sitting in. It began at house parties, moved to the Upstage in the late sixties and later to the Stone Pony as well as a whole slew of other clubs such as the Student Prince, the Fast Lane, Mrs. Jay's, and the High Tide Cafe.

Right from the very beginning, there were some bands that began overshadowing the others. Down around Asbury Park, Sonny and the Starfires ruled. Sonny Kenn, a guitarist influenced by the likes of Link Wray and Lonnie Mack, was the bandleader and frontman. The Starfires' backbeat was kept by a self-taught drummer named Vini Lopez. Out in the Freehold area, it was the Motifs, the band that came closest to turning professional and reaching beyond the Jersey Shore, and the Castiles, which included two respected guitarists, George Theiss and Bruce Springsteen. Up in Red Bank, The Source, led by Steve Van Zandt, was making itself known by playing in local battle-of-the-bands contests and playing high school dances.

To take advantage of the wealth of young rock talent at the Shore in the mid-sixties and of the seemingly insatiable appetite of kids there for live rock 'n' roll, a host of nonalcoholic teen clubs sprouted throughout the area. The Hullabaloo chain of teen clubs was especially popular. Sonny and the Starfires became regulars at the Asbury Park Hullabaloo club. Here is how Sonny Kenn remembers those days:

"We wore gold lamé suits and fancy boots, and we had Ampeg and Fender amplifiers. We'd get up there onstage at around 8 P.M. and we'd play 55 minutes with a five-minute break. Then we'd go back and play again. It was just enough time to have a cigarette and a soda. We played there all summer and gained a tremendous amount of experience. By this time Vini [Lopez] had introduced me to this kid from Garden Grove,[4] Johnny Lyon [later known as Southside Johnny], and he started coming to all our gigs and practice sessions. Whenever we played at Hullabaloo or a school dance or something, he'd go out in the audience to make sure our amps were turned up high enough."

The competition between bands at the Jersey Shore in the mid-sixties was certainly keen, but it was not cutthroat. Instead, there was a subtle yet strong bond between musicians that later made the Upstage experience such a valuable one for them. Despite the occasional squabble, such camaraderie allowed for the frequent trading of ideas and riffs, and enabled musicians and bands to grow.

Even though the mid-sixties saw the rise of a large number of bands at the Shore, few groups played anywhere but the Shore. What with teen clubs, high school and CYO dances, and battles of the bands, of which there were many, there were plenty of places to perform locally without having to venture to New York.

One group, the Castiles, had more drive than most. It also had a manager, Tex Vinyard, who took it upon himself to push the group musically and force it to seek brighter horizons. Because of him, the Castiles were one of the few mid-sixties Shore bands to make a record (a self-produced, self-recorded single, "That's What You Get" backed with "Baby I"). Vinyard also worked the Castiles into a regular set of gigs at New York's legendary club, the Cafe Wha?, where groups like the Blues Project and artists such as Jimi Hendrix and Bill Cosby got their start.

"Tex was a big ego builder," George Theiss remembers. "He would sit there and tell you how the girls were going crazy over you. At 16 or 17, that's just what you wanted to hear. He made sure we were confident."

Confidence. That's the key word. Vinyard instilled a sense of sureness in the Castiles, especially Springsteen, that never really left them. Vinyard also exposed the group to a whole new level of rock in New York City that most other Shore bands missed during this era. Such things enabled Springsteen to leave the Castiles when the Jersey Shore music scene was about to enter a new stage in the late sixties and to form his own bands fueled by his own rock visions.

From this point on, it was Springsteen who set the pace, who broke the most new ground, and, as Theiss says, who acted "as if he already had a plan . . . and knew exactly where he was heading."

Much has been written about the Upstage. "It was really a unique place, the Upstage," said Van Zandt. "I've never ever run across another club like it anywhere else in the world."

"Everybody went there 'cause it was open later than the regular clubs and because between one and five in the morning you could play pretty much whatever you wanted, and if you were good enough, you could choose the guys you wanted to play with," wrote Springsteen in the liner notes for *I Don't Want to Go Home,* the debut album of Southside Johnny and the Asbury Jukes.

"It was like going to school," recalled Sonny Kenn a few years ago. "Upstage, when you think about it, really was a school. Better yet, for those of us who used to play at Hullabaloo and the teen clubs, it was almost a college of sorts."

The entire Jersey Shore music scene revolved around the Upstage for the two years or so in the late sixties that it was open. Run by Tom and Margaret Potter, it was a meeting place, a proving ground, and a musical laboratory all in one. More groups were formed there, and more groups broke up there, than anywhere else.

Musicians at the Upstage were part of a large pecking order. The best—Springsteen, Van Zandt, and other guitar players like Billy Ryan, Ricky DeSarno, and Sonny Kenn, drummers such as Vini Lopez and Big Bobby Williams, harp players like Southside Johnny, and keyboard players such as David Sancious—had first dibs on stage time. Other musicians worked their way onstage when they were good enough to play with the first team.

The Upstage acted as a springboard for what was to follow at the Jersey Shore in the 1970s. No one could ever have deliberately planned a club so crucial to the development of so many musicians. The incredible thing is that it worked. The informality, the competition, Tom Potter's zany, slapstick-like organizational skills, and the madness that never really surfaced long enough to blow the whole thing out of control, all created an atmosphere of intense apprenticeship.

It was during this time that Bill Chinnock's Downtown Tangiers Band gained notoriety and respect as far north as New York, that Maelstrom (Southside on bass and harp, Kenn on guitar, and Ronnie Romano on drums) practically became the house band at the downstairs coffeehouse section of the Upstage, and that Steel Mill, the first of the truly great Shore bands, was born.

Steel Mill's best lineup was Springsteen on guitar and vocals, Steve Van Zandt on bass, Danny Federici on organ, and Vini Lopez on drums. On a bad night Steel Mill was still the best outfit on the Shore, perhaps in all of Jersey. On a good night, the band was, well, simply amazing.

I remember going to see the band in concert at Ocean County College in Toms River, New Jersey. It was a typically hot and humid night at the Shore. I think it was August 1970. The gymnasium was packed with sweaty, anxious souls. The word had spread about Steel Mill. Anticipation filled the air. Even though Springsteen had briefly attended Ocean County College, and Toms River is part of the Jersey Shore, it wasn't part of Steel Mill's true stomping grounds. Many people in the audience that night had only heard about how good the band was supposed to be.

For the two hours or so that Steel Mill played, Springsteen and company simply overwhelmed everyone on the other side of the stage. Had his brand of blues-rock been available on record at the time, or had that concert been somehow made into a live album and rushed to radio stations and record stores, it would have rivaled Led Zeppelin's best, I swear.

People who had seen Steel Mill for the first time walked out of that show as if they had participated in a mystical musical experience. Springsteen's manager, Jon Landau, saw the future of rock 'n' roll four years later in 1974. A lot of us at the Shore saw it that night.

There were other fine bands at the Shore during this time. Southern Conspiracy was one. Sunny Jim was another. Both opened for Steel Mill on a regular basis. It was an era of shared apartments and skimpy meals, and of free outdoor concerts at local parks and at Monmouth College in West Long Branch, when the weather was good.

It was also an era of restlessness. Steel Mill made a trip to California and played the Fillmore West. Afterwards, rock impresario Bill Graham offered the band free recording time. They recorded three songs for him but turned down his contract offer. Back in Jersey a few months later, Springsteen formed Dr. Zoom and the Sonic Boom, which represented a classic case of musical absurdity and was the result of wild experimentation never before seen at the Shore.

Musicians came and went. Garry Tallent, David Sancious, Southside Johnny, and others left Asbury Park and headed to Richmond, Virginia, a town that became a home away from home for Asbury Park players. Others split for California, Colorado, and New England. Springsteen's restlessness is well documented. He broke up Steel Mill. He formed the Bruce Springsteen Band. He broke up the Bruce Springsteen Band. He became a folksinger. He commuted to New York's Greenwich Village and played the clubs there. And then he got a recording contract.

❖   ❖   ❖

Springsteen's signing with Columbia Records was enough of an event to bring most everyone back to Asbury Park in 1972 and 1973. The scene, which had become disjointed and lost its purpose, was about to be righted.

"Bruce needed a band to make *Greetings from Asbury Park, N.J.* with," recalled Garry Tallent. "So the word went out and people came home." A new version of the Bruce Springsteen Band was formed, the record was made, and the boys hit the road to promote it.

"It was an interesting time," remembers Big Danny Gallagher, who acted as the band's road manager. "We played all these weird places and drove hundreds of miles to do it again the next night. Nobody saw much in the way of money. We practically starved."

Back home, musicians, caught up in the enthusiasm of one of their own actually making a record and going on tour, formed new bands and hoped to follow in Springsteen's footsteps. One such group was the Blackberry Booze Band.

"The kind of music we played was blues," says David Meyers, the Booze Band's bass player. "Steve [Van Zandt] was in the band and so was Southside. We played the kind of stuff that might have been heard during the Upstage days, but we did it with more polish, I think. We also played a lot of material that no one else had ever heard before. We were a band rather than a bunch of musicians that simply showed up and jammed, although at times that did happen when friends asked to sit in."

By this time a new club had opened up on Ocean Avenue in Asbury Park, called the Stone Pony. Its owners were looking for a house band that would draw locals to the club on a regular basis. Using some of the ideas worked out in the Blackberry Booze Band, Miami Steve Van Zandt and Southside Johnny formed just the group the Pony was searching for, Southside Johnny and the Asbury Jukes.

Van Zandt, who had toured with the Dovells after Steel Mill broke up, and who had always been infatuated with black music, formed the Asbury Jukes around a horn section and a pepper-hot rhythm section. Not prepared to take center stage himself, he gave that task to Southside. Armed with a blazing harp and an encyclopedic knowledge of blues and R&B, Johnny sang and moved like his heroes—Jackie Wilson, Otis Redding, Sam Cooke, and Ray Charles—and the Pony began to fill up.

When Springsteen and his band came off the road, they found the Stone Pony the place to hang out. Gradually, the club became the unofficial meeting place of Jersey Shore musicians, especially those with strong links to Asbury Park.

"It filled a gap," says Kevin Kavanaugh, an original member of the Asbury Jukes who still plays keyboard in the band. "When the Upstage closed, there was really no place where you knew you could go on a given night and find plenty of musicians. The Pony became that place."

It was in 1976 that the music scene of the Jersey Shore, particularly in Asbury Park, had matured into one worthy of national attention. Springsteen's *Born to Run*, released the year before, had been critically acclaimed in virtually every nook and cranny of the rock media. The *Time* and *Newsweek* stories had introduced him to mainstream America. All the hype that surrounded Springsteen nearly destroyed his career, but it did wonders for Asbury Park and the Stone Pony.

When record company executives came looking for another Springsteen in the back alleys and beer joints of Asbury, they almost certainly wound up at the Pony, where they were introduced to the Asbury Jukes. Springsteen praised the band and helped open important doors at Epic Records. Soon Southside and the Jukes had a record deal. On Memorial Day 1976 they celebrated the release of *I Don't Want to Go Home* with a Stone Pony concert broadcast live on the radio.

David Sancious, who had left the E Street Band, along with drummer Boom Carter, to start a solo career as a jazz-rock fusion artist, also scored a record deal. His album, *Forest of Feelings*, although not nearly as commercially popular as *I Don't Want to Go Home*, scored high critical marks nonetheless.

Other Asbury Park–based bands such as the Shakes, Cold, Blast and Steel, Lord Gunner, and the Cahoots scrambled to be the next in line. None ever did land a contract, but they came close. All this added up to what many locals consider the heyday of Jersey Shore music. Asbury Park was, in a word, music-rich. It was primarily a rock-R&B blend that one heard echoing out of area clubs, flavored with the sounds of a saxophone and the gritty vocals of a lead singer well versed in soul and Motown. Black leather jackets, newsboy caps, and earrings were in. Bands like Paul Whistler and the Wheels and the Shots kept the musical momentum strong.

Eventually the scene diversified enough to allow bands such as Kinderhook Creek, with deep-seated ties to country and Southern rock;

Salty Dog, the Shore's answer to heavy metal; and Sam the Band, perhaps the best Top 40 bar band, to develop large, devoted followings.

One would have thought, though, that with all the musical energy coming out of the Shore and with the large number of bands—and good bands at that—vying for a chance at stardom, at least one or two other outfits would have signed their names on record contracts.

"You have to take into consideration the 'Springsteen curse,'" says one prominent Shore musician who asked to remain anonymous. "As much as Bruce was good for the local scene, he was also bad for it. Every band that was worthy of a recording contract in the late seventies was branded a Springsteen clone, it seemed. That's why nobody got signed in those years. Record companies heard you were from Asbury Park and right away they shut their doors. The hype was over. A lot of good bands were denied their chance to get a deal because of the whole Springsteen bit. Now don't get me wrong. I ain't saying it was his fault. It just happened that way."

Consider the case of Billy Chinnock. An Upstage veteran and longtime member of the Shore music scene, it was Chinnock's bad luck to be labeled an Asbury Park artist with an R&B-styled sound that closely resembled Springsteen's. Chinnock even looked and sounded like Springsteen at times. But worse, even though he was one of the precious few to sign a recording contract in the late seventies (with Atlantic), what did he call his debut album? *Badlands*.

"I had no idea Bruce had a song with the same name," said Chinnock in an interview. "I couldn't help it that I sort of have the same features as he does. And we came from the same roots, so why should my music sound all that different from his?

"It was like no matter what I did or where I turned, there was this Bruce-ghost following me. I knew I'd never get the proper attention in Jersey, so I moved to New York, then Maine, then back to Jersey, and finally to Nashville. It was there that I got a record company (CBS Associates) to take another look at my songs. It took a long time and a lot of running."

Gradually, disappointment and frustration began to take a toll in Asbury Park. Bands broke up. Some musicians turned away from music altogether. Disco was hot elsewhere in America, so many club owners sought out DJs or Top 40 dance bands to fill the dance floors on the Shore. Even the Stone Pony began booking cover bands.

What saved the scene was the opening of a new club in Asbury Park, the Fast Lane. Its booking agent and manager, Jim Giantonio, sought out national acts when no one else would, and hired local bands which played original music to open for them. Almost overnight it became the Shore's premier club. Not only did acts like Joe Jackson, the Ramones, Robert Gordon, and seemingly countless New Wave bands from Britain play the club in the early eighties, but "honorary" Shore groups such as Beaver Brown and Norman Nardini and the Tigers developed strong followings.

Giantonio actively encouraged area bands to focus on original music. He was, for example, responsible for pushing a band called The Rest, which included a lead singer named John Bongiovi (later to be known as Jon Bon Jovi), to deal seriously with its image and stage presence as well as its original songs. The result? The Rest became the best on the Shore in the early eighties.

The success of the Fast Lane prompted the Stone Pony to change gears and revert to its old policy of featuring original music bands. Another club, Big Man's West, owned by E Street Band member Clarence Clemons, opened in nearby Red Bank. A whole new generation of Shore bands filled these clubs: Clarence Clemons and the Red Bank Rockers, Sonny Kenn and the Wild Ideas, Hot Romance, Cats on a Smooth Surface, Junior Smoots and the Disturbers. At the Pony, E Street Band members were back hanging out, and Springsteen would routinely show up on Sunday nights to sit in with Cats on a Smooth Surface. Suddenly the Shore music scene was back on its feet.

Sidenote: While all this was happening in Asbury Park and Red Bank, a hardcore punk offshoot of the Shore music scene sprouted in nearby Long Branch. The host club was the Brighton Bar. It permitted slam-dancing and gave the rowdiest punk bands a place to perform.

"Hardcore at the Shore is just a violent reaction to all the hype that surrounds Asbury Park and the bands that play there," said The Mutha, owner of Long Branch's Mutha Records and a leader of the local punk movement a couple of years ago. "We don't want any part of that crap." Brighton bands openly resented bands that played the Asbury Park/ Red Bank circuit and repudiated the R&B roots of the area in grand fashion.

Yet there were ties. John Eddie played the Brighton as much as he played Big Man's West. So did Sonny Kenn. Little Steven was even known to sign in at the Brighton when he was at the Shore. And some very good bands came out of the scene, bands that, with the proper guidance, could have gone much farther than they did. One such group was Secret Syde. Another was the Wallbangers.

All this brings us to the present. The Fast Lane is gone, as is Big Man's West. The Stone Pony has reclaimed its right to be called the Shore's most prestigious rock club, though redevelopment plans for Asbury Park will probably mean the demolition of the club's Ocean Avenue site. The Brighton Bar lives on. And there are some new clubs—the Deck House in Asbury Park, the Green Parrot in Neptune, Jasons in South Belmar— that regularly book the best local bands and carry on the tradition of the Jersey Shore music scene.

There is yet another generation of artists and bands worth noting, too. John Eddie is at the top of the list, and right behind him is Glen Burtnick. Then there are the Cruisers and LaBamba and the Hubcaps, two bands with strong links to R&B; the Fairlanes, the Shore's best blues act; and new entries like Mike Wells and the Wage, Big Danny and the Boppers, Beyond the Blue, Baby Boom, and the World.

"The Shore music scene is still something special," says Stone Pony DJ Lee Mrowicki. "Overall, the quality of bands is quite good, and you'll never know who might jam on any given night. It's a tight scene, too, just like it's always been. Maybe that's what makes it so special. If you play in a Shore band, I think you feel like you belong to something bigger than the three or four guys in your group. You feel like you're part of a legacy or a tradition. Few other scenes have that. And I know most of us are pretty proud of it."

Notes

1. Springsteen was born at Monmouth Memorial Hospital, Long Branch, New Jersey.
2. *Crawdaddy!* is back in circulation again.
3. For a look at the current Asbury Park music scene, see Gary Wien, *Beyond the Palace* (Victoria, B.C.: Trafford Publishing, 2003).
4. Johnny Lyon grew up in Ocean Grove, a seaside community immediately south of Asbury Park.

Charles R. Cross

■

Backstreets wasn't the first Springsteen fanzine to be published, although it is the most enduring (the honor of the first magazine devoted to Springsteen belongs to *Thunder Road,* published and edited by Ken Viola and Lou Cohan between 1977 and 1982).[1] The following article by *Backstreets* founder Charles Cross originally appeared in the Winter 1991 issue, written on the tenth anniversary of the magazine.

The Promise
Backstreets

■"ONE SOFT INFESTED SUMMER, me and Terry became friends, trying in vain to breathe the fire, he was born in." So begins Bruce Springsteen singing "Backstreets," for my money one of the most emotional and affectionate songs ever penned. Within this one tune, Springsteen addresses all the major elements to his work: rebellion; liberation; love; death; friendship; and salvation. These are themes that speak to my own human experience and no doubt, to yours too.

This magazine is ten years old this month and when I started it in my basement, typing on this same typewriter, I couldn't have imagined that I would today be finishing up the anniversary issue. At the time I started the mag I knew that Springsteen's music moved me and I wanted to share my feelings with others so I started this forum. It has led me into many uncharted directions and it has brought me friendships with many wonderful people all over the world. I simply had no idea that the ties that bind run so deep and run so true.

If I were to sum up the reason for this magazine to exist—an existence that has at times seemed tenuous—I would go back to that first line of the song "Backstreets" since it starts the ride we were all upon. This is [a] world where isolation leaps up at us from all sides and where only infrequently do we overcome it. . . . Fellowship is far too rare in this world of ours but fellowship is what this magazine is about. It is what brings together all of us as readers of this mag and as fans of Springsteen's music. And it is what in many ways has saved me numerous times from a life I found full of isolation. In some strange way, Bruce Springsteen's music has always played a role for me in our universal fellowship.

This recently hit home for me one night when I was driving around with my friend Carl. It was in early August of this year and it seemed at the time like both our lives were going to seed faster than we could blink an eye. We'd both recently ended relationships with women we had great hopes for, women we loved dearly. And I think we'd both seen our dreams turn to nightmares with a few hateful words. I thought my particular case was horrid: The woman I had been in love with, and had been shopping for wedding rings with, suddenly up and left town with no explanation except a few hurtful volleys my way. I still haven't had the heart to go back into the jewelry store and ask for my $200 deposit back because I don't think I ever want to face that thing inside of me again that knows what it feels like to have a promise broken. Carl's saga is not unlike mine: He also had fallen for an emotionally unavailable woman and he'd given a lot away. As Springsteen has said many times, it's easy to lose yourself. I think I've found that out the hard way in this world and the lesson continues to sting at me every day I live, like a bee in my shoe that I can't ever find. Back in August, for me, the world looked like a place filled with loss.

We were driving through the seamy part of town and I popped the Winterland '78 tape in the stereo as Carl had never heard the '78 version of "Backstreets," the one that includes the "Sad Eyes" segue.[2] I think it's the best thing Springsteen has ever done, the emotional zenith to his body of work. I can't listen to it without feeling a tear come to my eye, a tug of a raw nerve on my heart.

Carl had never heard this version of "Backstreets" before and he was instantly transfixed by it. "I'd drive all night, just to buy you some shoes and to taste your tender charms / to have you hold me in your arms, for just one kiss / for just one look from your sad eyes," Bruce sang in the song. "Just one look."

Springsteen only played the song this way for a few months in 1977 and 1978 and they edited it off the *Live* album for reasons that have never been clear to me. He'd always vary the story told in the song, but it always was intense and true. The version from Orlando in 1977 with the story about watching some kids burn down a barn, and watching the fields catch on fire and how the flames rushed towards him and his lover sitting on the hood of a car, is monumental. I've liked all I've heard but particularly am moved when Bruce added the line "Just to hear you tell me that you loved me." It was as tender as Bruce Springsteen gets, as tender as I can take it. And it was what I wanted so bad that August night: Just to hear it from her one more time.

The woman I'd looked at wedding rings for had those sad eyes herself. They were these little puppy dog eyes that turned slightly down on the ends and even when she was happy they always looked a little sad. She thought it made her ugly but to me it made her all the more beautiful. I can remember just what it sounded like when she told me "I love you," and I can remember every little inflection in her voice and yet I knew I'd never, ever hear it again.

Which is why I understood the depth of emotion in Springsteen's voice when he gets to the part in the song where he literally screams "But baby YOU LIED!" It is as close to a primal scream as I've ever heard and it's a scream that sums up his loss, Carl's loss, my loss, and the loss of every other broken-hearted hero who ever looked into someone's eyes and felt a spark.

Carl was stunned. He'd later say that listening to the tape was one of those experiences where the world just stops around you and there's nothing but you and it and it is looking you in the face and you can't turn around and you can't go back. You just can't.

It wasn't like anything else happened. That's really all there is to the story. I thought about driving by my old girlfriend's house and blasting out the tape so loud she could hear the "YOU LIED" stuff up in her room but I decided against it. In the song Bruce tells how the object of his affection comes back but Carl and I knew in our lives there was no going back. No one was going to be knocking on my door saying "Baby, I'm sorry." Nothing was going to happen and nothing was going to change anything.

Carl and I looked at each other. We looked at each other and we both knew. And because we knew we didn't need to say anything. We both knew what we felt inside and we knew that at one point Bruce Springsteen felt this same darkness too. And I don't want to get too ethereal here, but what we felt was connection. What we felt was fellowship. We felt it and nothing that could happen to us would change that.

In some ways, that connection is exactly what this magazine is about. It is about the fellowship and friendship between people like Carl and

I, and what Bruce Springsteen's music does to bring that out in us. It has to do with trying to learn to walk like the heroes we thought we had to be. But we're not heroes: We're just like all the rest. And Bruce Springsteen isn't a hero either—he's heroic in that he can sing and write about how he feels but he faces the same struggles we all do.

Almost four months later both Carl and I are long beyond the driving around late at night stage. Yet for me, another chapter in my life has begun and Bruce Springsteen is once again there with a song for me. "Mr. Trouble come walking this way," he sang on stage at the Christic Institute shows, "year gone by seems like one long day, but I'm alive and I'm feeling alright / Well I ran that hard road down heartbreak city, and a roadside carnival of hurt and self-pity / It was all wrong, but now I'm moving on." It's the real world out there and it's the only place I live these days. Love may be hopeless, hopeless at best, but I'll keep trying to breathe that fire, and I'll keep breathing it with my friends. I'm going out tonight, and I'm going with the tumbling dice.

Notes

1. See Robert Santelli, "'Thunder Road': The First Bruce Fanzine," *Backstreets,* Summer 1987, p. 11.
2. "Sad Eyes" appears on *Tracks* (1998).

Dave Barry

∎

Humorist Dave Barry wrote this tongue-in-cheek column on July 10, 1994. The Rock Bottom Remainders—the makeshift group that he refers to in the piece—consisted of a pickup band of writers, which included Barry, Dave Marsh, Stephen King, Amy Tan, Matt Groening, and at various times a few other literary souls, such as Roy Blount Jr., Barbara Kingsolver, and Robert Fulghum. In May 1993 the Remainders "reunited" for a nine-city tour of the East Coast, an account of which was released as *Mid-Life Confidential: The Rock Bottom Remainders Tour America with Three Chords and an Attitude*, edited by Dave Marsh with photographs by Tabitha King (1994).

Glory Days
Miami Herald

∎BRUCE SPRINGSTEEN PLAYED my guitar. I am not making this up. It was the high point of my musical life. It was even better than the time when, for a few minutes, I was in the same airport as Ray Charles. I am never going to wash my guitar again. (Not that I ever did before.)

I should explain that I belong to a band called the Rock Bottom Remainders. It consists mostly of writers. The original concept was that people who spend all their time writing would enjoy a chance to express their musical talent. The flaw here is that most of us don't have any musical talent. So we compensate by playing amplified instruments loud enough to affect the weather. Also we stick to songs that are so well known that even when WE play them, people sometimes recognize them.

For example, we play "Louie Louie," an extremely well-known song. You know how scientists have been trying fruitlessly for years to contact alien beings by broadcasting radio signals to outer space? Well, I think they should broadcast "Louie Louie." I bet alien beings would immediately recognize this song and broadcast a response ("PLAY SOMETHING ELSE").

For a change of pace, the Rock Bottom Remainders also play "Wild Thing," a song performed in a style known to classical musicians as "molto accelerando con carne," which means "basically the same as 'Louie Louie.'" We employ two powerful musical weapons when we perform this song. One is Roy Blount Jr., a great humor writer who has the raw natural musical talent of a soldering iron. At the end of the first verse, the band pauses dramatically, and Roy is supposed to say, "I LOVE you"; at the end of the second verse, he's supposed to say, "You MOVE me." These two lines are Roy's sole musical responsibility for the entire night, and he takes it seriously, pacing around before the performance, muttering his lines over and over to himself. So when we get to the end of the first verse, we stop, and everybody turns expectantly to Roy, waiting for him to say "I LOVE you," and Roy, frowning with deep concentration, inevitably says: "You MOVE me." And then the rest of us, in a smooth professional manner, stagger around and try not to wet our pants.

Our other big musical weapon on "Wild Thing" is Joel Selvin, a writer and rock critic for *The San Francisco Chronicle,* who plays a flute solo, using a plastic flute that looks like the kind you get from gum ball machines, only cheaper. Joel, like most of your top international flute players, learned this solo by watching an instructional videotape at home. The problem is, when he gets on stage with the band, he tends to get nervous and blow REALLY HARD, so that instead of notes, the flute emits a series of extremely high-pitched squeaks, like a gerbil that fell into a french-fry machine. Sometimes Joel's entire solo is above the range of human hearing. He'll be wailing away, his face red, his fingers moving in the manner prescribed by the videotape, and it LOOKS really dramatic, but nobody can hear anything. Meanwhile, for hundreds of miles around, dogs are jerking their heads up and thinking: "Hey! Somebody's playing 'Wild Thing'!"

I play lead guitar in this band. My sole musical qualification is that I am slightly more experienced than the guy who plays rhythm guitar, Stephen King, well-known author of children's books (*The Little Engine That Could Sneak into Your Room at Night and Eat Your Eyes*). Stephen has a custom-made black guitar with little white mother-of-pearl spiders crawling up the neck. One time I was showing him how to play a certain chord, and I pointed at a spot on the neck and said, "Put your finger here, " and he said, "Oh, on THAT spider."

In May, the Rock Bottom Remainders performed at a party in Los Angeles at the annual convention of the American Booksellers Association. It went very well. The audience members were receptive, by which

I mean they had been drinking. Some people got so receptive that they demanded an encore, so we decided to play "Gloria," which we like because it's even simpler to play than "Louie Louie." You can throw a guitar off a cliff and as it bounces off rocks on the way down, it will, all by itself, play "Gloria."

So we went back on stage, and I picked up one of the two guitars I'd been using, and just as we were about to start, Stephen tapped me on the shoulder and said, "We have a special guest." I turned around, and there was Bruce Springsteen. I still don't know how he came to be at this convention; I don't believe he's a bookseller. All I know is, he was picking up the other guitar. My guitar.

"Bruce," I said to him. "Do you know the guitar part to 'Gloria'?"

This is like asking James Michener if he knows how to write his name.

"I think so," he said. So we played "Gloria," and I say in all modesty that it was the best version of that song ever played in the history of the world, going back thousands of years. I would shout, "G—L—O—R—I-I-I-I-I A"; and the band, including Bruce Springsteen, would respond, "GLORIA!" and the crowd would scream as only truly receptive booksellers can scream. I could have died happy right then.

Anyway, now I'm back in my office, tapping at my computer, being a columnist again. But from time to time my mind drifts back to that night, remembering how it sounded. I haven't polled the other members of the Remainders, but I think we would definitely let Bruce join the band, if he wrote a book.

I would even let him play lead guitar.

Elizabeth Wurtzel

■

Prozac Nation (1994) by Elizabeth Wurtzel is a sad book, but it's also a darkly funny and wickedly incandescent memoir of a young woman's harrowing experience with clinical depression. During her descent into hell, rock helped keep her afloat. "When I was in the worst way with my depression, I found solace in music, in Bruce Springsteen, in Joni Mitchell, in Bob Dylan, and in so many other fleeting bits of rock 'n' roll, from Pink Floyd to Flipper to the Joy of Cooking to Janis Joplin. . . . I wanted to write like someone who has been stuck somewhere for so long that by the time she got un-stuck none of the rules mattered anymore." In short, she says, "I wanted to write like rock 'n' roll."[1] Springsteen's songs in particular seemed to speak directly to her soul. In Wurtzel's mind, he seemed to understand, to empathize, and to offer insights that she so desperately sought.

from *Prozac Nation:*
Young and Depressed in America

■SOMETIMES I LIE in my own bed and listen to music for hours. Always Bruce Springsteen, which is weird, I have to admit, because I'm becoming this really urban punked-out kid, and he is kind of the spokesman of the rumpled, working-class suburbs. But I identify with him so completely that I start to wish I could be a boy in New Jersey. I try to convince my mother that we should move out there, that she should work in a factory or as a waitress in a roadside diner or as a secretary at a storefront insurance office. I want so badly to have my life circumstances match the oppressiveness I feel internally. It all starts to seem ridiculous: After all, Springsteen songs are about getting the hell *out* of the New Jersey grind, and here I am trying to convince my mom that we ought to get *into* it. I'm figuring, if I can just become poor white trash, if I can just get in touch with the blue collar blues, then there'll be a reason why I feel this way. I will be a fucked-up Marxian worker person, alienated from the fruits of my labor. My misery will begin to make sense.

That is all I want in life: for this pain to seem purposeful.

The idea that a girl in private school in Manhattan could have problems worth this kind of trouble seemed impossible to me, and listening to rock and roll all day was probably no way to discover it. I didn't know about Joni Mitchell or Djuna Barnes or Virginia Woolf or Frida Kahlo yet. I didn't know there was a proud legacy of women who'd turned overwhelming depression into prodigious art. For me there was just Bruce—and the Clash, the Who, the Jam, the Sex Pistols, all of those punk bands talking about toppling the system in the U.K., which had nothing to do with being so lonesome you could die in the U.S.A.

Maybe I could have picked up a guitar myself and written some rants of my own, but somehow the Upper West Side of Manhattan as a metaphor for lost and embittered youth was not nearly as resonant as Springsteen's songs about hiding in the back streets or riding the Tilt-A-Whirl or the sound of a calliope on the Jersey Shore. Nothing about my life seemed worthy of art or literature or even of just plain life. It seemed too stupid, too girlish, too middle-class. All that was left for me to do was shut down and enter the world of Bruce Springsteen, of music about people from somewhere else, for people doing something else, that would just have to do, because for the moment, there was nothing else.

That summer, I am just thirteen, everything sucks and I am stuck at camp wondering about the Olympics. One day right after clean-up period, right after our beds have been inspected for hospital corners and our cubbies have been checked to make sure all the Archie comics are piled neatly, I sit on the porch of my bunk listening to Bruce Springsteen's first album. Paris, a girl I also go to school with, comes outside to sit with me. Paris is, I guess, what I would call a friend. I've known her since kindergarten, and like everyone else who's been in my life for a while, she's just kind of waiting for me to snap out of this funk so that we can have play dates and polish our nails in baby pink like we used to do when we were seven. She lives across the street from me so we still walk home from school together sometimes, which can't be any fun for her because all I want to talk about is the oncoming apocalypse in my brain.

Paris tries to be understanding. I don't make this process very easy for people. After weeks of haranguing the girls in my bunk about the genius of Bruce Springsteen, when they finally say that they're getting to like him, when they ask to borrow tapes or make requests to hear *Born to Run,* I just start yelling that they're all a bunch of unoriginal copycats and Bruce belongs to me alone. I make them swear that if they ever meet anyone new and claim to like any Springsteen songs, they'll remember to footnote me. And they all throw up their hands and say, Look, we're trying. So Paris comes and sits down beside me, and I make her a little nervous when I tell her that she's got to listen to this song called "For You." She's afraid I'll be cross if she doesn't like it, or—even worse—that I'll be really furious if she does. I explain that the song is about a girl just like me who kills herself. We listen to the first verse, to the cryptic lines about a girl's fading presence, about "barroom eyes shine vacancy," about someone whose grip on life is so vague that to see her you have to look hard.

That's me, I say to Paris. I'm the girl who is lost in space, the girl who is disappearing always, forever fading away and receding farther and farther into the background. Just like the Cheshire cat, someday I will suddenly leave, but the artificial warmth of my smile, that phony, clownish curve, the kind you see on miserably sad people and villains in Disney movies, will remain behind as an ironic remnant. I am the girl you see in the photograph from some party someplace or some picnic in the park, the one who looks so very vibrant and shimmery, but who is in fact soon going to be gone. When you look at that picture again, I want to assure you, *I will no longer be there.* I will be erased from history, like a traitor in the Soviet Union. Because with every day that goes by, I feel myself becoming more and more invisible, getting covered over more thickly with darkness, coats and coats of darkness that are going to suffocate me in the sweltering heat of the summer sun that I can't even see anymore, even though I can feel it burn.

Imagine, I suggest to Paris, only knowing that the sun is shining because you feel the ache of its awful heat and not because you know the joy of its light. Imagine being always in the dark.

I am going on and on this way to Paris, who is still uneasy, and is not quite sure what to say. You know, I continue, I'd be just like the girl in the song except for one thing. One thing. And that's that he says she's all he ever wanted. He loves her so much. The whole song is about how he's come to take her to the hospital, to rescue her from suicide.

I start, as if on cue, to cry. I am so caught up in the idea that nobody would actually try to save me if I were to slit my wrists or hang myself from one of the rafters in the bunk. I can't believe anyone might care enough to try to keep me alive. And then I realize that, yes, of course they would, but only because it's the thing to do. It's not about true caring. It's about not wanting to live with the guilt, the insult, the ugly knowledge that a suicide took place and you did nothing. Once I make a suicidal gesture, then everyone indeed will come running because my problems leave the realm of the difficult, workaday, let's-talk-it-through stuff and I become an actual medical emergency. I will qualify as a trauma case that Aetna or MetLife, or whatever insurance carrier I've got, will actually cover. They'll pump my stomach, stitch my wrists, apply cold packs to the bruises on my neck, do whatever it is they have to do to keep me alive—and then the heavy-duty, institutional-size mental health professionals take over.

But day after day of depression, the kind that doesn't seem to merit carting me off to a hospital but allows me to sit here on this stoop in summer camp as if I were normal, day after day wearing down everybody who gets near me. My behavior seems, somehow, not acute enough for them to know what to do with me, though I'm just enough of a mess to be driving everyone around me crazy.

I cry some more and go on and on about how nice it must be to have someone so in love with you they'd sing about the day you died. Paris opens her mouth, probably to say something about how people would like to help, people would like to let me know they care, they just don't know what to do, but I shut her up. I don't want to hear the company line right now. And if anyone ever loved me enough to write such a beautiful song about me, you know I wouldn't kill myself, I continue. In the end I have to think the girl in "For You" is totally crazy because she decided to die when there was so much love for her right here on earth.

Yes, Paris says, talking to me only to offer the comfort of a human voice, not because she can say anything that will make a difference. I see what you mean.

Oh, Paris. I cry some more. No one is ever going to love me that way because I'm so awful and all I ever do is cry and get depressed.

If I were another person, I go on, *I* wouldn't want to deal with me. I *don't* want to deal with me. It's so hopeless. I want out of this life. I really do. I keep thinking that if I could just get a grip on myself, I could be all right again. I keep thinking that I'm driving myself crazy, but I swear, I swear to God, I have no control. It's so awful. It's like demons have taken over my mind. And nobody believes me. Everybody thinks I could be better if I wanted to. But I can't be the old Lizzy anymore. I can't be myself anymore. I mean, actually, I am being myself right now and it's so horrible.

Paris just puts her arms around me and hugs me. Lizzy, everyone likes you fine just the way you are, she says, because that's what people say in these situations.

I sit there with my face in my hands as if to catch my head, to keep it from falling off and rolling across girls' campus like a soccer ball that someone might kick by accident.

Note

1. Elizabeth Wurtzel, Afterword, *Prozac Nation: Young and Depressed in America* (Boston: Houghton Mifflin, 1994; New York: Riverhead Books, 1995), p. 359.

Neil Strauss

■

Neil Strauss writes about pop music for the *New York Times* and other publications. In the following article that ran in the *Times* (May 7, 1995), a loquacious Bruce Springsteen discusses topics that aren't usually associated with the so-called decadent rock lifestyle, timeless issues such as Who am I? or Where am I going? "A lot of rock-and-roll music was concerned with the outlaw," he acknowledges. "My characters . . . were misfits more than outlaws."

Springsteen Looks Back but Keeps Walking On

New York Times

■"BROOOOOOOCE!" So WENT the cries of nearly a dozen police officers as Bruce Springsteen walked past the 18th Precinct station house on West 54th Street. As he strolled through midtown Manhattan on a sunny weekday afternoon, no other pedestrians stopped him or yodeled his first name. They just looked at him as he passed by, trying to quietly absorb his presence with their gaze in the jaded way that New Yorkers respond to fame. It was only the police officers who reacted, pulling out their summons pads for Mr. Springsteen to sign and yelling, "You're the best!" as he complied.

"I have a healthy fan base in law enforcement," Mr. Springsteen, 45, said with a staccato laugh as he turned on to Eighth Avenue, beginning one of the few interviews he has granted during his two-decade career, which has recently taken yet another upswing. Rock musicians and police officers aren't supposed to mix. It's a tradition that goes back to the day the blues musician Robert Johnson went to the crossroads and supposedly made a deal with the Devil. But since Mr. Springsteen emerged from Asbury Park, N.J., in the early 1970's, firing off hit songs like "Born to Run," "Hungry Heart" and, more recently, "Streets of Philadelphia," he has changed the rules of rebellion.

He imbued the daily struggles of those in the working class with a quotidian heroism, telling them they mattered and assuring them that there was nothing wrong with trying to realize a dream, even if their attempt failed. "Spend your life waiting for a moment that just don't come," he sings in "Badlands," a 1978 song on his newly released *Greatest Hits* album on Columbia. "Well, don't waste your time waiting."

"A lot of rock-and-roll music was concerned with the outlaw," Mr. Springsteen said. "But I liked the idea of *High Noon* and the ambivalent sheriff. My characters were people who had something to be gained and lost by stepping in either direction. They were misfits more than outlaws."

Since Mr. Springsteen's heyday in the early and mid-1980's, times have changed—and so has Mr. Springsteen. In 1989, he divorced his first wife, the model Julianne Phillips, and started dating the woman who would become his second, Patti Scialfa, a member of his backup group, the E Street Band. That same year, he dismissed the band and, in 1990, bought his third home, a $14 million estate in Beverly Hills (he also has a farm near his hometown, Freehold, N.J., and a house in nearby Rumson).

For fans who saw Mr. Springsteen as one of the few rock stars who hadn't forgotten what it was like to be a regular human being, these actions were confusing. The relative lack of enthusiasm with which fans and critics greeted his 1992 albums, *Human Touch* and *Lucky Town*, led some to wonder how relevant Mr. Springsteen was in the '90's.

But in the past year, the pendulum has started to swing in Mr. Springsteen's direction again. He received four Grammys and an Oscar for his title song to the movie *Philadelphia*, reunited with the E Street Band to record six additional songs for *Greatest Hits* (three of which ended up on the record) and watched the album shoot to No. 1 on the pop charts the week it was released. Its first new hit, a previously unreleased 1982 song called "Murder Incorporated," about the proliferation of guns and the devastation of human life, sounds even more appropriate today than it did when it was written.

"I believe that the basic ideas and the values that I wrote into all those songs on the album are still relevant," Mr. Springsteen said. "When I wrote them, I wanted to write about things that people always have to go through at some point in their lives. My music wasn't going to be about fashion or style. It was going to be about family and struggle and identity questions, spiritual questions: Who am I? Where am I going? How do you live an honest life, and is it possible? How do you make the kinds of connections that keep you from the worst of yourself and bring out the best of yourself? And then there's fun and good times—how do you find them?"

During that afternoon walk, Mr. Springsteen had his choice of good times: he could find them in Central Park or he could find them in Hannah's Cocktail Lounge, a few blocks from the police station. It took two seconds for Mr. Springsteen to choose the latter. He settled into a table near the window in the front of the small, empty bar, then changed his mind. He wanted a table in the back corner, where no sunlight penetrated. His age didn't show in his ruddy cheeks, tousled dark hair, husky frame and cross-shaped earring. "If anybody could make you dream, it's Bruce Springsteen," says Melissa Etheridge, who models her impassioned performances after Mr. Springsteen's. But on that day, he seemed more ready to shatter dreams than inspire them.

He downed a shot of tequila, took a sip from his beer chaser and talked about his recent metamorphosis. Having children—Evan James, 4, Jessica Rae, 3, and Sam Ryan, 1—pulled himself out of his solipsistic world, he said, and not just because he now has to wake up every morning at 8:30 and drive the two oldest to school in his black Ford Explorer.

"I think that before I had kids, I was waiting for my life to begin," he said. "It was always, 'When this happens, when that happens.' And all of a sudden one morning I woke up and that feeling was just gone. It felt to me like the beginning of some life that I had worked really hard and waited very long to get to. I was 40 years old when I had kids, and so I was already at the point where the interesting things for me felt like they were going to be over there—away from bars and running around—and closer to children and relationships and deeper satisfactions."

On *Greatest Hits,* one can hear these changes taking place. It begins with visions of freedom and the open road in "Born to Run," matures with the 35-year-old father in "My Hometown" who knows he's lying to himself when he talks of packing his bags and escaping, and ends with the fatalistic wisdom of "Blood Brothers," a song about the E Street Band. In his slightly hoarse voice he sings, "The hardness of this world slowly grinds your dreams away, making a fool's joke out of the promises we make."

"The songs are not literally autobiographical," he said. "But in some way they're emotionally autobiographical. As they go by, you see your own take on the world and how it's changed since you were a kid. You create a variety of characters, and the thing they have in common is some emotional thread you've tried to use to make your own way through what can feel like a particularly imponderable existence."

Songs have not always been enough for Mr. Springsteen to help him weave his way through life. One of the biggest steps he ever had to take, he said, was 13 years ago, when he decided to undergo therapy, which he continues sporadically. "I grew up in a working-class family," he said. "It was very, very difficult for me to ever get to a place where I said I needed some help. I stumbled into some different, very dark times where I simply had no other idea of what to do. It's not necessarily for everybody, but all I can say is, I've accomplished things personally that felt simply impossible previously. The leap of consciousness that it takes to go from playing in your garage to playing in front of 5,000, 6,000, 7,000 people or when you experience any kind of success at all can be very, very demanding."

Mr. Springsteen has made the transition from garage-rocker to arena-rocker better than most rock singers. He doesn't have to try to be sincere; it comes naturally. In the 1970's, at the height of rock-star decadence, Mr. Springsteen set himself apart from his contemporaries by rarely indulging in anything but a sweaty, energetic three- or four-hour show. In the 1990's, it's now vogue for rockers to resent their large following, but Mr. Springsteen continues to embrace his wholeheartedly. His vision from the beginning was that the band should be a fan's rock group. In fact, "Murder Incorporated" was included on *Greatest Hits* solely because of one fan's persistence.

"For years, there's this guy that's been following me around with a 'Murder Incorporated' sign," Mr. Springsteen said. "I see him in the audience like every five shows. I have never played the song, ever, in concert and would have no intent to do so, and yet this guy follows me around with this sign and flashes it during the entire show. So it was he who I had in mind when we put the song on the album. We said, 'Let's put this on for that guy, whoever he is.'"

In the introduction to a book about Mr. Springsteen, one fan describes his idol in bold capital letters as "real." Mr. Springsteen prefers the word "grounded," but real is what comes to mind when one meets him. Sitting at Hannah's Cocktail Lounge, he came on like a good-natured lumberjack ready to chop down the trees that separate him from his audience. He urged on the conversation with lines like "Let's not stop now" and ordered new beers every time one started to get warm. He seemed ready to talk about each subject for an hour or two—if only to avoid an awkward silence.

The topic Mr. Springsteen constantly returned to was the E Street

Band, which has been with him through the best years. A poet in auto mechanic's clothing, he was first signed to a record label during the tail end of the Nixon years; he and the band were one of the few groups in a politically cynical time that still thought rock could change the world. Mr. Springsteen and the band's fame peaked during the Reagan 1980's, when they gave voice to those grasping for a meaningful life in a system that did not seem to value them. Now that Congressional Republicans are trying to undo 60 years of social reform, perhaps there's no better time for Bruce Springsteen and the E Street Band to return and let those blue-collar voices be heard from again.

"It's very strange that the Republicans are coming back now," Mr. Springsteen said. "Because my idea in the early and mid-1980's was to put forth an alternate vision of the America that was being put forth by the Reagan-era Republicans. They basically tried to co-opt every image that was American, including me. I wanted to stake my own claim to those images, and put forth my own ideas about them. The band drew me in that direction, and that's the direction that I want to work in in the future with them."

Mr. Springsteen's reunion with the E Street Band, whom he hasn't recorded with in 10 years, is not just symbolic. In his view, people perceived his solo work, on albums like *Nebraska, Tunnel of Love* and *Lucky Town,* as very personal and psychological. The E Street Band, he said, is like a bridge connecting him with his fans, broadening the scope of his writing. Equally important, he said the band's easy camaraderie keeps him from slipping into what he called "the abyss of self-destructiveness."

A prolific songwriter but notoriously slow when it comes to releasing records, Mr. Springsteen, nonetheless, wants to finish recording a solo album in the next few weeks and record an album with the band this summer. He hopes to change his relationship with the band. "I simply want to do both things, like what Neil Young does with Crazy Horse," he explained. "He'll go and do a project with different musicians, and then he'll come back and play with Crazy Horse when he has something that feels right for them."

Steve Van Zandt, the guitarist who left the E Street Band in 1984 but has rejoined it, said Mr. Springsteen's plan made sense. "We talked about it years ago," he said. "I really felt that was the way to go."

In addition to the new songs on the *Greatest Hits* album, Mr. Springsteen also recently completed a song for the Sean Penn film *The Cross-*

ing Guard and wrote for and helped produce a forthcoming album by Joe Grushecky, a Pittsburgh rock musician. The thrill of playing blues guitar with the roots-rock band Blasters at a recent concert of theirs, he said, has led him to start "toying around with the idea of making a record that's centered around loud guitars." He has also been listening to the punk band Social Distortion and Wayne Kramer, the former guitarist with the proto-punk group MC5.

Mr. Springsteen is less enthusiastic about the Grammy and Academy Awards he recently won for "Streets of Philadelphia." "I didn't win any awards for so long, so I devalued them because it was necessary," he said, guffawing so hard that his shoulders shook. "Those are pretty conservative organizations, and all the actual rock records I've made over the years have been ignored. But I had a nice night at the Oscars, and I was really sort of appreciative, and my mother came and got to see me win instead of lose. In the early 1980's, we did a benefit for the Vietnam Veterans Association, and all the guys gave me a helmet that they had signed. So I think that was the nicest award I've ever received."

Growing older has enabled Mr. Springsteen to look back at his past with perspective and, at times, curiosity. In "Thunder Road," recorded in 1975, the protagonist tries to explain to the woman he is speaking to that she is not too old to escape her dead-end life. "So you're scared and you're thinking that maybe we ain't that young anymore," he tells her.

"I was 24 when I wrote that," Mr. Springsteen said, pausing to laugh at himself. "I listen to that now and think, 'Hey, wait a minute.' It's really strange, that line, and the one in 'Rosalita'—'Someday we'll look back on this, and it will all seem funny.' Those were two good ones, you know. I have no idea where I was conceivably coming from at that time."

Mr. Springsteen can make fun of his songs and ambition now. But the truth is, he tried to make music and plan his career so that he would regret nothing: "I didn't want to be rocking on my porch when I was 70 years old going, 'Oh, man, I should have taken a shot at this.'"

When it was pointed out to him that in an interview he did three years ago, he used the same image about sitting on his porch, but that the age he mentioned was 60 instead of 70, he laughed again. "There you go," he said. "The older you get, the younger you are. At 60, I plan to be still doing it. We're moving it up as we go. It will be 80 in another five years."

Hope Edelman

■

This essay, perhaps more than any of the selections in the *Reader*, captures the special relationship that exists between Springsteen and his fans. To Hope Edelman and countless others like her, Springsteen was writing about her, about her friends, about her way of life, especially so in the first few recordings, when the Jersey Shore featured so prominently in his lyrics. Fans turned to his songs for inspiration, for insight, for advice, and always for hope amid the darkness. "Over the years," writes rock critic and historian Gene Santoro, "Springsteen has become part of the soundtrack of our lives, as the Animals were for his."[1] "Bruce Springsteen and the Story of Us" also offers a fairly rare glimpse of a female perspective of the singer and his music.[2] Alas, we all must grow up, which sometimes means leaving our heroes behind. Thus, the release of *Nebraska* in 1982—full of fractured dreams and quiet desperation—left Edelman cold. Springsteen, she writes, had gone from being "the prophet of one generation's rhapsody to the chronicler of another's demise." The essay originally appeared in the January 1996 issue of the *Iowa Review*. An excerpt follows.

Bruce Springsteen and the Story of Us

Iowa Review

■THE FIRST TIME I heard a Bruce Springsteen song performed live was in 1979, when I was in the tenth grade and Larry Weinberger and A.J. DeStefano stood in our high school parking lot shouting all the words to "Thunder Road" from start to finish, zipping right through that tune at fast-forward speed. Eyes squeezed shut into brief black hyphens, shoulders pumping to an imaginary drumbeat, they sang to an audience of ten or twelve sophomores sprawled against the hoods of their parents' old cars, their red and green and blue looseleaf binders strewn right side up and upside down like blackjack hands along the pavement at their feet.

This was October, the second month of the school year, and the time between 3:40 P.M. and dinner was still a flat landscape of vast and open hours. A single cigarette slowly made its way around the circle, passed between the tight Vs of fingers and held just long enough for each of us to blow a smoke ring for effect. Across the parking lot, students called to each other by last name ("Yo, Speee-VAK!"), car doors slammed, engines revved like short-lived lawn mowers. Larry and A.J. finished their song and started on "Jungleland," pausing after "The Magic Rat drove his sleek machine over the Jersey state line" just long enough to allow:

"Into Rockland County!"

"The Ramapough Inn!"

"Yo mama's backyard!"

"Hey! Your sister's bedroom, *asshole.*"

We all knew the words to Springsteen's songs, and we knew, firsthand, most of the places they described. Some of them practically were in our parents' backyards. We were living in New York, just over the New Jersey border in the tiny towns that dot the bottom of the state map like scattered flecks of black pepper, a county filled with minor suburbs most frequently described by their relative position to somewhere else: thirty-three miles northwest of Manhattan, less than a one-hour drive from two international airports, and a half tank of gas north of the Jersey shore.

Springsteen Country, our bumper stickers read, though most of us took thick black magic markers and crossed out the second R. Springsteen County was far more accurate for a place where high school principals considered "Jungleland" appropriate music to play over the hometown P.A. system; where parents routinely dropped off their children in front of Ticketron offices fortified with sleeping bags and pastrami sandwiches, returning the next morning to carpool them to school; and where sixteen-year-olds held parties in empty parking lots on heavy, humid, late-summer nights, where they sat on the hoods of cars and swirled beer around in the can, listening to Springsteen sing about a barefoot girl on the hood of a Dodge drinking warm beer in the soft summer rain. It was enough to make you wonder where the scene ended and the song began, or if there really were a difference, at all.

Those were our years of music, back when we still could find simple, one-step answers to life's most complex problems in the lyrics of the songs we sang, back when a deejay's mellifluous voice could still smooth out all the rough edges of a day. In those years, the late '70s and early '80s, we plucked our role models from the FM dial—Bruce Springsteen, John Cougar, Joan Jett, a cast list of sensitive survivors, underdogs with good intentions, minor idols who neatly met our critical adolescent need to constantly feel wronged without ever actually *doing* anything wrong, and we aligned our frustrations with the lyrical mini-dramas scripted for us in advance. Our mythology was created and recycled, and recycled and recycled, every day.

Though we liked to imagine ourselves as the kind of characters that peopled Springsteen's songs—he was, after all, *writing about us*—the fit was never quite right. We had pretty much the same anxieties, but the socioeconomics were all wrong. He sang of working-class kids stuck in dead-end towns who grabbed their girlfriends by the wrists, leapt into their rebuilt '69 Chevys and peeled out of town in search of their futures. Our hometown was an upper-middle-class suburb where a college education was more an expectation than an exercise in free will. Most of us would grow up to become just what our parents had planned, and to do just as they had done. *Doctor, lawyer, C.P.A.* But in the time we had before our decisions became too intractable to erase, we were free to try on and shrug off whatever clothing best fit our erratic moods. Even the most intelligent, even the most affluent among us had visions of a utopia free of parents, P.E. teachers, and pop quizzes. Springsteen offered us his version of that place, his promises surrounding us like audio wallpaper— hogging the airwaves on our car radios, piped into our homerooms, pumped into every store in our local indoor shopping mall, encircling us with songs of hot desire and escape.

This was 1978, 1979, and in the magazine interviews we passed from desk to desk in social studies class Springsteen told us he would never change, would never, essentially, grow up. His was a world of perpetual adolescence, an eternal seventeen. "I couldn't bring up kids," he told *Rolling Stone.* "I couldn't handle it. I mean, it's too heavy, it's too much. . . . I just don't see why people get married. It's so strange. I guess it's a nice track, but not for me."

Back then, like us, Springsteen was still living among his history, shuffling along the Asbury Park boardwalk with his hands jammed down deep in the front pockets of his jeans but his eyes fixed on the gulls that dipped and cawed on the horizon. He held tight to the Jersey towns where he began, always swore he'd never forget the people or the place, but he also knew where he wanted to go, and this duality pervaded his songs like a restless, wanton motif. His lyrics told us precisely what we wanted to hear: that when the pressures of adulthood started squeezing too tight we could just peel out, leaving skid marks as our contemptuous farewell, and his music could, in the course of only three minutes, transform a solitary harmonica wail into a full band battle cry, the cymbals crashing *one, two, three* like a bedroom door slamming shut over and over again.

But I'm talking early Springsteen here, vintage Springsteen, those pre-1980 songs that put you in a fast car and took you on a one-way ride through images that came quick and fast as lightning, no time to bother with a chorus you could return to and repeat when you lost your place in the stream of consciousness lyrics that rambled on and on like Kerouac sentences in search of a period. The songs that gave you hope there was a simpler, gentler world out there somewhere, and that the happiness missing from your own backyard could be found in the next town. This was back before he cut his hair short and sprouted biceps, back when the guitar chords still came down angry and loud and an unshaven, scrawny Springsteen rooted himself behind the mike with a guitar pressed tight against his groin, his shoulders and neck twitching spastically in time with the beat. Back when you could still tell a lot about a man by the lyrics that he sang, and when you thought Bruce Springsteen knew a lot about you, as you lay alone on your twin bed with the door slammed shut and the hi-fi turned up to 9, listening to him play the piano introduction to "Jungleland" the way he did it every time, with his left hand firmly anchored in the bass chords as his right hand skittered manically up and down the soprano notes, flailing like a frantic fish, fluttering like wings.

When I met Jimmy T., I was seventeen and still a virgin, and three weeks later I was neither anymore. We did it for the first time on a Saturday afternoon in his lumpy double bed underneath guitars that hung suspended from a ceiling rack like electric pots and pans. He had a chair jammed under the doorknob and WPLJ turned up loud enough to mask our noise, and sometimes when the radio hit a bass note, a guitar string buzzed above my head. Two hours of songs must have played that afternoon, but the only one I remember is Springsteen's "Hungry Heart," because as soon as he heard the opening chords Jimmy T. started to hum and thrust in rhythm to the song. *Got a wife and kids in Baltimore Jack, I went out for a ride and I never went back.* Jimmy T. assured me that losing his virginity at age thirteen made him eminently qualified to relieve me of mine without unnecessary pain or pomp. He was right, on both counts, but I was disappointed nonetheless. I'd been prepared for several unsuccessful attempts, searing pain, and the kind of hysterical bleeding Sylvia Plath had described in *The Bell Jar.* The ease of it made me wonder, at first, if we'd done it right.

I was the last among his friends to lose it but the first among mine, and when I left his parents' house I drove straight to my friend Jody's, walked down the hall to her room, sat down carefully on her white-ruffled canopy bed, and started to cry.

"Holy shit . . ." she whispered, and when I nodded she threw her arms around my chest and hugged me, hard.

"Holy shit!" she shouted, bouncing her butt up and down on the bed. "Holy SHIT! TELL ME WHAT IT'S LIKE!"

What was it like? What was any of it like? Like one long manic car ride on an open stretch of road with a driver whose license had wisely been revoked. And I'm not talking just about the sex part. It was like that all the time with Jimmy T. He could get a whole room of people singing with no more than five words of encouragement and a chord on his guitar, and when we went to the movies he'd have met everyone in our row and even collected a phone number or two by the time I came back with the popcorn and Junior Mints. The intersection of a precocious intellect with a cool-guy delivery had him performing monologues about hypothetical conversations between Hitler, Santayana, and Christ ("So, the Nazi dude would have said to the Jewish dude, man . . .") to his small group of smoking-section disciples during lunchtime, after he'd cut three classes that morning and had to beg his English teacher to give him a passing grade. His mother once told me his I.Q. was 145, a fact I found suspicious considering he'd never learned how to spell.

Jimmy T. Just look at his name. James Anthony Spinelli was the full version, but he wouldn't answer to James or Jim and he always included the T. For Tony. When I reminded him that his middle name was Anthony, and shouldn't he then be Jimmy A.? he gave me a crooked half-smile and raised his open palms in a shrug. I told him Jimmy T. sounded like a name he got from a fourth-grade teacher with too many Jimmys in one class, and he laughed and created a list of last names he might have had, had this been true: Tortoni, Turino, Testarossa. Jimmy Traviata at your service, he'd say, opening the car door for me with a flourish of the wrist and a bow. Jimmy Tortellini here to escort you to Spanish class. My mother would have called him a man with presence, like Frank Sinatra or Tom Jones. The kind of man, she said, who can take your heart away.

Jimmy T., I'm certain, would have considered this a compliment. In fact, if it'd been on paper, he probably would have tried to autograph it. At seventeen he already envisioned himself as a celebrity of sorts, with an existence worth chronicling as it unfolded. Write the story of us, he used to say, assigning the task to me, because I was the one who would conform to the rules of grammar and could spell. But he was the story-teller among us, the one with the elaborate narratives of drag races and secret meetings with record executives, and of playing his guitar in smoky SRO bars where audiences lifted their brown beer bottles and shouted for more. Stories I would have immediately thought unbeliev-able had they not been told with such authority, such grace. Write the story of us, he would say, the "us" squeezing implied chapters between its two characters, but when I tried I could never get past our first, un-remarkable conversation at a party in a cheap motel room at the New Jersey shore. The people who appeared on my pages were insipid and one-dimensional, nothing at all like the characters we aspired to be, and my efforts turned into crumpled wads of paper I tossed against his bed-room walls.

I spent most of my after-school hours between those walls, preferring to close a bedroom door against the silence of Jimmy T.'s house than against the disorder of my own. This was 1982. The summer before, my mother had died of cancer, quickly and unexpectedly, leaving my father to care for three children, ages seventeen, fourteen, and nine. When we returned from the hospital he looked at us and blinked quizzically, as if to ask, Have we met? and I realized for the first time how fragile a bal-ance life must be, if it can be tipped so swiftly, so dramatically and ir-revocably by the force of a single event. Only after my mother was gone did I understand she'd been the only adhesive that had held us together, and as the empty Scotch bottles multiplied on the kitchen counter my fa-ther began to spout increasingly weird and existential rhetoric about how the individual is more important than the unit, and how we all must learn to fend for ourselves. I'm doing just *fine,* thank you, he hollered when he found me one evening pouring honey-colored streams of alco-hol down the avocado kitchen sink. And I don't need *you* or anyone *else* to tell me how to live my life. Then don't you tell me how to live mine, I screamed back in a defensive panic, and he yelled *Fine!* and I yelled *Fine!* and everything, perhaps, would have been just fine, except that very soon I began to feel like a tiny, solitary satellite orbiting way out there, connected to nothing and no one, even after my father apologized and sent me on vacation to Florida to show how much he really meant it. I just smiled and kept saying everything was fine.

That was the fall I became obsessed with J. D. Salinger, read each of his books four times and began to quote esoteric Zen koans at wholly inappropriate cafeteria moments, and for an entire week that winter I ate nothing but ice cream and wore nothing but black. When teachers kept me after class to ask how I was doing, I said, with great conviction, I am doing just fine. But when you're out there spinning solo, it's only a matter of time before you get close enough to someone else's gravitational pull. That spring, Jimmy T. came trucking across the dirt-brown motel room carpet, black curls flapping and motorcycle boots clomping with each step, to sit next to me on the orange bedspread. He was a senior with a fast car, a reputation, and a Fender Stratocaster electric guitar. I didn't say anything as plebian as hello. . . .

It didn't take me much to fall in love at seventeen—the graceful arc of a smooth-shaven jaw, the smell of freshly washed hair, the sound of a telephone ringing at precisely the moment of the promised call. After Jimmy T. and I returned from the beach that Sunday, we intertwined our fingers and we held on tight. Two weeks later, we were officially in love.

We spent every afternoon together, in his bedroom at the top of the stairs. Jimmy T. played songs he said he'd written for me, on the beat-up acoustic guitar he'd bought with birthday money when he was twelve. He and his friend George had written a song on it they'd sold to a record label the previous year, a tune Jimmy T. played for me over and over again as I sat crosslegged on his bed. We kept the curtains drawn. His room was dark and womblike, like a tight hug, and far removed from the bright yellow-and-green pep of my own. The verve of my bedroom had become a hypocrisy in my father's house, where dust had settled on the living room tables and a television droned constantly in the background to give the illusion of discourse. The downstairs bedroom that once had been my sanctuary from mother-daughter strife had transformed into something foreign and surreal. I'd grown much older than seventeen that year, but every time I walked into my room the geometric mobiles and kitten posters along its perimeter told me I'd once been that age, and not so very long ago.

Jimmy T.'s room, on the other hand, was testimony to postmodern teenage chaos: stereo components and recording equipment stacked schizophrenically against the walls; cassette and eight-track tapes scattered like loose change across the floor; Muppet dolls hanging in nooses from the ceiling; six-year-old posters of Bruce Springsteen taped to the sliding closet doors; and pages and pages of handwritten sheet music layered like onion skin on top of his dresser, desk, and bed. Jimmy T. was working on a project, he said, a big one that the record company was anxiously waiting to see. It would take him another two years, he said, maybe three. He couldn't reveal its content yet, but he said it had the potential to change the world. Three years, maybe four. He didn't think the world could wait much longer than that.

He'd chosen music as his medium, he said, because it was the most influential, *the most powerful* forum for widespread philosophical reform, our last-gasp hope to save our youth from an impending spiritual decline, and he was certain he'd be the one who'd one day use his guitar to make the difference that mattered. But he'd have to get moving soon, he said, seeing as how he was already certain he wouldn't live past forty.

"I mean, shit," he said. "Look at Springsteen. He's already pushing thirty-five. All right, the man's a genius, he's changed my life, but how many years does he really have left? Okay, I'm seventeen now, right? So say I take off at twenty, maybe twenty-one. Can you *imagine* how much I'd get done if I got started then?"

He told me this the night we met, as we walked along the beach before dawn. It was no surprise that our conversation quickly skidded into music, one of the few common denominators that fused the three distinct groups—Italians, Blacks, and Jews—that comprised our high school student body. In English class that year we all read Shakespeare and Keats, but our real poets were the ones whose song lyrics we carefully copied onto our spiral notebook covers. When our teacher asked three students to bring in their favorite poems for the class to interpret the next day, Elisa Colavito showed up with the lyrics to "Born to Run." It was worth every five-paragraph essay we had to write that year to see Mrs. Bluestein squint at the blackboard, trying to scan and analyze *Just wrap your legs round these velvet rims, and strap your hands 'cross my engines.*

My yearbook is filled with hand-scribbled verses like these, all the Jackson Browne and James Taylor and Bruce Springsteen aphorisms we reached for in moments of passion or distress. *I don't know how to tell you all just how crazy this life feels. Close your eyes and think of me, and soon I will be there. Baby, we were born to run.* They were the greatest hits of pre-packaged sentiment, providing me with words that sounded like what I thought I was supposed to feel. I had no blueprint for emotion, no adult I trusted to tell me what I should do with my mother's winter coats, or how to feel when I heard my siblings crying alone in their rooms, or what to say to a father who drank himself to sleep each night. In the absence of any real guidance or experience, Jackson Browne's advice to hold on and hold out was as good as any I could divine on my own.

Discussing music our first night together gave Jimmy T. a convenient chance to introduce his favorite topic—Bruce Springsteen—and engage in open idolatry, which he did at every available moment. By our senior year, Jimmy T. had re-created himself almost entirely in the musician's late '70s image, adopting the appearance (long, dark hair, faded jeans, half smile), the voice (a gravelly just-got-outa-bed-and-smoked-a-packa-Marlboro grumble), the transportation ('69 Chevy with a 396, and a motorcycle, no license), and the look (chin down, eyes up, head tilted slightly to one side) we saw on album covers and in music magazine photo spreads. Jimmy T. wasn't content to merely listen to the man; he actually wanted to *be* him. Which meant that I, in turn, got to be his Wendy-Annie-Rosie-Mary-Janey, his co-pilot in passion and impulse. It gave me a clear persona, straightforward and well-defined. The first time we walked hand-in-hand between the rows of metal lockers, I metamorphosed from the girl whose mother had died of cancer last year into the girl who was dating Jimmy T.—the girl who rode tandem and helmetless on his motorcycle, the girl who didn't care about safety or the law. I'd been waiting all year for someone to hand me a costume that fit so well.

It wasn't a bad deal. After all, the scenery changed every day and I never had to drive. . . .

I knew other girls like me in high school who saw their boyfriends as their saviors, turning to them for the nurturing and attention they couldn't get from home. We were everywhere, holding on to our textbooks with one hand and our boyfriends' belt loops with the other as we maneuvered through the halls; scratching their names into our arm skin with safety pins during study hall, making little love tattoos; sitting knee-to-knee in Planned Parenthood conference rooms while a counselor named Joe waved flat-spring diaphragms and Pill packets in the air as he talked about "shared responsibility." Outside in the waiting room, another group sat clutching their bouquets of ten-dollar bills, waiting to file in. There were so many of us, so many rooms of women, all waiting to be saved.

When Jimmy T. and I were juniors, the year before we met, his best friend Billy D'Angelo died. The local newspaper reported it as an accident, no other victims involved. It happened in late May, just a few weeks before Billy would have graduated. I'd known Billy from fifth-period lunch, when we sometimes stood in the same circle in the smoking section outside with our shoulders hunched together to protect our matches from the wind. It was no secret that his grades hadn't been good enough to get him into any college, or that his parents were beginning to turn up the volume about enlisting in the military. "The fucking *army*, man," he said, flicking his cigarette butt into the grass. "Like I'm really going to cut my hair and do pushups. Right."

Wild Billy, his friends called him, after Springsteen's song "Spirit in the Night." *Crazy Janey and her mission man, were back in the alley trading hands, 'Long came Wild Billy with his friend G-man, all duded up for Saturday night.* It's sort of a lonely song, about old friends and drugs and a single night's attempt to get away from it all, but Billy didn't seem to mind the name.

I didn't know Billy all that well, but up until the time he died I still believed the universe was a largely benevolent place run by a judicious management. In this cosmos of my imagination, people didn't die young. My mother was still alive, and though she'd been diagnosed with breast cancer the previous spring, it hadn't yet occurred to me that she might actually do something as radical as *die*. Her own optimism blanketed the family with a false security, allowing us to believe we could all go on living just as we always had, treating cancer and chemotherapy as temporary boarders on a month-to-month lease.

Before Billy died, death was more than just an abstraction to me. It was damn near incomprehensible. When it caught up with him, it caught up with me, too, and I was left struggling to understand the insidious speed and finality of it. One day Billy was cupping his hand around a lit match, trying to light a cigarette in the wind, and the next he was gone, a quenched flame. For the first few days after he died, I kept half-expecting him to sidle up next to me outdoors with an unlit Marlboro dangling from his mouth. I just couldn't wrap my mind around the idea that someone who'd always been there could suddenly be so . . . well, *nowhere,* as far as I could see.

The accident—which is what we were calling it then—had happened on a Saturday night, in a state park about fifteen miles north of town. Jimmy T. and Billy and their crowd of high school friends used to go up there after dark and race cars on the narrow roads that hugged the mountain curves. Billy had convinced Jimmy T., don't ask me how, to lend him his '65 Mustang for the ride. Kimmy Rinaldi, Billy's unofficial fiancée, pulled him over to the gravel shoulder and pleaded with him not to race. Afterward she said she'd just had a bad feeling about that night. Not bad like you were on an airplane and suddenly thought it might be on its way down, she told me, but bad enough to say something, you know? Billy told her not to worry, popped a quick, dry kiss against her mouth, and caught the key ring Jimmy T. tossed his way with a quick twist of his wrist.

What happened next happened quickly. Moments after the two cars squealed off, everyone jogged up the road to see beyond the first bend. Jimmy T. was the first to arrive, just in time to see the Mustang take a sharp right turn off the edge of the road and to hear the sickening crash and thump of metal against granite and bark as the steep forest rejected the car all the way down the mountain's side.

Jimmy T. took off running to where the other driver stood, already out of his car, pounding its roof with a bruised fist and crying without tears. *Crying without tears,* they said. "I don't get it, man. He was on the *inside.* I don't *get* it man. I don't get it." A couple more people ran over, and there was a bunch of noise and some crying, and a lot of spinning around without any real direction before someone decided it would probably be a good idea to call the cops. When Kimmy finally realized what had happened, she started screaming Billy's name, over and over again. It took three people to hold her back, to keep her from going over the edge after him.

The funeral was six days later, in a church around the corner from our school. A wave of students outfitted in tan poly-blend suits and white peasant skirts left after the third period that day, all absences excused. After the service, Jimmy T. and some other friends paid their respects to Mrs. D'Angelo and told her how they hoped she'd have "Wild Billy" engraved somewhere on the headstone. They said they knew Billy would have wanted it that way. She was very kind and courteous and said Bill had been so lucky to have had friends as nice as them, but when the stone went up a few weeks later, it read *William Christopher D'Angelo, Beloved Son and Brother, 1963–1981*, and nothing more.

The story of Billy's death quickly became a dark legend told and re-told up and down the hallways of our school, increasing in macabre and explicit detail until even those who'd been there couldn't separate the imaginary from the real. The car did a complete flip as it went over the cliff, or was it two, or three? Billy had called "Kimmy!" as he went down, or was it "Jimmy!" or "Why me?!" Overnight, Billy became our roman-tic hero, the boy who'd died at the same fast speed at which he'd lived. Never mind that he'd really spent most of his days red-eyed and only marginally coherent in the smoking area outside. Never mind that his car left no skid marks. In myth you have no mortal limits. You can do anything. You can become a god. . . .

College, Jimmy T. said, was just a place where all the problems of the world masqueraded as department names, but I might as well go any-way. "Someone's got to help me undo all the damage that's been done, and they'll take us more seriously if you have a college degree," he ex-plained. Before I'd even met Jimmy T. I'd been accepted at a school in Illinois, and throughout the summer my departure date hung over like a heavy Great Plains sky. As August merged into September, Jimmy T. still wasn't sure what he'd do in the fall. Maybe take some courses at the community college in town: philosophy, or religion, or poetry or film. He once casually mentioned coming to Chicago with me. My evasive "Yeah . . ." surprised us both, and told him not to offer again. We both knew he was only grasping for a plan as he watched his previously reli-able audience begin to disperse, moving on to college, the military, and jobs in other states.

This hadn't been the promise. The promise had been that we'd stay young together, follow our dreams, and one day land on the cover of *Newsweek* or *Rolling Stone*. It hadn't accounted for the powerful force that smoothly propels upper-middle-class kids out of high school and into whatever it is they're expected to do next.

We'd counted on Springsteen, at least, to keep his original vow, but even he couldn't sustain it forever. With the release of *Nebraska* in the fall of 1982, he made the sudden transition from the prophet of one gen-eration's rhapsody to the chronicler of another's demise. The album was a veritable avalanche of fractured dreams, filled with stories of plant shutdowns, home foreclosures, and debtors driven to desperate means.

Springsteen was just describing the times, I suppose, but they weren't my times anymore. The first time I listened to *Nebraska* and heard *Everything dies, baby that's a fact, but maybe everything that dies some-day comes back,* was the first time I'd ever listened to a Bruce Spring-steen song and thought, You are wrong. You are so completely wrong.

The night before I left for college, I tacked a calendar on Jimmy T.'s bed-room wall and counted off the days until I'd be home for Thanksgiving break. "Seventy-four," I told him with manufactured optimism as he sat sullenly on the edge of the bed, wrists dangling between his knees. "When you wake up in the morning, it'll be only seventy-three."

"I know how to subtract."

Overnight, I had become the traitor, he the betrayed. "Don't leave me," I pleaded, as I held onto him at the door.

"What?" he said. "You're the one who's getting on the plane without me."

Which I did, in the middle of September, on a direct flight to Chicago from New York. The first friend I made in my dorm became my closest one that year, a prep school graduate from Massachusetts with Mayflower ancestry and an album collection filled with Joni Mitchell, Johnathan Edwards, and Neil Young. "Bruce Springsteen?" she asked, scrunching up her nose in thought. And then, after a pause, "Isn't he that short guy from New Jersey?" By the second week of school, I'd buried all my cas-sette tapes in the bottom of a desk drawer. It's frighteningly easy to aban-don the familiar when you discover it might be cliché.

Jimmy T. mailed me a letter in late September saying he couldn't con-tact me again until Halloween, because he was going on the road with his new band. So you can imagine my surprise when, in mid-October, I returned from an anthropology class on a Thursday afternoon and found him sitting alone in the first floor lounge of my dormitory, his black leather jacket with the chrome zippers at odd angles hopelessly out of place in the sea of Izod sweaters and wool peacoats from Peck & Peck. He looked like a page from one short story ripped out and used as the bookmark in another, and when I first saw him I pulled my books into my chest and took a step back. He understood that step, he told me later. Hey! he said. Jimmy T. is no fool.

I didn't know exactly what pushed—or pulled—me back into the protective pocket of the glass-in entryway. All I knew was in that moment after I instinctively withdrew, I suddenly understood something about relationships, something important. I understood there was a third kind of man my mother never told me about, the kind who *you* need, regardless of how he feels about you. The kind who offers you shelter when no one else even knows how to open a damn umbrella. The kind you can love but can never stay with for long, because the reason you ran to him in the first place was to gather the strength you needed to leave.

Jimmy T. stayed with me in Chicago for three days. We argued the whole time. We apologized in harmony, and then we argued some more. He wanted me to come back with him. I wanted him to leave alone. He wrote prose poems and taped them to my mirror when I was in class. *The Chicago wind blows back your hair, you're living your art, your part. Long camel hair and scarf.* We couldn't get past metaphor. "My axe has broken strings," he told me late one night, and I asked him to please for God's sake just drop the poetry and get to the point.

Our conversation, at the end: He said I came here to ask you to do something with me, and I said What? and he said But now I see you won't, and I said *What?* and he said I can't tell you, exactly, but it has to do with a quest I can't fulfill alone, and I said Please. *Please* would you just tell me what you mean. And he said All right, but you can't tell anyone, you swear? So I swore, and he nodded, and then he told me, very simply, that he was the Second Coming of Christ.

After he'd gotten back on the plane alone, after I'd called his mother from the pay phone at O'Hare, after the iceberg in my stomach finally began to thaw, I spent long nights wondering about the role I'd played in all this. Could I have prevented it somehow? Could I have been the cause? As the letters addressed to Jimmy T. came back marked "Return to Sender" in an angry scrawl, I lay on my bed and stared at the ceiling, looking for the words that would help me understand.

I was lying like this in my dorm room one night with the clock radio tuned in to Chicago's WXRT when I heard the first few bars of Jimmy T.'s song, the one he and his friend George had sold to the record company, come through on the air. I lay very still, barely breathing, trying to identify whose voice was singing the familiar words. I didn't dare move, too afraid I'd miss the end of the song and the name of the band.

I had to wait through two more songs before the deejay returned

". . . and before that we heard the Greg Kihn Band," he said, as the music faded away. "Doing a remake of an old Bruce Springsteen tune."

Somewhere in the distance, I imagine, an engine revved and purred. Somewhere far beyond my reach, another boy shifted into high gear and pressed the pedal to the floor, believing he could sail on and on into the night.

Notes

1. Gene Santoro, "Hey, He's Bruce," *Nation,* September 16, 2002.
2. For another—and more humorous—view, see Joyce Millman, "To Sleep, Perchance to Dream About the Boss," *Salon,* August 8, 1997.

Judy Wieder

■

Bruce Springsteen has the image of being one of the most heterosexual of men.[1] The following interview that ran in the April 2, 1996 issue of *The Advocate,* a gay magazine, offers another side of the singer. In it, he discusses the film *Philadelphia* and his Grammy- and Oscar-winning title song, "Streets of Philadelphia," his reputation in the gay press, his ideas about homosexuality while growing up in New Jersey, the price of fame, and raising children.

Bruce Springsteen:
The *Advocate* Interview

The Advocate

"THE BONUS I GOT *out of writing 'Streets of Philadelphia' was that all of a sudden I could go out and meet some gay man somewhere and he wouldn't be afraid to talk to me and say, 'Hey, that song really meant something to me.' My image had always been very heterosexual, very straight. So it was a nice experience for me, a chance to clarify my own feelings about gay and lesbian civil rights," says rock's most thoughtful megastar, Bruce Springsteen. Sitting in the dimly lit living room of a West Hollywood hotel suite, the man the world calls "the Boss" is talking about his 1994 Oscar and Grammy award-winning song from the film* Philadelphia—*a song detailing the feelings of a gay man facing the final turmoil of his struggle with AIDS.*

Now, with his second Oscar-nominated song, "Dead Man Walking," and his stark new acoustic album, The Ghost of Tom Joad, *the 46-year-old Springsteen seems relieved to have returned once again to the deliberately noncommercial core of his best social-commentary songwriting skills. Like "Streets of Philadelphia" and 1982's daring* Nebraska— *recorded on his home tape recorder—Springsteen's latest album and tour strip his muscular stadium rock down to a dark one-man stage show. No E Street Band, no mania-driven masses waving lighters from the balconies and shrieking "Bru-u-u-ce!" Just Springsteen, alone onstage, singing out from the shadows of all that's gone wrong between people in the world today.*

For many skeptics, the idea of a hard-core rocker from the mean streets of New Jersey growing up, growing rich, and aligning himself with those who have not is pretty far-fetched. Yet that's essentially the Springsteen way. Although he has sold millions of albums, filled thousands of concert arenas, and won mantelsful of Grammy and American Music awards, over the years he's still managed to lend his support directly or indirectly to people and causes as diverse as Amnesty International, feeding the starving in Africa ("We Are the World"), the plight of immigrants, AIDS awareness, and the struggles of gays and lesbians. "After Bruce supported me by appearing on my VH1 special last year, we became friends," says out lesbian rocker Melissa Etheridge. "I think the experience of having his song in Philadelphia led him to meet a lot of gay people and learn a lot about our lives. My girlfriend, Julie, is always with me when we go to his house, and he always treats us as a couple. I've often talked to him about my frustration over not being able to get legally married, and he's always supportive and sympathetic."

Springsteen's own struggles with finding love and settling down have been well documented in both his songs and the press. After his herculean 11-year rise to superstardom—which began with Greetings from Asbury Park, N.J. *in 1973 and culminated in 1984 with* Born in the U.S.A.*—he married model-actress Julianne Phillips. The marriage ended in the tabloids four years later when Springsteen fell in love with his backup singer, Patti Scialfa. They were married in 1991 and have three children.*

JUDY WIEDER: You think you'll win another Oscar for your song "Dead Man Walking"?[2]

BRUCE SPRINGSTEEN: [Laughing] Oh, I don't know. When those Disney pictures are out there [*Pocahontas*], you don't stand a chance. "Dead Man Walking" is another song that's pretty offbeat, so I am not really expecting one.

JW: Still, offbeat subject matter served you well in "Streets of Philadelphia." You say you're pleased that gays and lesbians began approaching you after that song?

BS: Oh, yeah! I had people come up to me in the streets or in restaurants and say, "I have a friend" or "I have a lover" or "I have a partner" or "I have a son."

JW: Why do you think Jonathan Demme—the director—asked you to write a song for *Philadelphia*?

BS: Demme told me that *Philadelphia* was a movie he was making "for the malls." I'm sure that was one of the reasons why he called me, I think he wanted to take a subject that people didn't feel safe with and were frightened by and put it together with people that they did feel safe with like Tom Hanks or me or Neil Young. I always felt that was my job.

JW: How could you make people feel safe?

BS: When I first started in rock, I had a big guy's audience for my early records. I had a very straight image, particularly through the mid '80s.

JW: But why could you reach them?

BS: I knew where the fear came from. I was brought up in a small town, and I basically received nothing but negative images about homosexuality—very bad. Anybody who was different in any fashion was castigated and ostracized, if not physically threatened.

JW: Did you have some personal inspiration for the song?

BS: I had a very close friend who had a sarcoma cancer and died right around that time. For me, it was a very devastating experience, being close to illness of that magnitude. I had never experienced what it calls on or asks of the people around the person who is so ill. Part of that experience ended up in the song.

JW: You caught a particular isolation that many gay AIDS patients experience. When there are walls between people and there is a lack of acceptance, you can reach for that particular kind of communion: "Receive me, brother" is the lyric in the last verse.

BS: That's all anybody's asking for—basically some sort of acceptance and to not be left alone. There was a certain spiritual stillness that I wanted to try to capture. Then I just tried to send in a human voice, as human a voice as I possibly could. I wanted you to be in somebody's head, hearing their thought—somebody who was on the cusp of death but still experiencing the feeling of being very alive.

JW: Were you surprised the song was a hit?

BS: I would never have thought in a million years it was going to get radio airplay. But people were looking for things to assist them in making sense of the AIDS crisis, in making human connections. I think that is what film and art and music do; they can work as a map of sorts for your feelings.

JW: Because you come from the streets of New Jersey, was there a personal journey for you in accepting and learning about homosexuality? Did it ever frighten you?

BS: I don't know if frighten would be the right word. I was pretty much a misfit in my own town, so I didn't buy a lot of those negative attitudes. Sure, you are affected and influenced by them. But I think that your entire life is a process of sorting out some of those early messages that you got. I guess the main thing was that the gay image back then was the '50s image, the town queen or something, and that was all anyone really knew about homosexuality. Everybody's attitudes were quite brutal. It was that real ugly part of the American character.

JW: When you said you were a misfit, what did you mean?

BS: Basically, I was pretty ostracized in my hometown. Me and a few other guys were the town freaks—and there were many occasions when we were dodging getting beaten up ourselves. So, no, I didn't feel a part of those homophobic ideas. Also, I started to play in clubs when I was 16 or 17, and I was exposed to a lot of different lifestyles and a lot of different things. It was the '60s, and I was young, I was open-minded, and I wasn't naturally intolerant. I think the main problem was that nobody had any real experience with gay culture, so your impression of it was incredibly narrow.

JW: So you actually met gay people?

BS: Yeah, I had gay friends. The first thing I realized was that everybody's different, and it becomes obvious that all of the gay stereotypes are ridiculous. [Laughs] I did pretty good with it.

JW: Because of your macho rock image, I didn't know if you were going to tell me, "Oh, yeah, there were years when I didn't want anybody to feel that I had any sympathy for that."

BS: No, I always felt that amongst my core fans—because there was a level of popularity that I had in the mid '80s that was sort of a bump on the scale—they fundamentally understood the values that are at work in my work. Certainly tolerance and acceptance were at the forefront of my music. If my work was about anything, it was about the search for identity, for personal recognition, for acceptance, for communion, and for a big country. I've always felt that's why people come to my shows, because they feel that big country in their hearts.

JW: You mean a country big enough for everyone?

BS: Yes. Unfortunately, once you get a really big audience, then people come for a lot of different reasons. And they can misunderstand the songs.

JW: You even had to deal with President Reagan thinking "Born in the U.S.A." was about his values.

BS: Yes, at that one point the country moved to the right, and there was a lot of nastiness, intolerance, and attitudes that gave rise to more intolerance. So I'm always in the process of trying to clarify who I am and what I do. That's why I wanted to talk to you.

JW: On *The Ghost of Tom Joad,* you have a song, "Balboa Park," and in it you say, "Where the men in their Mercedes / Come nightly to employ . . . / The services of the border boys." Are you talking about drugs or sex or both?

BS: I'm talking about sex, hustling.

JW: What do you know about this subject?

BS: I read about it in a series of articles the *Los Angeles Times*[3] did about border life. It fit into the rest of the subject matter in the album.

JW: It's impossible for most people to imagine the kind of fame you have. Everyone in the world knows who you are. Does it make you feel alienated?

BS: The only thing I can say about having this type of success is that you can get yourself in trouble because basically the world is set open for you. People will say yes to anything you ask, so it's basically down to you and what you want or need. Yes, you can get isolated with an enormous amount of fame or wealth. You can also get isolated with a six-pack of beer and a television set. I grew up in a community where plenty of people were isolated in that fashion.

JW: How do you keep your personal life connected to the real world?

BS: Over the years I think you may have to strive for some normalcy. Like you need to say, "Hey, I'm not going to lock myself up in my house tonight. I'm going to go to the movies or maybe down to a club or take my kids to Universal Studios."

JW: What keeps you connected?

BS: You have to want to be included. I always saw myself as the kid who got the guitar and was going to hold it for a while and play it and pass it on to somebody else. I always saw a lot of myself in my audience.

JW: But that changed when you got so big.

BS: True, and by anybody's measure I have an extravagant lifestyle. But I never felt that I've lost myself in it. I want to feel that essential spiritual connection that you make with your deep audience, your true audience.

JW: So that's how you've kept it balanced?

BS: Yeah. I just felt that what I was doing was rooted in a community—either real or imagined—and that my connection to that community was what made my writing and singing matter. I didn't feel that those connections were casual connections. I felt that they were essential connections. I was a serious young man, you know? I had serious ideas about rock music. Yeah, it was also a circus and fun and a dance party—all of those things—but still a serious thing. I believed that serious things could be done with it. It had a power; it had a voice. I still fucking believe that. I really do.

JW: And I assume that your being here today means that you want gays and lesbians to feel they're a part of this community—this big country?

BS: Yeah, very much so. The ongoing clarification of the way I feel, of my ideas, where I stand on different issues: That's my work now. That's why this interview is a great opportunity for me. Hey—you write, and you want your music understood.

JW: When you fell in love with your wife Patti, there was a lot of negativity in the press because your marriage to Julianne Phillips was breaking up. Did your experience with this kind of intrusion into your private life give you any idea what it's like for gays and lesbians, who constantly get criticized for who they love?

BS: It's a strange society that assumes it has the right to tell people whom they should love and whom they shouldn't. But the truth is, I basically ignored the entire thing as much as I could. I said, "Well, all I know is, this feels real, and maybe I have got a mess going here in some fashion, but that's life."

JW: But that's everything: This feels real.

BS: That's it. Trust yourself in the end. Those are the only lights that can go by, and the world will catch up. But I think it would be much more difficult to be gay, particularly in the town that I grew up in. Divorce may have been difficult for me, but I don't know what it would be like to have your heart in one place and have somebody say, "Hey, you can't do that." So all anybody can do is do their best. Like when President Clinton came into office, the first thing he tried to do was have gays in the military. I thought, Wow! A leader. I just felt that was leading.

JW: What did you feel when it all fell apart?

BS: Initially I felt surprised at the reaction. I was surprised that it was such a big deal. But that's what the federal government is supposed to do: It is supposed to encourage tolerance. If you can't get acceptance, tolerance will have to do. Acceptance will come later. That's what the laws are for. So I was saddened by the fate of the whole thing and the beating that he took.

JW: Were you surprised when Melissa Etheridge was able to come out and still have success in rock and roll?

BS: It was tremendously groundbreaking. The rock world is a funny world, a world where simultaneously there is a tremendous amount of macho posturing and homophobia—a lot of it, in my experience—and yet it has as its basic rule the idea that you are supposed to be who you are. When I first heard about Melissa, I was very happy to see that that was where some of the seeds of what I had done had fallen. I said, "Wow, a lesbian rock singer who came up through the gay bars! I don't believe it!" [Laughing] I felt really good about it.

JW: I understand you and Patti and Melissa and her Julie have become friends.

BS: We have gotten to know each other since her VH1 special. Since then, we've got a nice relationship going.

JW: She told me she's talked with you about the fight gays and lesbians are in to have the right to be legally married. Some people, especially heterosexuals, think it isn't that important. I've had well-meaning people say, "But you know that loving is all that's important. Getting married isn't."

BS: It does matter. It does matter. There was actually a long time when I was coming from the same place: "Hey, what's the difference? You have got the person you care about." I know that I went through a divorce, and it was really difficult and painful and I was very frightened about getting married again. So part of me said, Hey, what does it matter? But it does matter. It's very different than just living together. First of all, stepping up publicly—which is what you do: You get your license, you do all the social rituals—is a part of your place in society and in some way part of society's acceptance of you.

JW: You and Patti decided you needed that?

BS: Yes, Patti and I both found that it did mean something. Coming out and saying whom you love, how you feel about them, in a public way was very, very important. Those are the threads of society; that's how we all live together in some fashion. There is no reason I can see why gays and lesbians shouldn't get married. It is important because those are the things that bring you in and make you feel a part of the social fabric. The idea that Melissa and Julie can't be married—that seems ridiculous to me. Ridiculous!

JW: So you, a rock star, a symbol of counterculture earlier in your life, have come to defend the importance of traditions?

BS: Yeah, oh, yeah. It's like, my kids are sort of little heathens at the moment. [Laughs] They have no particular religious information. Ten years ago I would have said, "Who cares? They'll figure it out on their own." But you are supposed to provide some direction for your children. So you look for institutions that can speak to you and that you can feel a part of and be a part of and that will allow you to feel included and be a part of the community.

JW: What about gays and lesbians having children?

BS: Being a good or bad parent is not something that hinges on your particular sexual preference. I think that people have some idea of what the ideal parent is. I don't know any ideal parents. I have met single mothers who are doing an incredible job of raising their kids. I don't feel sexual preference is a central issue.

JW: You have three children. What would you do if one of them came to you and said, "I think I'm gay"?

BS: Whatever their sexual preference might be when they grow up, I think accepting the idea that your child has his own life is the hardest thing to do. That life begins, and you can see it the minute they hit the boards. I think when I was growing up, that was difficult for my dad to accept that I wasn't like him, I was different. Or maybe I was like him, and he didn't like that part of himself—more likely. I was gentle, and generally that was the kind of kid I was. I was a sensitive kid. I think most of the people who move into the arts are. But basically, for me, that lack of acceptance was devastating, really devastating.

JW: Your father didn't accept you?

BS: Yeah, and it was certainly one of the most devastating experiences. I think your job as a parent is to try to nurture and guide. If one of my kids came and said that to me—hey, you want them to find happiness, you want them to find fulfillment. So they're the ones who are going to have to decide what that is for them.

JW: Does it get harder and harder for you, in terms of being a father, as your children define themselves more and more?

BS: Yeah, because you are caught up with your children's identities. You try not to be rigid, but you do find out the places where you are rigid. And you do get caught up in really some of the great cliches of parenting, whether it is wanting them to excel at some particular sport—I mean, really, just some of the dumbest things.

JW: It's hard to separate?

BS: Yeah, it's the separation.

JW: And then to have your child's sexuality be different from your own, that would be difficult, right?

BS: I think that with a lot of these issues, you just don't know until they truly enter your life in some really personal way. You have your lights that you are trying to steer by, everybody has those. But then you have all that stuff that's been laid on you that you're working your way through. Sure, I can sit back and say I know how I would want to react. I know what I would want to say and how I would want to feel. But unless those things enter my life in some personal fashion, I don't know how I will act.

JW: I think that is very honest. Do you have any family members who are gay?

BS: No. [Laughing] I have a very eccentric family, but, no, nobody gay in my immediate family.

JW: In your whole career, have you ever had a man ask you out or make a pass at you?

BS: Once or twice when I was younger. Yes [laughs]—I mean, no, not exactly directly—[laughs again] but you know how those things are.

JW: Being gay or lesbian is a unique minority in the sense that we can pretend we're straight if we don't want to encounter homophobic feelings, including our own. Unfortunately, we'll never change the world that way. To that end it's important to identify ourselves so that people learn how many people really are gay. As always, there is a tremendous conflict going on in the gay community about pushing people to come out—especially celebrities, because of their wide visibility. Do you have any strong feelings about it?

BS: I have to come at it from the idea of personal privacy. To me, that is a decision that each individual should be free to make. I don't know if someone should make as profoundly a personal decision as that for you. I'm not comfortable with that.

JW: But would you encourage them?

BS: Sure, you can say, "Hey, come on, step up to the plate" or "We need you" or "It'll make a big difference," and that would be absolutely true and valid. But in the end—hey, it's not your life.

JW: Do you think they could get hurt professionally?

BS: If you're in the entertainment business, it's a world of illusion, a world of symbols. So I think you're talking about somebody who may feel their livelihood is threatened. I think you've got to move the world in the right direction so that there is acceptance and tolerance, so that the laws protect everybody's civil rights, gay, straight, whatever. But then you also have got to give people the room to make their own decisions.

JW: But on a very personal level, what would you tell somebody who asked you for advice about whether or not he or she should come out?

BS: First of all, I can only imagine that not being able to be yourself is a painful thing. It's awful to have to wear a mask or hide yourself. So at the end of my conversation, I'd just say, "Hey, this is how the world is; these are the consequences, and these are your fundamental feelings." Because a person's sexuality is such an essential part of who he is, to not be able to express it the way that you feel it [sighs] has just got to be so very painful.

Notes

1. See Martha Nell Smith, "Sexual Mobilities in Bruce Springsteen: Performance as Commentary," *South Atlantic Quarterly* 90, no. 4 (Fall 1991): 833–54, for her interpretation of Springsteen and Clarence Clemons's "soul kiss" and the homoerotic undercurrent of Springsteen's recorded and live performances. "On the surface of things," she writes, "Bruce Springsteen seems so male, so heterosexual, so frank, so knowable. But close attention to his artistic production reveals not only how inscrutable he may be, but also how tenuous knowledge is of that most basic element of human nature—sexuality. Homoeroticism permeates his performances, assumption of the feminine is one of his repeated artistic maneuvers, and, though he writes and sings about Adam, he finally seems much more like Eve in his approach to knowledge." (See p. 849.) Springsteen, the most inclusive of rock singers, has also written from a female perspective. See "Car Wash" on *Tracks* (Columbia, 1998).
2. As it turns out, he did not win the Oscar for "Dead Man Walking."
3. See Sebastian Rotella, "Children of the Border: Caught in a Makeshift Life, Immigrants, Youths Eke Out a Living in San Diego's Balboa Park," *Los Angeles Times,* April 3, 1993; and Mark Arax and Tom Gorman, "California's Illicit Farm Belt Export," *Los Angeles Times,* March 13, 1995.

Bryan K. Garman

■

Bryan Garman, the author of *A Race of Singers: Whitman's Working-Class Hero from Guthrie to Springsteen* (2000), teaches history at the Sidwell School in Washington, D.C. The following selection is a variation of an earlier piece of writing that appeared in the Summer 1996 issue of *Popular Music and Society*. In it, Garman describes a particular type of song, "the hurt song," and Springsteen's contribution to the genre.

The Ghost of History:
Bruce Springsteen, Woody Guthrie,
and the Hurt Song

Popular Music and Society

■BRUCE SPRINGSTEEN HAS long associated himself with a lineage of artists who have used popular culture to address social injustices in America, particularly those endured by the American working class, a subject he has seriously explored since the release of *Darkness on the Edge of Town* (1978). Inspired both by Springsteen's austere working-class upbringing and the legal battle in which he and his manager were engaged after the release of *Born to Run* (1975), *Darkness* claims its cultural roots in John Steinbeck's *The Grapes of Wrath* as well as John Ford's film based on the novel. With the release of *The Ghost of Tom Joad* (1995), Springsteen recalls this influence, but also pays homage to perhaps the best-known poet of the Dust Bowl, Woody Guthrie, who since the early 1980s has profoundly shaped Springsteen's work. Although a number of journalists have identified Springsteen as the wearer of Guthrie's mantle, none have seriously analyzed the ways that Guthrie's legacy has shaped Springsteen's art and politics.

Steinbeck, Ford, and Guthrie were not strangers, of course. A native of Oklahoma, Guthrie was consulted about the soundtrack for the film, and admired Ford and Steinbeck enough to record a ballad named for their protagonist, Tom Joad. Despite his affection for this character, the folksinger distanced himself from the novelist and director. Although he praised the film for having "more thinkin' in it than 99% of the celluloid that we're tangled up in in the moving pictures today," he maintained that his job was "to pick stories about Dust Bowl people that John Steinbeck did not write about." Guthrie was convinced that only folk music, a form which captured the voice of the people, could represent "the real stuff" of class struggle and "use the Truth . . . like a spring of cold water" to bring about social reform. Steinbeck and Ford had done much to publicize the plight of America's displaced farm workers, but because they had not lived the experience as completely as Guthrie had, they could not, in Guthrie's view, understand the Okie and working-class "hurt songs" as well as he did.

Born in Okemah, Oklahoma, in 1912, Guthrie learned the traditions of the hurt song at a very young age. As a newspaper boy, he "picked up" songs on street corners, "learned to jig and dance along the sidewalks to things called portable phonographs," and listened carefully to the folk songs his parents sang at home. Because the Guthrie family faced economic uncertainties, personal tragedies, and sickness, their songs were often inflected with sorrow. His mother, Nora, sang "the sadder songs in a loster voice" and began "to follow her songs out and up and over and away from it all, away over yonder in the minor keys." As her Huntington's chorea worsened, Guthrie "heard all of the hurt songs over in a wilder way. These were the plainest days that I remember and the songs were made deepest in me along in these seasons. This was the time that our singing got the saddest." Written in working-class language, hurt songs express the collective pain, suffering, and injustice working people have historically suffered, and articulate their hopes and dreams for a less oppressive future.

By embracing the hurt song and its history, Springsteen reclaims popular music as a cultural space in which class relations are both taken seriously and historicized. He places his work in the context of a recognizable cultural and political tradition which affords his characters dignity and opens possibilities for social change. Throughout his folk-inspired albums *Nebraska* (1982) and *The Ghost of Tom Joad* (1995), Springsteen connects this tradition to the social and economic traditions that shaped it, reconstructing a history which often contrasts sharply with conventional histories written about the United States. Speaking in a working-class language, his characters narrate histories that link class experiences across generations, representing these experiences not in terms of indi-

vidual success or failure, but as products of complex social and historical forces.

Springsteen began to cultivate an interest in history when he read Henry
Steele Commager and Allan Nevins's *A Pocket History of the United
States of America* during the *Darkness on the Edge of Town* tour of
1978–79. As he became more historically aware, Springsteen gradually
acquired a political consciousness, performing benefit concerts in 1979
for Musicians United for Safe Energy, an antinuclear power alliance, and
in 1981 for the Vietnam Veterans of America, an organization which lob-
bies for veterans' rights. Meanwhile, he became interested in traditional
folk and classic country recordings. In the late 1970s he began to listen
to Jimmie Rodgers, Johnny Cash, Hank Williams, and the performers on
the standard collection of American folk music, *The Folkways Anthology*. As Springsteen continued to write about working-class lives, he
found that for inspiration he went "back further all the time. Back into
Hank Williams, back into Jimmie Rodgers. Because the human thing in
those records is just beautiful and awesome." Captivated by the deep
emotions that Rodgers and Williams expressed, Springsteen drew on the
pain embedded in their hurt songs "to make a record like today, one
that's right now." Several songs on *The River* (1980) were influenced by
his studies. The title song was based on Williams's "Long Gone Lonesome Blues," and "Wreck on the Highway" reworked Roy Acuff's 1943
ballad of the same title.

   While Williams exerts a discernible influence on Springsteen,
Guthrie developed into his most important cultural ancestor. Following
a performance in Phoenix in November 1980, Springsteen acquired a
copy of Joe Klein's biography, *Woody Guthrie: A Life*. Intrigued by the
folksinger's political and cultural activities, Springsteen began to cover
Guthrie's "This Land Is Your Land" during his concerts, a practice he
continued throughout *The River* and *Born in the U.S.A.* tours. Introducing the song at Uniondale, New York, that December, Springsteen
referred to Klein's biography and explained that "This Land" was written as an "angry" response to Irving Berlin's "God Bless America." Influenced by the Communist Party, Guthrie wrote "This Land" in 1940
and originally gave the song the ironic title "God Blessed America for
Me." Historians have tended to overlook this irony, however, focusing on
Guthrie's picturesque descriptions of the American landscape, and

largely ignoring the highly critical and radical content of the original manuscript. School children from California to the New York Island can sing about Guthrie's "ribbon highway" and "golden valley," but few have heard the criticism leveled in the following lines:

> *In the Relief office I saw my people*
> *As they stood hungry, I stood there wondering if*
> *God blessed America for me.*

Springsteen proclaimed "This Land" "the most beautiful song ever written," emphasizing aesthetics rather than politics, and choosing not to perform these verses. When he discussed Guthrie elsewhere, however, he acknowledged the folksinger's politics, emphasizing that Guthrie had "a dream for more justice, less oppression, less racism, [and] less hatred." By performing a song written by this well-known labor activist and antiracist, Springsteen placed himself squarely within a cultural struggle for social justice, explaining that he covered Guthrie's song "[b]ecause that is what is *needed* right now. . . . I sing that song to let people know that America belongs to everybody who lives there: the blacks, Chicanos, Indians, Chinese and the whites. . . . It's time that someone took on the reality of the eighties." When he finished *The River* tour in September 1981, Springsteen had not developed a coherent political ideology, but he understood that if in theory America belonged to everyone, in reality vast segments of the population were excluded from the fundamental promises it offered. To address the economic and social realities of the 1980s, he drew on the spirit embedded in the lost verses of "This Land" and demonstrated that in 1982 many working people did not feel so blessed to live in the United States.

According to Springsteen, *Nebraska* "was about . . . American isolation: what happens to people when they're alienated from their friends and their community and their government and their job." Once this alienation develops, he explained, "you start to exist in some void where the basic constraints of society are a joke, then life becomes kind of a joke." An acoustic album recorded in Springsteen's home, *Nebraska* documents the desperate acts people commit under such circumstances—suicides, mass murders, barroom brawls, and petty crimes. Creating an emotional tautness which threatens to unravel at any moment, Springsteen narrates tales of desperation and defiance, clearly articulating class-conscious lyrics over sharp harmonica blasts and bare acoustic guitars. Grounded in the language, themes, and representational strategies of traditional working-class musicians, *Nebraska* demonstrates a profound sense of musical history. Its somber storyteller twice reiterates the plea for deliverance that Chuck Berry utters in "School Days" (1957), and captures the despondency of Dylan's "The Ballad of Hollis Brown" (1964) at nearly every turn. Indeed, Dylan's influence is particularly apparent, but the roots of Springsteen's representation of working people extend far beyond the 1960s. While Dylan constructs his working-class characters as passive "pawns" who are wholly manipulated by historical and social forces beyond their control, Springsteen's characters make their own history, but they do so under very difficult circumstances. Kindred spirits of the Guthrie character who travels "down that road feeling bad" but defiantly declares "I ain't gonna be treated this-a-way" (*Dust Bowl*), Springsteen's working-class narrators proudly and faithfully proclaim, "Mister, I ain't a boy, no I'm a man / And I believe in a Promised Land" (*Darkness*).

"Johnny 99," a song about an unemployed autoworker who kills a man in a moment of drunken desperation, demonstrates this assertion and illustrates the ways in which Springsteen connects working-class struggles of the present to the past. As he was writing songs for *Nebraska,* Springsteen listened to the *Folkways Anthology of American Folk Music* (1952) where he heard Julius Daniels's "Ninety Nine Year Blues" (1927) and the Carter Family's "John Hardy Was a Desperate Little Man" (1930), two songs which informed Guthrie's understanding of the hurt song and provided the narrative and thematic structure for "Johnny 99."[1] While we cannot be certain that Guthrie heard Daniels's recording, he was undoubtedly familiar with the type of "blueses" that came from the Daniels's region of the country, having frequently played with such North Carolina–based bluesmen as Brownie McGhee and Sonny Terry. Moreover, he was an ardent fan of the Carters, modeling his guitar playing after Maybelle and reworking their version of "John Hardy" in the 1940s. The social and cultural history embedded in "Ninety Nine Year Blues" and these two versions of "John Hardy" enable us to understand how the language, themes, and representational strategies of the hurt song are mediated through Guthrie and Springsteen, and to consider how Springsteen preserves and adapts these "residuals" to historicize class relations and render a critique of capitalism in the 1980s.

Springsteen blends and adapts the traditions of Daniels, the Carters, and Guthrie to ground "Johnny 99" in the socioeconomic conditions of the 1980s and to understand these conditions in historical terms. Focusing on the life of a young autoworker who loses his job at a plant in Mahwah, New Jersey, "Johnny 99" is based in part on an actual event. In June 1980, the Ford Motor Company closed its Mahwah plant, a facility they had opened in 1955. Two years after the shutdown, more than half of the 3,359 workers who lost their jobs remained unemployed; many of those who found other positions accepted drastic cuts in pay or left their homes to find work in other regions of the country. Douglas Fraser, the president of the United Auto Workers who saw nearly 250,000 workers lose their jobs in the early 1980s, explained that the "kind of permanent layoff at Mahwah [was] much more shattering than anything that happened in the Depression. At least in the 1930s workers had hopes of being called back to work. In Mahwah they don't." For many working people, particularly those in Mahwah, the 1980s seemed hauntingly reminiscent of Guthrie's 1930s. In the shadow of Ronald Reagan's decidedly antilabor policies, the unemployment rate reached a post-Depression high of 11% in 1982, union membership fell by 29%, industrial cities rapidly decayed, and homelessness became a visible national problem.

To represent these economic transformations, Springsteen replicates the narrative techniques of the traditional ballad, locating his actors in a specific social-geographical context which establishes a sense of contemporary relevance and veracity.

While the Carters and the Guthries use geography to confirm and contest the values of identifiable communities, Springsteen's working-class geographies illustrate the dissolution of working-class communities. Dismissed from his job, Ralph unsuccessfully pounds the pavement and heads to the Club Tip Top, a working-class bar segregated from the more affluent suburban districts of Mahwah "in the part of town where when you hit a red light you don't stop." Springsteen suggests that these markers—the industrial town, the factory, and the neighborhood bar—have become so marginalized that it is impossible to forge a collective working-class identity which provides people a sense of self-worth. Throughout the 1980s factories relocated outside of the United States, union halls emptied, and people left many traditional working-class communities to search for employment elsewhere. When Ralph tells the judge that the bank was threatening to foreclose on his mortgage, he alludes to the literal and figurative displacement that many working people experienced. The impending foreclosure represents a clear financial crisis, but it also indicates the profound sense of displacement he will feel when he is detached from the coworkers, the neighborhood, and the culture he has known. In the wake of such fragmentation and historic changes in the economy, the collective alliances and sense of community that Woody Guthrie sought to build were in the 1980s becoming increasingly difficult to imagine, let alone forge.

As Springsteen's characters tell their stories, they speak in a working-class language which locates them in a specific social space, but also empowers them to push against the boundaries that delineate this space. In nearly all of his material, including "Johnny 99," Springsteen sings in colloquialisms, drops the endings to his words, relies on such slang words as "ain't," and often uses improper verb tenses. Although Springsteen himself speaks in this idiom, the use of nonstandard English represents the unequal educational opportunities afforded to working people and corresponds to the lack of political and cultural power and influence that they wield in the vast social spaces claimed by the middle class.

As Guthrie would say, "Johnny 99" is not the story of "just another bad man gone wrong"; it is a representational history of class relations in the United States which illustrates the cost of these relations in human terms.

While this murder ballad considers a rather drastic means of resistance, "Mansion on the Hill" represents the daily humiliations that characterize working-class life. As the title suggests, "Mansion" is a rewriting of the 1947 Hank Williams song. Retaining the class consciousness of the original, Springsteen relies on geography to demarcate class relationships, and locates his mansion on the outskirts of town where we see it "[r]ising above" the working-class geographies of "the factories and fields" located "down here in Linden town." In the narrator's memory, the mansion symbolizes the history of class relations in this industrial locale. Geographically isolated from the town, the mansion is "completely surround[ed]" by "gates of hardened steel." Obviously produced by the millworkers driving home from work, the cold, hard steel recalls the lovelessness of Williams's mansion, and, more importantly, emphasizes the workers' place in their community. As the fruits of their labor are transformed into the ornaments of wealth which segregate them from the comfort and success the mansion represents, Springsteen suggests that labor does not deliver workers to the American dream, but rather isolates them from it.

A multilayered work of revisionist history narrated in working-class language, *Nebraska* represents the history of class in the United States and places the social problems of the 1980s in the context of change over time.

The Ghost of Tom Joad (1995) indicates a rekindled interest in the Guthriesque political and aesthetic traditions of the hurt song, addresses the social problems caused by racial and class oppression, and sharpens the historical critique of capitalism he advances on *Nebraska*. Like this artistic forebear, *Ghost* is a strikingly uncommercial, largely acoustic album on which minimalist guitar, organ, and harmonica arrangements provide a background for an unsettling collection of narratives.

Ford and Steinbeck certainly influenced the album, but it has strong connections to Guthrie's *Dust Bowl Ballads* (1940), a collection which in addition to including "Vigilante Man" and "I Ain't Got No Home"[2] contains the two-part ballad "Tom Joad." Folksingers often write lyrics that fit traditional tunes, but Guthrie's choice to set this Okie ballad to the tune of "John Hardy" is particularly significant because it enmeshes the song in a complex network of historical and cultural connections. Guthrie associated Hardy's struggles with a number of black and white outlaws who fought for their freedom, and used them to point out the limitations of individual resistance and to promote collective political action. Placing Steinbeck's character in this musical and cultural context, Guthrie emphasizes the collectivist vision outlined by *The Grapes of Wrath* character Preacher Casy and reiterated by Joad at the end of the ballad: "Everybody might be just one big soul / Well it looks that a-way to me." The connections that Guthrie musically forges between working-class blacks in McDowell County and migrant workers from Oklahoma places all working peoples, regardless of race, in the same struggle for social justice.

Reawakening Joad's ghost and putting his spirit to work in contemporary America, Springsteen reconnects with the hurt song tradition and strengthens his cultural ties to Guthrie. Drawing on the history contained in Guthrie's "Tom Joad," he recalls the struggles that shaped *Nebraska*, affirming his commitment to an alternative political tradition which distinguishes itself from middle-class commercial culture and criticizes the morality this culture engenders. *The Ghost of Tom Joad* subjects the American conscience to tough moral questions, dismantles the national and religious myths that structure conventional historical narratives, and once again constructs a repressed history which represents the brutality of "the real world."

The powerful first verse of the album's title track condenses the emotional content of *Dust Bowl Ballads* in eight lines. Helicopters from the highway patrol watch the homeless from the skies, families sleep in their cars, and migrants cook soup on campfires they build beneath bridges, while a "shelter line" welcomes the listener "to the new world order" that George [H. W.] Bush promised would follow the Gulf War. Springsteen has been outspoken about what he considers the New Right's failure to address American social issues constructively, but in "Ghost" the former president's promise is just one of many that has been broken. A homeless preacher reveals the limitations of a conservative, individualistic Christian tradition which, instead of preaching the social gospel, has retreated into complacent passivity and arrogant moralizing. Whereas Preacher Jim Casy in both Steinbeck's *Grapes* and Guthrie's "Vigilante Man" renounces the practice of saving individual souls and instead tries to organize working people into "one big soul that ever'body's a part of," Springsteen's preacher helplessly and ironically sits in a cardboard box waiting "for when the last shall be first and the first shall be last."

Much of *Ghost* considers the politics of race, something that both Ford and Steinbeck overlook. Influenced by folk blues such as Daniels's as well as the soul music of the sixties, Springsteen has always performed with interracial bands, often embracing saxophonist Clarence Clemmons [*sic*] in long on-stage "soul kisses" that symbolize racial unity. Moreover, Springsteen has spoken publicly about a relationship between economic exploitation and racial oppression, but until he released *Ghost* his work did not explicitly address racial issues. The album contains four songs which confront the politics of Mexican immigration and its relationship to the labor market. The clear antecedent for these border ballads is Guthrie's "Deportee (Plane Wreck at Los Gatos)," a song that Springsteen performed in concert in 1981 and that Guthrie's son Arlo recorded with Emmylou Harris for *A Vision Shared*.

When Springsteen reconstructs Joad's farewell speech in the final verse of "The Ghost of Tom Joad," he implicitly offers his vision of community to all struggles for justice. Like Steinbeck's and Ford's Joad, Springsteen's will be with unsuspecting victims who are beaten by the police and with children when they are hungry. But when Springsteen sings that Joad will be *"wherever* somebody's strugglin' to be free,"* he specifically signifies the hurt song of Guthrie, who, unlike the novelist and filmmaker, allows Joad to transcend the class politics of the Okie community and travel *"wherever* people ain't free."* If Steinbeck and Ford author collective visions which include only members of the white working class, Guthrie and Springsteen suggest that the fight for social justice must be much more inclusive, particularly when it comes to matters of race.

Notes

1. Writes Eric Alterman, "Like Dylan, Springsteen drew directly on Harry Smith's anthology. Song number seventy-four on the collection is a bluesy dirge called "Ninety-Nine-Year Blues" recorded by a North Carolina native named Julius Daniels in February 1927. The song concerns a young black man who is arrested while visiting a new town under the 'poor boy law.' (In other words, he is guilty of being poor and black.) The judge sentences him to ninety-nine years in 'Joe Brown's coal mine,' and the injustice inspires the boy to express a desire to 'kill everybody' in town. Springsteen's response is 'Johnny 99.'" See Eric Alterman, *It Ain't No Sin to Be Glad You're Alive: The Promise of Bruce Springsteen* (New York: Little, Brown, 1999), pp. 133–34.
2. Springsteen's renditions of Guthrie's "Vigilante Man" and "I Ain't Got No Home" appear on *A Vision Shared* (Folkways, 1988).

Jim Cullen

■

Jim Cullen is a former lecturer in history and literature at Harvard University and the author of numerous books that examine the effects of pop culture on various aspects of American society. Many of his works also plumb the meaning behind the American dream. Among his titles are *The Civil War in Popular Culture: A Reusable Past* (1995), *The Art of Democracy: A Concise History of Popular Culture in the United States* (1996), *Restless in the Promised Land: Catholics and the American Dream* (2001), and, most recently, *The American Dream: A Short History of an Idea That Shaped a Nation* (2003). In *Born in the U.S.A.: Bruce Springsteen and the American Tradition* (1996), Cullen argues not only that Springsteen is an important icon of American culture but also that he is an heir to the tradition of Walt Whitman, Abraham Lincoln, John Steinbeck, and even Martin Luther King Jr.—heady company indeed. Or as Jefferson Cowie once wrote, "If he rarely proselytizes about politics and collective action, his evangelical rock does preach a secular American faith through an appeal to what Abraham Lincoln called 'the better angels of our nature.'"[1] In the following excerpts, Cullen discusses the Springsteen-Steinbeck-Guthrie connection and the Jersey rocker's adventures in Graceland during the height of the *Born to Run* hype.

Tom Joad's Children

from *Born in the U.S.A.: Bruce Springsteen and the American Tradition*

The nonchalance of boys who are sure of a dinner, and would disdain as much as a lord to do or say aught to conciliate one, is the healthy attitude of human nature.

—Ralph Waldo Emerson, "Self-Reliance"

I'll be in the way kids laugh when they're hungry and they know supper's ready.

—Tom Joad, protagonist of John Steinbeck's
(and John Ford's) *The Grapes of Wrath*

■On March 3, 1940, Woody Guthrie appeared at New York's Forrest Theater in a benefit performance for what was billed as "The John Steinbeck Committee for Agricultural Workers." Steinbeck's novel *The Grapes of Wrath,* chronicling the mass migration of displaced farm workers from Guthrie's beloved Oklahoma, had been published the previous spring, and was still a major bestseller. The film version of the novel, directed by John Ford, had premiered in New York with great fanfare six weeks before. The *Daily Worker,* a Communist newspaper, promoted Guthrie's appearance with a picture of him strumming a guitar and with the caption "'Woody'—that's the name, straight out of Steinbeck's 'Grapes of Wrath'—sings People's Ballads."

It was a great night for Guthrie. Explaining that he was pleased to perform in a "Rapes of Graft" show, he amused and moved the audience, which included Alan Lomax, the budding ethnomusicologist who would go on to lasting fame by recording Guthrie's work and that of other folk musicians. Shortly after the benefit, Lomax persuaded Victor Records to produce an album of Guthrie's dust bowl ballads.[2] "The Victor people want me to write a song about *The Grapes of Wrath,*" Guthrie told his friend Pete Seeger, asking him if he knew where he could find a typewriter. Seeger directed him to the apartment of a friend, where, with a half gallon of wine, Guthrie sat down to work. The song that resulted, "Tom Joad," was a seventeen-verse ballad that tracked the plot of the book and the movie.

It should be noted that there are significant differences between the two. This is not only because a movie must necessarily condense a novel, but also because director Ford softened some of the novel's more radical edges. Steinbeck, for example, ends with the Joad family in very desperate straits, fleeing a rising flood and finding only temporary refuge in an abandoned barn (where, in a scene that underlines the importance of women, Rose Joad nurses a starving man). Ford, by contrast, ends with a battered-but-stabilized family on the road again, and Ma Joad commenting on the endurance of the people—not the necessity for change in the system.

Nevertheless, both book and movie share fundamental values. As historian Alan Brinkley noted in an essay comparing book and film, as far as both Steinbeck and Ford were concerned, "neither despair nor rage could adequately convey the real meaning of the Great Depression. Instead, the novel and film suggest, the true lesson of the time was the importance of community: not community defined in traditional, geographical terms; not in the community of a neighborhood or a town, or a region—but in a community of the human spirit."

This point is made in Tom Joad's pivotal parting words to his mother, which are similar in book and film (the following comes from the latter because it's shorter and uncluttered with reference to other characters in the story):

> "I'll be all around in the dark. I'll be everywhere. Wherever there's a fight so hungry people can eat, I'll be there. Wherever there's a cop beatin' a guy, I'll be there. I'll be in the way guys yell when they're mad; I'll be in the way kids laugh when they know supper's ready. And when the people are eatin' the stuff they raise, and livin' in the houses they build, I'll be there, too."

Woody Guthrie's version adapted the core of this passage for the climax of "Tom Joad":

> *Wherever people ain't free*
> *Wherever men are fightin' for their rights*
> *That's where I'm gonna be, ma*

These words lack the crisp clarity of book and film, but their musicality is apparent even on the page.

However urgent and moving the work of Steinbeck, Ford, and Guthrie, all were in some sense being outpaced by history. By the time Guthrie appeared at the Steinbeck benefit, many of the displaced Okies he sang about were finding jobs in California defense plants gearing up for World War II. That war, and the energies it unleashed, transformed the United States in the four years between the time Guthrie wrote the first draft of his response to "God Bless America" in February 1940 and his first recording of the song as "This Land Is Your Land" in the spring of 1944. Twenty years later, starving migrants were hosting backyard cookouts; the defining voice of California life (itself increasingly the defining voice of American life) was not Woody Guthrie, but the Beach Boys.

Of course, poverty did not disappear in California or anywhere else in America. And other struggles, most notably the Civil Rights movement, were only beginning. But with the exception of the early years of the movement, there was a steady ebbing of the egalitarian spirit—a spirit suffusing [Walt] Whitman even as he wrote "Song of Myself"—that had animated the artists of the thirties.

Springsteen's discovery of Woody Guthrie in 1980 coincided with the advent of an era of accelerating inequality in the United States, a development he chronicled on *Nebraska* and subsequent records. But by the end of the decade even Springsteen had retreated somewhat from his concern with social injustice. Records like *Tunnel of Love, Human Touch,* and *Lucky Town,* while hardly rejecting the political stance of his earlier records, lacked the sense of active engagement that had characterized his music in the early eighties.

But during a sleepless night in early 1995 while trying to write new songs, Springsteen picked up *Journey to Nowhere,* a book on the new American underclass written by Dale Maharidge with photographs by Michael Williamson (they would go on to share a Pulitzer Prize in 1990 for *And Their Children After Them,* which traced the subsequent history of Alabama sharecropping families first chronicled in James Agee's classic 1940 study *Let Us Now Praise Famous Men*). *Journey to Nowhere* had originally been published in 1985, which is when Springsteen bought it, but only now was he actually reading the book. Maharidge's and Williamson's depictions of the decaying industrial city of Youngstown, Ohio, and their portraits of contemporary boxcar hoboes were the direct inspiration for two new songs, "Youngstown" and "The New Timer." "What Springsteen is trying to do is something so incredible," said Maharidge in 1996, when *Journey to Nowhere* was reissued (with a new introduction by Springsteen). "He's a musical Steinbeck."[3]

Springsteen made this political and artistic connection clear in his decision to title the ensuing album *The Ghost of Tom Joad,* and in the song of the same name that opens it. But his primary tie to *Tom Joad,* as he has made clear in interviews and in source notes that accompany the album, is the John Ford version. Whatever the lineage, though, it's apparent that Springsteen sought to make his own imprint on the material.

He does this in a number of ways. One is the use of contemporary details that anchor the songs in the present even as they resonate with the past. So, for example, "The Ghost of Tom Joad" opens with men walking along railroad tracks—and highway patrol choppers coming over a ridge. Steinbeck/Ford/Guthrie focus on poor white Southerners; Springsteen's locus is the Southwest, and many of his characters are nonwhite (this was true of some of Steinbeck's other fiction). While the original Tom Joad sought to navigate the shoals of the Great Depression, Springsteen's narrator, observing a line of people waiting for shelter, dryly welcomes "the new world order" proclaimed by George [H. W.] Bush. Indeed, there's a bitterness in "The Ghost of Tom Joad" that may even exceed that of Steinbeck. "The highway's alive tonight," begins the chorus on a hopeful note—only to end with an acerbic "But nobody's kiddin' nobody about where it goes." Thunder Road, it would seem, is a dead end.

The Bars of Graceland

We [the E Street Band] wanted to play because we wanted to meet girls, we wanted to make a ton of dough, and we wanted to change the world a little bit, you know?

—Bruce Springsteen, 1984

In our day, the term "American Dream" has become a cliché most commonly invoked by real-estate agents and Hollywood screenwriters. The former use it in a tireless effort to sell home ownership, the most concrete vision of the Dream. The latter use it to sell a vision of wealth, fame, and power all the more alluring for its seeming effortlessness.

It may be logical, then, that both these versions of the American Dream converge at [Elvis] Presley's baronial home. Here, he took care of his beloved mama, and here he fed his bottomless appetites (sustained via income from his movies). Its very name, Graceland, testifies to its almost totemic power as the supreme expression of the Dream, heavenly grace in earthly form.

But however potent a symbol, Graceland cannot wholly represent the American Dream in its many dimensions. It has gone by different names: "the American Creed," "the American Way of Life," or, simply, the "American Way." All are united by a common underlying faith that runs through the many versions of the Dream. This faith is rarely articulated explicitly, and it has never been formally codified. But it can be summed up in the following assertion:

Anything is possible if you want it badly enough.

Americans may invest in this Dream so heavily because America itself is a product of it. Its earliest formulation was perhaps best expressed by John Winthrop, the first governor of the Massachusetts Bay Colony, in a lay sermon he delivered to the Puritans in 1630 while still sailing the Atlantic. "We shall find that the God of Israel is among us, when ten of us shall be able to resist a thousand of our enemies; when he shall make us a praise and glory that men shall say of succeeding plantations, 'the Lord make it like that of New England,'" he reputedly said. "For we must consider that we shall be as a city upon a hill."

The heart of the Puritans' American Dream was what they called their "covenant," an implicit pact with God that he would provide for them spiritually if they formed a community to honor him according to his precepts as they understood them. This American Dream was a religious dream, as were many subsequent versions of the Dream, including the massive evangelical revivals known as the "Great Awakenings" of the mid-eighteenth and early nineteenth centuries. As time passed, these versions of the Dream tended to become more individualistic, less focused on salvation through community than through personal redemption. But the original energy persisted, even as it diffused across the country at large, most obviously in the case of an increasingly secular work ethic.

By the end of the eighteenth century, another version of the Dream, this one more political, was articulated by the signers of the Declaration of Independence. Thomas Jefferson's assertions to the contrary, it was by no means "self-evident," then or now, that "all Men are created equal, that they are endowed by their Creator with certain inalienable rights," and that these rights can be summed up as "life, liberty, and the pursuit of happiness." But such was the will and good fortune of the Founders that they did achieve political autonomy from Britain, and bequeathed to us a vision of possibility that we have honored—if all too imperfectly realized—ever since.

There were a number of American Dreams in the nineteenth century. Some, like the Transcendentalists' quest for self-realization, were relatively modest in scope. "I have learned this, at least, from my experiment: that if one advances confidently in the direction of his dreams, and endeavors to live the life he has imagined, he will meet with a success unexpected in common hours," wrote Henry David Thoreau after his sojourn in the woods of Walden. Others, like the so-called "Manifest Destiny," were far more collective, though not especially communitarian. Coined by journalist John L. Sullivan, the term referred to the drive for a continental empire that stretched to the Pacific, the American Dream as imperial conquest.

In the decades following the Civil War, with capitalism ascendant and technology triumphant, the primary expression of the Dream was economic. In its most powerful and durable formulation, it was a hope that one's children would enjoy a higher standard of living than oneself. A variation on this Dream was expressed in the fictional characters of novelist Horatio Alger, whose poor boys made good *because* they were good (and lucky). Still others, like Andrew Carnegie, tried to couch this American Dream in terms of progress that allows those of modest means to achieve happiness no less than the millionaire. "Material prosperity is helping to make the national character more unselfish, more Christlike," Reverend William Wallace, Episcopal bishop of Massachusetts, wrote in 1901.

Whether or not this was really true, the maturation of American industrial capitalism in the early twentieth century led to yet another reorientation of the American Dream. Now it was less about religion, politics, empire, or money—though each continued to have its adherents—than about personal freedom and pleasure. Athletes like Babe Ruth and movie stars like Mary Pickford were enviable not simply because they were rich and powerful, but because they always seemed to be having a good time. This vision was expressed most perfectly not in real life, but in another fictional character: James Gatz, an ordinary boy from small-town Minnesota, who transformed himself into the fabulous Jay Gatsby to win the heart of the beautiful Daisy Buchanan in F. Scott Fitzgerald's *The Great Gatsby* (1925).

Fitzgerald had a sophisticated grasp of the American Dream. Gatsby, of course, fails to attain his; the woman to whom he pins his hopes is not really worthy of him. Not that Gatsby is so "great" either; in the end, he seems little more than a pathetic man who confuses appearances with reality. But even the clear-eyed narrator Nick Carraway cannot help but be moved by the intensity of the man's vision, a vision comparable to that of a European explorer who encountered a continent "commensurate with his capacity for wonder."

Ten years after the publication of *The Great Gatsby*, Elvis Aaron Presley was born in Tupelo, Mississippi. In an important sense, Presley was the opposite of Gatsby, because he really did achieve his Dream. That Dream has been vividly described by Greil Marcus in his now classic essay "Presliad,"[4] whose very title suggests the degree to which Presley's life evokes a myth of origin. Marcus's point of entry is country music, and the way in which Presley was nurtured by—and broke from—it. Marcus argues that while the Protestant work ethic in the North "set men free by making them strangers," Southerners, black and white, emphasized (segregated) community, one bound through rituals like music, which could provide solace for the heartbroken and consolation for rebels whose cause was lost. To be sure, there was plenty of hell-raising and good times to be had on Saturday night. But that's as far as it went. Come Sunday morning, there was a service to attend, and on Monday morning, everyone returned to work. What made Presley and his fellow rock and rollers special, Marcus says, was their attempt to make Saturday night last forever. "You had to be young and a bit insulated to pull it off," he conceded. But the promise of the idea was irresistible:

> Reality would catch up sooner or later—a pregnant girlfriend and a fast marriage, the farm you had to take over when your daddy died, a dull and pointless job that drained your desires until you could barely remember them—but why deal with reality before you had to? And what if there was a chance, just a chance, that you didn't have to deal with it?

Presley himself put it more succinctly: "When I was a boy, I was the hero in comic books and movies. I grew up believing in a dream. Now I've lived it out. That's all a man can ask for."

As Presley learned, however, the Dream itself turned out to be a "dull and pointless job." In this regard, he was just like Gatsby: his Dream was an unworthy one. Presley became a latter-day King Midas; by 1956, any song his voice touched went gold (a singer far more than a composer, by contractual arrangement he nevertheless received songwriting credit for many records), and simply appearing before the camera guaranteed profits for any of his movies. Lacking an essential curiosity or even simple business acumen about his future, he left most of the crucial decisions shaping his career to the rapacious "Colonel" Tom Parker, who committed Presley to projects that were beneath him. Before long, his work was a profitable joke, and by the late sixties, it wasn't even so profitable anymore.

Presley's career was not simply a tale of perfect decline. All through this period, he showed flashes of commitment, and when it became unmistakably clear to him that he'd lost his touch, he turned Colonel Parker's plans for a 1968 Christmas special into an astonishing display of his resiliency and the springboard for his celebrated comeback. He recorded some of the best work of his life at this time, went back on the road for the first time in a decade, and conquered America all over again. But after the first few appearances in Las Vegas, Presley acted like a man with "talent so vast it would be demeaning to apply it." In his words, becoming a hero onstage "was all a man could ask for," and after attaining this goal in the fifties, losing it in the sixties, and recapturing it in the seventies, he apparently had no idea what else to do except to take refuge in the dreamless sleep of narcotics. And so Presley's American Dream became his prison, and, ultimately, his tomb.

Reflecting on Presley's life and death in 1987, a decade after his death (and a decade after his own pilgrimage to Graceland), Springsteen called Presley's dream "a cult of personality" in which fame and wealth were the only objectives. He did so as a superstar in his own right, featured as the lead interview in the twentieth-anniversary issue of *Rolling Stone*.[5] Once the voice (and even conscience) of the counterculture, the magazine was now itself devoted to cults of personality, attaining its commercial preeminence in the 1980s by stoking sleek, updated versions of Presleyesque fantasies.

But if Springsteen was in this world, he was not quite of it. "When I jumped over that wall to meet Elvis that night, I didn't know who I was gonna meet,"[6] he reflected. "And the guard who stopped me at the door did me the biggest favor of my life. I had misunderstood. It was innocent, and I was having a ball, but it wasn't right. In the end, you cannot live inside that dream."

Notes

1. See Jefferson Cowie, "Fandom, Faith, and Bruce Springsteen," *Dissent*, Winter 2001.

2. Woody Guthrie, *Dust Bowl Ballads* (1940; Buddha, 2000).

3. See Dale Maharidge and Michael Williamson, *Journey to Nowhere: The Saga of the New Underclass*. Introduction by Bruce Springsteen (New York: Hyperion, 1996; Doubleday, 1985). In *Born in the U.S.A.: Bruce Springsteen and the American Tradition*, Cullen also cites Tom Schoenberg, "Professor's Research Inspires a Rock Star," *Chronicle of Higher Education*, January 19, 1996.

4. Greil Marcus, "Elvis: Presliad," in *Mystery Train: Images of America in Rock 'n' Roll Music* (New York: E. P. Dutton, 1976), pp. 137–205.

5. See Mikal Gilmore, "Twentieth Anniversary Special: Bruce Springsteen Q & A," November 5–December 10, 1987, in *Bruce Springsteen: The Rolling Stone Files* (New York: Hyperion, 1996), pp. 238–46.

6. Ibid., p. 246. Springsteen discusses the night he tried to meet Elvis at his Graceland mansion with Kurt Loder of *Rolling Stone*. See Kurt Loder, "The Rolling Stone Interview: Bruce Springsteen," in *Bruce Springsteen: The Rolling Stone Files* (New York: Hyperion, 1996), pp. 162–63.

Tom Perrotta

■

Tom Perrotta is the bard of a particular brand of adolescent New Jersey angst. His Jersey-inflected fiction includes *Bad Haircut: Stories of the Seventies* (1997), a collection of short stories that follow the life of Buddy, a small-town New Jersey boy; *Election* (1998), set in a New Jersey high school on the eve of the election of the school president (and adapted as a smart 1999 movie starring Reese Witherspoon and Matthew Broderick); and *Joe College* (2001), a novel about college life circa 1982. His coming-of-age stories are astute and universal in their observations, and often wickedly funny. In *The Wishbones* (1997), from which the following excerpt is taken, we meet Dave Raymond, a thirty-one-year-old musician (he plays guitar in a wedding band) who is not quite ready to give up his dream of adolescent freedom—as the ubiquitous presence of New Jersey's favorite son, Bruce Springsteen, looms over him.

from *The Wishbones*

■DAVE HAD TWO courier runs that afternoon—a quick in-and-out to Wall Street, followed by a trip to Morristown to drop off some X rays at a doctor's office. He liked driving for a living, especially since it meant he got paid for time spent listening to tunes on his car stereo. There was no better way to experience music, cranking the volume as high as it could go in an enclosed space, singing at the top of his lungs as he zigzagged like a stuntman through slow-moving traffic on the Pulaski Skyway. He could never understand how people managed to survive entire days cooped up in an office, with nothing to listen to but ringing phones and hushed voices. Even worse, a few of the places he visited had piped-in Muzak, the sound track of living death. Just thinking about it gave him the willies.

Another cool thing about his job was that it brought him into the city two or three times a week. Manhattan was always a jolt of crazy energy, a reminder that life wasn't meant to be safe or easy, the way it was in the suburbs. Dave even appreciated the stuff that gave most drivers headaches—the insane cabbies and squeegee men, the pedestrians who swarmed around his car at red lights like ants around a piece of candy, the whistle-tooting bike messengers and Rollerbladers who zipped past his windshield in suicidal blurs. Just making it in and out of this mess in one piece qualified as a triumph, an achievement he could carry around for the rest of his day.

Sometimes he wondered if things would have turned out differently if he'd moved into the city after dropping out of college instead of drifting back to his parents' house and the routine of familiar places and faces that had consumed his life ever since. Maybe it would have sharpened him somehow, having to live in a dingy, roach-infested shoe-box apartment, eating canned soup and SpaghettiOs, following in the footsteps of Dylan and Lou Reed and Talking Heads and the zillions of wannabes who'd journeyed to the city to test themselves against the myth Sinatra sang about. It wasn't something he brooded about, just a possibility he turned over in his mind every now and then when he found himself trying to answer the thorny question of how it was he'd ended up a Wishbone instead of a star.

In the car, he was able to consider his predicament more clearly, without the edge of panic that had clouded his morning thoughts. The first thing he realized was that it wasn't the idea of marrying Julie that frightened him; it was the idea of *being married,* of joining this big corny club of middle-aged men that included his father, Julie's father, his uncles, and every scoutmaster, Little League coach, and voluntary fireman he'd ever known. There were some exceptions—Bruce Springsteen and Buzzy came to mind—but in general, marriage seemed to require that a man check his valuables at the door: his dreams, his freedom, all the wildness that had defined the secret part of his life, even if, like Dave, he wasn't all that wild in reality.

It was easier if you were a woman. Women were supposed to *want* to get married, to go through life with a husband and children. A man's job, as far as Dave could see, was simply to resist for as long as possible before surrendering to the inevitable. You didn't have to play guitar in a wedding band to know that there was something at least slightly pathetic about a bridegroom.

Beyond his personal fears, though, he identified a deeper, more philosophical question: Was marriage something you chose, or was it something that happened whether you wanted it to or not, one of those mysterious, transforming events on the order of birth or death? The no-brain answer, of course, was that you chose. You were an adult in a free country; there were no arranged marriages in America. You didn't have to do anything you didn't want to.

He accepted all that, but on another level, it was hard to say that he and Julie had actually chosen each other in some rational, adult way. Fifteen years ago—half their lifetime—she had walked up to him in the hallway of Warren G. Harding Regional High School and told him that Exit 36 had put on a great show at the spring dance and predicted that they would someday be famous. A week later he took her to see *Midnight Express*. Two months after that they split a six-pack purchased by her older sister's boyfriend and had sex for the first time. It just *happened*, in some urgent hormonal haze that had little to do with concepts like choice or intention, and they hadn't been free of each other since. And now, apparently, unless he thought of something fast, they were going to get themselves married.

Glenn was further along on the path to musical enlightenment. He put his own mark on "The Sky Is Crying," transforming it from an almost exuberant bellow of pain to something more muted and matter-of-fact, as though, in his world, the crying of the sky were the ordinary state of things rather than a strange and sinister change in the weather. His voice was less gruffly expressive than Stevie Ray Vaughan's, his licks more furtive, less self-assured; instead of wild anguish you felt a dull pain motivating the song, an ache that wouldn't go away when the sun came out. Glenn was Stevie Ray without the swagger and the cowboy hat, and these were the blues the dead man might have known if, instead of being a famous guitar hero, he'd been a lonely guy in green gym shorts who hadn't gotten laid in a long time and didn't expect the future to deliver anything better than the shrunken-down life he already had.

Glenn was one of the few guitarists Dave knew who didn't make big faces when he soloed; he just hunched down over his Strat and went to work. Every once in a while he looked up, squinting in mild perplexity, his fingers spider-walking over the fret board as though directed by an entirely separate intelligence. Watching him, Dave thought of "Bobby Jean," Bruce Springsteen's tribute to Steve Van Zandt, his musical soul mate from high school all the way through the glory days of the E Street Band. If things had worked out the way they were supposed to, he and Glenn might have had a similar trajectory, instead of a story that began and ended on a single night.

Dave never expected to find himself home at eleven o'clock with no one to talk to on the night before his wedding, but here he is. He figured he'd be out getting drunk or watching some nearly naked woman hump a metal pole, doing *something* to mark the passing of the last night of the first phase of his life. But when the time came, no one was available. Ian and Tammi had another party to go to. Glenn was wiped out; he said his new medication was wreaking havoc with his sleep/wake cycle. Even Buzzy begged off. He was making an effort to cut down on his drinking and be a more responsible husband and father, and had promised JoAnn he'd be home as soon as the dinner ended.

His own family didn't have much more to offer in the way of company. Chuck and Linda disappeared upstairs as soon as they got into the house, both looking exhausted. (They're sleeping on the twin beds in Dave's room, leaving him to fend for himself on the furry couch in the TV room, hardly luxury quarters for his last night in the family home.) His parents stayed up for a brief, self-congratulatory postmortem on the dinner, then hightailed it up to bed, repeatedly reminding Dave and themselves of the fact that they all had "a big day coming up."

Dave gives some serious consideration to calling Julie, but resists the temptation, knowing how concerned she is about looking fresh and rested on her wedding day. He wants to tell her again how surprised and moved he was by her slide presentation, which she'd introduced to the dinner guests as *Dave and Julie: Fifteen Years in Fifteen Minutes.*

"Some of you might have been wondering what took us so long," she said. A few people giggled, even though Julie didn't seem to be making a joke. "It's a question I've asked myself more than once. This was the only answer I could come up with."

What followed was a blizzard of images, arranged in no particular order. Prom pictures, vacation snapshots, photographs from weddings, retirement parties, graduations, picnics, birthdays, Christmases, and countless forgotten occasions. Julie making a human pyramid with some college friends. Dave singing with the Tragics, his short-lived New Wave band, wearing his trademark dinner jacket and ascot. Julie in a pink bikini and sunglasses, sitting atop a tall lifeguard chair, whistle around her neck. Dave with his shirt off, posing beneath his father's prize sunflower. Dave and Julie mugging in a photo booth, looking impossibly young and happy. The boys from Löckjaw. A chorus line of Julie and her sisters, all three wearing identical flannel nightgowns and kneesocks, kicking for the camera. The Wishbones rehearsing in street clothes. Julie as a bridesmaid. Dave in an ugly suit. Julie acting in a college play Dave never saw, due to the fact that she was living with Brendan at the time.

Four of the five members of Lost Cause standing in front of a kiddie airplane ride on the boardwalk at Asbury Park, looking like contestants in a Bruce Springsteen wannabe contest. Julie and her young-looking father carrying boxes into a dorm. Sensitive Dave singing at an open mike, during an abortive attempt to reinvent himself as a folkie. Julie glamorous in a black leather jacket, cigarette planted between bright red lips. Five-year-old Dave, wearing an Indian warbonnet, blowing on a toy trumpet. Five-year-old Julie, dressed like a bride for Halloween.

It wasn't just the pictures, though. Julie had put together a sound track of songs performed by bands Dave had played in over the past decade and a half. Exit 36 doing a credible rendition of "Angie." Lost Cause covering "Should I Stay or Should I Go?" The Tragics playing "Scared of the Light," probably the best song Dave had ever written. And finally, the Wishbones' exuberant version of "Brown-Eyed Girl," from a promo tape they'd put together about a year ago.

The show ended with a rapid-fire series of Dave and Julie kissing. Some of them were little pecks obviously staged for the camera, but others were candid shots. They kissed in a pool. In a photo booth. At someone's wedding. On Christmas morning. Passionately. On a couch. Under a tree. As sixteen-year-olds. Just the other day. Dave sat there laughing as the memories rolled by, and for a minute or two, his life seemed to have consisted of nothing but love and music, and it seemed to him as good a life as he ever could have wished for.

Nicholas Dawidoff

■

Nicholas Dawidoff's interests tend to hover between sports and music, especially country music. He is probably best known, though, for being the author of *The Catcher Was a Spy: The Mysterious Life of Moe Berg* (1995) and as the editor of *Baseball: A Literary Anthology* (2002). But he has also written *In the Country of Country: A Journey to the Roots of American Music* (1997), in which he profiles some of the genre's greatest performers, from Jimmie Rodgers and Bill Monroe to Emmylou Harris and Jimmie Dale Gilmore. "[W]hat has bound traditional country together . . . ," he wrote, "is that it is simply worded, string-driven, melodic music concerned with subjects that are both quotidian and universal: faith, love, family, work, heartbreak, pleasure, sin, joy, and suffering." And he finds that the American singer whose influence has a deep and abiding social significance is not a country singer but a rock star—Bruce Springsteen. "Like Harlan Howard, Merle Haggard, or Hank Williams, Springsteen requires only three or four minutes to tell stories that pack the emotional force of great short fiction."[1] The following long profile ran in the January 26, 1997, issue of the *New York Times Magazine*. Dawidoff notices details that other writers have either neglected or ignored—such as what he calls Springsteen's "Jersey-Pennsylvania lilt" or his relationship with his children. It makes for a revealing portrait.

The Pop Populist
New York Times Magazine

■ON THE LAST Sunday in October, just over a week before Election Day, 2,000 people gathered in front of the Federal Building in the downtown Westwood section of Los Angeles for an old-time liberal political rally. Among the most strident of the many issues Californians would soon decide was Proposition 209, which sought the sharp reduction of affirmative-action programs across the state. Opposition to this bill had brought the crowd together.

It was, in many ways, an entirely familiar tableau. Aging lefties wearing beards and tie-dye stood shoulder to shoulder with comely U.C.L.A. undergraduates wearing very little. People waved signs that said things like "No on 209, Yes on Opportunity," "Let Me Dream Too" and "The Klan Supports 209." Up on the steps of the Federal Building, a cast of veteran speech makers stepped forward one by one. Representative Maxine Waters had her say, as did State Senator Tom Hayden and Dolores Huerta, a founder of the United Farm Workers. The president of the Fund for a Feminist Majority, Ellie Smeal, said a few words, before giving way to the Rev. Jesse Jackson, who gave a ringing address, which he described as "A call to healing, a call to hope." Then he turned and said, "Ladies and gentlemen: Mr. America—Bruce Springsteen!"

This was something different. For 30 years Springsteen has been writing and singing songs about ordinary people struggling through life on the hard side of the American dream. For all of the social tension crackling through his music, however, Springsteen has been a notably circumspect man. He has never been interviewed on a talk show, endorsed a political candidate or advertised a commercial product, much less given a political speech. In 1984, the year Springsteen and his E Street Band released an album, *Born in the U.S.A.*, that would sell 20 million copies, Ronald Reagan was running for re-election. During a campaign stop in central New Jersey, Reagan blithely inserted several references to Springsteen into his stump speech that were downright cousinly. It was Springsteen's belief that Reagan's presidency was the worst thing to happen to the American workingman in years. Yet his response was muted. Constitutionally cautious, he didn't want to enter any national dialogues. Nor did he view himself as someone who was qualified to indulge in political repartee. Springsteen hoped only to write songs that helped people put themselves for a moment into the next fellow's shoes.

Yet now here he was, dressed in jeans with his shirt sleeves rolled up, pulling some index cards from his hip pocket. Looking out at the crowd, he said, "I'm not used to this," and he did appear a bit jittery. But Springsteen acquitted himself well during a short talk in which he said that he felt America should be a country where everyone could find "work that fulfills you, brings meaning and purpose to your life." He chastised "cynical" conservative politicians who would have people believe that the United States was a race-and-gender-blind society—"We won't be fooled," he warned—and said, "I believe that the Promised Land is still attainable, but we're not there yet. Let's stand together in defense of that Promised Land."

Then he produced a guitar and sang "The Promised Land," his song about an American workingman who has grown weary of living in a country that urges you to dream and then leaves "you nothing but lost and brokenhearted." There was such prolonged applause that Jackson had time to raise joined fists with Springsteen before collecting him into a hug. The crowd wanted an encore. Jackson suggested "Born in the U.S.A.," but Springsteen instead chose "No Surrender."

Afterward, as Springsteen walked to his car, people behind crowd barriers yelled greetings, and policemen walked up to him and gripped his hand. Springsteen was smiling.

"So how does it feel to be a protest singer?" somebody asked him.

"Well," Springsteen said, "there's something about that direct connection between what you're singing and what's happening. It's no longer abstract. It steps out from being an idea or an esthetic and becomes physical. That's an exciting transformation." He seemed very relaxed.

Bruce Springsteen looks very much the way you would expect Bruce Springsteen to look. He dresses in battered boots, faded jeans, faded thermal undershirts with faded work shirts over them and a battered, faded leather jacket. His walk is stiff and a little chesty. One of his knees is always grinding, and the leg drags some. "You played basketball, right?" a doctor asked him once. "Well," Springsteen told him, thinking of all the years of bounding around arena stages, "I used to do a lot of jumping." Springsteen drives a Ford, hasn't gone to church in years—he is a lapsed Catholic—and usually forgoes his sunglasses too, if not his baseball cap. He is slow to get up in the morning and sometimes slower to fall asleep at night. Not that a wild time is getting in his way. He drinks— Jack Daniels—but usually doesn't even finish his first one. Once he is on his feet, he begins his day with the newspaper. Lately he ends it with an Erskine Caldwell novel.

Like many men who are well read and largely self-taught, Springsteen is attracted to polysyllables and sometimes mispronounces them. When he speaks, it is often his practice to leave off the hard consonant at the end of a word. There is a Jersey-Pennsylvania lilt to some of his inflections— he says "hill-larryus" for "hilarious"—and, at times, a hint of an Alabama drawl may slip in. (His childhood neighbor was a transplanted Southern truck driver.) His laugh is a guttural, chuckly thing, and it gets produced— usually without apparent provocation—just about every other sentence.

He adores his second wife, Patti, doesn't have anything unkind to say about his first, Julianne Phillips, loves his mother, is pretty devoted to his aunts too, and is in territory well beyond that when it comes to his three small children. (They like his pancakes. Nobody else does.) His father has taken him some time, but they've finally worked it out. If someone says, "Bruce, I have one of your records," he replies, "Good news for me!" He likes to watch old movies and the fights. Peanut butter and jelly is fine by him. "Those god-damned Republicans" are, of course, another matter.

He wasn't always such a regular guy. When he was a teenager, Springsteen had shaggy hair that made him the local misfit in his hometown, the central New Jersey village of Freehold. When drivers saw him hitch-hiking out on Route 9, they would try to nudge him into ditches. "The town was on the rednecky side, and they didn't like it if you were different," Springsteen says. "Meant you had to watch out for yourself. Made getting around a lot harder. But, you know, hey, I got to be me."

Even then, as a taciturn loner, Springsteen had rather extravagant ambitions about cultivating people like the ones he grew up with. They might not fathom him, but he understood what they were about with the clarity of perspective that comes from being the outsider, standing along the penumbra of a small community. He didn't see himself as so eccentric—he just looked that way—and he wanted to spend his life making music about his concerns for people who he was sure truly shared them.

And he succeeded. Not since Hank Williams have the common people—Williams's phrase—so thoroughly embraced someone who was singing about them. Springsteen's audience came to revere him as "the Boss" because he imbued ordinary lives with heroic qualities. His songs were set in places that might bear details drawn from the actual New Jersey landscape, but were also recognizable as American anytowns. They featured vivid characters like the Magic Rat, Sandy (of Asbury Park) and patrolman Joe Roberts, whose experiences—their bright hopes and harsh disappointments, their outer docility and inner turbulence—told a much broader story. Here was how it was going for the little guy in the Promised Land.

As Springsteen's audience grew huge in the mid-1980's, he became something more than an entertainer—as the voice of the regular people, he became a man of significant influence. This was a mantle he wore uneasily. He was a millionaire several times over by then, but he still saw himself as a rock-and-roll greaser from a blue-collar neighborhood who hadn't even made it through a year of community college. Springsteen was chary of telling people what to think or do, and he took care to remain an observer rather than an ideologue. He was preaching sympathy, compassion and understanding, not telling anyone how to think about welfare or immigration reform.

Still, it was always Springsteen's desire to make rock-and-roll grapple with the issues that confronted people over the full span of their lives. "I want my work to be about something, to mean something, to be useful" was how he so often put it. Springsteen is now 47, the first seminal rock-and-roll singer to reach middle age after growing up listening to the music. (He is eight years younger than Bob Dylan, who was born six years after Elvis Presley.) But the concerns of a 25-year-old who just wants to grab his girl and drive away from it all are different from those of a man with three children and some gray in his goatee.

Rock singers from Presley to Jim Morrison to Kurt Cobain never made that adjustment. After drawing their early songs from a fund of personal experience, they either found themselves bereft of inspiration or they burned out on fame. As for the rock-and-roll coming out of the radio today, it is solipsistic stuff, dense with self-loathing and anomie. ("Help me believe in anything / I want to be someone who believes," sings Adam Duritz of Counting Crows.) Springsteen, however, seems to have achieved a level of personal equipoise that has helped him to look out into the world and broaden himself as an artist. Twenty-five years ago he was anointed rock-and-roll's future. This month, Springsteen's most recent album, the largely solo and acoustic *Ghost of Tom Joad,* received a Grammy nomination for Best Contemporary Folk Album.

With its cast of immigrants, drifters and damaged veterans, *Tom Joad* taps directly into the populist political sensibility that always lurked in his music. Tom Joad is, of course, the protagonist of John Steinbeck's Dust Bowl novel, *The Grapes of Wrath,* and Springsteen's decision to link himself so explicitly with Steinbeck, an artist-activist competing for the public conscience if ever there was one, cast him into similarly charged terrain.

If this starkest Springsteen record hasn't yielded a string of hits, it has sold two million copies and enabled him to reconfigure his career. With the E Street Band dissolved, he is crossing the country in folkie musical raiment—alone with his harmonica and acoustic guitar—beginning his solo concerts with a song by that apostle of all liberal protest singers—Woody Guthrie—and making gingerly forays into radical social activism.

As he stands up on stage, describing jobless men in the Rust Belt, illegal immigrants running drugs in California and people sleeping under bridges, it's clear that what sets Springsteen apart from his peers is that he has succeeded in bringing a mature perspective to the music of youth. And to hear Springsteen explain it, that was always the plan.

It was halfway through October and Springsteen was making his way through the Middle West, telling audiences about the first time he saw the film adaptation of *The Grapes of Wrath*. "I grew up in a house where there wasn't a lot of culture, art or books around," he would say, cradling his guitar. "Everybody was busy trying to keep their heads above water. I was 26 when a friend showed me John Ford's film. I remember thinking that's what I wanted my work to be. I wanted it to have something to do with people's lives, to be about how people fall back upon love, and faith, and hope, and ultimately each other, even after the world reveals itself." Then he'd sing "Across the Border," his pretty song about hopeful tidings, which he delivers in a lush falsetto that is so different from his usual worn carburetor of a singing voice that people who haven't heard him do it before are astonished.

These concerts were full of conversational intervals. Springsteen talked about "people who spent 30 or 40 years of their life doing something they thought would provide them with some security and then they were deemed expendable," before singing his song about a fading industrial city, "Youngstown." He described himself as a kid listening to Elvis on the radio, explaining, "It was music that gave me a sense that life could be and should be about more than I had in front of me." He suggested that the scant wages paid to migrant workers for "backbreaking work" in the California produce fields might explain why so many Mexicans were working for drug dealers. A song on just that subject, "Sinaloa Cowboys," followed. Fatherhood, he said, made him realize that children "are a window onto the grace in this world." Then he said, "This is what happens when that grace gets violated," and sang "Balboa Park," which is about San Diego child prostitutes.

In Kalamazoo, Mich., Springsteen urged people to contribute to a local food bank—"especially now with the quote, unquote welfare reform." (Springsteen donates all of the income from the sale of T-shirts and other merchandise at his concerts to selected soup kitchens, veterans' groups and homeless shelters.) At every show he also spoke about his romantic disappointments, explaining that he was in the same relationship "for 30 years with a lot of different women" before a psychiatrist charged him "200 freaking bucks an hour" to figure out how to make something last.

An extremely private, even remote man for much of his life, Springsteen has never been diffident on stage. He might withhold himself from his family, girlfriends, band mates and the press, but his concerts have always been strewn both with picaresque monologues drawn from real events in his life, and with moments of straight personal revelation that can be jarringly frank. Audiences have heard him talk about being man-handled by the sadistic grammar-school nuns at St. Rose of Lima school in Freehold—stuffing him into a garbage can was just the start of it—and they've listened to Springsteen recount the details of his tortured relationship with his father. "When I was growing up there were two things that were unpopular in my house: me and my guitar," he might begin, before describing the day during the Vietnam War his father told Springsteen he hoped he'd be drafted, so the Army would "make a man out of you."

Over a grilled-cheese sandwich at a greasy spoon in Akron, Springsteen told me that even as a teen-ager he aimed to create a loyal audience that he could sing to over a lifetime. To do this he tried to let his audience know him. If people saw that the man stood for the same things the songs did, his music could be trusted. "I very consciously set out to develop an audience that was about more than buying records," he said. "I set out to find an audience that would be a reflection of some imagined community that I had in my head, that lived according to the values in my music and shared a similar set of ideals."

The next night, outside the Hill Auditorium on the University of Michigan campus in Ann Arbor, I had a talk with a woman who wouldn't tell me her name because she had called in sick at her job, got in the car and driven—she didn't like to say from where—many hours clear to Michigan to see Springsteen. "He's very real," she said. "He's not like a rock star who sets himself above everybody. These things he's talking about, the homeless, drug use, well, when the Boy Scouts come around now you're willing to contribute, not because you're a blind follower, but because he makes me think about my own life. I know people who vol-unteer at food banks because he always donates to food banks. You lis-ten to his music and these things are in your mind so it becomes the natural thing to do. I'm his age exactly. It's an adult outlook." She gestured to the clusters of Michigan undergraduates strolling into the theater. "There are a lot of college kids who listen to him now," she said. "I don't feel a generational barrier with them. He creates a common bond, a sense of community."

Standing nearby was Amanda Beaumont, a freshman from Grand Rapids. "I like him because he seems like he knows what the common people are going through," she said. "He seems like a different kind of rock star. I think people my age listen to him because he conveys a more meaningful message than Smashing Pumpkins or Pearl Jam."

They heard him exactly as he wanted them to, and it wasn't just in Ann Arbor. Everywhere I went, the audience Springsteen had imagined for himself seemed to be thriving. The allegiance was such that, as a woman in Kalamazoo put it, "By now we'd come to see this guy sing about anything, even about walking out to the driveway in the morning to pick up his newspaper." A California woman named Elizabeth Stanley, who began listening to Springsteen when she held a job installing dashboards on a General Motors assembly line, says: "He was talking about the kinds of things I saw people go through every day in the plant. Yearning for a better life. The contradiction between the fact that people are working hard and doing all the right things and that at the same time the possibilities for them are shrinking. It's amazing. He really captured the spirit of the work." Today Stanley's 13-year-old son is listening to Springsteen. Springsteen has done it. He is an intergenerational rock star with more than an audience. He has a public.

What made people so loyal to Springsteen was the extent of his musical commitment to them. Not only did he write songs which made it clear that he shared their concerns; he also gave performances that were epic displays of fidelity. For years his filial distress was such that when he faced a crowd he was looking for unconditional love. He was a kinetic performer, one who could make concert halls of any size feel intimate as barrooms as he catapulted himself about the stage, leaped out into the crowd, sweat like a spot welder, sang—and talked—himself hoarse. His band went to extraordinary lengths to keep up with him. The drummer Max Weinberg's hands routinely bled, while the guitar player Nils Lofgren drank so much espresso on stage that after concerts he lifted weights for hours before he could sleep. "You talk about James Brown as the hardest-working man in show business," says the soul singer Sam Moore, of Sam and Dave. "It's not true. This man was phenomenal."

When the show was over, Springsteen would return to his motel room, settle onto the edge of his bed with a notebook, a dictionary and a thesaurus and stay up until morning frantically writing songs with titles like "Prove It All Night." By creating music about people who trudged out of factories at the end of the day, he could honor such lives while avoiding the rug mill himself. His songs were full of romantic desperation, and they were his life. Springsteen was bent on impressing the importance of what he was doing upon his father, his hometown and his audience—the people who had given him a ticket out of Freehold. So he never touched drugs, never got too close to women, never did anything that might interfere with his work. Out on the road, when the E Street Band guitar player Steve Van Zandt and the saxophonist Clarence Clemons felt like going out to strip bars after shows, they kept their plans quiet. "Bruce was a very strong and mysterious person in those days," Van Zandt says. "People were afraid of him."

There are two films that Springsteen relies upon as the touchstones of his life. One is *The Grapes of Wrath,* which guides him as a writer. The other is another John Ford picture, *The Searchers.* It stars John Wayne as Ethan Edwards, a former Confederate soldier who, years after Appomattox, has been unable to put the war behind him and rejoin society. When his young niece (played by Natalie Wood) is kidnapped by Comanches, he spends years trying to find her. Finally he tracks her down and returns her to her people. Then he walks off again into the plains, alone.[2]

One Saturday, just after watching *The Searchers,* Springsteen was driving along the Jersey back roads. It was clear that he saw John Wayne's pistol as his guitar. "At the end of the film John Wayne has some realization as he reconstitutes that family that he can't join it," he said. "His inability to do that resonated with me. I spent 20 years playing on the road with no real home life or connections except when I played at night. Once I walked off the stage I didn't know how to do it, be part of it. Too much fear. I didn't have confidence that I could be accepted in the real world outside my work.

"I took my music just about as seriously as I could take anything," he went on. The Ford was zipping past road signs for Asbury Park, the blue-collar Jersey seaside resort town 15 miles east of Freehold that Springsteen's music has made famous. "I felt like I needed to. I don't know if I felt a lot of people had blown it before me. I was young and I was very intense about it. I saw it as redemptive. I was also so influenced by James Brown, and he took it real seriously, too. But there was a point where I was using the music for things that weren't so healthy—to play out my psychological problems. I needed a lot of distance. I was always fearful of coming too close. I finally decided music's a lot. But it's not everything."

In 1984 Springsteen made some signal changes in his life. Deciding that the band was too much of a "boy's club," he hired Patti Scialfa, an old friend from Asbury Park, to sing background vocals. He also bought a house. The next year he met and married Phillips, a blond former model from Oregon whom he had first seen acting in a 38 Special music video. The match was not popular with his audience. "People went into mourning when he married Julianne," says Elizabeth Stanley. "People felt he should have married a Jersey factory girl."

Springsteen says: "My first wife's one of the best people I've ever met. She's lovely, intelligent—a great person. But we were pretty different, and I realized I didn't know how to be married."

In 1988 Springsteen broke up the band, explaining that there were things he needed to try out on his own. He was separated from Phillips and headed for divorce when tabloid photographers in Italy sent back early word that Springsteen had fallen in love with his harmony singer. He married Scialfa, who grew up 10 miles away from him, in 1991 in Deal, the New Jersey town where her father owned a television shop. These days when fans spot Springsteen walking with his wife, they sometimes yell, "Hey, Patti, thank you for making him so happy!"

During the early years of his [first] marriage Springsteen would go off for lonely drives through central Jersey, ending up in Freehold, where he'd idle in front of the houses he'd grown up in, brooding about the past. From the stage he talked about feeling so unwelcome at home as a teen-ager that he spent the night in telephone booths. Then he'd sing a selection from the medley of downcast songs he wrote about his father over the years—"Adam Raised a Cain," "Independence Day," "My Father's House" and "Walk Like a Man." They all said, in effect, "I don't know what it always was with us."

Springsteen says he finally decided that "writing a song about something hoping somebody hears it is not the best way to work out your problems." He began visiting the psychiatrist and it helped. So did a certain softness that his father was betraying. After one show, Douglas

Springsteen was sitting in a chair backstage. "Bruce," he said, "I want you to come over here and sit in my lap."

"Dad, you sure?" said Springsteen.

"Son, I want you to sit on my lap," he said.

"So," says Springsteen, "I did."

Today, with no band on hand, things on stage are obviously quite different. Yet Springsteen is such a charismatic performer that his concerts remain stirring occasions. His concern for musical precision is, if anything, keener than ever. After each song, a man hands Springsteen a new, freshly tuned guitar. (In all, there are 17 guitars, each tuned to the specifications of a different song, lined up every night just off stage right.) During his early years playing in bar bands with names like Steel Mill in the towns around Asbury Park, Springsteen was known primarily as a guitar impresario. He's still awfully good—he never misses a note and gets enough noise out of the instrument that he's tantamount to a small band up there, picking the melody, adding tempo, supplementing it with a couple of strands of harmony, tapping out rhythm on the body, switching to slide once in a while and sometimes whacking the strings the way a drummer might his skins. His voice is neither smooth nor graceful, but his music is about emotion and the vocal imperfections fit the material as comfortably as old flannel. Not every singer learns the full capabilities of his voice. Springsteen, however, is someone who goes to the Metropolitan Opera just to admire what a gifted set of pipes can do with a song. He has visited every corner of his own voice, and he knows how to work them all. No singer ever made more of less.

He isn't plunging into the crowd anymore, but in quieter ways he remains an athletic performer, a butane showman who can make a noir ballad like "Highway 29" broil with sexual hostility. In Ann Arbor, by the end of Springsteen's sixth encore, people were standing on their chairs extending their arms the way fundamentalist worshipers do during church services. Suddenly Springsteen came out for yet another "last one." This turned out to be a song which he'd just dashed off called "Michigan." "It's a stinker, folks," he warned, and it was, but nobody minded. Then he leaned out to the crowd, shook some hands and pounded his heart.

An hour later, with the auditorium now clear, he wandered out into the empty seats and sat down by himself. Watching him carefully, as always, was a burly Vietnam Special Forces veteran named Terry Magovern. Springsteen met him 25 years ago in the Captain's Garter, the Jersey Shore bar Magovern was running at the time. They liked each other, and Magovern was soon convinced to become Springsteen's aide de camp. Gazing at Springsteen now, Magovern said that Springsteen will often stick around the concert hall for hours after shows while he waits for the "mental adrenaline" to stop whirring through his head. "He begins to feel a deep closeness to the building," Magovern said. "He really feels the place, and he can't easily tear himself away."

For all of Springsteen's potent skills as a musician and performer, his lyrics are what bring the real drama to his shows. The best of his songs have all the tension and complexity of great short fiction. "'Jungleland' and 'Meeting Across the River' pack as much punch in a few minutes as I got into *City of Hope,* which is a whole movie," says the filmmaker and novelist John Sayles. The same might be said of Springsteen's best song on the *Joad* album, "Youngstown." Nominally the story of the bitterness a family of iron scarfers feels after the big blast furnace they call Jenny closes, the song also expresses Springsteen's most familiar theme, the juxtaposition of a mythical America where anything is possible with the crushing reality of a country that keeps letting hardworking people down:

> *Well my daddy worked the furnaces*
> *Kept 'em hotter than hell*
> *I come home from 'Nam, worked my way to scarfer . . .*

When Springsteen played "Youngstown" in the Middle West, the audiences kept so still that you could hear people being moved.

Springsteen's writing has evolved nearly as profoundly over the years as have his emotions. The early albums, *Greetings from Asbury Park, N.J.* and *The Wild, the Innocent & the E Street Shuffle* are crammed with free-form wordplay—"Dethrone the Dictaphone, hit it in its funny bone, that's where they expect it least"—and colorful images of switchblade lovers and factory girls promenading the boardwalk. Then came the adolescent anthems to go-for-broke freedom like "Thunder Road," "Backstreets" and "Born to Run." Vividly poetic language—"There were ghosts in the eyes / Of all the boys you sent away / They haunt this dusty beach road . . ."—was set to layers of brass and keyboards that owed a lot to the pop producer Phil Spector. Over the next few years Springsteen responded to books he was reading by Flannery O'Connor and James M. Cain and to the country songs of Hank Williams and Merle Haggard by writing spare, hard-boiled ballads like "Stolen Car" and "Atlantic City." Today his songs are stripped down even further, so that nearly all of the lyrical bravura is gone and what remains are chiseled vignettes of people whose troubles will be familiar to anyone who reads the newspapers as carefully as Springsteen does.

"I've always been trying to write about what it's like to be my age in this particular point in history," Springsteen was saying. "People don't stay the same. When I wrote *Greetings from Asbury Park*, those lyrics felt like life to me. I wouldn't know how to do that now. I couldn't write another 'Thunder Road' now either. I wouldn't want to. It was who we were then. In those days my writing came out of things that influenced me musically. I was drawing from classic American images that I found in the songs of Chuck Berry, Bob Dylan and the Beach Boys, and in my own life.

"But there was a point where some of the issues rock-and-roll addressed stopped. You've got your Saturday night, but you're gonna have to wake up the next morning, pal, and you'll have to face the consequences of the choices you make. Rock had been mainly about avoiding those choices. Country musicians like Hank Williams and Merle Haggard asked the hard questions I was beginning to ask myself. After *Born to Run*, it was, O.K., now what? Country was concerned with how you go on living after you reach adulthood.[3] I said, well why can't rock ask those same questions. Because the audience is going to be asking those questions real soon. Then, at a certain point, the questions country music was asking seemed to stop, so I moved into listening to a lot of Woody Guthrie. He seemed to me to have a bigger, broader canvas."

If Springsteen has relied on other artists to guide his ideas about how to tell a story, for most of his career he took his actual subjects directly from what he saw around him. He could write songs like "Night" and "Racing in the Street," about how people with dreary jobs get through life, because he was the son of a man who drove a truck route, worked at a rug mill and lost some of his hearing on the night shift at a plastics factory. It wasn't just his father: life was a scrimmage for just about everyone Springsteen grew up with, and they responded in different ways. The "Jungleland" kids who frolic " 'neath that giant Exxon sign"—it's still there in Freehold—are the kind of people Springsteen knew. The girl who gets pregnant at 17 in *The River* is his older sister. Springsteen was making a drama out of his life in the Jersey flats, but because every town has similar people enduring similar struggles, the appeal was universal.

Lately his inspirations are people he hasn't had such sustained and intimate contact with. Springsteen came upon the millworkers in "Youngstown" by reading a book about the dispossessed in America called *Journey to Nowhere*. "Balboa Park," his song about San Diego street kids, occurred to him after he saw an article headlined "Children of the Border" in *The Los Angeles Times*.[4] (He has never been to Balboa Park.) Another *Los Angeles Times* article called "California's Illicit Farm Belt Export"[5] helped him to write "Sinaloa Cowboys," the ballad of two Mexican brothers who work in a central California drug lab.

Critics of these songs have written that the lyrics fail to suggest a means of change, in the way folk music often does, or that they lack musical variety—they are wooden, too unmelodic and glum. There are also those who think Springsteen has become pretentious and say they wish he would get back to what he knows: "Shh. Artist at work" sneered the British rock magazine *Q*.

Springsteen was shaking his head. He said that the flesh of his new songs might be different, but the impulses remained the same as ever. The struggling blue-collar workers he wrote about in records like *Darkness on the Edge of Town* and *The River* and the edgy, alienated types who populate *Nebraska* are, he said, confronting the same issues as the cast of immigrants and Californians in *Tom Joad*. "Today it's just different people with different skin color. But there's the same sense that people have been abandoned in some fashion. They're not rebels. They're on the outside trying to find their way in, and the forces that are keeping that from happening are social forces or their own internal psychology. These things all overlap."

He was sitting beside the fireplace in his rambling colonial house in Jersey horse country with a guitar in his lap. There is never one far from him. "I had an interest in writing about the country—all of it. I was creating intimate portraits of individuals that you can draw back from and look at them in the context of the country they live in. You have to find circumstances where those characters resonate with psychological, emotional and, by implication, political issues."

Picking up the guitar, Springsteen began singing "The Line," a song on *Tom Joad* about a widower named Carl who, after taking a job as a California border patrolman, walks into a Tijuana bar where he encounters a pretty Mexican woman looking to go north. After singing four lines Springsteen said: "That's the personal side, that's the motivation for the guy's behavior. You've got somebody in a volatile state who's placed himself in a volatile job." He sang a few more lines in which another patrolman says, "We send 'em home and they come right back again / Carl, hunger is a powerful thing."

"That sets up the social context," Springsteen said. "Now you've got an internal and an external point of view. You're set up for something to happen and you've got to decide what it'll be." The next lines describe some of the people Carl finds himself turning back into Mexico. "The border's not what it appears," Springsteen said. "Hey, there's kids, women with children, mountain people, farm people. All of a sudden there's ambivalence mixed up with unresolved social issues, and with unresolved personal issues, and they come crashing together. Now I'm not thinking this when I'm writing it. I'm just trying to find a story. You're operating on your instinct, your feelings and ultimately, something you're trying to say about yourself. You're writing on because it's working."

Very few American popular musicians of Springsteen's stature have managed to keep writing on over a lifetime. In Springsteen's generation, only Paul Simon and Merle Haggard wrote great American popular songs as young men and continue to do so at a high level now. Johnny Cash, Bob Dylan, Chuck Berry, Joni Mitchell, Brian Wilson—they are all long past their primes. There are many reasons for Springsteen's continued vitality as a songwriter. Like Simon, he won't schedule a concert tour until he has new songs to sing, and when fans clamor for the old hits he'll cheerfully say: "Let me put you right at ease. I ain't gonna do none of those suckas tonight." He hasn't abused his body with drugs or liquor. And he always refused to let record companies—or anyone else—push him to produce new albums sooner than he was ready to. Primarily, though, the explanation is that he has never lost interest in the world.

"We compliment you on what you said to Dole," Sam Venti was saying.

"Well, I try to mind my own business, but enough's enough," Springsteen replied.

It was early October, and two days before, during a presidential campaign tour of the Northeast, Bob Dole had pulled into Springsteen's part of central New Jersey, with Springsteen's song "Born in the U.S.A." blaring from his bus. The following afternoon *The Asbury Park Press* received this brief letter from Springsteen: "I read in *The Press* this morning that my music was appropriated for the Republican rally for Bob Dole in Red Bank yesterday. Just for the record, I'd like to make clear that it was used without my permission and I am not a supporter of the Republican ticket."

"Shoulda gave 'em four barrels," Sam Venti crowed.

Springsteen looked pleased. "I've got a lot of support locally," he said.

He was in Freehold, just driving around. It's not a large place, and it hadn't taken long to pass by St. Rose of Lima, the Catholic church where he'd gone to parochial school as a boy, the office that his mother walked to every day for her job as a legal secretary and the abandoned rug mill where his father once worked. Springsteen lived for a while in Los Angeles, where he still owns a home, but he now spends most of his time back in New Jersey, a few towns away from Freehold. He is always taking his children—the eldest is now 6—through Freehold to visit their great aunts. At the moment, he was even plotting to give a concert in the gymnasium at St. Rose of Lima. "Imagine that," Springsteen said, and he chuckled.

Not far from the Nescafé factory—"On a rainy day you'd smell coffee through the whole town"—was the two-family house on Institute Street where he lived as a kid for eight years. Suddenly, he switched off the engine, got out of the Ford and walked over to his old kitchen window. "Hey Mike," he shouted. "Mike, it's me!" A moment later a delighted man in a Penn State sweatshirt was handing him a beer.

The apartment where Springsteen's truck-driver neighbor used to live now belongs to Sam Venti's daughter, Joan Kress, a somewhat voluble middle-aged woman, and no sooner did Joan hear the laugh that her door flung open and she was bustling Springsteen into her kitchen. "I got pork chops in the oven," she said. Several other people were in the kitchen as well, and quickly enough they were all filling Springsteen in on who was going senile, how someone else had looked in the casket and letting him know that they, too, appreciated him taking on that muckety-muck Bob Dole. Springsteen was eyeing the pork chops.

"Joan, I can't," he said finally. "Patti's got the whole thing going and I got to go home with an appetite." And home he went—for turkey and mashed potatoes. There was broccoli too, but Springsteen skipped it. "Only thing I have in common with George Bush," he said, and he laughed. Then he said, "Boy, those pork chops, they looked good."

Springsteen is both an enthusiast and a person who is interested in other people's enthusiasms. During his free time in the Middle West, Springsteen went for walks to look over the old factory towns he was singing in. With his weathered coat and creaky gait he fit right in, and in Akron at least, nobody recognized him. Not that he would have objected. How could he? At age 25, on a visit to Memphis, Springsteen scaled the wall at Graceland in the middle of the night in the hope of glimpsing Elvis Presley. ("The King" was off in Lake Tahoe, it turned out.) Springsteen loves to meet people. Sixteen years ago in St. Louis, a young man walked up to him in a theater after a Woody Allen movie and said hello. They talked for a while and then the man invited him home to his mother's house for dinner. Springsteen went, had a fine time and still keeps in touch.

"How'd you get into that?" he's always asking, once people tell him what they do. There are obvious benefits to such encounters. On a motorcycle trip across Arizona, a Mexican man Springsteen met in a small-town cafe told him about his dead brother. Springsteen was thinking of him when he wrote "Sinaloa Cowboys."

What anyone who spends even a little time with Bruce Springsteen comes to appreciate is his complete lack of affect. "He's a very honest, gentle guy," says the folk singer Pete Seeger. "Not showoffish. I once read an interview with him where he said that a rock musician can stay honest if he can look down into the footlights and see his own face reflected there. I wrote his manager, Jon Landau, a letter after I saw that saying that it's really great that you've managed [to] stay normal good people despite the huge amount of publicity and big sales. Think of how many people's lives have been ruined by fame."

The rarefied celebrity existence never held any appeal for Springsteen. In 1975, on his first trip to Europe, he arrived in London to find posters describing him as the future of rock-and-roll all over town. He tore down every one he saw. Even his move to Los Angeles in the 1980s—much reviled by his fans—was actually predicated on his desire for normalcy. After *Born in the U.S.A.* made him a pop idol, a city that was inured to movie stars like Los Angeles was an easier place to get around than New Jersey. "Ninety percent of rock-star isolation is invented," Springsteen says. "I think a lot of people choose to withdraw from the world. To me, I go to the grocery store. It's not an issue. If somebody on the way there says to me, 'Hey, I like your music,' well, if that bothers you, stay home. I believe when I had some success my world expanded. I had to try not to think of myself as the Boss, but it always seemed ridiculous to me. It seemed silly. You draw your music from your experiences."

Springsteen lives in a home scattered with toys. He is always willing to sing for the class, and never misses a birthday party or a fireman's fair. His concerts are rarely on weekends anymore, and when he is abroad he remains on his family's time schedule, sitting up reading, writing and telephoning home several times during the night. "I didn't work 30 years as hard as I could to miss my kids' growing up," he says.

Springsteen was always a man who took great interest in life around him, but parenthood seems to have sharpened his concerns about the kind of world he's sending his children into. It's perhaps for that reason that he has become more aggressive in expressing his feelings on the political and social issues of the day. Where in the past he appealed to people of conservative mind as easily as liberals, in these less reticent times his decidedly progressive views can create tension both in his songs, and within his audience.

Five days before the affirmative-action rally in Los Angeles, Springsteen gave a concert in Fresno. The city is the hub of the Central Valley, and many of the produce growers who hire migrant workers to do their harvesting live there. They liked it when Springsteen said he had decided that it was time to stop writing songs about his father. "Done that," he said. "Slap me if I do it again." The reaction was cooler when he introduced "Sinaloa Cowboys" by saying, "Sixty years after John Steinbeck wrote *The Grapes of Wrath,* people are working under conditions in the Central Valley that as Americans we really shouldn't tolerate." When he talked about his belief in affirmative action, people were shaking their heads and frowning. Afterward, two women asked for—and were given—their money back. But an old Mexican man walked up to Springsteen and said: "Tonight I felt the spirit of God in there. Bless you, sir."

Three days later, Jon Landau flew out from New York to see Springsteen sing in the largely Republican city of Santa Barbara. Landau seemed somewhat nonplussed by the spectacle of Springsteen saying things like,

"If you believe that California has metamorphasized into a race-and-gender-blind society, you also believe in a Santa Claus."

"A transformation is taking place," Landau said. "For Bruce Springsteen it always used to be just to be as creative as possible. Now with Steinbeck and Woody Guthrie, they did something he's drawn to. How does it suit him? He's figuring that out now."

In the past, Springsteen says, he held back from such commentary because "I was a little frightened. Not completely sure of myself. I haven't had an extensive education and I was also trying to sort out my personal life and having a tough time doing it." If he couldn't handle himself, was his thinking, who was he to tell other people how to live. Springsteen also fretted that perhaps it was inappropriate for a millionaire to be stepping forward to describe how it was for the less fortunate.

There were other reservations. Ever conscious of how his public saw him, Springsteen, the man of the people, didn't want to court the perception that he was getting above his raising. Nor did he like the idea that he might be viewed as a charlatan. This is a concern that yet runs deep in him. "I never claim to have any big social conscience," he says.

It was Steinbeck's example that pushed him forward. Once, when he was explaining what he admired so much about the novelist, Springsteen said simply, "he risked himself—he hung it all out there." Ultimately, that's the kind of guy Springsteen wants to be, too.

"Look," he says, "I don't see myself as the voice of whatever. I think a lot of the motivation for the music I've written comes from my own background. I understand joblessness like I do because I grew up in a house with a sense of dispossession. That sort of results in frustration and anger. I didn't start out with a specific political point of view. I don't sit down and write with political intentions. It's much more internal. The things I've written about best over my entire career are things I know about. The idea of the wasted life. The idea of the pure unkindness of the world. In some fashion I always felt that I wrote about those things feeling a connection with my own father that I didn't have growing up. It was a way of saying, 'I remember this.'"

As someone who has spent his life advocating fairness and opportunity, it was with growing disgust that Springsteen watched another presidential election season unfold featuring candidates who struck him as unlikely to take an interest in improving the lives of the kinds of people he writes about. "The old story," he said. "I didn't see anybody, not Clinton or Dole, addressing the concerns of working people. Holding onto the things you've worked for, the deep fear of displacement, the fact that you're useful only as long as you're useful. I always thought, gee, people should be guaranteed the right to work. You know, being 45 or 50, you've worked your whole life, and then there's somebody telling you that's it. Your work's caught up so deeply in who you are. The ability to have a job, support a family, create a home, feel a part of a community, those are the things that keep people sane and bring them fulfillment. To have such a large percentage of people in such a wealthy country whose basic needs haven't been met, that's a terrible moral failing. That should be our bridge to the 21st century, to straighten these things out."

Backstage in San Diego, a little boy asked Springsteen why he was speaking out so vigorously against Proposition 209. "Because it's bad," he said, "and sometimes you've just got to stand up and say, 'Hey.'"

Notes

1. Nicholas Dawidoff, *In the Country of Country: A Journey to the Roots of American Music* (New York: Vintage, 1998), p. 311.
2. Film critic Richard Blake, who is also a Jesuit priest, analyzes John Ford's classic movie *The Searchers* from a Catholic perspective. The John Wayne character, Ethan Edwards, writes Father Blake, "is completely alienated from any notion of home . . . [h]e embodies 'the search,' and when it ends, he has nothing else to live for." See Richard A. Blake, *Afterimage: The Indelible Catholic Imagination of Six American Filmmakers* (Chicago: Loyola Press, 2000), p. 160.
3. Dawidoff refers to Springsteen writing a "batch of what he offhandedly refers to as 'South Jersey cowboy songs.'" See *In the Country of Country*, p. 311. In a related vein, Springsteen biographer Dave Marsh has referred to the *Nebraska* demos as having "the quality of stillness associated with the great Library of Congress folk recordings of the 1930s and 1940s. . . ." See Dave Marsh, *Glory Days: Bruce Springsteen in the 1980s* (New York: Pantheon, 1987), p. 112.
4. See Sebastian Rotella, "Children of the Border," *Los Angeles Times*, April 3, 1993.
5. See Mark Arax and Tom Gorman, "California's Illicit Farm Belt Export," *Los Angeles Times*, March 13, 1995.

Mikal Gilmore

∎

Mikal Gilmore, one of the finest journalists around today, has written about rock and culture for the *Los Angeles Times,* the *Los Angeles Herald Examiner, L.A. Weekly,* and *Rolling Stone.* He was music editor for *L.A. Weekly* and the *Los Angeles Herald Examiner.* His first book, *Shot in the Heart* (1994), a devastating account of growing up the brother of murderer Gary Gilmore, won the L.A. Times Book Prize and the National Book Critics Circle Award, and was a *New York Times* Notable Book of the Year. The following essay—a combination of pieces that appeared in *Rolling Stone* and the *Los Angeles Herald Examiner,* as well as some new material—is a brilliant analysis of Springsteen's career from *Greetings from Asbury Park, N.J.* to *The Ghost of Tom Joad,* and what it means to be an American. It is taken from *Night Beat: A Shadow History of Rock & Roll* (1998).

Bruce Springsteen's America

from *Night Beat: A Shadow History of Rock & Roll*

■ON THE NIGHT of November 5, 1980, Bruce Springsteen stood onstage in Tempe, Arizona, and began a fierce fight for the meaning of America. The previous day, the nation had turned a fateful corner: With a stunning majority, Ronald Reagan—who had campaigned to end the progressive dream in America—was elected president of the United States. It was hardly an unexpected victory. In the aftermath of Vietnam, Watergate, the hostage crisis in Iran, and an ongoing economic recession, America had developed serious doubts about its purpose and its future, and to many observers, Reagan seemed an inspiring and easy response to those hardships. But when all was said and done, the election felt stunning and brutal, a harbinger for the years of mean-spiritedness to come.

The singer was up late the night before, watching the election returns, and stayed in his hotel room the whole day, brooding over whether he should make a comment on the turn of events. Finally, onstage that night at Arizona State University, Springsteen stood silently for a moment, fingering his guitar nervously, and then told his audience: "I don't know what you guys think about what happened last night, but I think it was pretty frightening." Then he vaulted into an enraged version of his most defiant song, "Badlands."[1]

On that occasion, "Badlands" stood for everything it had always stood for—a refusal to accept life's meanest fates or most painful limitations—but it also became something more: a warning about the spitefulness that was about to visit our land, as the social and political horizon turned dark and frightening. "I want to spit in the face of these badlands," Springsteen sang with an unprecedented fury on that night, and it was perhaps in that instant that he reconceived his role in rock & roll.

In a way, his action foreshadowed the political activism and social controversy that would transform rock & roll during the 1980s. As the decade wore on, Springsteen would become one of the most outspoken figures in pop music, though that future probably wasn't what he had in mind when he vaulted into "Badlands" on that late autumn night. Instead, Springsteen was simply focusing on a question that, in one form or another, his music had been asking all along. In a way it was a simple and time-old question: Namely, what does it mean to be born an American?

Well, what does it mean to be born in America? Does it mean being born to birthrights of freedom, opportunity, equity, and bounty? If so, then what does it mean that so many of the country's citizens never truly connect with or receive those blessings? And what does it mean that, in a land of such matchless vision and hope, the acrid realities of fear, repression, hatred, deprivation, racism, and sexism also hold sway? Does it mean, indeed, that we *are* living in badlands?

Questions of this sort—about America's nature and purpose, about the distance between its ideals and its truths—are, of course, as old as the nation itself, and finding revealing or liberating answers to those questions is a venture that has obsessed (and eluded) many of the country's worthiest artists, from Nathaniel Hawthorne to Norman Mailer, from D. W. Griffith to Francis Coppola. Rock & roll—an art form born of a provocative mix of American myths, impulses, and guilts—has also aimed, from time to time, to pursue those questions, to mixed effect. In the 1960s, in a period of intense generational division and political rancor, Bob Dylan and the Band explored the idea of America as a wounded family in works like *The Basement Tapes, John Wesley Harding,* and *The Band;* in the end, though, the artists shied from the subject, as if something about the American family's complex, troubled blood ties proved too formidable. Years later, Neil Young (like the Band's Robbie Robertson, a Canadian with a fixation on American myths) confronted the specter of forsworn history in works like *American Stars 'n' Bars, Hawks and Doves,* and *Freedom.* Yet, like too many artists or politicians who come face to face with how America has recanted its own best promises, Young finally didn't seem to know what to say about such losses. When all is said and done, it is chiefly pre-rock singers (most notably, Robert Johnson, Hank Williams, Woody Guthrie, Charley Patton, and a few other early blues and country singers) and a handful of early rock & roll figures—Elvis Presley, Chuck Berry, Jerry Lee Lewis—who have come closest to personifying the meaning of America in their music. In particular, Presley (a seminal influence on Springsteen) tried to seize the nation's dream of fortune and make himself a symbol of it. But once Presley and those others had seized that dream, the dream found a way of undoing them—leading them to heartbreak, decline, death. American callings, American fates.

Bruce Springsteen followed his own version of the fleeting American Dream. He had grown up in the suburban town of Freehold, New Jersey, feeling estranged from his family and community, and his refusal to accept the limitations of that life fueled the songwriting in his early, largely autobiographical albums. Records like *Greetings from Asbury Park; The Wild, the Innocent, and the E Street Shuffle;* and *Born to Run* were works about flight from dead-end small-town life and thankless familial obligations, and they accomplished for Springsteen the very dream that he was writing about: That is, those records lifted him from a life of mundane reality and delivered him to a place of bracing purpose. From the outset, Springsteen was heralded by critics as one of the brightest hopes in rock & roll—a consummate songwriter and live performer, who was as alluring and provoking as Presley, and as imaginative and expressive as Dylan. And Springsteen lived up to the hoopla: With his 1975 album *Born to Run,* Springsteen fashioned pop's most form-stretching and eventful major work since the Beatles' *Sgt. Pepper's Lonely Hearts Club Band.* But for the praise and fame the album won him, it couldn't rid Springsteen of his fears of solitude, and it couldn't erase his memory of the lives of his family and friends. Consequently, his next work, *Darkness on the Edge of Town*, was a stark and often bitter re-flection on how a person could win his dreams and yet still find himself dwelling in a dark and lonely place—a story of ambition and loss as ill-starred (and deeply American) as *Citizen Kane*.

With *The River*, released in 1980, Springsteen was still writing about characters straining against the restrictions of their world, but he was also starting to look at the social conditions that bred lives split between dilemmas of flight and ruin. In Springsteen's emerging mythos, people still had big hopes, but often settled for deluded loves and fated families, in which their hopes quickly turned ugly and caustic. In the album's haunting title song, the youthful narrator gets his girlfriend pregnant, and then enters a joyless marriage and a toilsome job in order to meet his obligations. Eventually, all the emotional and economic realities close in, and the singer's marriage turns into a living, grievous metaphor for lost idealism. "Now, all them things that seemed so important," sings Spring-steen, in a rueful voice, "Well, mister, they vanished into the air. . . ." In *The River*'s murky and desultory world—the world of post-Vietnam, post-industrial America—people long for fulfillment and connection, but often as not, they end up driving empty mean streets in after-midnight funks, fleeing from a painful nothingness into a more deadening nothingness. It's as if some dire force beyond their own temperaments was drawing them into inescapable ends.

The River was Springsteen's pivotal statement. Up to this point, Springsteen had told his tales in florid language, in musical settings that were occasionally operatic and showy. Now he was streamlining both the lyrics and the music into simpler, more colloquial structures, as if the re-alities he was trying to dissect were too bleak to bear up under his ear-lier expansiveness. *The River* was also the record with which Springsteen began wielding rock & roll less as a tool of personal mythology—that is, as a way of making or entering history for personal validation. Instead, he began using it as a means of *looking* at history, as a way of under-standing how the lives of the people in his songs had been shaped by the conditions surrounding them, and by forces beyond their control.

This drive to comprehend history came to the fore during the singer's remarkable 1980–81 tour in support of *The River*. Springsteen had never viewed himself as a political-minded performer, but a series of events and influences—including the near-disaster at the Three Mile Island nu-clear reactor, and his subsequent participation in the No Nukes benefit, at New York City's Madison Square Garden in September 1979—began to alter that perception. Springsteen had also read Joe Klein's biography of folk singer Woody Guthrie and was impressed with the way popular songs could work as a powerful and binding force for social consciousness and political action. In addition, he read Ron Kovic's harrowing personal account of the Vietnam War, *Born on the Fourth of July*. Inspired by the candor of Kovic's anguish—and by the bravery and dignity of numerous other Vietnam veterans he had met—Springsteen staged a benefit at the L.A. Sports Arena in August 1981, to raise funds and attention for the Vietnam Veterans of America (a group whose causes and rights the American Legion and Veterans of Foreign Wars had steadfastly refused to embrace). On one night of the Los Angeles engagement, Springsteen told his audience that he had recently read Henry Steele Commager and Allen [*sic*] Nevin's *Short History of the United States* and that he was profoundly affected by what he found in the book. A month earlier, speaking of the same book, he had told a New Jersey audience: "The idea [of America] was that there'd be a place for everybody, no matter where you came from . . . you could help make a life that had some decency and dignity to it. But like all ideals, that idea got real corrupted. . . . I didn't know what the government I lived under was doing. It's important to know . . . about the things around you." Now, onstage in Los Angeles, getting ready to sing Woody Guthrie's "This Land Is Your Land," Springsteen spoke in a soft, almost bashful voice, and told his largely well-off audience: "There's a lot in [the history of the United States] . . . that we're proud of, and then there's a lot of things in it that you're ashamed of. And that burden, that burden of shame, falls down. Falls down on everybody."

In 1982, after the tour ended, Springsteen was poised for the sort of massive breakthrough that people had been predicting for nearly a decade. *The River* had gone to the top of *Billboard*'s albums chart, and "Hungry Hearts" [*sic*] was a Top 10 single; it seemed that Springsteen was finally overcoming much of the popular backlash that had set in several years earlier, after numerous critics hailed him as rock & roll's imminent crown prince. But after the tour, the singer was unsure about what direction he wanted to take in his songwriting. He spent some time driving around the country, brooding, reading, thinking about the realities of his own emotional life and the social conditions around him, and then settled down and wrote a body of songs about his ruminations. On January 3, 1982, Springsteen sat in his home and recorded a four-track demo cassette of the new songs, accompanied for the most part only by his ghostly sounding acoustic guitar. He later presented the songs to producer Jon Landau and the E Street Band, but neither Landau nor the musicians could find the right way to flesh out the doleful, spare-sounding new material. Finally, at Landau's behest, Springsteen released the original demo versions of the songs as a solo effort, entitled *Nebraska*. It was a work like very few in pop music history: a politically piercing statement that was utterly free of a single instance of didactic sloganeering or ideological proclamation. Rather than preach to or berate his listeners, Springsteen created a vivid cast of characters—people who had been shattered by bad fortune, by limitations, by mounting debts and losses— and then he let those characters tell the stories of how their pain spilled over into despair and, sometimes, violence. In "Johnny 99," he told the story of a working man who is pressed beyond his resources and in desperation, commits robbery and impulsive murder. Johnny doesn't seek absolution for what he's done—he even requests his own execution. Just before sentence is passed, Johnny says: "Now judge I got debts no honest man could pay. . . . But it was more'n all this that put that gun in my hand." In "Highway Patrolman," Springsteen related the tale of an idealistic cop who allows his brother to escape the law, recognizing that the brother has already suffered pain from the country he once served.

There was a timeless, folkish feel to *Nebraska*'s music, but the themes and events it related were as dangerous and timely as the daily headlines of the 1980s—or of the 1990s, for that matter. It was a record about what can occur when normal people are forced to endure what cannot be endured. Springsteen's point was that, until we understood how these people arrived at their places of ruin, until we accepted our connection to those who had been hurt or excluded beyond repair, then America could not be free of such fates or such crimes. "The idea of America as a family is naïve, maybe sentimental or simplistic," he told me in a 1987 interview, "but it's a good idea. And if people are sick and hurting and lost, I guess it falls on everybody to address those problems in some fashion. Because injustice, and the price of that injustice, falls on everyone's heads. The economic injustice falls on everybody's head and steals everyone's freedom. Your wife can't walk down the street at night. People keep guns in their homes. They live with a greater sense of apprehension, anxiety, and fear than they would in a more just and open society. It's not an accident, and it's not simply that there are 'bad' people out there. It's an inbred part of the way that we are all living: It's a product of what we have accepted, what we have acceded to. And whether we mean it or not, our silence has spoken for us in some fashion."

Nebraska attempted to make a substantial statement about the modern American sensibility in a stark and austere style that demanded close involvement. That is, the songs required that you settle into their mournful textures and racking tales and then apply the hard facts of their meaning to the social reality around you. In contrast to Springsteen's earlier bravado, there was nothing eager or indomitable about *Nebraska*. Instead, it was a record that worked at the opposite end of those conditions, a record about people walking the rim of desolation, who sometimes transform their despair into the irrevocable action of murder. It was not exulting or uplifting, and for that reason, it was a record that many listeners respected more than they "enjoyed." Certainly, it was not a record by which an artist might expand his audience in the fun-minded world of pop.

But with his next record, *Born in the U.S.A.,* in 1984, Springsteen set out to find what it might mean to bring his message to the largest possible audience. Like *Nebraska, Born in the U.S.A.* was about people who come to realize that life turns out harder, more hurtful, more close-fisted than they might have expected. But in contrast to *Nebraska's* killers and losers, *Born in the U.S.A.'s* characters hold back the night as best they can, whether it's by singing, laughing, dancing, yearning, reminiscing, or entering into desperate love affairs. There was something celebratory about how these people faced their hardships. It's as if Springsteen were saying that life is made to endure and that we all make peace with private suffering and shared sorrow as best we can.

At the same time, a listener didn't have to dwell on these truths to appreciate the record. Indeed, Springsteen and Landau had designed the album with contemporary pop style in mind—which is to say, it had been designed with as much meticulous attention to its captivating and lively surfaces as to its deeper and darker meanings. Consequently, a track like "Dancing in the Dark"—perhaps the most pointed and personal song Springsteen has ever written about isolation—came off as a rousing dance tune that had the effect of working against isolation by pulling an audience together in a physical celebration. Similarly, "Cover Me,"

"Downbound Train," and "I'm on Fire"—songs about erotic fear and paralyzing loneliness—came off as sexy, intimate, and irresistible.

But it was the terrifying and commanding title song—about a Vietnam veteran who has lost his brother, his hope, and his faith in his country—that did the most to secure Springsteen's new image as pop hero and that also turned his fame into something complex and troubling. Scan the song for its lyrics alone, and you find a tale of outright devastation: a tale of an American whose birthrights have been torn from his grasp, and paid off with indelible memories of violence and ruin. But listen to the song merely for its fusillade of drums and its firestorm of guitar, or for the singer's roaring proclamation, "*BORN* in the U.S.A. / I was *BORN* in the U.S.A.," and it's possible to hear it as a fierce patriotic assertion—especially in a political climate in which simpleminded patriotic fervor had attained a new and startling credibility. Watching Springsteen unfurl the song in concert—slamming it across with palpable rage as his audience waved flags of all sizes in response—it was possible to read the song in both directions at once. "Clearly the key to the enormous explosion of Bruce's popularity is the misunderstanding [of the song 'Born in the U.S.A.']," wrote critic Greil Marcus during the peak of Springsteen's popularity. "He is a tribute to the fact that people hear what they want."

One listener who was quite happy to hear only what he wanted was syndicated conservative columnist George Will, who in the middle of the 1984 campaign that pitted Walter Mondale against Ronald Reagan attended a Springsteen show, and liked what he saw. In a September 14, 1984, column that was read by millions, Will commended Springsteen for his "elemental American values" and, predictably, heard the cry of "Born in the U.S.A." as an exultation rather than as pained fury. "I have not got a clue about Springsteen's politics, if any," Will wrote, "but flags get waved at his concerts while he sings about hard times. He is no whiner, and the recitation of closed factories and other problems always seem punctuated by a grand, cheerful affirmation: 'Born in the U.S.A.!'"

Apparently, Reagan's advisors gave a cursory listening to Springsteen's music and agreed with Will. A few days later, in a campaign stop in New Jersey, President Ronald Reagan declared: "America's future rests in a thousand dreams inside your hearts. It rests in the message of hope in songs of a man so many young Americans admire: New Jersey's Bruce Springsteen. And helping you make those dreams come true is what this job of mine is all about."

It was an amazing—even brain-boggling—assertion. Reagan's tribute to Springsteen seemed about as stupefying as if Lyndon Johnson, during the awful uproar over Vietnam, had cited Bob Dylan for his noble influence on America's youth politics, or as unnerving as if Richard Nixon, with his strong disregard for black social realities, had honored Sly Stone for the cutting commentary of his 1971 classic *There's a Riot Goin' On*. Clearly, to anybody paying attention, the fierce, hard-bitten vision of America that Springsteen sang of in "Born in the U.S.A." was a far cry from the much-touted "new patriotism" that Reagan and many of his fellow conservatives claimed as their private dominion. And yet there was also something damnably brilliant in the way the president sought to attach his purposes to Springsteen's views. It was the art of political syllogism, taken to its most arrogant extreme. Reagan saw himself as a definitional emblem of America; Bruce Springsteen was a singer who, apparently, extolled America in his work; therefore, Springsteen must be exalting Reagan as well—which would imply that, if one valued the music of Springsteen, then one should value (and support) Reagan as well. Reagan was manipulating Springsteen's fame as an affirmation of his own ends.

The president's gambit left Springsteen with a knotty challenge: Could he afford to refute Reagan's praise without also alienating his newly acquired mass audience? Or should he use the occasion to challenge the beliefs of the audience—maybe, in the process, helping to reshape those beliefs? *Or* should he simply ignore the hubbub, and assume that his true fans understood his viewpoint?

A few nights later, Springsteen stood before a predominantly blue-collar audience in Pittsburgh and, following a rousing performance of "Atlantic City" (a song about American decay), decided to respond to the president's statement. "The president was mentioning my name the other day," he said with a bemused laugh, "and I kinda got to wondering what his favorite album might have been. I don't think it was the *Nebraska* album. I don't think it was this one." Springsteen then played a passionate, acoustic-backed version of "Johnny 99"—the song about a man who commits impulsive murder as a way of striking back against the meanness of the society around him—a song he wrote, along with other *Nebraska* tunes, in response to the malignant public and political atmosphere that had been fostered by Reagan's social policies.

Springsteen's comments were well-placed: *Was* this the America Ronald Reagan heard clearly when he claimed to listen to Springsteen's music? An America where dreams of well-being had increasingly become the province of the privileged, and in which jingoistic partisans determined the nation's health by a standard of self-advantage? When Reagan heard a song like "My Hometown," did he understand his own role in promoting the disenfranchisement the song described? If Reagan *truly* understood that the enlivening patriotism of "Born in the U.S.A." was a patriotism rooted in pain, discontent, and fury, perhaps he would have been either a better president or an angrier man. More likely, of course, he probably would have dismissed any such notions with his characteristic shrug of contempt—which is no doubt what he did when he finally heard Springsteen's response.

But Reagan's attempt to co-opt Springsteen's message also had some positive side effects. For one thing, it made plain that Springsteen now commanded a large and vital audience of young Americans who cared deeply about their families, their futures, and their country, and that Springsteen spoke to—and perhaps *for*—that audience's values in ways that could not be ignored. The imbroglio also forced Springsteen to become more politically explicit and resourceful at his performances. After Pittsburgh, he began meeting with labor and civil rights activists in most of the cities that he played, and he made statements at his shows, asking his audience to lend their support to the work of such activists. He also spoke out more and more plainly about where he saw America headed, and how he thought rock & roll could play a part in effecting that destiny. One evening in Oakland, when introducing "This Land Is Your Land," he said: "If you talk to the steelworkers out there who have lost their jobs, I don't know if they'd believe this song is what we're about anymore. And maybe we're not. As we sit here, [this song's promise] is eroding every day. And with countries, as with people, it's easy to let the best of yourself slip away. Too many people today feel as if America has slipped away, and left them standing behind." Then he sang the best song written about America, in as passionate a voice as it had ever been sung.

But none of this action was enough. In November 1984, Ronald Reagan was reelected president by an even more stunning mandate than the first time. It seemed plausible that many (if not most) of the millions of fans of voting age who had made *Born in the U.S.A.* the year's biggest success had cast their votes for the man to whom Springsteen so obviously stood in opposition. Perhaps it nettled him, but Springsteen was finally facing the answer to the question he had been asking during the length of the decade: To be born in America, to be passionate about the nation's best ideals and to be concerned over the betrayal of those ideals, meant being part of a nation that would only believe about itself what it wanted to believe. It also meant that one still had to find a way to keep faith with the dream of that nation, despite the awful realities that take shape when that dream is denied.

In 1984, America had not had enough of Ronald Reagan, or it would not have reelected him. It had also not had enough of Bruce Springsteen: After an international tour, he returned to the States a bigger, more popular artist than ever. It may seem like a contradiction that a nation can embrace two icons who differed so dramatically, but the truth is, Reagan and Springsteen shared an unusual bond: Each seemed to stand for America, and yet each also was largely misunderstood by his constituency. Reagan seemed to stand for the values of family and improved opportunity for the working class at the same time that he enacted policies that undermined those values. Springsteen seemed to stand for brazen patriotism when he believed in holding the government responsible for how it had corrupted the nation's best ideals and promises.

To his credit, Springsteen did his best to make his true values known. In the autumn of 1985, he embarked on the final leg of his *Born in the U.S.A.* tour, this time playing outdoor stadium-sized venues that held up to 100,000 spectators. Playing such vast settings was simply a way of keeping faith with the ambition he had settled on a year or two earlier: to see what it could mean to reach the biggest audience he could reach. It was also an attempt to speak seriously to as many of his fans as possible, to see if something like a genuine consensus could be forged from the ideals of a rock & roll community. And of course, the gesture also entailed a certain risk: If Springsteen's audience could not—or would not—accept him for what he truly stood for, then in the end, he could be reduced by that audience.

In some surprising respects, Springsteen's ambition succeeded. At the beginning of the stadium swing, many fans and critics worried that he would lose much of his force—and his gifts for intimacy and daring— by moving his music to such large stages. But if anything, Springsteen used the enlarged settings as an opportunity to rethink many of his musical arrangements, transforming the harder songs into something more fervid, more moving, more aggressive than before, and yet still putting across the more rueful songs from *The River* and *Nebraska* with an uncompromised sensitivity. If anything, he made the new shows count for more than the election-year shows, if only because he recognized that addressing a larger audience necessarily entailed some greater responsibilities. In Washington, D.C., on the opening night of the stadium shows, Springsteen told a story about a musician friend from his youth who was drafted and who, because he did not enjoy the privilege of a deferment, was sent to Vietnam and wound up missing in action. "If the time comes when there's another war, in some place like Central America," Springsteen told his audience of 56,000, "then you're going to be the ones called on to fight it, and you're going to have to decide for yourselves what that means. . . . But if you want to know where we're headed for [as a country], then someday take that long walk from the Lincoln Memorial to the Vietnam Veterans Memorial, where the names of all those dead men are written on the walls, and you'll see what the stakes are when you're born in the U.S.A. in 1985." By the last few nights of the tour, at the Los Angeles Memorial Coliseum, he had added Edwin Starr's 1970 hit "War" to the show, coming down hard on the line, "Induction, destruction / Who wants to die—in a war?" There was something heartening about watching a man who gazed into his audience and who—in defiance of the country's political mood and perhaps even the beliefs of that audience—cared enough about them to hope they would not die in a futile or demoralizing military action.

But for all his intensified fervor, Springsteen was gracious at the end of the tour. At the end of "Dancing in the Dark," in that moment when he generally pulled a female fan from the audience to dance with, Springsteen brought out his new wife, Julianne Phillips, danced with her sweetly, then took her in his arms and gave her a long kiss. Maybe it was his way of saying that this new relationship was where he would live, now that his tour was ending; or perhaps that his marriage was a way of attempting to live up to the best ideals of his own music. Later, at evening's end, Springsteen stood before his band, his friends, and his audience and said: "This has been the greatest year of my life. I want to thank you for making me feel like the luckiest man in the world." Indeed, Springsteen had begun the tour as a mass cult figure; he was leaving it as a full-fledged pop hero—a voice of egalitarian conscience unlike any rock had yielded before, with a remarkable capacity for growth and endurance.

In short, Springsteen seemed to emerge from the tour occupying the center of rock & roll, in the way that Presley, or the Beatles and Dylan and the Rolling Stones had once commanded the center. And yet the truth was, in 1980s pop, there was no center left to occupy. Rock was a field of mutually exclusive options, divided along racial, stylistic, and ideological lines,[2] and each option amounted to its own valid mainstream. In fact, by the decade's end, even the American and British fields of rock—which had dominated the pop world thoroughly for a quarter-century—were gradually losing their purism and dominance, as more and more young and adventurous musicians and fans began bringing African, Jamaican, Brazilian, Asian, and other musical forms into interaction with pop's various vernaculars. In modern pop, as in the modern globe, America no longer overwhelmed the international sensibility.

In any event, Springsteen seemed to step back from rock & roll's center at the same moment that he won it. In 1986, he assembled a multidisc package of some of his best performances from the previous ten years of live shows—a box set intended as a summation of his artistic growth and his range as a showman. In a sense, it was the most ambitious effort of his career, but also the least satisfying and least consequential. It didn't play with the sort of revelatory effect of his best shows or earlier albums, and it didn't captivate a mass audience in the same way either. Then, the following year, Springsteen released *Tunnel of Love*. Like *Nebraska*, the work with which he had begun the decade, *Tunnel of Love* was a more intimate, less epic statement than its predecessor—a heartbreaking but affirming suite of songs about the hard realities of romantic love. Maybe the record was intended to remind both Springsteen and his audience that what ultimately mattered was how one applied one's ideals to one's own world—or maybe the songs were simply about the concerns that obsessed Springsteen most at that time. In any event, *Tunnel of Love* was one of Springsteen's most affecting works, and it fit into his life with painfully ironic timing. A few months later, Springsteen separated from his wife of three years, Julianne Phillips, and was rumored to be seeing the backing vocalist in his band, Patti Scialfa. Eventually, Springsteen divorced Phillips and married Scialfa. In life, as in music, sometimes one's best hopes take unexpected, somewhat hurtful turns.

At the end of the decade, Springsteen was on tour again. Reluctant to continue playing oversized venues, he returned to the arena halls where he had done some of his most satisfying work in the years before, and restored a more human scale to his production. It was another election year, and while he still spoke out about issues from time to time,

Springsteen seemed wary of being cast as merely a rock politician or statesman. Perhaps he realized that America's political choices just couldn't be affected very tellingly from a rock & roll stage, or maybe he was simply discouraged by what he saw around him. To be sure, there was plenty to be disheartened about: It was a season when Oliver North enjoyed status as a cultural hero, and when George [H. W.] Bush turned patriotism and flag-waving into brutal, vicious, and effective campaign issues. (Though one night in New Jersey, in a burst of inspiring temper, Springsteen went on record with an electoral choice of sorts. "Don't vote for that fucking Bush," he told his audience, "no matter what!")

At the same time, Springsteen remained committed to the idea of turning the rock & roll audience into an enlightened and active community. After the *Tunnel of Love* tour, he headlined Amnesty International's Human Rights Now! world tour in the fall of 1988. Along with Live Aid, the Amnesty tour was one of the most ambitious political campaigns in rock's history. And the fact that it could occur at all and could reach an audience that was both massive and ready was in some ways a testament to the sort of idealism for which Springsteen had fought throughout the 1980s.

With his first records in the 1990s, Springsteen retreated further from his role as an icon and spokesperson, and attempted to redefine the scope of his songwriting. *Human Touch* and *Lucky Town* (the double offering from 1992) worked on smaller scales: They were dark and complex works about personal risks, and as such, they seemed to say much about the internal realities of Springsteen's own life, as he went from a highly publicized failed marriage to an apparently sounder second one, in which he became the father of three children. It was as if, in both his art and his life, Springsteen was attempting to say that to make your best hopes and ideals count for anything real, you have to bring them into your own home and heart, and see if you can live up to them.

Meantime, though, much changed about the larger family that Springsteen and the rest of us live in—that tormented home we still call America—and too little of it for the better. Back in the 1980s there was a vital argument to be waged about what it meant to be an American, and which visions and dreams best delineated our collective soul and destiny. In the 1990s, that argument hasn't been settled so much as it's been shunted to the side, or compromised between the maleficence of a Republican Congress and the artful ambitions of Bill Clinton's presidency. Some of our most valuable and necessary instruments of economic opportunity and social justice have been curtailed or ended—tools such as affirmative action, immigration rights, and welfare protection for children and families in poverty conditions—and our criminal justice system is imprisoning poor and young people at increasing rates (indeed, no other democracy in the world locks up as many of its citizens as America). The message is clear: No more help for people on the fringe, no more chances for the losers. These are pitiless times, and there have been too few voices in either our arts or our politics who dare to tell us that the America we are making will be a more perilous, bloodier place than we might ever have imagined.

The 1995 album *The Ghost of Tom Joad* was Bruce Springsteen's response to this state of affairs—you could even call it his return to arms. In any event, it was his first overtly social-minded statement since *Born in the U.S.A.*, eleven years earlier. *Joad* isn't an easy record to like immediately. Its music is often sorrowful and samely, its words soft-spoken, sometimes slurred. In addition, it creates an atmosphere as merciless in its own way as the world it talks about. That is, it is a record about people who do not abide life's ruins—a collection of dark tales about dark men who are cut off from the purposes of their own hearts and the prospects of their own lives. In this album, almost none of the characters get out with both their beings and spirits intact, and the few who do are usually left with only frightful and desolate prayers as their solace. "My Jesus," Springsteen intones at one song's end, "your gracious love and mercy / Tonight I'm sorry could not fill my heart. . . ." At the end of another song, a man prays: "When I die I don't want no part of heaven / I would not do heaven's work well. . . ." Plaintive, bitter epiphanies like these are far removed from the sort of anthemic cries that once filled Springsteen's music, but then, these are times for lamentations, not anthems.

On the surface, *Tom Joad* bears obvious kinship to *Nebraska*. Like that album, *Joad*'s musical backings are largely acoustic, and its sense of language and storytelling owes much to the Depression-era sensibility of Guthrie and such authors as John Steinbeck, James M. Cain, John Fante, and Eric Knight (the author of *You Play the Black and the Red Comes Up*). The stories are told bluntly and sparsely, and the poetry is broken and colloquial, like the speech of a man telling the stories he feels compelled to tell, if only to try and be free of them. That's where the similarities end. In *Nebraska,* Springsteen wrote about people living their lives at the edges of hopelessness and suppression—people whose lives could turn dangerous and explode—and the music conveyed not just their melancholy but, at moments, also their escape into rage. In *Tom Joad,* there are few such escapes and almost no musical relief from the numbing circumstances of the characters' lives. You could almost say that the music gets caught in meandering motions, or drifts into circles that never break. The effect is brilliant and lovely—there's something almost lulling in the music's blend of acoustic arpeggios and moody keyboard textures, something that lures you into the melodies' dark dreaminess and loose mellifluence. But make no mistake: what you are being drawn into are scenarios of hell. American hell.

Many of *Tom Joad's* characters are caught in this place, waiting for some event to make sense of their existence, or to explain to them their fates. A man sits by a campfire under a bridge, not far from endless railroad tracks. He is waiting on the ghost of Tom Joad, the hero of John Steinbeck's *The Grapes of Wrath,* who at the end of John Ford's 1940 film version of the novel, says: "'Wherever there's somebody fightin' for a place to stand / Or decent job or a helpin' hand / Wherever somebody's strugglin' to be free / Look in their eyes . . . you'll see me.'" But such hopes of salvation in the mid-1990s aren't really much more palpable than ghosts, and the man sitting, praying by the fire, will wait a long time before his deliverance comes. In "Straight Time," an ex-con takes a job and marries, and tries to live the sanctioned life. But the world's judgments are never far off—even his wife watches him carefully with their children—and he waits for the time when he will slip back into the deadly breach that he sees as his destiny. In "Highway 29," a lonesome shoe clerk surrenders to a deadly sexual fever that leads him into an adventure of robbery and murder and ruin, and he realizes that it is *this*— this dead-end flight of rage and self-obliteration—that his heart has always been headed for.

The most affecting stories on *Joad,* though, are the ones that Springsteen tells about a handful of undocumented immigrants, and their passage into Southern California's promised land. Some of these tales are drawn from real-life instances, as reported in the *Los Angeles Times.* In "The Line"—an achingly beautiful song, with a melody reminiscent of Bob Dylan's "Love Minus Zero/No Limit"—a border patrol cop falls in love with an immigrant woman, Louisa, and he helps her and her child and younger brother sneak into the States. But in a confrontation with another officer, he loses track of her, and never again finds her. In "Sinaloa Cowboys," two young brothers, Miguel and Louis, come from north Mexico to the San Joaquin Valley orchards to make money for their hungry families, and get involved in dangerous and illegal drug manufacturing. One night there is an explosion in the shack where they work; one brother is killed, and the other is left to bury him and tell their family. And in "Balboa Park," an undocumented teenage immigrant called Spider gets caught up working in San Diego as a sex hustler and drug smuggler, until one night, during a border patrol, he becomes victim of a hit-and-run. These people come to their fates quickly—much like that doomed planeload in Woody Guthrie's "Deportees"—one of the first songs that awakened Springsteen's political awareness. In one moment, these characters' "undocumented" lives are over, and the world takes no note of their passing or shot hopes.

People like Spider, Louisa, Miguel, and Louis are not people we hear much about in the popular music and literature of our time. In fact, they are the people that politicians like California governor Pete Wilson and Republican presidential candidate Pat Buchanan tell us are part of our national problem: folks who do not speak our language or share our birthrights. It is a testament to Bruce Springsteen's continuing vitality as one of our greatest writers that he has found the stories of these people—and the stories of the other characters caught in *Tom Joad*'s lower depths—worthy of being comprehended and told. By climbing into these people's hearts and minds, Springsteen has given voice to people who rarely have one in this culture—and that has always been one of rock & roll's most important virtues: giving voice to people who are typically denied expression in our other arts and media. In the midst of confusing and complex times, Bruce Springsteen has written more honestly, more intelligently, and more compassionately about America than any other writer of the last generation. As we move into the rough times and badlands that lie ahead, such acts might count for more than ever before.

Notes

1. See also Greil Marcus, "The Next President of the United States," in this volume.
2. Although Springsteen's enduring popularity transcends cultural, geographical, and generational lines, the racial divide remains strong. In August 1999, African Ameri-

can essayist and *Village Voice* staff writer Greg Tate attended a Springsteen and the E Street Band concert—his first—at the Meadowlands in New Jersey, looked around the stadium, and promptly asked himself, "Where are all my Negroes at? Why aren't there more Black people out here screaming Bruuuuce like Dolly Earshatterer to the rear of my right lobe?" He leaves the concert, though, a convert: ". . . [T]o finally see Springsteen live is to become some kind of believer." As Tate notes, Springsteen doesn't accept indifference for an answer "and you'd have to be dead to not respond to his shock tactics," he admits. Much to the journalist's surprise and delight, he discovers that Springsteen is "a shameless ham" who "lives to leave an already hysterical crowd limp or speaking in tongues. . . . Springsteen's rapport with his folks staggers not only for the degree of adulation present, but for his ability to move them from vulgarity to deep thought in a heartbeat." See Greg Tate, "Tear the Roof Off Jungleland," *Village Voice,* August 11–17, 1999.

R. C. Ringer

■

R. C. Ringer's short stories have been published in various publications, including *Witness, Midstream, The Quarterly,* and *Quarter After Eight.* "Asbury
Park" appeared in *Shore Stories: An Anthology of the Jersey Shore,* edited by
Rich Youmans (1998). Written in the late 1980s, it is set in the late 1960s
to early 1970s, a time when the fortunes of the former resort town were on
the wane. The story Ringer tells here is a rather sordid little tale of a father
who takes his young son to Asbury Park to meet up with his mistress. It captures the decay and the sadness—the ruined splendor—that permeates the
town to this day. "There's something very haunting about it," Ringer told me.
"I can't think of Asbury Park without thinking of *Greetings,*" he said, referring
to Springsteen's first album, *Greetings from Asbury Park, N.J.* And rightly so.
Springsteen's music provides the unofficial soundtrack to this story.

Asbury Park

from *Shore Stories: An Anthology of the Jersey Shore*

■"COME ON, BUTCH," my father says to me. He puts his large hand
on the back of my head and gives me a gentle shake. "Let's get going."

He waits for me while I finish tying my sneaker laces into knots. Then
we walk out to the car. He doesn't tell me where we are going—just out
for another Saturday drive. I suppose that we will end up at the Ten-Two
Lounge or the Alibi or some other bar where we can watch the ball game.

The way we are going, though, isn't the way to any of those places. We
drive through Morristown and then we keep driving along Route 24. We
are driving for a long time and the sunlight coming in through the windows is making the stale car air hot and lazy. I am drifting off to sleep.
My father is whistling along to songs on the radio, tapping one hand on
the steering wheel in not quite accurate time. Every so often he smiles, a
great happy smile. When he does this, his whistling fades away. He seems
lost in some happy memory, some hot and lazy happy memory.

I wake up because something is different.

It's the air.

I sit up straight in the seat. My wrist is sore from having been leaned on while I was napping.

It's the air. It smells like the shore.

I look around at the houses we are passing. They seem smaller, more fragile than the houses in Morristown. There is a feeling of flatness, of the low buildings, of the land. I see seagulls flying.

"Where are we going?" I ask.

"To visit a friend," my father says.

"I mean, where are we going?" I say.

"You'll like it there. You can play all the pinball you want and even eat ice cream."

I don't ask again. I know when I am not going to get an answer from him. There are some things about my father that I know, and this is one of them.

Here's another thing about him: I don't know what his job is. I don't ask that anymore, either. He's told me he has a top secret job working for the government and will be put in jail if he tells me what it is; he's told me that he's the one who squeezes the toothpaste into the tubes; he's told me that he tests light bulbs, one by one. I don't believe any of his stories, he tells even more of them than my sister does.

I have my own ideas about his job. Sometimes I think that he's an executive. Sometimes I think he drives a forklift.

We pass a few signs that show the mileage to Asbury Park. This is probably where we are going. Or nearby.

I begin to feel uneasy. This is a long way away from Morristown. And we aren't dressed for the shore. I'm wearing long pants and sneakers. And my father, he's wearing tan slacks and one of his white shirts, the ironed-in wrinkles making it seem more clean and new. His shoes are polished. And his smile is glorious. But most of all, it is his aftershave that is making me uneasy. He only wears aftershave when he and my mother go out to dinner or parties. Never on a Saturday drive.

Asbury Park is the shore, but not the shore where we usually go to in the summer. Long Beach Island is where we usually go. And we all go together, not just two of us. My father spreads the worn green army blanket over the hot sand, my mother calls us over one by one to rub suntan lotion all over our backs. Then there are the interminable hours and hours, dull hot hours, of sitting or lying in the blazing sun. The breeze from the ocean is minimal comfort, only felt when lying absolutely still and listening to the waves. When the sun becomes too unbearable, there is the cold relief of the ocean—cold, salty, gritty relief, until my mother comes to the edge of the water and yells for me to come out, my lips are turning blue. I go back to the blanket. My sister sits apart from us on her own blanket. It's really a large white towel with a green stripe down the middle and HOLIDAY INN spelled out in green letters. Later, when it's time to go home, there is sand everywhere. I can't put on my socks or sneakers because of the sand biting into my skin. My father yells about the sand getting all over the car and the wet bathing suits ruining the car seats. My mother spreads towels out on the hot seats, checks us one last time for sunburn, and then we begin the long hot drive home. When we arrive home, the one with the most sunburn gets to take a shower first. All of the bathing suits are left to soak in soapy water in the sink. In the shower I scrub and scrub and even use soap but the sand, never visible to my eye, can't be washed away. And later yet, during the night, I wake from my dreams brushing imaginary sand out of the bed.

We don't have the blanket with us, or towels.

Besides, Asbury Park isn't like that. At least, not what I've heard. There are boardwalks and nightclubs. And the boardwalk has all sorts of rides and merry-go-rounds and games and ice cream stands. I don't re-member having been here before.

We pass a sign welcoming us to Asbury Park. Looking around, I feel disappointed. This is not what I had expected of Asbury Park. It's noth-ing more than a town, really, with neat old homes and small front lawns of grass forever dying in the sandy dirt and salty air.

I turn anxiously, twisting on the seat, trying to see out of all the win-dows at the same time, disappointed with all I see.

My father is also looking out of the windows. He's stopped whistling and is looking carefully at the street signs as we drive slowly past. We turn off the main road on which we had been driving and continue straight for several blocks. My father slows down, sticks his head out of the car to see house numbers. Then he looks for a parking space along the curb. We find one, halfway down one of the blocks, and park.

He turns off the motor.

"Are we here yet?" I ask.

My father laughs.

"Yes," he says. "We're here. We're always here."

He's out of the car and five or six steps away before I can unbuckle the seatbelt. I have to run to catch up to him, to keep up, to make sure I don't lose him in this unfamiliar town. He walks to a white three-story house at the corner.

It's a high, narrow house and rather odd looking. There is a wooden staircase on the outside leading to the porch and then on up to the second and third stories. These stairs feel flimsy under my feet as we climb up. I stop at the second story landing, one of my sneaker laces has come untied. I try not to look down as I tie the lace into more knots. I am afraid of these stairs, of the height.

"Come on," my father calls down to me from the third-story landing.

I have to hold my breath and not look down or anywhere except at the whitewashed walls of the house as I continue climbing up. The steps are worn smooth, some of them are loose. I would close my eyes except for fear of missing a step and falling all the way down to the ground.

Somehow I make it up.

My father is not waiting for me on the landing. He's gone into the house and has left the door open for me to follow. I can't quite see in there, the sunlight outside making it difficult to see anything inside. I hold onto the wooden railing and turn to look out, away from the house. What I see are roofs of other houses stretching along for blocks and blocks and after the roofs I see some larger buildings, some with flags on them, and a Ferris wheel and the top rails of a roller coaster. And beyond that I can see the ocean; an enormous flat gray-green expanse with toy-like clouds hanging in the blue sky above it.

From inside the house my father calls out to me, "Hey Butch, what are you doing out there? Aren't you coming in?"

I go in.

The first thing I do is sneeze. This room stinks of perfume.

My father is sitting on a sofa drinking beer from a glass. He looks relaxed; one leg crossed over the other, his arm stretched out along the back of the sofa. He is alone on the sofa, we are alone in this room.

"Sit down," he says.

I look around for a place to sit. There a few armchairs, mismatched colors, the white stuffing falling out of the cushions. There is a folding card table with some dirty glasses on top of it. On the floor is a stereo, with records scattered nearby, some of the records in their cardboard sleeves and others not. The floor is partially covered with a rug. Nowhere is a place that I want to sit.

A woman comes into the room from one of the other rooms. She is wearing a long green velour bathrobe. There are no buttons on the bathrobe and empty loops where there had once been a velour belt. She is haphazardly holding the bathrobe closed with her hand. Under it she is wearing shorts and a blouse that doesn't match. Her hair is wet and matted down but her face is almost fully made-up.

She smells of this perfume.

Everywhere is the smell of this perfume. It is inside the furniture, the walls.

It makes me sneeze again. I squeeze my nose between my fingers to keep myself from sneezing some more.

My father gets up from the sofa, but he doesn't go anywhere. He just stands there.

"This is Peg," he says. "She's an old friend of mine."

The woman, Peg, laughs and says, "I'm not that old."

I look closely at her, at her eyes and mouth and hands, to see if I can see how old she is. This light, and her make-up, make it impossible to guess. She's old enough, I'd say. She's an adult. And then it occurs to me that she might not have meant age.

"Can I get you something to drink?" she asks.

She giggles at that, raises one hand to cover her mouth as she giggles. "A soda, I mean."

I shake my head.

She says, "Just help yourself if you change your mind." She waves her arm toward another part of the apartment, where I suppose the kitchen is. Her bathrobe falls open. Both my father and I look. She pulls the bathrobe together. "You two boys will have to excuse me while I go make myself decent."

While she's gone, my father gets up from the sofa and bends down to the floor to put a record on the stereo. He gathers all of the albums together into one large stack. Once the record he has chosen is playing, he gets back up and goes to the kitchen. He returns with a can of beer for himself and a glass of soda for me.

A little while later Peg comes back into the room wearing a light green dress, stockings and high heels. She's carrying a black pocketbook. She stops at the doorway and looks at my father. My father looks over at me. I look down at my sneakers, at a spot on the floor three feet in front of me, then back at my father. He's already looking at Peg.

"That's nice," my father says. "That's real nice."

"Thank you," she says.

My father turns to me. "Hey, Butch, how's about a walk along the boardwalk. And that pinball I promised you?"

Peg says, "Butch? I thought you said his name was John."

"Butch. Everyone calls you Butch, right?" my father says. "Let's go out to the boardwalk and see those pinball games they have here."

Peg turns off the stereo. The three of us leave the apartment. We stand on the landing while Peg locks the three locks on the door. Then we go back down the nearly collapsing wooden steps.

My father goes down fast. Peg is slower, grabbing onto the railing so she doesn't tip over on her high heels. I follow behind, two steps, three steps, four, slowly making my way down. They are waiting for me on the sidewalk when I reach the front porch. I hurry, afraid that they might leave without me.

When I catch up to them, my father says, "He wants to be a mountain climber, except he's afraid of heights."

Peg puts her hand on my shoulder. "He's adorable," she says. When she takes her hand away, I can smell her perfume on my shirt.

We walk along in the direction of the ocean. The sidewalk is narrow. The smells of salt and fish get stronger with each step we take. There are a few other people walking along the sidewalk, mostly old men and women. Certainly no one we pass looks like they would spend their time sitting on the beach had it been twenty degrees warmer. As we pass these people, we huddle on our side of the sidewalk and they on theirs.

It is not long before I can see the end of the street and the steps leading up to the boardwalk.

The buildings that had seemed so far away when I was standing on Peg's landing are now so close. I can see that most of them are amusement halls, with big, indoor merry-go-rounds and Skee Ball games. There are cotton candy stands, ice cream stands, and salt water taffy shops everywhere.

On the boardwalk itself are even more shops and amusement halls. There are wheel of fortune games where it is possible to win cartons of cigarettes (18 or older only) and coin toss games and more ice cream stands and salt water taffy shops. Everything looks like it belongs in a carnival.

There aren't many people around and not all of the stands are open. This place has a half-deserted air about it. It looks like an empty, abandoned carnival. And the fading, peeling paint of the once jolly decorations on the buildings and stands makes everything seem even more abandoned and decaying.

My father and Peg walk along the boardwalk in front of me.

Peg is holding my father's arm. Every so often one of her high heels catches or slips and my father puts his arm around her waist to hold her up. After this happens a couple of times, he keeps his arm around her waist.

We stop in front of one of the amusement halls. Inside are pinball games and the latest electronic and video games. There is a shooting gallery along one wall and Skee Ball games in the back.

"How's this place look to you, Butch?" my father says.

I don't say anything. He reaches into his pocket and pulls out some money. Not coins, but bills. He stuffs them into my pants pocket, then pulls up my pants so they don't sag below my waist.

Peg watches as he does this.

He says, "Peg and I are going for a walk. Don't worry about us, we'll be back for you. There's plenty of money there to keep you occupied for a couple of hours—even enough for a hot dog if you get hungry."

I don't know what to say. Certainly I'm not hungry.

"You'll be okay," he says. "Just don't leave here or we won't be able to find you when we come back. Okay?"

I nod.

They begin walking away. Peg turns around, comes back. She leans down and hugs me, surrounding me with perfume. She kisses me on the mouth.

"You're a dear," she says. Then, walking carefully on her high heels, she catches up with my father. Together they walk along the boardwalk back in the direction we just came from.

Two and a half hours pass and I am still here. I may not know left from right, but I have learned how to tell time. I have also learned that two and a half hours does not always equal two and a half hours. Sometimes it is forever.

I still have plenty of money to play pinball. I have eaten two hot dogs.

Every fifteen minutes, according to the large clock in here, I go out to the boardwalk and look for my father and Peg. I walk in the direction that they went, but not too far. I am afraid that they will be coming back the other way and I'll miss them, so I hurry back to the amusement hall.

The man who gives out the change has been keeping an eye on me. Whenever I return from the boardwalk, he asks, "Find them yet?" When I shake my head no, he says, "Don't worry, they'll be back soon."

He's given me some free games on the pinball machines. And he even let me play the water shoot for nothing. I had been watching people at the water shoot for some time before I got to play it. What it is is you aim a water gun at the mouth of a wooden clown's head, and the water makes a balloon on top of the clown blow up. The better your aim, the faster the balloon blows up. Whoever's balloon pops first, wins.

I won twice.

Even so, time passes slowly.

I am about to walk down the boardwalk to the hot dog stand for my third, when I hear my father yelling to me.

"Hey Butch!" he yells. "Wait up."

He's half walking and half running along the boardwalk. He's alone. He's waving to me and smiling and I wave back. I can't help but smile. I run to him and he catches me in a great big hug.

"I'm back," he says. His breath smells of beer and he smells of her. "I told you I'd be back. Did you have a good time playing pinball?"

I tell him that I did. I tell him about eating two hot dogs.

"Two!" he says. "How about if I buy you an ice cream to top it off?"

We walk to the nearest ice cream stand and he orders two large soft ice cream cones with sprinkles on top. Vanilla ice cream.

I watch my father while he pays for the ice cream. I am looking for a clue, something that will tell me what has changed. Something has changed.

I look around to see if Peg might be anywhere.

Between licks of my ice cream, I ask where she is.

"Peg? She wasn't feeling well, she had to go home. But she really liked you. She said you were 'a good little soldier.' That's just what she said, 'a good little soldier.'"

We walk along the boardwalk toward the street where Peg lives and the car is parked. My father messes up my hair with his hand.

"Don't tell your mother about this," he says. He winks at me. "We'll both get into trouble for it."

I say I won't say anything.

"Promise?"

I promise.

"Cross your heart and hope to die?"

I hold up my hand. "Promise," I say. I would say anything he told me to say. He's my father.

Sheri Tabachnik, Joseph Sapia, and Kelly Jane Cotter

■

The following obituary announcing the death of Douglas Springsteen appeared in the May 2, 1998, issue of the *Asbury Park Press*.

Father of Bruce Springsteen Dies at 73

Asbury Park Press

■FREEHOLD—WHEN MICHAEL HANSEN arrived at school Thursday and was asked to go into church for the funeral Mass of Douglas "Dutch" Springsteen, he understood the importance of having a hometown. Hansen, 12, a student and altar boy at St. Rose of Lima, was proud to assist in the service. Dutch Springsteen, Bruce Springsteen's father, was a childhood friend of Hansen's grandfather. "He couldn't wait to come home and tell his mother," said Frank "Spat" Federici Jr., Hansen's grandfather and owner of Federici's Pizzeria on Main Street. "He said Bruce told them they did a nice job."

Dutch Springsteen, 73, died Sunday, in Belmont, Calif. A borough native who graduated from St. Rose of Lima School in 1939, he lived in California with his wife, Adele, and daughter Pamela Springsteen since moving from the borough about 30 years ago. Dutch Springsteen is also survived by another daughter, Virginia Shave, of Lakewood, six grandchildren and two great-grandchildren. The family did not disclose the cause of death.

In a statement released last night, Bruce Springsteen said: "My father and I had a very loving relationship. With family all around, he celebrated his 73rd birthday, and my parents recently marked 50 years together. They had a warm and caring marriage. I feel lucky to have been so close to my dad as I became a man and a father myself. My mother, my sisters and I love him and will miss him very much."

A World War II veteran, Dutch Springsteen grew up in his parents' Randolph Street home. His father, Fred, a painter, and his mother,

Alice, also had a daughter, but she died after being hit by a car when she was a young child, Federici said. "He used to come into the restaurant and we'd talk about old times," Federici said. "He was a very quiet teenager, but very handsome."

Vini "Mad Dog" Lopez, who played drums in Bruce Springsteen–led bands including the E Street Band, recalled Dutch Springsteen as a friend to the band members. "To all the guys in the band, he was very nice, a very nice fellow," said Lopez, who lives in Ocean Grove. "He always treated us, when we were around, like part of the family."

In an onstage anecdote told during his 1978 tour, Springsteen described his father's intolerance for his musical aspirations. The tale, according to Dave Marsh's book *Born to Run,* is as follows: "When I was growin' up, there were two things that were unpopular in my house. One was me, and the other was my guitar. He always used to call the guitar, never a Fender guitar or a Gibson guitar, it was always the God-damned guitar. Every time he'd knock on my door, that was all I'd hear—'Turn down that God-damned guitar.' He musta thought everything in my room was the same God-damned brand—God-damned guitar, God-damned radio, God-damned stereo."[1]

But Joan Kress, 54, whose parents' Parker Street home was around the corner from the Springsteen house on Institute Street, said that all happened long ago. Dutch Springsteen "was very proud of Bruce," she said.

Note

1. Springsteen sang about the often turbulent relationship with his father in numerous songs, such as "Adam Raised a Cain," "My Father's House," "Factory," "Mansion on the Hill," and especially "Independence Day" and "Walk Like a Man." In the British magazine *Uncut,* he talks about how, as he ages, he has grown to physically resemble his father. "Your features change," he told interviewer Adam Sweeting. "When I was young I looked Irish, when I was a little kid I had the little Irish features, as my children have had, up until 12 or 13 and then zoom! Your face lengthens out and you see the Italian features. I had that for most of my life, I kinda got used to looking at myself. Then as you get a little older, for some reason I see a little of the Irish creeping back in. . . . occasionally I'll look in the mirror and he'll be looking back at me." See Adam Sweeting, "Into the Fire," *Uncut,* September 2002.

Part Three

■

REBIRTH

In the early 1990s, the rock world that Springsteen had conquered only a few short years before seemed somehow altogether different. A new generation had come of age, a generation, like all generations before and since, that was searching for its own sound, its own particular meaning: for music that spoke to them directly and to their experiences. Clearly, Springsteen belonged to another era. He found himself trying to find his place in this strange new land.

And yet this period of waning popularity seemed only to energize him, giving him the freedom to create a truly personal music. Much of his new work in the 1990s is intensely introspective and genuinely touching, as a middle-aged Springsteen confronts life issues: the importance of family, the unfortunate breakup of relationships, the devastating effects of illness—all of which lead to the sudden realization that time is no longer on our side. Springsteen, once hailed as the future of rock and roll, now glimpses his own mortality.

And yet, as the dawn of the new millennium approached, Springsteen experienced an artistic rebirth of sorts and rediscovered his own voice. The physical and emotional wreckage of 9/11 gave him further pause. In the aftermath of the tragedy, he found his purpose once again: to write songs that really matter.

In other words, the role of this singer is to celebrate, to eulogize, to bear witness, and to offer moments of genuine hope.

Pellegrino D'Acierno

■

Pellegrino D'Acierno is a fellow at the Italian Academy for Advanced Studies at Columbia University and a former professor of Italian and comparative literature at Hofstra University. The following excerpts are taken from "Italian American Musical Culture and Its Contribution to American Music" (originally published in full by Robert Connolly and Pellegrino D'Acierno), and consists of one of twenty-seven essays that make up *The Italian American Heritage: A Companion to Literature and Arts* (1999), which explores Italian American identity from numerous perspectives. Springsteen, of course, is primarily of mixed Italian and Irish ancestry, but he seems to have much in common with other Italian Americans. Like one of his musical predecessors and idols, Frank Sinatra, he returns to his ethnic tradition "without making a point of it"—and editor in chief George Leonard in the Preface makes exactly that distinction.[1] In this excellent essay, D'Acierno examines the effect of the Italian American singing tradition on pop culture, from the Philadelphia teen idols who were mostly of Italian heritage to the gorgeous harmonies of white doo-wop groups to Springsteen's Martin Scorsese–style "street" Catholicism.[2]

Roll Over, Rossini:
Italian American Rock 'n' Roll

from *The Italian American Heritage*

■The Italian American impact on popular singing continued well into the rock era, that is, well after the "death of the crooner," or, what amounted to the same thing, the institutionalization of the crooner—no longer perceived as having a dangerous edge—within the pop mainstream, Las Vegas, and television.

The second-generation singers would be replaced, in the late 1950s, by two new musical types. The first type was the "teen idol" as epitomized by the south Philadelphia "dreamboats," Frankie Avalon, Bobby Rydell, Fabian Forte, a fabricated role in which a group of teenage Italians who had absorbed the ethos of rock 'n' roll were typecast by the industry, "as music left the streets and moved into the studios," as heartthrobs to capitalize on their good looks—clean-cut and nondangerous versions of the dark other—and to produce a rock 'n' roll consumable by the teeny-bopper audience targeted by American Bandstand. The second type was the White "doo-wop group," a role into which inner-city Italians naturally placed themselves, living out the "Street Corner Symphony"—the singing a capella on the Lexington Avenue IRT is in no way apocryphal—and through which they expressed their own urban anguish and "mean streets" desire: "There's a Moon Out Tonight." The Italian American doo-wop groups (Dion and the Belmonts, Johnny Maestro and the Crests and later the Brooklyn Bridge, Tony Canzano and the Duprees, Frankie Valli and the Four Seasons, the Regents, Vito Picone and the Elegants, and so forth) represent a genuine border crossing between urban-Black and Italian musical cultures. As John Javna, a doo-wop enthusiast, observes: "Unlike previous white artists who had made their fortunes by 'covering' (read: 'stealing') black groups' tunes, the new white doo-woppers learned their art on America's street-corners. They developed their own styles [the 'Italian style' exemplified by the Elegants' 'Little Star'] and wrote their own songs."

Sociologically, it is interesting that the crucibles for both phenomena were big-city Italian neighborhoods. The teen idols were drawn from the south Philly subculture, which was relocated in the television studio where it became a model for mass-mediated teen culture of the late fifties and sixties. The doo-wops crystallized in the boroughs of New York City and the metropolitan area: the Crests in Brooklyn, the Belmonts in the south Bronx, the Capris in Queens, the Four Seasons in Newark. But there was a tremendous difference in the packaging of the two types. Self-styled impresario Bob Marcucci, whose exploits are recounted in the 1980 film *The Idolmaker,* picked the best-looking kids from the area, regardless of their vocal attributes or lack of the same, and set about making them stars. The formula produced Frankie Avalon (Francis Thomas Avallone) and the "Tiger Man" Fabian (Fabio Forte), both of whom, together with Bobby Rydell (Robert Ridarelli), defined the Philadelphia sound. Of the three, Rydell, with his sweeping pompadour, was probably the most accomplished musician, and between 1959 and 1964 he scored nineteen Top Thirty smashes, including "Kissin' Time," "Volare," a rocking version of the Domenico Modugno tune, "Swingin' School," "Wild One" and "Forget Him." From a sociological point of view, the teen-idol phenomenon is interesting because it packages these good-looking teenagers of moderate talent as simulacra of the Italian American identity, as ethnic signifiers without ethnic or musical substance. As such, they served as images by which the ethnic look is rendered a spectacle suitable for the fantasy consumption of White American adolescent girls.

On the other hand, the doo-wops, whether Black or Italian, were part of the New York City street-corner scene and did not receive the benefit of the star-manufacturing machinery in place in Philadelphia. With the exception of Dion and the Belmonts and Frankie Valli and the Four Seasons, most of the Italian American doo-wop groups produced one or two hits and then faded from view, only to be recycled on the rock 'n' roll revival circuit. In any case the era of Italian American rock 'n' roll is embodied most authentically in the genealogy of street-corner vocal-harmony groups that extends from Johnny Maestro and the Crests and Dion and the Belmonts to Frankie Valli and the Four Seasons and Joey Dee and the Starlighters. Their songs—"Sixteen Candles," "I Wonder Why," "Teenager in Love," "Where or When," "The Wanderer," "Barbara Ann" (the Regents), "Little Star" (the Elegants), "Sherry," "Big Girls Don't Cry"—embody the street-corner ethos of the 1950s and the pre-Beatles 1960s. (For an account of the way in which Italian Americans bought into rock 'n' roll culture, see Ed Ward's "Italo-American Rock" in Miller's *Rolling Stone Illustrated History of Rock & Roll* [1980]. The article begins: "In my hometown, Eastchester, New York, there was only one ethnic group that knew anything about rock and roll. They liked loud, flashy colors, and they seemed to have a natural sense of rhythm and an inborn musical ability. They excelled in the school band, and at dances they cut everybody." Here Ward is deliberately projecting the standard Black stereotype onto Italians, as the remainder of the piece makes clear. . . ."

The list of Italian American teen idols is extensive: Freddie Cannon (Frederick Picciarello), Terry Randazzo, James Darren, Johnny Restivo, Sal Mineo, the actor who also sang, and the like. Of these, the most important was Bobby Darin (Robert Walden Cassotto), who was born in 1936 in a "mean streets" section of New York City's East Harlem. As the story goes, he took his name from a broken neon sign on a Chinese restaurant that was missing the first three letters of the word "Mandarin." He came on the scene as a rock singer in 1958, quickly becoming an idol of the teenage crowd. He won two Grammy Awards in 1960 for his recording of "Mack the Knife" and made a dozen films. By 1967 he had sold thirty-five million records. Ambitious and talented, he had won over an adult audience and was being taken seriously as an artist of stature—Sinatra-influenced—when he died of a heart ailment at the age of thirty-seven.

After the Long Good-bye: From Frank Zappa to Bruce Springsteen and Madonna

As the great divide between taste cultures—adult and teenager—grew more absolute, the second-generation crooners became the staples— caught in the time warp of television and Las Vegas—of the pop mainstream tradition, where they were joined by younger crossover singers like Bobby Darin, occasionally producing an anthem like Tony Bennett's "I Left My Heart in San Francisco" (1962). Their hegemony over popular singing was no longer in effect, and their attempt to translate the *bel canto*[3] into American terms had long since run its course. Their successors, the teen idols, were history by the mid-1960s, and the doo-wop groups, with the notable exception of the Four Seasons, did not survive the invasion of the Beatles. Of course, Sinatra, who had called rock 'n' roll that "rancid, putrid aphrodisiac," continued to defy the laws of pop entropy, surviving his own institutionalization.

After 1965 three Italian American groups would remain dominant: Frankie Valli and the Four Seasons; Felix Cavaliere and the Young Rascals (later the Rascals), a recycled version of Joey Dee's Starlighters, a "blue-eyed soul" quartet formed in 1965 in New York City featuring, along with Cavaliere, Eddie Brigati, Gene Cornish, and Dino Danieli; and Mitch Ryder (William Levise) and the Detroit Wheels, a White soul-rock group. Also deserving of mention is Jim Croce (1943–1973), a singer, guitarist, and songwriter whose breakthrough hits "You Don't Mess Around with Jim" (1972) and "Operator" (1972) were followed by his classical character-song "Bad Bad Leroy Brown" (1973) and the posthumously released "Time in a Bottle" (1973). He was clearly headed for the top of the rock world when he was killed in a plane crash while nearing the end of a tour.

Three Italian American performers play definitive roles in the musical culture of the 1970s and 1980s: Frank Zappa (1940–1993), whose band the Mothers of Invention had already become a fixture of the counterculture of the 1960s, the exponents of a free-form mixture that would come to define acid, or psychedelic, rock; the Italian Irish Bruce Springsteen (1949–), whose mother's name is Adele Zerilli; and Madonna Ciccone (1958–). All three define their musical identities primarily in American terms and without specific reference to the Italian musical tradition. They do, however, elaborate complex personae in keeping with their status as postmodern performance artists. The emphasis is on "postmodern" because all three fashion their musical and personal identities ironically in terms of pastiche and recycling. Unlike their predecessors— from Sinatra and the other balladeers, to such doo-woppers as Dion Di Mucci and Frankie Valli, and other rockers like Felix Cavaliere and Mitch Ryder (the latter two would be points of reference for Springsteen)— who defined themselves in terms of the Italian American subculture and constructed themselves as strong Italian American hybrids (the "blue-eyed soul" of the Young Rascals, none of whom had blue eyes, designates this hybridization, the "blue eyes" alluding to Sinatra as well), these three construct their identities as "texts," as collage constructions in which rock 'n' roll (not ethnicity) serves as the primary subculture. Although the figure of Italianness, especially as mediated through Catholicism, does come into play in their performances of the self, it does so as a trace among other traces. This is especially true of Madonna, the last ethnic and the first postethnic diva, who fashions her persona by perpetually deconstructing it. From this perspective, all three can be seen as meta- and postethnic artists as Italian Americans. . . .

The second Italian American influencing the musical culture of the 1970s, 1980s, and beyond is the singer, songwriter, guitarist, and band leader Bruce Springsteen, the New Jersey–born son of an Italian mother and a predominantly Irish father. Because he is not marked nomenclaturally— his family name is, in fact, Dutch—and also because his musical persona is an all-American rock 'n' roll construction, his Italianness is encrypted, vaguely glimpsed through physiognomy and body image and, even more vaguely, through his pulsiveness. Thomas J. Ferraro[4] quite convincingly recuperates Springsteen's Italianness through the figure of blue-collar rock 'n' roll Catholicism. It is thus no accident that Springsteen's musical persona involves a recycling of Presley and Dylan through the filter of an urban Catholic—"It's Hard to Be a Saint in the City"—sensibility incubated by the New Jersey shore scene. It is interesting, however, that

John [*sic*] Landau, in a May 1974 piece for the *Real Paper* that had the effect of a shot heard round the rock 'n' roll world ("I saw rock 'n' roll future last night and its name is Bruce Springsteen!"), would describe him as "a rock 'n' roll punk, a Latin street poet, a ballet dancer, a joker, a bar band leader. . . ." Here in this mix are the traces of a postmodern ethnic—"Latin"—identity that has reconstructed itself in terms of the subculture of rock 'n' roll. But there is much more to Springsteen than a jukebox identity. By way of experimenting with our perception of ethnicity, consider what would happen if he were named matrilineally Bruce Zerilli. Would the name change alter substantially our response to him? Would it oblige us to read him as an ethnic signifier in the way Sinatra and Madonna are securely read? This is no easy exercise, for it raises the question of the way in which ethnicity—especially third- or fourth-generation ethnicity, which, as in Zerilli-Springsteen's case, is compounded by intermarriage (the typical destiny of Italian Americans, a group that tends to intermarry)—is just one element in a complex system of traces by which identity is rendered a transitional category. Furthermore, with a rock star like Springsteen, who is jockeying to find a position in the rock genealogy that extends from Elvis through Dylan and Hendrix, we are dealing with the construction of an image that involves the organization of the signs of a performer's personality, of which ethnicity is no longer the determining sign.

That Springsteen, however, is sometimes mistaken for being Jewish is symptomatic of the fact that his image is generically ethnic, vaguely Other. That Otherness is elaborated in the explicit class terms of a blue-collar, "street" Catholicism in the Scorsese mold as thematized in the lyrics of Springsteen's songs and then expanded into the archetypal rock persona of the outlaw qua "renegade priest." Springsteen does acknowledge his Italianness, attributing his art of storytelling to his grandfather Zerilli and treating in his songs the blue-collar Oedipalism of his family life: "There ain't a note I play on stage that can't be traced directly back to my mother and father (Lynch 1984)."[5] If the figure of Italianness were applied to his work, it would both bring into focus and distort aspects of his persona: his bravado as the Boss, his attempt to "naturalize" rock 'n' roll (the great Italian American stereotype of the "natural," the instinctive White artist who brings into play pulsive rhythms), and, above all, the whole contradictory ethnic search for the American Dream, displaced into the no less contradictory search for the authentic voice of rock 'n' roll.

Notes

1. George Leonard, editor in chief, *The Italian American Heritage: A Companion to Literature and the Arts*. Edited by Pellegrino D'Acierno (New York: Garland Publishing, 1999), xvi.

2. In an interview with *Publishers Weekly* editor Mark Rotella, Bill Tonelli, editor of *The Italian American Reader*, admitted that "In Italy, there's never been a strong book culture. The more Americanized Italians become, the more they read. . . . It's partly that Italian Americans don't tell too much to the outside—they don't give it up easily." See Mark Rotella, "Bueno Sera: Trio of Italian American Writers Draw Hundreds to B&N," *PW Daily for Booksellers*, March 31, 2003, and Bill Tonelli, ed., *The Italian American Reader* (New York: William Morrow, 2003). In recent years, there have been a number of books examining Italian American heritage. Of special interest are Regina Barreca, ed., *Don't Tell Mama! The Penguin Book of Italian American Writing* (New York: Penguin, 2002) and Maria Laurino, *Were You Always an Italian? Ancestors and Other Icons of Italian America* (New York: W. W. Norton & Company, 2000) as well as the work of Fred Gardaphé, an Italian American scholar/activist and director of the Italian American Studies Program at the State University of New York at Stony Brook. Gardaphé in particular has been instrumental in presenting a new face of the Italian American to mainstream culture. See his *Italian Signs, American Streets: The Evolution of Italian American Narrative* (Durham, N.C.: Duke University Press, 1996), *Dagoes Read: Tradition and the Italian American Writer* (Tonawanda, N.Y.: Guernica, 1997), and *Leaving Little Italy: Essays in Italian American Culture* (Albany, N.Y.: State University of New York Press, 2003). With Anthony Tamburri and Paolo Giordano, he edited *From the Margin: Writings in Italian America* (West Lafayette, Ind.: Purdue University Press, 1991), and in 1993 he wrote the introduction—Studs Terkel wrote the preface—to a revised paperback edition of the classic Italian American 1939 novel *Christ in Concrete* by Pietro di Donato (New York: Signet Classic). For another look at the Italian American experience, this time from a West Coast perspective, see the work of the Los Angeles–based writer John Fante (1909–1983). *The John Fante Reader*, edited by Stephen Cooper (New York: William Morrow, 2002) conveniently includes excerpts from his novels and short stories as well as never-before-published letters and exposes the poverty and prejudice that were such common features among working-class Italian Americans of his time.

3. In *The Italian American Heritage*, *bel canto* is defined as "literally, 'beautiful singing'; a style of operatic singing characterized by rich tonal lyricism and brilliant display of social technique. It has come to be used as a generic term to describe the art of singing in the Italian style." See Pellegrino D'Acierno, ed., *The Italian American Heritage: A Companion to Literature and Arts* (New York: Garland Publishing, 1999), p. 707.

4. Observes Ferraro, "The idiom in which Bruce Springsteen operates—the language and imagery of his oeuvre, the ethos of his shows, and the very shape of his career—is that of a renegade priest turned prophet to the East Coast working classes, women included (no male star since Elvis Presley has had as female an audience). In his songs, he describes last-ditch efforts to salvage broken American dreams—

'redemption,' he calls it—that he himself offers, in turn, in relentless stage shows, alternately evocative of homosocial street camaraderie and heterosexual romance yet intuitively modeled in its larger rhythms on the High Masses of feast days. For those in the audience, the experience is, as they always report, that of religious transport, the cleanest of ecstasies yielding the most good-willed and least self-indulgent of rock 'n' roll crowds, and this effect is no surprise: Listen to the contrasting messages and styles of the first three performances on *Bruce Springsteen Live, 1975–85,* and you will hear secularized versions of the gathering, the Confiteor-Kyrie, and the Gloria, distinctly articulated and in the correct order. As the decades proceeded, Springsteen himself moved from small-scale cult following to stadium megastar to a persisting but scaled-down middle age, with a typically Catholic self-reflexiveness regarding the life cycle: The Boss has been aging less like the eternally rebellious Mick Jagger or the precociously wise Billie Holiday and more like, not coincidentally, the Chairman of the Board: In the early 1990s, a father of two, he began sporting crosses as more than a fashion statement, recorded children's ballads, and offered varying testimonies to his 'leaps of faith.'" See Thomas J. Ferraro, "Catholic Ethnicity and Modern American Arts," in *The Italian American Heritage: A Companion to Literature and Arts,* Pellegrino D'Acierno, ed. (New York: Garland Publishing, 1999), pp. 347–48.

5. Quoted in Kate Lynch, *Springsteen: No Surrender* (New York: Proteus, 1984).

Will Percy

■

Will Percy is the nephew of the late novelist Walker Percy. In the Spring 1998 issue of *DoubleTake* magazine,[1] Percy and Springsteen engaged in a wide-ranging and revealing interview that touched on many subjects, not the least of which was Springsteen's admiration of Walker Percy's work as well as the damage wrought by the country's ongoing obsession with the cult of celebrity. Unfortunately, novelist and singer never did meet, but Percy's influence on Springsteen's songwriting was considerable.

Rock and Read:
Will Percy Interviews Bruce Springsteen

DoubleTake

In early 1989, Walker Percy penned a fan letter "of sorts"[2] to Bruce Springsteen, praising the musician's "spiritual journey" and hoping to begin a correspondence between them. At the time, Springsteen hesitated in responding, but he later picked up a copy of The Moviegoer *and began a new journey into Dr. Percy's writing. Walker Percy died in May 1990, and the two never met, but Percy's novels and essays, among other books and films, have had a most profound impact on Springsteen's songwriting. In 1995, Springsteen recorded* The Ghost of Tom Joad, *a richly lyrical album that forged a new purpose for his music, linking him in some ways to the tradition of such artist-activists as John Steinbeck (Joad is the radical hero of* The Grapes of Wrath) *and folk music icon Woody Guthrie. Springsteen's songs tell us, in their familiar narrative style, about ordinary people struggling through life's twists and turns, presenting a cast of characters that includes immigrant families, border patrolmen, Midwestern steelworkers, and America's poor and disenfranchised. The populist sensibility of Guthrie can be heard throughout: it is music competing for public conscience.*

Following an Atlanta concert promoting the album, Will Percy, Walker's nephew, met Springsteen backstage, and the two talked for hours. When Springsteen mentioned his regret at never having written back to Will's uncle, Will encouraged him to write to his aunt, Walker's widow. A few

*months later, Springsteen, who likes to say that "it's hard for me to write
unless there's music underneath," sat down and wrote four pages—a letter years in the making.*

    *Last fall, Will Percy and Springsteen had the chance to meet again, this
time on the Springsteen farm in central New Jersey, not far from the small
town where Springsteen grew up or from the Jersey Shore clubs where he
first made his mark in the 1970s. With a tape running, the two explored
the importance of books in Springsteen's life, most recently his discovery of Dr. Percy's essays in* The Message in the Bottle.[3] *Like the long-
in-coming letter to Mrs. Percy, perhaps this is part of the conversation
that Bruce Springsteen might have had with Walker Percy.*

**WILL PERCY: When did books start influencing your songwriting and
music? I remember as early as 1978, when I saw you in concert, you
mentioned Ron Kovic's *Born on the Fourth of July*,[4] and you dedicated
a song to him.**

BRUCE SPRINGSTEEN: I picked up that book in a drugstore in Arizona
while I was driving across the country with a friend of mine. We stopped
somewhere outside of Phoenix, and there was a copy of the paperback in
the rack. So I bought the book and I read it between Phoenix and Los
Angeles, where I stayed in this little motel. There was a guy in a wheel-
chair by the poolside every day, two or three days in a row, and I guess
he recognized me, and he finally came up to me and said, "Hey, I'm Ron
Kovic"—it was really very strange—and I said, "Oh, Ron Kovic, gee,
that's good." I thought I'd met him before somewhere. And he said, "No,
I wrote a book called *Born on the Fourth of July*." And I said, "You
wouldn't believe this. I just bought your book in a drugstore in Arizona
and I just read it. It's incredible." Real, real powerful book. And we talked
a little bit and he got me interested in doing something for the vets. He
took me to a vet center in Venice, and I met a bunch of guys along with
this guy Bobby Muller who was one of the guys who started VVA, Vietnam
Veterans of America.

    I go through periods where I read, and I get a lot out of what I read,
and that reading has affected my work since the late seventies. Films and
novels and books, more so than music, are what have really been driving
me since then. Your uncle once wrote that "American novels are about
everything," and I was interested in writing about "everything" in some
fashion in my music: how it felt to be alive now, a citizen of this country
in this particular place and time and what that meant, and what your

possibilities were if you were born and alive now, what you could do, what you were capable of doing. Those were ideas that interested me.

The really important reading that I did began in my late twenties, with authors like Flannery O'Connor. There was something in those stories of hers that I felt captured a certain part of the American character that I was interested in writing about. They were a big, big revelation. She got to the heart of some part of meanness that she never spelled out, because if she spelled it out you wouldn't be getting it. It was always at the core of every one of her stories—the way that she'd left that hole there, that hole that's inside of everybody. There was some dark thing—a component of spirituality—that I sensed in her stories, and that set me off exploring characters of my own. She knew original sin—knew how to give it the pesh [*sic*] of a story. She had talent and she had ideas, and the one served the other.

I think I'd come out of a period of my own writing where I'd been writing big, sometimes operatic, and occasionally rhetorical things. I was interested in finding another way to write about those subjects, about people, another way to address what was going on around me and in the country—a more scaled-down, more personal, more restrained way of getting some of my ideas across. So right prior to the record *Nebraska* [1982], I was deep into O'Connor. And then, later on, that led me to your uncle's books, and Bobbie Ann Mason's novels—I like her work.

I've also gotten a lot out of Robert Frank's photography in *The Americans*.[5] I was twenty-four when I first saw the book—I think a friend had given me a copy—and the tone of the pictures, how he gave us a look at different kinds of people, got to me in some way. I've always wished I could write songs the way he takes pictures. I think I've got half a dozen copies of that book stashed around the house, and I pull one out once in a while to get a fresh look at the photographs.

WP: I find it interesting that you're influenced a lot by movies—you said you're more influenced by movies and books than music. In the liner notes of *The Ghost of Tom Joad* you credited both the John Ford film and the book *The Grapes of Wrath* by Steinbeck.

BS: I came by the film before I really came by the book. I'd read the book in high school, along with *Of Mice and Men* and a few others, and then I read it again after I saw the movie. But I didn't grow up in a community of ideas—a place where you can sit down and talk about books, and how you read through them, and how they affect you. For a year, I went to a local college a few miles up the road from here, but I didn't really get much out of that particular place. I think I'm more a product of pop culture: films and records, films and records, films and records, especially early on. And then later, more novels and reading.

WP: Where did you draw your musical influences in your earlier writing as compared with this last album?

BS: Up until the late seventies, when I started to write songs that had to do with class issues, I was influenced more by music like the Animals' "We Gotta Get Out of This Place" or "It's My Life (And I'll Do What I Want)"—sort of class-conscious pop records that I'd listen to—and I'd say to myself: "That's my life, that's my life!" They said something to me about my own experience of exclusion. I think that's been a theme that's run through much of my writing: the politics of exclusion. My characters aren't really antiheroes. Maybe that makes them old-fashioned in some way. They're interested in being included, and they're trying to figure out what's in their way.

I'd been really involved with country music right prior to the album *Darkness on the Edge of Town* [1978], and that had a lot of effect on my writing because I think country is a very class-conscious music. And then that interest slowly led me into Woody Guthrie and folk music. Guthrie was one of the few songwriters at the time who was aware of the political implications of the music he was writing—a real part of his consciousness. He set out intentionally to address a wide variety of issues, to have some effect, to have some impact, to be writing as a way to have some impact on things: playing his part in the way things are moving and things change.

I was always trying to shoot for the moon. I had some lofty ideas about using my own music, to give people something to think about—to think about the world, and what's right and wrong. I'd been affected that way by records, and I wanted my own music and writing to extend themselves in that way.

WP: I notice that you talk about "writing" and not "songwriting." Do you sit down and write lyrics and then look for music?

BS: When I'd write rock music, music with the whole band, it would sometimes start out purely musically, and then I'd find my way to some lyrics. I haven't written like that in a while. In much of my recent writing, the lyrics have preceded the music, though the music is always in the back of my mind. In most of the recent songs, I tell violent stories very quietly. You're hearing characters' thoughts—what they're thinking after all the events that have shaped their situation have transpired. So

I try to get that internal sound, like that feeling at night when you're in bed and staring at the ceiling, reflective in some fashion. I wanted the songs to have the kind of intimacy that took you inside yourself and then back out into the world.

I'll use music as a way of defining and coloring the characters, conveying the characters' rhythm of speech and pace. The music acts as a very still surface, and the lyrics create a violent emotional life over it, or under it, and I let those elements bang up against each other.

Music can seem incidental, but it ends up being very important. It allows you to suggest the passage of time in just a couple of quiet beats. Years can go by in a few bars, whereas a writer will have to come up with a clever way of saying, "And then years went by. . . ." Thank God I don't have to do any of that! Songwriting allows you to cheat tremendously. You can present an entire life in a few minutes. And then hopefully, at the end, you reveal something about yourself and your audience and the person in the song. It has a little in common with short-story writing in that it's character-driven. The characters are confronting the questions that everyone is trying to sort out for themselves, their moral issues, the way those issues rear their heads in the outside world.

WP: While your previous albums might all come from personal experience— from the people and places you grew up with in New Jersey and elsewhere— you seem to have started writing more about other people and topics now, Mexican immigrants, for instance, in songs like "Sinaloa Cowboys." With that song, I remember you said in concert that it started out when you met a couple of Mexican brothers in the desert once when you were traveling.

BS: There's no single place where any of the songs come from, of course. True, I drew a lot of my earlier material from my experience growing up, my father's experience, the experience of my immediate family and town. But there was a point in the mid-eighties when I felt like I'd said pretty much all I knew how to say about all that. I couldn't continue writing about those same things without either becoming a stereotype of myself or by twisting those themes around too much. So I spent the next ten years or so writing about men and women—their intimate personal lives. I was being introspective but not autobiographical. It wasn't until I felt like I had a stable life in that area that I was driven to write more outwardly—about social issues.

A song like "Sinaloa Cowboys" came from a lot of places. I'd met a guy in the Arizona desert when I happened to be on a trip with some friends of mine, and he had a younger brother who died in a motorcycle accident. There's something about conversations with people—people you've met once and you'll never see again—that always stays with me. And I lived for quite a while in Los Angeles, and border reporting and immigration issues are always in the paper there. I've traveled down to the border a number of times.

WP: Why would you travel down to the border?

BS: With my dad, I'd take trips to Mexico a few years back. We'd take these extended road trips where we'd basically drive aimlessly. The border wasn't something I was consciously thinking about, it was just one of those places that all of a sudden starts meaning something to you. I'm always looking for ways to tell a particular story, and I just felt the connection, I can't explain what it was exactly—a connection to some of the things I'd written about in the past.

I don't think you sit down and write anything that isn't personal in some way. In the end, all your work is a result of your own psychology and experience. I never really write with a particular ideology in mind. As a writer, you're searching for ways to present different moral questions—to yourself because you're not sure how you will respond, and to your audience. That's what you get paid for—from what I can tell. Part of what we call entertainment should be "food for thought." That's what I was interested in doing since I was very young, how we live in the world and how we ought to live in the world. I think politics are implicit. I'm not interested in writing rhetoric or ideology. I think it was Walt Whitman who said, "The poet's job is to know the soul." You strive for that, assist your audience in finding and knowing theirs. That's always at the core of what you're writing, of what drives your music.

It's all really in your uncle's essay "The Man on the Train,"[6] about the "wandering spirit" and modern man—all that's happened since the Industrial Revolution when people were uprooted and set out on the road into towns where they'd never been before, leaving families, leaving traditions that were hundreds of years old. In a funny way, you can even trace that story in Chuck Berry's "Johnny B. Goode." I think that we're all trying to find what passes for a home, or creating a home of some sort, while we're constantly being uprooted by technology, by factories being shut down.

I remember when my parents moved out to California—I was about eighteen. My folks decided that they were going to leave New Jersey, but they had no idea really where to go. I had a girlfriend at the time and she was sort of a hippie. She was the only person we knew who'd ever been to California. She'd been to Sausalito and suggested they go there. You can just imagine—Sausalito in the late sixties! So they went to Sausalito, three thousand miles across the country, and they probably had only three grand that they'd saved and that had to get them a place to live, and they had to go out and find work. So they got to Sausalito and realized this wasn't it. My mother said they went to a gas station and she asked the guy there, "Where do people like us live?"—that's a question that sounds like the title of a Raymond Carver story!—and the guy told her, "Oh, you live on the peninsula." And that was what they did. They drove down south of San Francisco and they've been there ever since. My father was forty-two at the time—it's funny to think that he was probably seven or eight years younger than I am now. It was a big trip, took a lot of nerve, a lot of courage, having grown up in my little town in New Jersey.

But that story leads back to those same questions: how do you create the kind of home you want to live in, how do you create the kind of society you want to live in, what part do you play in doing that? To me, those things are all connected, but those connections are hard to make. The pace of the modern world, industrialization, postindustrialization, have all made human connection very difficult to maintain and sustain. To bring that modern situation alive—how we live now, our hang-ups and choices—that's what music and film and art are about—that's the service you're providing, that's the function you're providing as an artist. That's what keeps me interested in writing.

What we call "art" has to do with social policy—and it has to do with how you and your wife or you and your lover are getting along on any given day. I was interested in my music covering all those bases. And how do I do that? I do that by telling stories, through characters' voices— hopefully stories about inclusion. The stories in *The Ghost of Tom Joad* were an extension of those ideas: stories about brothers, lovers, movement, exclusion—political exclusion, social exclusion—and also the responsibility of these individuals—making bad choices, or choices they've been backed up against the wall to make.

The way all those things intersect is what interests me. The way the social issues and the personal issues cross over one another. To me, that's how people live. These things cross over our lives daily. People get tangled up in them, don't know how to address them, get lost in them. My work is a map, for whatever it's worth—for both my audience and for myself—and it's the only thing of value along with, hopefully, a well-lived life that we leave to the people we care about. I was lucky that I stumbled onto this opportunity early in my life. I think that the only thing that was uncommon was that I found a language that I was able to express those ideas with. Other people all the time struggle to find the language, or don't find the language—the language of the soul—or explode into violence or indifference or numbness, just numbed out in front of TV. "The Language"—that's what William Carlos Williams kept saying, the language of live people, not dead people!

If I'm overgeneralizing, just stop me. I'm not sure if I am or not, but in some fashion that's my intent, to establish a commonality by revealing our inner common humanity, by telling good stories about a lot of different kinds of people. The songs on the last album connected me up with my past, with what I'd written about in my past, and they also connected me up with what I felt was the future of my writing.

WP: Do you think your last album, which wasn't a pop or rock-and-roll record, had the same impact on the larger public that other records of yours had?

BS: I've made records that I knew would find a smaller audience than others that I've made. I suppose the larger question is, How do you get that type of work to be heard—despite the noise of modern society and the media, two hundred television channels? Today, people are swamped with a lot of junk, so the outlets and the avenues for any halfway introspective work tend to be marginalized. The last record might have been heard occasionally on the radio, but not very much. It's a paradox for an artist—if you go into your work with the idea of having some effect upon society, when, by the choice of the particular media, it's marginalized from the beginning. I don't know of any answer, except the hope that somehow you do get heard—and there are some publishing houses and television channels and music channels that are interested in presenting that kind of work.

I think you have to feel like there's a lot of different ways to reach people, help them think about what's really important in this one-and-only life we live. There's pop culture—that's the shotgun approach, where you throw it out and it gets interpreted in different ways and some people pick up on it. And then there's a more intimate, focused approach like I tried on *Tom Joad*. I got a lot of correspondence about the last album from a lot of different people—writers, teachers, those who have an impact in shaping other people's lives.

WP: Do you think pop culture can still have a positive effect?

BS: Well, it's a funny thing. When punk rock music hit in the late 1970s, it wasn't played on the radio, and nobody thought, Oh yeah, that'll be popular in 1992 for two generations of kids. But the music dug in, and now it has a tremendous impact on the music and culture of the nineties. It was powerful, profound music and it was going to find a way to make itself heard eventually. So I think there's a lot of different ways of achieving the kind of impact that most writers and filmmakers, photographers, musicians want their work to have. It's not always something that happens right away—the "Big Bang"!

With the exception of certain moments in the history of popular culture, it's difficult to tell what has an impact anymore, and particularly now when there's so many alternatives. Now, we have the fifth *Batman* movie! I think about the part in the essay "The Man on the Train" where your uncle talks about alienation. He says the truly alienated man isn't the guy who's despairing and trying to find his place in the world. It's the guy who just finished his twentieth Erle Stanley Gardner Perry Mason novel.[7] That is the lonely man! That is the alienated man! So you could say, similarly, the guy who just saw the fifth *Batman* picture, he's the alienated man. But as much as anyone, I still like to go out on a Saturday night and buy the popcorn and watch things explode, but when that becomes such a major part of the choices that you have, when you have sixteen cinemas and fourteen of them are playing almost exactly the same picture, you feel that something's going wrong here. And if you live outside a major metropolitan area, maybe you're lucky if there's a theater in town that's playing films that fall slightly outside of those choices.

There's an illusion of choice that's out there, but it's an illusion, it's not real choice. I think that's true in the political arena and in pop culture, and I guess there's a certain condescension and cynicism that goes along with it—the assumption that people aren't ready for something new and different.

WP: Do you think that the culture of celebrity is a cause of some of those problems? You seem to have escaped some of the problems that go along with being a celebrity.

BS: I don't know, it's the old story—a lot of it is how you play your role. My music was in some sense inclusive and pretty personal, maybe even friendly. I've enjoyed the trappings from time to time, but I think I like a certain type of freedom. Of course, I enjoy my work being recognized, and when you get up on stage in front of twenty thousand people and you shake your butt all around, you're asking for some sort of trouble. I hope I've kept my balance. I enjoy my privacy.

I don't think the fascination with celebrities will ever really go away. An intellectual would say that people in the Industrial Age left their farms and their towns, so they couldn't gossip with their neighbors over the fence anymore—and all of a sudden there was a rise of a celebrity culture so we could have some people in common that we could talk about.

The substantive moral concern might be that we live in a country where the only story might be who's succeeding and who's number one, and what are you doing with it. It sure does become a problem if a certain part of your life as a writer—your "celebrity," or whatever you want to call it—can blur and obscure the story that you're interested in telling. I've felt that and seen that at certain times. One of the most common questions I was asked on the last tour, even by very intelligent reviewers, was, "Why are you writing these songs? What are you complaining about? You've done great." That's where your uncle's essay "Notes for a Novel About the End of the World"[8] was very helpful to me and my writing. Your uncle addresses the story behind those same comments: "The material is so depressing. The songs are so down."[9] He explains the moral and human purpose of writing by using that analogy of the canary that goes down into the mine with the miners: when the canary starts squawking and squawking and finally keels over, the miners figure it's time to come up and think things over a little bit. That's the writer—the twentieth-century writer is the canary for the larger society.

Maybe a lot of us use the idea of "celebrity" to maintain the notion that everything is all right, that there's always someone making their million the next day. As a celebrity, you don't worry about your bills, you have an enormous freedom to write and to do what you want. You can live with it well. But if your work is involved in trying to show where the country is hurting and where people are hurting, your own success is used to knock down or undercut the questions you ask of your audience. It's tricky, because American society has a very strict idea of what success is and what failure is. We're all "born in the U.S.A." and some part of you carries that with you. But it's ironic if "celebrity" is used to reassure lots of people, barely making it, that "Look, someone's really making it, making it big, so everything is all right, just lose yourself and all your troubles in that big-time success!"

WP: Do you think you're through making music videos?

BS: I don't know. I probably am. There's nobody waiting with bated breath out there for my next video right now. I've never been much of a video artist. I was "prevideo," and I think I remain "prevideo," though maybe I'm "postvideo" now.

Music videos have had an enormous impact on the way that you receive visual images on television and in the theaters—and it sped up the entire way the music world worked, for better or for worse. When I started, you had a band, you toured two or three, four years, you did a thousand shows or five hundred shows, that's how you built your audience, and then maybe you had a hit record. I feel sorry for some of these talented young bands that come up: they have a hit record, a video or two, and then it's over. I think it might have made the music world more fickle. In some ways, it may be more expedient for some of the young acts, but I think it's harder also, because you don't have the time to build a long-standing relationship with your audience.

There was something about developing an audience slowly—you'd draw an audience that stood with you over a long period of time, and it got involved with the questions you were asking and the issues you were bringing up. It's an audience who you shared a history with. I saw the work that I was doing as my life's work. I thought I'd be playing music my whole life and writing my whole life, and I wanted to be a part of my audience's ongoing life. The way you do that is the same way your audience lives its life—you do it by attempting to answer the questions that both you and they have asked, sometimes with new questions. You find where those questions lead you to—your actions in the world. You take it out of the aesthetic and you hopefully bring it into your practical, everyday life, the moral or ethical.

"Man on the Train" helped me think about these things in some fashion, where your uncle dissects the old Western movie heroes.[10] We have our mythic hero, Gary Cooper, who is capable of pure action, where it's either all or nothing, and he looks like he's walking over that abyss of anxiety, and he won't fail. Whereas the moviegoer, the person watching the movie, is not capable of that. There's no real abyss under Gary Cooper, but there is one under the guy watching the film! Bringing people out over that abyss, helping them and myself to realize where we all "are," helping my audience answer the questions that are there—that's what I'm interested in doing with my own work.

That's what I try to accomplish at night in a show. Presenting ideas, asking questions, trying to bring people closer to characters in the songs, closer to themselves—so that they take those ideas, those questions— fundamental moral questions about the way we live and the way we behave toward one another—and then move those questions from the aesthetic into the practical, into some sort of action, whether it's action in the community, or action in the way you treat your wife, or your kid, or speak to the guy who works with you. That is what can be done, and is done, through film and music and photography and painting. Those are real changes I think you can make in people's lives, and that I've had made in my life through novels and films and records and people who meant something to me. Isn't that what your uncle meant by "existentialist reflection"?

And there's a lot of different ways that gets done. You don't have to be doing work that's directly socially conscious. You could make an argument that one of the most socially conscious artists in the second half of this century was Elvis Presley, even if he probably didn't start out with any set of political ideas that he wanted to accomplish. He said, "I'm all shook up and I want to shake you up," and that's what happened. He had an enormous impact on the way that people lived, how they responded to themselves, to their own physicality, to the integration of their own nature. I think that he was one of the people, in his own way, who led to the sixties and the Civil Rights movement. He began getting us "all shook up," this poor white kid from Mississippi who connected with black folks through their music, which he made his own and then gave to others. So pop culture is a funny thing—you can affect people in a lot of different ways.

WP: Did you always try to affect the audience like that? When you first started out, when you were young?

BS: We were trying to excite people, we were trying to make people feel alive. The core of rock music was cathartic. There was some fundamental catharsis that occurred in "Louie, Louie." That lives on, that pursuit. Its very nature was to get people "in touch" with themselves and with each other in some fashion. So initially you were just trying to excite people, and make them happy, alert them to themselves, and do the same for yourself. It's a way of combating your own indifference, your own tendency to slip into alienation and isolation. That's also in "Man on the Train": we can't be alienated together. If we're all alienated together, we're really not alienated.

That's a lot of what music did for me—it provided me with a community, filled with people, and brothers and sisters who I didn't know, but who I knew were out there. We had this enormous thing in common, this "thing" that initially felt like a secret. Music always provided that home for me, a home where my spirit could wander. It performed the function that all art and film and good human relations performed—it provided me with the kind of "home" always described by those philosophers your uncle loved.

There are very real communities that were built up around that notion—the very real community of your local club on Saturday night. The importance of bar bands all across America is that they nourish and inspire that community. So there are the very real communities of people and characters, whether it's in Asbury Park or a million different towns across the land. And then there is the community that it was enabling you to imagine, but that you haven't seen yet. You don't even know it exists, but you feel that, because of what you heard or experienced, it could exist.

That was a very powerful idea because it drew you outward in search of that community—a community of ideas and values. I think as you get older and develop a political point of view, it expands out into those worlds, the worlds of others, all over America, and you realize it's just an extension of that thing that you felt in a bar on Saturday night in Asbury Park when it was a hundred and fifty people in the room.

What do you try to provide people? What do parents try to provide their children? You're supposed to be providing a hopeful presence, a decent presence, in your children's lives and your neighbors' lives. That's what I would want my children to grow up with and then to provide when they become adults. It's a big part of what you can do with song, and pictures and words. It's real and its results are physical and tangible. And if you follow its implications, it leads you both inward and outward. Some days we climb inside, and some days maybe we run out. A good day is a balance of those sort of things. When rock music was working at its best, it was doing all of those things—looking inward and reaching out to others.

To get back to where we started, it can be difficult to build those kinds of connections, to build and sustain those kinds of communities, when you're picked up and thrown away so quickly—that cult of celebrity. At your best, your most honest, your least glitzy, you shared a common history, and you attempted both to ask questions and answer them in concert with your audience. In concert. The word "concert"—people working together—that's the idea. That's what I've tried to do as I go along with my work. I'm thankful that I have a dedicated, faithful audience that's followed along with me a good part of the way. It's one of my life's great blessings—having that companionship and being able to rely on that companionship. You know, "companionship" means breaking bread with your brothers and sisters, your fellow human beings—the most important thing in the world! It's sustained my family and me and my band throughout my life.

WP: Do you think you've extended your audience to include some of the kinds of people that you're writing about now: Mexican immigrants, homeless people? Do you feel that you're doing something for those people with your music?

BS: There's a difference between an emotional connection with them, like I think I do have, and a more physical, tangible impact. There was a point in the mid-eighties where I wanted to turn my music into some kind of activity and action, so that there was a practical impact on the communities that I passed through while I traveled around the country. On this last tour, I would meet a lot of the people who are out there on the front line—activists, legal advocates, social workers—and the people that they're involved with. It varied from town to town, but we'd usually work with an organization that's providing immediate care for people in distress, and then also we'd find an organization that's trying to have some impact on local policy. It helped me get a sense of what was going on in those towns, and the circumstances that surround the people that I'm imagining in my songs, in the imagined community I create with my music.

I'm sure I've gotten a lot more out of my music than I've put in, but those meetings and conversations keep me connected so that I remember the actual people that I write about. But I wouldn't call myself an activist. I'm more of a concerned citizen. I think I'd say that I'm up to my knees in it, but I'm not up to my ass!

I guess I'm—rock bottom—a concerned, even aroused observer, sort of like the main character of Ralph Ellison's *Invisible Man.*[11] Not that I'm invisible! But Ellison's character doesn't directly take on the world. He wants to see the world change, but he's mainly a witness, a witness to a lot of blindness. I recently heard two teachers, one black and one white, talking about that novel, and it sure got to them; it's what Ellison wanted it to be, it's a great American story—and in a way we're all part of it.

Notes

1. Founded by Pulitzer Prize–winning author and child psychiatrist Robert Coles, *DoubleTake* magazine publishes literature and photography of social reflection. In early 2003, Springsteen performed two benefit concerts for the magazine after it experienced major financial problems. See Jacques Steinberg, "A Rocker and a Revered Author Bond for a Cause: Robert Coles and Bruce Springsteen, Pundits and Pals," *New York Times*, March 20, 2003.

2. The letter is dated February 23, 1989, and reads, in part:

> Dear Mr. Springsteen—
> This is a fan letter—of sorts. I've always been an admirer of yours, for your musicianship, and for being one of the few sane guys in your field.
> The immediate occasion is that my favorite nephew, Will Percy, has even a higher opinion of you. He is a level-headed perceptive young lawyer and generally knows what he is talking about.
> Of particular interest is learning—from an article in *America,* the Jesuit weekly—that you are a Catholic. If this is true, and I am too, it would appear that the two of us are rarities in our professions: you as a post-modern musician, I as a writer, a novelist and philosopher. That—and your admiration for Flannery O'Connor. She was a dear friend of mine, though she was a much more heroic Catholic than I. . . .
> That is to say that I am most interested in your spiritual journey, and if there is any other material about it I'd be obliged if you will tell me.
> Unfortunately, I have cancer and am taking radiation for it. I am far from well and am not able yet to receive visitors.
> Since I don't know your address I am handing this to Will who says he knows where to send it.
> All my best wishes for your superb career.
> Sincerely,
> Walker Percy

Springsteen replied—some several years later—to Mrs. Percy. By that time, Walker Percy had passed away. It is a contrite, apologetic, and touching letter:

> Dear Mrs. Percy,
> This is a letter so long in coming I'm almost embarrassed to write, but I've gotten to know Will a little bit and he's encouraged me on, so here we go.
> A few years back when I received Dr. Percy's letter, I wasn't very familiar with his work. . . . My memory has it that [his] letter was written on a yellow legal pad and, as is mine, his handwriting was not the easiest to decipher. It was a passionate letter about the comforts and difficulties of reconciling the inner life of a sophisticated man, a writer's life, with the Catholic faith. I recall Dr. Percy's explaining how one had brought depth of meaning to the other for him. He was . . . curious to know how I handled my issues of faith. . . .
> It is now one of my great regrets that we didn't get to correspond. A while after receiving Dr. Percy's letter, I picked up "The Moviegoer," its toughness

and beauty have stayed with me. The loss and search for faith and meaning have been at the core of my own work for most of my adult life. I'd like to think that perhaps that is what Dr. Percy heard and was what moved him to write to me. Those issues are still what motivate me to sit down, pick up my guitar and write. Today, I would have had a lot to put into that letter. . . .

I hope this letter finds you well and that some day when I'm down in your neck of the woods or you're up in mine we can meet. I'd love to have you come to a show, you might like it!

Best,

Bruce Springsteen

P.S. I'm in Australia at the moment and I've just begun *The Message in the Bottle.*

3. Walker Percy, *The Message in the Bottle* (New York: Picador USA, 2000), consists of a collection of essays that address those quintessential questions that continue to haunt humankind: Who are we and why are we here? See also Percy's *The Moviegoer* (Knopf, 1961; Vintage, 1998), *Second Coming* (Farrar, Straus and Giroux, 1983), *Love in the Ruins* (Farrar, Straus and Giroux, 1973), and another collection of essays, *Signposts in a Strange Land,* edited by Patrick Samway (Farrar, Straus and Giroux, 1991). Samway is also the author of *Walker Percy: A Life* (Loyola Press, 1999).

4. Ron Kovic, *Born on the Fourth of July* (New York: Pocket Books, 1981).

5. Robert Frank, *The Americans* (1959; New York: Random House, 1993).

6. Walker Percy, "The Man on the Train," in *The Message in the Bottle* (New York: Picador USA, 2000), pp. 83–100.

7. Percy's full quotation reads, "The only literature of alienation is an alienated literature, that is, a bad art, which is no art at all. An Erle Stanley Gardner novel is a true exercise in alienation. A man who finishes his twentieth Perry Mason is that much nearer total despair than when he started." Percy, ibid., p. 83.

8. Walker Percy, "Notes for a Novel About the End of the World," in *The Message in the Bottle* (New York: Picador USA, 2000), pp. 101–18.

9. "It's an old story with novelists. People are always asking, Why don't you write about pleasant things and normal people? Why all the neurosis and violence? There are many nice things in the world. The reader is offended. But if one replies, 'Yes, it's true; in fact there seem to be more nice people around now than ever before, but somehow as the world grows nicer it also grows more violent. The triumphant secular society of the Western world, the nicest of all worlds, killed more people in the first half of this century than have been killed in all history. Travelers to Germany before the last war reported that the Germans were the nicest people in Europe'—then the reader is even more offended." See Percy, ibid., p. 105.

10. Percy, "Notes for a Novel About the End of the World," pp. 93–95.

11. Ralph Ellison, *Invisible Man* (Reprint; New York: Random House, 2002).

Nadine Epstein

■

Certain places in the world are always associated with one person or persons: Elvis and Tupelo, Mississippi; the Beatles and Liverpool. With Springsteen, of course, it's Asbury Park (even though he was born in Long Branch and grew up in Freehold). Nadine Epstein, a Washington, D.C.–based freelance writer, hails from Asbury Park. In the following article, which ran in the August 23, 1999, issue of the *Christian Science Monitor*, she describes her "hometown."

Asbury Park, My Hometown

Christian Science Monitor

■ "WHERE ARE YOU FROM?" is one of those questions you run into a lot. When it comes out that I grew up on the Jersey Shore near Asbury Park, people under 60 get excited.

I can be halfway around the world and they ask: "Do you know Bruce Springsteen?" Their eyes shine, because Springsteen and Asbury Park are inextricably linked.

Yes, I answer, I "met" Springsteen in 1970 when he played the Jewish Community Center Tween Dance.[1] The girl who became his wife was my grade-school lunch-recess monitor, and saxophonist Clarence Clemons and other band members gave me a ride to school one morning on their way home from an all-night practice.

But what I really care about is Asbury Park—a sad place that no longer jives with its rock 'n' roll image. The city's mile-long stretch of ocean is as deserted as Berlin's Potsdamer Platz during the cold war, disappointing pilgrims from Berlin or LA who come in search of landmarks of Springsteen lyrics—the boardwalk, Madame Marie the fortune-teller, the Tilt-a-Whirl where Springsteen got his shirt caught.

Every time I walk down the boardwalk I know that we ought to save this place, that it is worth fighting soulless urban blight, and taking a stand, right here. Transforming a fallen city, even a small seaside city studded with rock 'n' roll icons, is an epic challenge—but it's not beyond the wealth and consciousness of the generation that reunited and is rebuilding Berlin.

When I was a child, and that wasn't that long ago, the boardwalk and beaches were packed. There were concerts, fireworks, Easter Parades, rides, amusements, and my grandparents and thousands of other middle-class senior citizens calmly rocking in green Adirondack gliders.

My first memories are of running around in the sand at the First Avenue Beach. Later, my mother and I, in white gloves, ate dainty datenut and cream cheese sandwiches at the department store on Cookman Avenue, once the anchor of the county's finest shopping strip. I had innocent afternoons in a blissfully integrated kindergarten class.

My own troubled teen years coincided with the city's rapid decline, and the birth of the rock 'n' roll culture that breathed a faster, wilder kind of life into the beachfront area for about 15 years. In the 1970s, life was about hot rodders and freaks and beach parties and seaside restaurants and bars and concerts in Convention Hall, where I climbed into dressing-room windows via the roof to see shows for free.

In the late 1980s, a great razing occurred after the city, in a misguided attempt to save itself, sold off most of its valuable beachfront property to a condo developer who went bankrupt.

So while most of the buildings that front directly on the boardwalk survive boarded up, there are blocks of "no-man's" land. Most of the clubs where I lied about my age are gone, as are the rides. Waist-high grass growing up through the ruins of the two miniature golf courses I once adored breaks my heart.

Still, the Atlantic pounds the beach, and I find joy walking along the faded gray boards. That smell of wood drenched with sea salt is everywhere, enriched by generations of human feet slathered in oil, and candy apple, taffy, and melted custard drippings.

And there's a lot I don't feel joy about. Like the complexities that cause a town to fall hard and not get up. The corruption. The ignorance and fear that stemmed from a riot (I watched from my raft in the ocean as the black part of town burned in 1970). The helpless feeling of a downtown sucked dry by shopping malls. The rundown hotels occupied by the mentally ill, placed there by deinstitutionalization.

But there are signs of hope: a new city council, fresh sand replenishment on the beaches, a group trying to save the smiling clown face on the Palace Amusements building, a local developer trying to save the Ferris wheel, and one restored hotel.[2] And there is potential: gorgeous beaches just 50 miles from New York, and surrounding towns filled with high-priced real estate.

Those are just the tangibles. What about the famous name and the rock nostalgia that touches so many? Reviving Asbury Park is an enormous job. People have been trying for years without much result. I think that's because not enough of us have gotten involved. For baby boomers this city transcends normal geography, and it needs our help. I've often wondered why we don't create a Save Asbury Park Foundation and fund it through a Save Asbury Park Tour starring Springsteen, and maybe some of the other musicians who cut their teeth there?

If Springsteen fans are spending $75 a ticket for his current tour, why not tack on a bit more for the city that inspired the lyrics so many who've never been there know by heart? After all, it was Springsteen's poetry that transformed Asbury Park into more than a regional resort and has kept Madame Marie (deceased, I hear) and the Palace (condemned) alive in our collective consciousness. Not that Springsteen has forgotten Asbury Park. He comes back to do charity benefits for good causes, and he comes back to play.

I have a wild idea inspired by the sweet old houses with wrap-around porches found in Asbury Park. Maybe some aging boomers might buy some of these houses and summer there as my grandparents did, and transform the city into an international senior citizen's rock-music mecca—a living museum.

Then natives can regale rock 'n' roll pilgrims with stories of famous people we hardly knew, the kind of stories that make people's eyes shine. Like, how the head of the Jewish Community Center recorded that 1970 Tween Springsteen concert, then taped over it at a rabbinical conference. In between reminiscences, we can hum "Jersey Girl" as we rock in our Adirondack gliders, that fresh salty sea wind blowing through our strands of gray.

Notes

1. Epstein's chronology may be a bit off. According to the Brucebase Web site (www.springsteen.org.uk/gig1970.htm), Springsteen and his band performed in Deal, New Jersey, at a Jewish-community-sponsored dance held in the Young Hebrew Association Clubhouse on March 18, 1971. The show was taped but then accidentally erased. Patti Scialfa, then a high school senior, reportedly was in the audience that night and was introduced to Bruce during the course of the evening. She had seen him perform with his band Steel Mill in fall 1970 at Monmouth College.

2. The Palace is affectionately known as Tillie, referring to the Cheshire-cat smiling clown that graces the sides of the building. Even though the Palace closed in 1988, it was nevertheless placed on the National Register of Historic Places in 2000. As of this writing, the city of Asbury Park and New Jersey's state historic preservation agency have agreed to demolish the building and build a new structure—similar in volume—that will consist of a hotel/retail complex with up to three floors of commerical space. The image of Tillie is expected to be incorporated into the new design. See "State office agrees to Palace rebuild," Asburypark.net, March 21, 2003. For a photographic history of the heyday of Asbury Park, see Helen-Chantal Pike, *Asbury Park NJ*, Images of America series (Charleston, S.C.: Arcadia, 1997).

Frederick Reiken

∎

The Lost Legends of New Jersey (2000), Frederick Reiken's second novel, recounts the dissolution of the Rubin clan, a family saga done up Jersey style. In this bittersweet and strangely touching coming-of-age tale, its young protagonist, Anthony Rubin, does his best to focus on the here and now, as his comically dysfunctional family slowly disintegrates before his eyes. Reiken captures the sometimes shabby elegance of the New Jersey Shore's beach towns, including Asbury Park, Belmar, Sea Bright, and Allenhurst. Often heard in the background is the music of Bruce Springsteen, offering an element of hope and salvation.

from *The Lost Legends of New Jersey*

∎DURING THE SECOND WEEK of August, the fecal coliform count got so high that all the beaches closed. Apparently, there was some sort of flesh-eating bacteria in the water. Shane Sullivan claimed that the bacteria came from raw sewage that had been dumped into the ocean. He also claimed that it caused human skin to molt and come off like a crab shell.

The beaches stayed closed for six days. Anthony, Jay, Bradley, and Andy midget-wrestled and became denizens of the Asbury Park arcade. One rainy afternoon the four boys stood around the prize counter. They discussed prize options and what they planned to cash in all their win tickets for come Labor Day. Andy and Bradley both wanted the Muhammad Ali boxing gloves. Jay, who had barely any tickets, said he would probably go for the plastic back scratcher. After much deliberation, Anthony found that the only thing he liked besides the boxing gloves was a ceramic winged horse that was actually a coin bank. When he pointed the horse out, Jay said, "That's Pegasus, from mythology, just like the constellation." They had seen Pegasus several times while starwatching that summer. Somehow this incidental correlation settled things. Anthony nodded and said, "Yeah, that's what I'm going for."

That was also the week Bradley started them listening to Bruce Springsteen. He had just purchased a small boom box. He had four

Bruce tapes and swore that his oldest sister had once sat right next to Bruce at a bar in Sea Bright. He started toting the boom box everywhere, playing all songs as loud as possible. One day while blasting the album *Born To Run,* Bradley suddenly stopped walking. He turned the volume down and looked at his friends dramatically. Then he said, "We are walking through Bruce's songs."

Jay and Anthony immediately got their parents to buy them *Born To Run* on cassette. They started listening to it religiously, and soon they knew every cryptic word of "Jungleland." Anthony found that *Born To Run* evoked a sadness, that certain songs were almost cinematic. Each time they listened to "Thunder Road," all of the lyrics would unfold again inside him. He'd always see a screen door slam. Then he would picture some wondrous girl named Mary, her dress waving as she danced across the floor of their house in Allenhurst.

Toward the end of that week of the closed beaches, they even had one Bruce-related miracle. They met two Teaneck girls, Denise and Jackie. The girls approached while Bradley was blasting "Rosalita" on his boom box. They started singing along and saying things like, "Totally awesome song!" Both went for Andy, of course, but he played soccer. Just a day after they met the girls, Andy left the shore in order to go to soccer camp in Maryland. This made things easier and soon they were all hanging out together on the boards.

Denise and Jackie were best friends. Jackie was fragile and quiet. She had short light brown hair and a gaze that always caused Anthony to wonder what she was thinking. Meanwhile Denise seemed the quintessential Jersey girl. She had thick black hair and plump breasts and would call out "Jinx!" whenever she and another person spoke the same word at the same time. Then she would punch the person's arm until the person named five movie stars or beer brands or whatever Denise asked for. Likewise Anthony always had to say "safety" if he burped, otherwise Denise would say "slugs" and then start punching. She had three brothers, which explained her sort of tomboy roughhouse nature. She even liked to midget-wrestle. Both she and Jackie got their own names, the Big Babe and Psycho Kitty.

There was an afternoon when Anthony wound up alone with Jackie on the boardwalk. He had a crush on her by then. Jackie was eating cotton candy. They were both leaning against a railing, talking and watching small children ride the Asbury Park carousel. He got his guts up and placed his hand on hers.

She didn't move her hand away, but also did not respond to his bold gesture. They continued chatting as Jackie ate her cotton candy, her captured hand still clasping the metal railing. Finally Jackie pulled her hand back. She held out the purple cotton candy and said, "Want some?" He took a bite.

She said, "You're Jewish, right?"

He nodded.

"Then why the heck is your name Anthony? I've never met a Jew named Anthony in my life."

"I had this cousin," he said. "Anthony Spignatelli. He was half Jewish, half Italian. He died two months before I was born. Until then my parents planned to name me Eric, or else Jill."

"How did he die?"

"It was a mystery."

"They have to know."

"They say they didn't."

He took her hand again. For a few seconds Jackie stared as if assessing the situation. Anthony smiled, clasped her hand tighter. "I barely know you," she said, and pulled her hand away.

Allenhurst Beach reopened on a Sunday in mid-August. By then Anthony, Jay, and Bradley were getting bored with being junior lifeguards. They'd make one garbage pass in the morning, then they would run off to find Denise and Jackie. The girls belonged to The Breakwater Club in Elberon. They had a freshwater pool and a snack bar, unlike Allenhurst. They had a shuffleboard court, and Anthony loved shuffleboard. . . .

Just before Labor Day weekend, Anthony's mother got arrested. It was a weekday. Anthony's father and Douglas Berkowitz were each at home that night in Livingston, which was an hour's drive from Allenhurst without traffic. Sometimes they stayed there on weekday nights instead of braving the Parkway after work.

Both Jess and Claudia got tanked at a bar called Tides, which was in Belmar. On the way home, Jess was pulled over in Asbury. She was arrested for drunk driving and locked up in an Asbury Park jail cell. All four children were there when Claudia returned in a kind of frenzy. She said the officers acted like rough jerks and had left her standing on the roadside. Clearly as plastered as Jess Rubin, she had walked back because she figured she'd get pulled over if she drove.

Michael arrived an hour later, after receiving his wife's phone call from the jailhouse. He explained the situation to his children. Then he and Claudia went out. Anthony didn't know what to feel. He kept on thinking that his mother was somehow part of a Bruce Springsteen song. She was behind bars in the Asbury Park jailhouse. She's had a cancer scare and wouldn't laugh at Yiddish constellations. Maybe it wasn't as mythical as "Jungleland," but it still seemed too confusing to be reality. He also knew that his mother would freak out when she got home.

Samuele F. S. Pardini

■

Bruce Springsteen has written many politically edged songs during his career but few are as controversial as "American Skin (41 Shots)," about the fatal shooting in February 1999 of an unarmed African immigrant in the vestibule of his Bronx apartment by four New York City police officers who reportedly mistook his wallet for a weapon. All four were acquitted of murder charges. "American Skin" made news when members of the New York Police Association claimed the song was an anti-police diatribe. Indeed, so incensed were the boys in blue that the Patrolmen's Benevolent Association of New York City called for a boycott of all Springsteen performances in the city. The president of the association even went so far as to call Springsteen a "dirt bag." In this provocative essay, Samuele F. S. Pardini, a student of the late Leslie Fiedler and a teacher at the State University of New York at Buffalo, offers his own interpretation of the song.

Bruce Springsteen's "American Skin"

Artvoice

A Killing and a Silence

■ON THE NIGHT of February 19, 1999, four New York Police Department Officers on duty fired 41 shots at Amadou Diallo, a young, black, street vendor who had emigrated to the U.S. from Guinea. Diallo was unarmed, he was trying to reach his wallet, presumably to show the officers his ID, as any good citizen of any country would do if stopped by the cops. At their murder trial (for some strange jurisdictional reason moved from New York to Albany), the officers testified they thought he was pulling out a gun. They were acquitted of all charges. The reactions to the acquittal divided the city and the country. The protest against the jury and NYPD was strong especially in New York City, where people gathered in sit-ins. Black communities in New York and elsewhere denounced the case as one of clear racial profiling. Newspaper columnists and television commentators debated the case. Politicians, congressmen, presidential candidates—everyone had something to say. President Clinton, the same president who in his 1998 State of the Union speech proposed putting 100,000 new officers on the streets of America, an idea that received the support and a long applause from both parties in Congress, declared that there's still a division between blacks and whites in America, that being black isn't the same as being white.

Then, a week after the tempest, silence. The momentum, as they call it, was over, gone. The case disappeared from the news, from the editorial page, from political campaigns. Nobody talked about it anymore, the economy kept booming, unemployment kept going down as never before in American history, the presidential primaries were basically over the first week of March, students went on Spring break in Florida or Mexico, and Diallo kept lying horizontal in his grave. Silent, dead, 41 holes in his black skin, forgotten by almost everybody. Until June 4.

The Night They Drove Old Dixie Down

Sunday, June 4, was the night Bruce Springsteen and the E Street Band performed their second concert in Atlanta, Georgia, part of their reunion tour begun more than a year ago in Europe, the same tour that stopped in Buffalo the past November. It was the last concert before a final stand of ten shows at Madison Square Garden that would begin June 10.

Springsteen's concerts are never the same, and the set list, though it has a basic structure, changes each night, especially if he performs two or three times in the same city. Since the beginning of the tour, he has included more than 70 songs. But nobody was expecting two new songs in just one night.

The first was "Further On Up The Road,"[2] a classic Springsteen song, with which he opened the show. After the sixth song, "Point Blank," which had been preceded by a cover of Jimmy Cliff's "Trapped," he stopped for a moment and did what he rarely did throughout the entire tour. He spoke a few words in order to introduce another new song, calling it "American Skin"[3] (though on the handwritten set list it was called "41 Shots"). Springsteen is a very meticulous musician and prepares his concerts maniacally. He does nothing, absolutely nothing at random. He sound-checks for hours if he feels it's necessary, he makes sure the sound is the best it can be everywhere in the arena, he exercises before the concert, he chooses his and the band's clothes, he refuses commercial sponsors. He wants the audience's attention on the stage and on his music. Buffalonians who attended the debut concert of the *Darkness* Tour at the Shea's in May 1978 will remember the rage on his face when the electric power went off during "She's the One." The band had rehearsed "Further On Up the Road" for months, but they hardly rehearsed "American Skin" at all. Reportedly, the song had been sound-checked only twice before Atlanta—in Raleigh and in Salt Lake City.

Nonetheless, its rendition was very powerful and by the end of it the crowd was chanting along with the intense and emotional refrain: "41 shots, 41 shots." I don't know what kind of reactions Springsteen expected, but certainly he knew there would be *some* reaction. He had the biggest misunderstanding a rock song has ever generated with "Born in the U.S.A.," a song mistakenly interpreted as a patriotic anthem. Any time there's a political campaign in New Jersey, politicians try to associate their names with his. So did Ronald Reagan in 1984, Bob Dole in 1992, and most recently New Jersey Governor Christine Whitman (guess what: they're all Republicans). Though Springsteen's audience these days is mostly white, he knew he was performing in Atlanta, where the vast majority of the population is black, where the mayor is black, where the history of the Civil Rights Movement is more important than, say, in Hawaii.

The same night, on "Light of Day," a guitar-oriented song during which he gives his "Minister of Rock and Roll" speech telling the fans that he knows they have been "analyzed, stigmatized, pokemonized" but that the ministry of rock and roll will save and free them, he also told them: "I know you've been re-publicanized, but it's not too late to repent!" I am sure he was preaching to the Reagan Democrats, especially numerous in the South: blue-collar workers, usually conservative, often racially biased, who shifted from the Democratic to the Republican side of the political electorate at the end of the 1970s, voting for Ronald Reagan. First, they lost their jobs as their factories moved to Mexico or someplace where work is cheaper, then they ended up in long lines in front of some food bank to collect a bowl of soup. In any city the tour stops, Springsteen makes a donation to a local food bank, he dedicates a song, usually "The Ghost of Tom Joad," to the people that work for that organization, and invites the audience to do the same "for the many many people the economy doesn't reach," as I heard him recently saying in Anaheim, California, and Las Vegas. He has worked with such organizations for more than fifteen years.

The Media Circle

The day after the Atlanta show, rumors of the new songs began to circulate among fans across the world. Web pages dedicated to Springsteen highlighted "American Skin" and the lyrics appeared on different websites. Three days later, on June 8, the *New York Post* reported that Springsteen played a song inspired by the killing of Amadou Diallo. The same day Patrick J. Lynch, president of the Patrolmen's Benevolent Association of the City of New York, released an official note about the song on the PBA website, accusing Springsteen of trying "to fatten his wallet by reopening the wounds of this tragic case at a time when police officers and community members are in a healing period." Lynch urged PBA's members to boycott Springsteen's concerts "as security or in any other kind of work" and "not to attend" them.

The same day, in Microsoft's web magazine *Slate*, Timothy Noah accused Springsteen of having written the song to help Hillary Clinton's New York senatorial race. Bob Lucente, the president of the New York state chapter of the Fraternal Order of Police, denounced the song for anti-police messages and called Springsteen a "dirt bag." The song and reaction to it were featured on television prime time news and newspaper front pages in Europe.

The day following the first concert at Madison Square Garden, the *New York Times* published a review of it along with an article by John Tierney in its Region section, in which the journalist defines "American Skin" [as] an "anthem against police brutality" and accuses the New Jersey resident of "crusading to preserve affirmative action programs, not exactly a popular case in his old neighborhoods." On June 17, the *Times* published an op-ed piece by George Molé, a lieutenant in the New York Police Department, who said that he was no longer a Springsteen fan because the song showed "contempt for me and my fellow officers."

Springsteen refused to comment on the episode or on any of the other attacks.[4] He performed the song in every one of the New York shows.

According to the *New York Daily News* (June 9), Amadou Diallo's mother called the song a "beautiful thought" and thanked Springsteen for keeping the memory of her son's case alive. Mr. Saikou Diallo, Amadou's father, said the same thing. The Diallos met with Springsteen before the first concert and attended the show, apparently enjoying it very much.

Why All This Fuss?

Despite all the clamor generated by the case, none of the commentators and the interpretations given of the songs really made an effort to answer the real questions that stand at the heart of all this fuss.

Did Springsteen write this song for money? The song has not been officially recorded yet, which means no royalty will fatten Springsteen's wallet. All the shows in New York were sold out since February and the tour generated more than $50 million without any sort of commercial sponsorship. Throughout his entire career, Springsteen has sold more than sixty million records and sold out hundreds of concerts. I don't know his annual income, but I would exchange mine with his, and I'm sure you would do the same.

Is "American Skin" a boost for Hillary Clinton? I have 20/20 vision and I can't see any sort of reference in the lyrics to the senatorial race. Moreover, on June 4, the day the song premiered in Atlanta, New York Mayor Rudy Giuliani had already abandoned the race.

Finally, I doubt there is anyone unaware of the fact that Springsteen is from New Jersey, where he resides and is probably registered to vote. Has he suddenly turned political, explicitly political, as never before in his career? This is the main argument used to explain the noise "American Skin" has generated by many commentators, including many of those that stand on Springsteen's side and know his music very well. This same argument, though reversed, has been used against Springsteen by those who accused him from time to time either of being a populist or of not being politically engaged.

This is the artist who wrote "Factory," "The River," "Atlantic City," "My Hometown," "Murder Inc.," "Souls of the Departed," "Streets of Philadelphia," "Youngstown," "Balboa Park," "The Line" among others, the artist who covered the songs of Woody Guthrie and thanked militant singer Pete Seeger for having kept Woody's flame alive for forty years, who performed at concerts against nuclear energy after Three Mile Island, toured the world for Amnesty International to celebrate the 40th anniversary of the Declaration of Human Rights, joined other musicians and Reverend Jesse Jackson to sing against Proposition 209 in California, and so forth. Those songs and those performances are precise and clear political acts. His music, and this tour in particular, are about the ideas of creating a community of people, about inclusion, and about the notion of work as something necessary to live a decent life, a right any individual has. Take a look at the set lists of this tour: no "Glory Days," no "I'm On Fire," no "Pink Cadillac" (unfortunately). These choices, for an artist, have a political value. Denying this fact is like denying that the earth turns around the sun.

Twice during this tour, both times last April, Springsteen dedicated "Dead Man Walking," a song about a man on death row he wrote for Tim Robbins' movie, to two organizations that work against the death penalty, an issue that is supported by 70% of the American people. But nobody accused him of being anti–death penalty. Finally, and more important, in "The Ghost of Tom Joad," the title song for his 1995 acoustic record, Springsteen borrows some lines from John Steinbeck's novel *The Grapes of Wrath:* "Mom, wherever there's a cop beating a guy / Wherever a hungry newborn baby cries / Where there's a fight 'gainst the blood and hatred in the air / Look for me Mom I'll be there. . . ." This same song has been performed in almost all "The Ghost of Tom Joad Tour" concerts in 1996 and 1997, and in 115 out of 130 concerts of the reunion tour—though not in the second show in Atlanta and the first three shows in New York, which should tell you something. Nobody said anything against it or Springsteen, no journalist, no police officer.

So why all this reaction for just one song? Wasn't Three Mile Island an important political issue? Isn't capital punishment an important political issue, especially now that one of the presidential candidates, George W. Bush, governor of the state that executes more prisoners than any other in the country, refuses to admit that the killing process is even worth a careful examination?

The reason why "American Skin" has become a "scandal" is exactly "American Skin" itself, what a few words tell about us and how these words are spoken to us.

What Is "American Skin" All About, Anyway?

The song is made of only 89 different words repeated over and over for a total of 412 words. The line "41 shots" is repeated 28 times, the Lena verse twice, the chorus four times, the "across this bloody river" and "we'll take that ride" lines twice. Scholars of oral culture, which in America often equals black culture, call this technique "incremental repetition." It has two main functions: it helps the speaker to remember the words and to get the message across. Why do you think politicians spend millions of dollars in TV commercials that are shown again and again? Try to listen to a song you never heard before ten times in a row. You won't forget it for the rest of your life and you'll be singing it every once in a while.

Here we have a mother who instructs her son on how to behave if stopped by police. Then, the speaker asks what is the cause of dying in an American skin, with a clear reference to the Diallo episode. Next, after the shooting, the people kneeling and praying in the verse "You're kneeling over his body in the vestibule / praying for his life" are the officers who realized Diallo was unarmed. After the chorus, the 41 shots and the Lena verses, come the verses "Across this bloody river to the other side . . . we're baptized in these waters and in each other's blood." These are the key verses of the song and this is what the song is all about. Rivers run through cities, they often cut cities in two parts, they divide cities: the division between blacks and whites that still kills Americans.

I read all the articles written about this song: nobody has remembered or noticed that Amadou Diallo was NOT an American citizen. He was a BLACK man and there's no doubt that Springsteen acknowledges that fact. That is the reason why in Atlanta he changed the title from "41 Shots" to "American Skin." This song is about the fact that if you are a black man or woman in this country, you are not as American as the other Americans. It is about any American city in which the poorest section, be it East Buffalo or South Central Los Angeles, is inhabited by black Americans and other minorities. It is about politicians like President Clinton and Governor Pataki, who put more policemen on the streets of America, cut funding to education and educational programs for minorities and inmates and keep building new jails. It is about Senator Charles Schumer, who in his commencement speech at SUNY at Buffalo last month complained about the fact that middle-class families struggle for sending their children to college, but didn't say one word for the poor families that can't even afford to send their children to college at all. It is about Governor Bush and all those like him who support the death penalty, that mostly kills black people, while they have the power to stop it. It is about the state of terror that the black skin produces in many Americans and in four honest policemen, that only because Diallo was black fired 41 shots at him and now they have to live with a nightmare for the rest of their lives.

This is not a song against the cops, it is a song about being American today. Lena could be anybody's mother, the policemen could be anybody's father, and, given the right circumstances, the right light, Amadou could be anybody at all. He could be me. He could be you.

Notes

1. Others, of course, have commented on the song and its meaning. Christopher Phillips, editor of *Backstreets,* quotes Hendrik Hertzberg in the *New Yorker*: "Unless any song suggested by the Diallo tragedy is deemed ipso facto anti-police—unless actual content does not matter—then this song is not anti-police. . . . What's striking about the song (especially in contrast to the obtuseness of the attacks on it) is its imaginative sympathy. The first verse takes the point of view of one of the officers, whose action is not exactly that of a murderer. . . . The second verse is in a mother's worried voice. . . . The third verse brings the two voices together in suffering with a subtle hint of redemptive hope. The refrain combines the voices, too, without quite blending them, in a way that makes clear that the American dilemma enmeshes us all." See Christopher Phillips, "41 Shots: The Sound and the Fury," *Backstreets,* Summer 2000, pp. 13–14. In the same issue, Michael Newall describes the song as "a perfect example of what Springsteen is capable of doing when he is at his best: allowing us to look into ourselves and into the society that we are all partly responsible for constructing." See Michael Newall, "Between What's Flesh and What's Fantasy," *Backstreets,* Summer 2000, p. 15. See also Jim Farber, "Views of the Boss," (New York) *Daily News,* June 14, 2000, and Jon Pareles, "Born to Run or at Least Be Redeemed," *New York Times,* June 14, 2000.
2. Appears on *The Rising* (2002).
3. Appears on *Bruce Springsteen & the E Street Band/Live in New York City* (2001).
4. In an interview with Robert Hilburn of the *Los Angeles Times,* Springsteen expressed surprise at the controversy that surrounded the song. ". . . I felt the song was simply an extension of the music I had been writing for my whole life. It was a meditation on what it means to be an American at a particular moment of time. . . . It felt to me like the most necessary issue to deal with at the turn of the century was the question of race in America and how we deal with one another. To some degree, the answer to that question is going to decide a lot about how the nation as a whole eventually rises or falls. I wanted to point out that people of color are viewed through a veil of criminality and that ultimately means they are thought of as somehow less American than other Americans, therefore people with less rights. Not just by law enforcement but the guy behind the counter at the convenience store and whoever." Robert Hilburn, "Under the Boss' Skin," *Los Angeles Times,* April 1, 2001.

Bob Crane

■

Bob Crane is founder of Save Tillie, a not-for-profit organization consisting of about 500 Springsteen fans that formed in July 1998 to save from destruction the Asbury Park landmark the Palace Amusements arcade, otherwise known as Tillie. Crane is also a Springsteen scholar and has spent a considerable amount of time studying the content of the singer's songs. In the process, he has come up with some rather interesting statistics: that Springsteen has more than 200 written references to home in his songs, that on Springsteen's first four albums he refers to more than 25 specific New Jersey places, and that Springsteen has mentioned 33 states and 46 U.S. cities or towns in his songs. The following selection is taken from Crane's *A Place to Stand* (2002), in which the author examines Springsteen's strong sense of place in his lyrics.

from *A Place to Stand:*
A Guide to Bruce Springsteen's Sense of Place

■BRUCE SPRINGSTEEN'S WORLD is one many of us have been visiting ever since Wild Billy organized an escapade out to Greasy Lake. Back then, in the early '70s, pop singers were bopping to the Crocodile Rock and joining hands to start up the love train, so the infinitely realistic geography and compelling narrative Springsteen wrote into "Spirit in the Night" took rock and roll for a brand new ride.

Now, nearly three decades after the release of *Greetings from Asbury Park, N.J.*, Springsteen's mastery of the power of place stands among his defining accomplishments as a songwriter. In his stories, place is the lyrical bedrock, the written equivalent of the rhythm line in his instrumentation. Seldom is place merely a geographic reference; instead, Springsteen allows it to take shape as a character, and, at its best, as a force that influences the choices and decisions of his protagonists.

Thus, Springsteen has created an intriguing landscape to the delight of those who love the particularity of his songs. We closely examine his changing treatment of Asbury Park, his denunciation of Balboa Park in San Diego, and the depiction of a killing vestibule in the Bronx, for insights into the intrinsic nature of a place, and the relationship between place and deed. We seek these places out, wanting to see them, to know everything we can about them, to understand how they affect the action in the songs, and, yes, to gain a greater sense of wonder about the world.

Twenty-three centuries ago, Plato observed in *The Republic* that the elements of music "find their way to the inmost soul and take strongest hold upon it."

No singer-songwriter has laid stronger claim to the secret places of the soul over the last 25 years than Bruce Springsteen. On stage more than 1,600 times, Springsteen has been dazzling, rocking with a visionary exhilaration that may never be matched. He has won an Oscar from the Motion Picture Academy, seven Grammys from the National Academy of Recording Arts & Sciences, a Polar Award—the equivalent of a Nobel Prize for music—from the Royal Swedish Academy, and was a shoo-in first ballot inductee to the Rock and Roll Hall of Fame.

Yet it is as a songwriter that Springsteen has had the greatest impact on the human soul. His ten albums of original compositions and more than 260 recorded songs are deeply in tune with the human spirit, filling his songbook with poignant vignettes of struggle and turmoil as his characters stand at decisive times and places, confronting strictures far too often beyond their control.

Surprisingly, despite the shelves of library space devoted to his life, career and honors, there has been comparatively little attention paid to the career-long implications of Springsteen's sense of place: how, in his narratives, we are aware of an interaction, a spirit that implies intimacy between person and place. *Glory Days,* by Springsteen biographer Dave Marsh, invited broader discussion by highlighting Springsteen's "remarkably specific sense of place." From the start, "Springsteen songs have been peppered with unforgettable places," Marsh wrote—even the fictitious ones are "vivid out of all proportion, compellingly rendered in the inflections of Springsteen's singing and recognizable archetypes for every American . . . (a)nd because these songs are unified by their emotional portraits, even 'Badlands' and 'The Promised Land' are genuinely international beyond the bounds of their all-American titles." To date, however, only a few have taken advantage of the invitation to look seriously at this aspect of his writing.

Given the tight limitations of rock and roll recordings, most rock songwriters ignore the power of place altogether. As a result, their characters engage in various preoccupations while interacting inconsequentially if at all with the inner geography of place. To them, a road is merely a conveyance, never a place where something happens. A home is seldom a place of influence or fear or social intercourse. Towns have no core, or sense of concrete reality. From the original "Rock Around the Clock" to today's trendy chart climbers, most rock writers skip right over the notion that to know who you are, you need to understand where you stand.

By any yardstick, Springsteen is the exception, writing with a place-infused consistency that puts him far more in sync with novelists such as Barbara Kingsolver (*The Bean Trees*), Tony Hillerman (the Navaho Reservation mysteries) and Jane Smiley (*A Thousand Acres*) than rock contemporaries. Reaching deep within the realm of personal experience, Springsteen links the voices of his characters to the landscapes where they stand, with metaphoric power and revelation. The natural place of congregation for his all-hot half-shots is beneath a giant Exxon sign; an empty hearted woman sits stranded on her father's porch; town boys polish their attitudes outside Woolworth's. By citing Asbury Park's Palace Amusements, he added nuance and complexities to "Born to Run." In less skillful hands, "The River" could have been boy meets girl, girl gets pregnant, and out comes the shotgun; Springsteen told the story as a topology of emotions set against the greens of the valley and the river's flow.

Colleen Sheehy, curator of the Weisman Art Museum exhibition "Springsteen: Troubadour of the Highway," has said Springsteen's landscape is "as rich a social and cultural place as William Faulkner's Yoknapatawpha County in Mississippi." Closely patterned on his adopted hometown of Oxford, Faulkner discovered early in his writing career that his "postage stamp of native soil" could support virtually every character and plot he could imagine. Much the same can be said for Springsteen's Monmouth County in New Jersey. This terrain of consciousness may never have existed exactly as Springsteen tells it, but it is as rich and deep as Faulkner's home turf, and has a real-life geography that can be mapped, and explored, and debated.

The essence of Springsteen's places is at times so stark and specific it has become part of their unique spirits. In "Soul Searching,"[1] the author Pythia Peay writes that Springsteen's Asbury Park, James Joyce's Dublin and impressionist painter Camielle [*sic*] Pissarro's Paris were in some ways "created by the artists who render them immortal as much as by the planners, construction workers, and business leaders who built them."

Delving into the works of songwriters, along with those of poets, fiction writers, and others, she writes, "deepens how we experience our home, imbuing commonplace reality with awareness, appreciation, and perhaps wonder."

Not every Springsteen song, of course, is rooted in place. "She's The One" and "Red Headed Woman," among others, affirm no particular place whatsoever, either primary or secondary. In others, place is a background element, adding a sense of texture to the stories without emerging as a fully defined character. On *The Rising*, Springsteen explores the entire range of human emotion ignited by terrorist attacks without once mentioning the World Trade Center, the Pentagon, or suicide bombers in the Middle East. Similarly, the vestibule in the Bronx where Amadou Diallo was slain by New York City Police is invoked, but never specifically mentioned, in "American Skin."

Yet in many of Springsteen's best works, the grace note hanging over it all—the line at the lyrical center tying together narrative and theme and music—is a real-life brick and mortar place, interacting with character, the one subjecting the other to its confinements, conditions and traps. For listeners, the reward is a deep involvement in the moment when people in love, in fear, or with nowhere to turn must make an irreversible decision. The reward for fans is a specific geography where, in the course of a visit, the stirrings of the soul connect with the reality of place.

Adolescents have been described as travelers, far from home with no native land. For Springsteen, the critical years were deeply defined by his isolation in Freehold, New Jersey, his hometown. During the 1950s and early '60s, Freehold was a fading industrial town of 12,000 hit hard by changing times and technologies, a place historian Kevin Coyne described as "confining, sustaining, maddening, inspiring."

For Springsteen, Freehold was suffocating, and became more so as social and economic conditions worsened. "I didn't have anything to hold on to," he once said, "or any connections whatsoever—I was just reeling through space and bouncing off the walls." Many times, from the stage, Springsteen has told of watching Freehold grind down his father, Douglas Springsteen, who "worked a whole lot of different places, worked in a rug mill for a while, drove a cab for a while, and he was a guard down at the jail for a while. I can remember when he worked down there, he used to always come home real pissed off, drunk." At 9 P.M., Douglas Springsteen would turn off the house lights and sit in darkness with a six pack and cigarettes.

In his more than 200 written references to home, Springsteen leaves little doubt these are among his most personal writings. These are places of great voids and shattered dreams, where angry, lonesome people move through empty rooms in search of someone to blame. On the rare occasions when a door is thrown open in hope and expectation, there is almost always a moment of terrible sadness when it slams shut again. "I burst through the front door, my heart pumping hard," he sang on "Downbound Train." "The room was dark, our bed was empty, then I heard that long whistle whine."

In moments such as these, Springsteen points his remarkable talent toward small details and uses them to give us a sense of personality interacting with setting. A masterful example is "Mansion on the Hill," a late night drive through the social-economic strata of Freehold. Springsteen recalls how "at night my daddy'd take me and we'd ride through the streets of a town so silent and still, park on a back road along the highway side, look up at that mansion on the hill." In the Chamber of Commerce version, Freehold was a "family community" where people lived and raised their kids in a measure of peace. Without a word spoken between father and son, Springsteen allows us to see Freehold as it was for him.

While he was growing up, the mammoth A & M Karagheusian rug mill a few blocks in from Main Street at Jackson and Center Streets employed 1,600 people—half the jobholders in Freehold. The quality of their rugs set industry standards, and it was a point of local pride that the United States Supreme Court building in Washington, D.C., and Radio City Music Hall in New York City were carpeted by Karagheusian. By the time Springsteen was ready to graduate from Freehold Regional High School, the mill was in its death throes, a symbol of lost jobs and broken dreams. Freehold already had its share of class and racial tensions, and as the economic problems deepened, Main Street merchants closed and boarded up their stores.

Incapable of finding his place in Freehold, Springsteen took refuge in the guitar, and a series of 6" by 9½" notebooks into which he poured his emotions. After early tries at creating allegorical places, Springsteen began experimenting with the use of literal places—penny arcades, highways, cheap little seaside bars—to define the search for safe haven and escape. Before long, he had taught himself to create powerfully connected metaphors by linking the voice of his characters to the ground on which they stood.

The technique figured prominently on Springsteen's earliest albums, powering both his writing, and his growing fame. By 1975, *Rolling Stone* record editor Jon Landau would rave that Springsteen had "far more depth than most artists because he really has roots in a place." In all, 67 of the 73 Springsteen songs released during the '70s—songs which took him from obscurity to the pantheon of rock and roll greatness—were enriched by his sense of place.

The more than 25 specific New Jersey places scattered throughout his first four albums came with a picturesque accuracy remarkable in rock and roll. On "Born to Run" and "4th of July, Asbury Park (Sandy)," he memorialized beach front landmarks that remain to this day, including the Casino and the Palace (now broken relics facing uncertain futures). In Freehold stands the high school on which he strafed revenge in "Growin' Up." Springsteen used the street grid of nearby Belmar— lettered streets intersecting with numbered avenues—for an allegorical wintery blast on "Tenth Avenue Freeze-Out," and took the name of his band from the E Street address of their early rehearsals.

There, too, are all the highways over which Springsteen plotted his eventual escape. To Springsteen, highways such as Highway 9 (actually Route 9) and the New Jersey Turnpike are places in their own right, where something is likely to happen and usually does. His earliest songs were full of romance for the open road and a belief that for anyone who wants it badly enough, there is a stretch of road that gives us one final shot at hope, love and opportunity. Then, gradually, as the idealized excitement over the open road gives way to dark stretches of lonely highway, you encounter either streets of pain or deadend highways leading to nowhere.

For his first offering of the '80s, and fifth overall, Springsteen spent 16 arduous months in the studio before settling on a 20-song double album hailed by critics as a neon New Jersey version of *Grapes of Wrath*. Its blue-collar regionalism hit fans in the heart, and they kept *The River* on the U.S. and British charts for nearly a year. It contained his first No. 1 hit, "Hungry Heart," and during their worldwide tour, Bruce Springsteen and the E Street Band sold out multiple dates in major arenas for the first time. But what almost no one then knew was that upon entering The Power Station studio in New York City, Springsteen had unleashed a harrowing drum-laced fire-on-the-fingertips three minute forty-seven second masterpiece of emotional and environmental landscaping that would eventually lead to a great cycle of songs exploring the sterility of contemporary places far beyond his formative landscape.

Early on March 28, 1979, two pumps at Unit 2 of the Three Mile Island nuclear plant shut down, leaving the turbine generator without water from the Susquehanna River to cool the reactor. The core rapidly overheated, and while 500,000 people slept nearby, radioactive gases escaped into the Pennsylvania atmosphere.

The first blast of released steam, superheated to 500 degrees and pressured at a thousand pounds per square inch, sounded like the roar of a jet. It shook homes a quarter mile away. Those who slept through it awoke several hours later to panic spreading rapidly over radio and telephones, for no one in authority seemed capable of answering even the most basic question: should we stay or should we go?

Springsteen was making final preparations that week for recording *The River,* and judging from what was to come, the crisis at Three Mile Island was all too reminiscent of the dehumanizing conditions of his childhood. For upon entering the studio a few days later, Springsteen's first order of business was to record "Roulette," a scathing account of Three Mile Island through the eyes of a fireman in a small unnamed town based on Cly, Falmouth, Yocumtown and a dozen other places near the Metropolitan Edison reactor.

The fireman had "grown up here on this street" in the shadow of the nuclear power plant, part of the fabric of the community. Yet within an astonishing span of a few hours, everything about the place—the sense of community, the sense of belonging, the sense of the familiar—vanished under a monstrous convergence of forces, the worst being the plethora of contradictory information from government and industry.

Left to make monumental decisions on his own, Springsteen's fireman rapidly saw that in the eyes of Three Mile Island operators and government regulators, he and his family were part of "the big expendable," abandoned by authorities in a game of nuclear roulette. As this unfathomable conclusion sank in, it transformed their attitudes toward the most fundamental elements of life: the town where the fireman and his family belonged became a place full "of worthless memories," their home a collection "of things that I can't touch," and their street an eerie byway where "nothin' moves, just a strange breeze" full of radioactive contamination.

Four years earlier, Springsteen had wondered aloud about "how important the settings are in the first place." Now, as his fireman reached the nuclear crossroads, Springsteen answered his own question, relying on a universally known place as the foundation for the most unambiguous depiction of fear and anger Springsteen had ever written.

Coming after eight years of metaphorical hints and allegorical clues, the discovery led him to a song cycle of stunning scope and magnitude. The song was also perfectly suited for *The River,* an album full of dangerous undercurrents at the point where our pasts and our presents are fused. But for reasons still a mystery, "Roulette" was kicked off the album and kept in the can until 1988, long after Springsteen had embraced its darker dimensions as the tone for the best of his future work.[2]

For someone who hated school, who said he suffered "daily defeat and humiliation in front of my peers" in school, who when September rolls around is "still glad that I don't have to go to high school," Springsteen has proven himself to be a remarkably astute student of the underside of America's industrial soul.

In his chronicles, Springsteen travels the side streets and dark alleys of 33 states and 46 U.S. cities and towns where good workers grow hard on the line, lovers meet in six-dollar motels, and life savings are risked in casinos. He takes us through factory gates to the places where stress, repetition, boredom, and hopelessness are accepted as a condition of employment. We see men go from the military to the mind-numbing tedium of the factory, spending their lives working the docks until, at the end of the day, they punch out with anger, hatred and betrayal in their eyes, and hearts. "You just better believe, boy," he sang on "Factory," "somebody's gonna get hurt tonight."

Drawing on the lessons of "Roulette," Springsteen is place-specific in his depiction of children who are condemned by their environment to almost certain fates: on "Seeds," sick kids and jobless parents sleep in Texas lumberyards; on "Souls of the Departed," a seven-year-old is slain on a playground contested by Los Angeles gangs; on "Youngstown," successive generations breathe the soot-filled air of their grandfathers and fathers.

To Springsteen, the price paid by children is far too great, but it gets worse as they grow up seriously impoverished and headed for trouble. Many end up trapped in a domain of moral darkness that spreads violently across the landscape.

There, in "My Hometown," black youths rampage through downtown Freehold when white officials canceled a black unity march. At the intersection of Route 33 and South Street, a white youth fired a shotgun into a parked car, costing a black youth an eye.[3]

There, across the stark and barren landscape of middle America, "Nebraska" psychopath Charles Starkweather and his teenage girl friend, Caril Fugate, randomly murder 10 people, including most of Fugate's family. Springsteen takes the story from Nebraska on a murderous ride through Wyoming, ending up in the electric chair at the Nebraska State Penitentiary.

There, stepping onto the porch of 2117 Porter St. in South Philadelphia, mob boss Philip C. Testa is blown to bits by a bomb in a battle for control of business and union-related activities in "Atlantic City."

On May 18, 2002, only days after the final recording sessions of *The Rising* in Atlanta, Springsteen was a surprise guest at the dedication of Vinyard Park, across from the old rug mill in Freehold. The park is the site of the former home of Tex and Marion Vinyard who mentored Springsteen's first band, The Castiles, another of the homes that somehow never made it into a Springsteen song.

Tex and Marion were among the "unsung heroes of rock and roll, without whom we wouldn't have had a place to practice and hone our craft," Springsteen said during the dedication. The Vinyards had, he said, opened their home and hearts and wallets to the band, the only adults who "allowed us to turn it up as loud as we wanted when all the other adults were trying to get us to turn it down."

The Vinyard home is gone now, but what happened there lives on with each new phase of Springsteen's career. "You carry with you," he explained on that day, "a big part of the texture of the town from which you came. It becomes a part of your internal life, and I've carried that with me long, long since I've moved out of Freehold."

Notes

1. Pythia Peay, *Soul Sisters: The Five Sacred Qualities of a Woman's Soul* (Tarcher/ Putnam, 2002).

2. Ironically, "Roulette" was the first song recorded for *The River*. Springsteen later said he felt the song was a bit too specific for the album since "the story I started to tell was more of a general one. I may have just gotten afraid—it went a little over the top, which is what's good about it. In truth it should have probably gotten put on. It would have been one of the best things on the record and it was just a mistake at the time—you get oversensitive when you're going to release the things." See Mark Hagen, "Interview," *MOJO*, January 1999. "Roulette" appears on *Tracks* (Columbia, 1998).

3. The incident, a precursor to the Asbury Park riots of 1970–1971, that Springsteen sings about took place in May 1969. According to the *Asbury Park Press*, "The police log for Monday night's racial disturbance (May 19, 1969) . . . Police said a carload of white youths pulled alongside a car of black youths and a shotgun was fired into the back seat of the car of black teenagers. The victims, Dean Lewis, 16, of 8 Monmouth Ave., who suffered buckshot wounds in the left side of his face and right eye, and Leroy Kinsey Jr., 19 Factory St., who was hit in the neck, were taken to Jersey Shore Medical Center, Neptune." *Asbury Park Press*, May 22, 1969. Both victims survived the attack but Lewis lost an eye.

Nick Hornby

∎

Nick Hornby is the author of several popular novels, including *High Fidelity* (1995), *About a Boy* (1998), *Fever Pitch* (1998), and *How to Be Good* (2001). In 2002 he wrote *Songbook,* in which he revisited his favorite songs, consisting of a varied selection of styles and artists ranging from Rod Stewart ("Mama, You Been on My Mind") and the Beatles ("Rain") to Van Morrison ("Caravan") to Richard and Linda Thompson ("Calvary Cross"). Another perennial favorite of Hornby's is Springsteen's classic "Thunder Road"—here, the very English Hornby meets up with the very American Springsteen. "It's one of the songs in Springsteen's repertoire that hasn't really aged," Hornby said.[1] "I like the way it starts with the harmonica and piano and kind of builds up—it really sounds like the end of an album, the closing credits, rather than the opening track."

Thunder Road
from *Songbook*

∎I CAN REMEMBER listening to this song and loving it in 1975; I can remember listening to this song and loving it almost as much quite recently, a few months ago. (And, yes, I was in a car, although I probably wasn't driving, and I certainly wasn't driving down any turnpike or freeway, and the wind wasn't blowing through my hair, because I possess neither a convertible nor hair. It's not that version of Springsteen.) So I've loved this song for a quarter of a century now, and I've heard it more than anything else, with the possible exception of . . . Who am I kidding? There are no other contenders. See, what I was going to do there was soften the blow, slip in something black and/or cool (possibly "Let's Get It On," which I think is the best pop record ever made, and which would easily make it into my top twenty most-played-songs list, but not at number two. Number two—and I'm trying to be honest here—would probably be something like "White Man in the Hammersmith Palais" by the Clash, but it would be way, way behind. Let's say I've played "Thunder Road" 1,500 times just over once a week for twenty-five years, which sounds about right, if one takes into account the repeat plays in the first couple of years); "White Man . . ." would have clocked up something like 500 plays. In other words, there's no real competition.

It's weird to me how "Thunder Road" has survived when so many other, arguably better songs—"Maggie May," "Hey Jude," "God Save the Queen," "Stir It Up," "So Tired of Being Alone," "You're a Big Girl Now"—have somehow become less compelling as I've got older. It's not as if I can't see the flaws: "Thunder Road" is overwrought, both lyrically (as Prefab Sprout pointed out, there's more to life than cars and girls, and surely the word "redemption" is to be avoided like the plague when you're writing songs about redemption) and musically—after all, this four and three-quarter minutes provided Jim Steinman and Meatloaf with a whole career. It's also po-faced, in a way that Springsteen himself isn't, and if the doomed romanticism wasn't corny in 1975, then it certainly is now.

But sometimes, very occasionally, songs and books and films and pictures express who you are, perfectly. And they don't do this in words or images, necessarily; the connection is a lot less direct and more complicated than that. When I was first beginning to write seriously, I read Anne Tyler's *Dinner at the Homesick Restaurant*,[2] and suddenly knew what I was, and what I wanted to be, for better or for worse. It's a process something like falling in love. You don't necessarily choose the best person, or the wisest, or the most beautiful; there's something else going on. There was a part of me that would rather have fallen for Updike, or Kerouac, or DeLillo—for someone masculine, at least, and certainly someone who uses more swear words—and though I have admired those writers, at various stages in my life, admiration is a very different thing from the kind of transference I'm talking about. I'm talking about understanding— or at least *feeling* like I understand—every artistic decision, every impulse, the soul of both the work and its creator. "This is me," I wanted to say when I read Tyler's rich, sad, lovely novel. "I'm not a character. I'm nothing like the author. I haven't had the experiences she writes about. But even so, this is what I feel like, inside. This is what I would sound like, if ever I were to find a voice." And I did find a voice, eventually, and it was mine, not hers; but nevertheless, so powerful was the process of identification that I still don't feel as though I've expressed myself as well, as completely, as Tyler did on my behalf then.

So, even though I'm not American, no longer young, hate cars, and can recognize why so many people find Springsteen bombastic and histrionic (but not macho or jingoistic or dumb—that kind of ignorant judgment has plagued Springsteen for a huge part of his career, and is made by smart people who are actually a lot dumber than he has ever been), "Thunder Road" somehow manages to speak for me. This is partly—and perhaps shamingly—because a lot of Springsteen's songs from this period are about becoming famous, or at least achieving some kind of public validation through his art: what else are we supposed to think when the last line of the song is "I'm pulling out of here to win," other than that he has won, simply by virtue of playing the song, night after night, to an ever-increasing crowd of people? (And what else are we supposed to think, when in "Rosalita" he sings, with a touching, funny and innocent glee, "'Cos the record company, Rosie, just gave me a big advance," other than that the record company has just given him a big advance?) It's never objectionable or obnoxious, this dream of fame, because it derives from a restless and uncontrollable artistic urge—he knows he has talent to burn, and the proper reward for this, he seems to suggest, would be the financial wherewithal to fulfill it—rather than an interest in celebrity for its own sake. Hosting a TV quiz show, or assassinating a President, wouldn't scratch the itch at all.

And of course—don't let anyone tell you otherwise—if you have dreams of becoming a writer, then there are murky, mucky visions of fame attached to these dreams too; "Thunder Road" was my answer to every rejection letter I received, and every doubt expressed by friends or relatives. They lived in towns for losers, I told myself, and I, like Bruce, was pulling out of there to win. (These towns, incidentally, were Cambridge—full of loser doctors and lawyers and academics—and London—full of loser successes of every description—but never mind. This was the material I had to work with, and work with it I did.)

It helped a great deal that, as time went by, and there was no sign of me pulling out of anywhere to do anything very much, and certainly not with the speed implied in the song, "Thunder Road" made reference to age, thus accommodating this lack of forward momentum. "So you're scared and you're thinking that maybe we ain't that young anymore," Bruce sang, and that line worked for me even when I had begun to doubt whether there was any magic in the night. I continued thinking I wasn't that young anymore for a long, long time—decades, in fact, and even today I choose to interpret it as a wistful observation of middle age, rather than the sharp fear that comes on in late youth.

It helped, too, that some time in the early-to-mid-eighties, I came across another version of the song, a bootleg studio recording of Springsteen alone with an acoustic guitar (it's on *War and Roses,* the *Born to Run* outtakes bootleg); he reimagines "Thunder Road" as a haunting, exhausted hymn to the past, to lost love and missed opportunities and self-delusion and bad luck and failure, and that worked pretty well for me, too. In fact, when I try to hear that last line of the song in my head, it's the acoustic version that comes first. It's slow, and mournful, and utterly convincing: an artist who can persuade you of the truth of what he is singing with either version is an artist who is capable of an awful lot.

There are other bootleg versions that I play and love, too. One of the great things about the song as it appears on *Born to Run* is that those first few bars, on wheezy harmonica and achingly pretty piano, actually sound like they refer to something that has already happened before the beginning of the record, something monumental and sad but not destructive of all hope; as "Thunder Road" is the first track on Side One of *Born to Run,* the album begins, in effect, with its own closing credits. In performance at the end of the seventies, during the Darkness on the Edge of Town tour, Springsteen maximized this effect by segueing into "Thunder Road" out of one of his bleakest, most desperate songs, "Racing in the Street," and the harmonica that marks the transformation of one song into the other feels like a sudden and glorious hint of spring after a long, withering winter. On the bootlegs of those seventies shows, "Thunder Road" can finally provide the salvation that its position on *Born to Run* denied it.

Maybe the reason "Thunder Road" has endured for me is that, despite its energy and volume and fast cars and hair, it somehow manages to sound elegiac, and the older I get the more I can hear that. When it comes down to it, I suppose that I too believe that life is momentous and sad but not destructive of all hope, and maybe that makes me a self-dramatizing depressive, or maybe it makes me a happy idiot, but either way, "Thunder Road" knows how I feel and who I am, and that, in the end, is one of the consolations of art.

Postscript

A few years ago, I started to sell a lot of books, at first only in the U.K., and then later in other countries too, and to my intense bewilderment found that I had somehow become part of the literary and cultural mainstream. It wasn't something I had expected, or was prepared for. Although I could see no reason why anyone would feel excluded from my work—it wasn't like it was difficult, or experimental—my books still seemed to me to be quirky and small-scale. But suddenly all sorts of people, people I didn't know or like or respect, had opinions about me and my work, which overnight seemed to go from being fresh and original to clichéd and ubiquitous, without a word of it having changed. And I was shown this horrible reflection of myself and what I did, a funfair hall-of-mirrors reflection, all squidged-up and distorted—me, but not me. It wasn't like I was given a particularly hard time, and certainly other people, some of whom I know, have experienced much worse. But even so, it becomes in those circumstances very hard to hang on to the idea of what you want to do.

And yet Springsteen somehow managed to find a way through. His name is still taken in vain frequently (a year or so ago I read a newspaper piece attacking Tony Blair for his love of Bruce, an indication, apparently, of the Prime Minister's incorrigible philistinism), and for some, the hall-of-mirrors reflection is the only Springsteen they can see. He went from being rock 'n' roll's future to a lumpy, flag-waving, stadium-rocking meathead in the space of a few months, again with nothing much having changed, beyond the level of his popularity. Anyway, his strength of purpose, and the way he has survived the assault on his sense of self, seem to me exemplary; sometimes it's hard to remember that just because a lot of people like what you do doesn't necessarily mean that what you do is of no value whatsoever. Indeed, sometimes it might even suggest the opposite.

Notes

1. As quoted in Andy Gill, "Thunder Road: The Power and the Glory," *Independent,* January 17, 2003.
2. Anne Tyler, *Dinner at the Homesick Restaurant* (New York: Knopf, 1982).

Colleen Sheehy

■

Colleen Sheehy is the curator of *Springsteen: Troubadour of the Highway,* the first traveling exhibition on Bruce Springsteen, which originated at the Weisman Art Museum in Minneapolis in September 2002. The following selection is the title piece, slightly edited, from the exhibition's catalog (2002). *Troubadour* examines Springsteen's use of car imagery and the road in his music and career through a multimedia presentation that features 65 color and black-and-white photographs by Edie Baskin, Joel Bernstein, David Gahr, Lynn Goldsmith, David Michael Kennedy, Annie Leibovitz, David Rose, Frank Stefanko, and Pamela Springsteen (Bruce's sister), including 41 photos from her *Ghost of Tom Joad* series; five Springsteen videos; and excerpts from Springsteen's lyrics. Sheehy is the museum's director of education and an adjunct faculty member in American Studies at the University of Minnesota.

Springsteen: Troubadour of the Highway

■"THERE'S AN OPENING harmonica line in many Bruce Springsteen songs, announced in the first strains of "Thunder Road," where it tries to break free as it lilts above the piano, then moves into a lonesome whine at the start of "Nebraska," reemerging as one long wailing high note in "The Ghost of Tom Joad." The movement of that musical line follows Springsteen's changing imagery of the highway, too, and the meaning of those images.

In "Thunder Road," recorded on his breakthrough 1975 album *Born to Run,* the highway is a path to liberation. When Mary's screen door slams at the beginning of the song, the car door opens, giving the lovers an escape from a dead-end town. They take to the highway, where "the night's bustin' open / these two lanes will take us anywhere" and head out "to case the promised land." The openness of the road, with its offer of movement, freedom, and new possibilities, is matched in Springsteen's performances of "Thunder Road," when he sings at full throttle, "we're pullin' outta here to wiiiii-iiin," screaming the last line as a promise and an oath.

That call of the road turns deadly by the time Springsteen gets to the 1982 title track of *Nebraska,* sung in the voice of mass murderer Charlie Starkweather. When he and his girlfriend take to the highways of Nebraska and Wyoming, "ten innocent people died." The emotional tone of the song is deadpan, and Springsteen's intonations are as flat as the Nebraska landscape, making the harmonica the most live part of the song, like the wind whistling across the Great Plains. When Springsteen arrives at "The Ghost of Tom Joad," the title track on his 1995 CD, the highway promises nothing. It's illusory, confusing, heartbreaking. "The highway is alive tonight, but nobody's kiddin' nobody about where it goes," he sings as a homeless immigrant, "with a one-way ticket to the promised land." Wandering the California desert and the ghettos of L.A., he searches for some sign of hope or act of kindness, seeking the spirit of John Steinbeck's Tom Joad from his novel of the Great Depression, *The Grapes of Wrath*. Now Springsteen's nameless character is no longer driving but walking along the road, sleeping under the overpasses, not racing on them.

From "Thunder Road" to "The Ghost of Tom Joad" and at every point along the way, Bruce Springsteen has employed images of cars and the highway as central features of his music. While these images are conventions in rock 'n' roll, Springsteen mines them more consistently and with more depth and complexity than any other rock artist. His restless characters are on the move, sometimes on the hustle, and often on the run. Speeding off to the edge of town, down the New Jersey Turnpike, or across the desert, their physical movement matches their psychic and spiritual searches. Like so many American film directors and authors, Springsteen uses the American landscape as the canvas on which he inscribes his characters' journeys. While his highways are getaway routes, they are counterpoised with fixed points on the map, whether that be a character's home, workplace, or the fabled boardwalk at Asbury Park, the New Jersey beach town immortalized in "Born to Run" and "4th of July, Asbury Park (Sandy)," among other songs. Over the course of Springsteen's career, he has expanded his view from the New Jersey towns and New York City of his youth to take on the entire expanse of the nation, moving into the Midwest, the South, and the West.

Springsteen's images work as metaphors for his meditations on both the promise and disappointments of America. Both are real, his music tells us, and the music itself moves restlessly between these paradoxical points of view, trying to reconcile American idealism with the smack of reality, individual freedom with connections to family and society. His songs alternate between lamentation and affirmation, emotions felt musically even within a single song by, as the singer has pointed out, verses steeped in the blues and choruses resounding with gospel music. This tension and duality, this lack of easy answers in his music, are important elements that have made Bruce Springsteen one of the world's most enduringly popular rock musicians in his thirty years as a recording artist.

Springsteen once told rock critic and biographer Dave Marsh that he felt invisible until the age of thirteen, when he stood behind his first guitar. Cars and guitars function in parallel ways in Springsteen's career and music. Both are vehicles of visibility and liberation. "Well I got this guitar and I learned how to make it talk," he sings in "Thunder Road," as he urges Mary to take "the long walk" from her porch to his car. "And I swear I found the key to the universe in the engine of an old parked car," he sang in his great paean to adolescence, "Growin' Up," one of the first songs he performed in his 1972 audition for Columbia Records legend John Hammond. Certainly in Springsteen's visual record, the number of photographs of the singer in, on, or next to cars is second only to images of him on stage with a guitar.

Springsteen loves cars and loves to drive, so his musical motif is not only a trope but also something rooted in his own life. The photographs of Springsteen with his many cars hold particular power and appeal because they resonate with a host of references from American music, film, and television history. A cool car gets you noticed, whether you're Elvis with his pink Cadillac, Kookie on *77 Sunset Strip,* James Dean in *Rebel without a Cause,* or, like Springsteen, a working-class guy from New Jersey. In Frank Stefanko's 1978 photograph of the tousle-haired singer leaning on his Corvette, Springsteen echoes the young James Dean, and in Annie Leibovitz's photograph of Springsteen sitting in his Cadillac convertible, looking over his shoulder, he could be Dean or Montgomery Clift.

Springsteen wrote in *Songs,* his 1998 book of lyrics, that in 1970s New Jersey, when he was first recording, the car was still an important symbol of success. A cool car is a sign of success in more than monetary terms. Many of Springsteen's car images express a fun-lovin' confidence characteristic of many rock 'n' roll car songs. These tunes entice us to forget our troubles and have a good time, and that alone can be a triumph in the face of whatever mean or meaningless stuff life throws our way. In this spirit, David Gahr's photographs of Springsteen, taken for promotion of the mid-1980s *Born in the U.S.A.* tour, show him laughing and lounging with the E Street Band on his 1964 Impala, given to him by singer Gary U.S. Bonds, whose career Springsteen had helped revive. These visual images find musical expression in many Springsteen songs. In the rollicking "Sherry Darling," for instance, Springsteen's character throws off life's tribulations, driving with his girlfriend: "Well I got some beer and the highway's free / I got you, and baby you got me / hey hey hey, whadya say, Sherry darlin'?" In concert, Springsteen rocks out with abandon on these types of songs, something that makes his live performances legendary and joyful marathon parties. His exuberance in concert can be hard to catch in still photos but can be glimpsed in David Rose's image showing Springsteen's dramatic gesture as rock 'n' roll preacher, captured at Madison Square Garden during the sold-out, ten-night run there in summer 2000.

Yet alongside Springsteen's sense of serious fun, he creates a counterpoint, an undertow, that turns back on and fights with those liberating images. The road *might* offer a fun time or a new chance, but it can just as often be a dead end. In "Wreck on the Highway" on *The River* (1980), the character is haunted by the memory of finding a dying man at the site of a car crash. And on the same album, the character in "Stolen Car" is an ancient mariner–like wanderer, driving each night in circles around town, on the run from a marriage gone sour, hoping to get caught. On the 1987 *Tunnel of Love,* an album full of questions about love and commitment, Bill Horton is the "cautious man" of one song's title. His marriage is marked by love and fear, words tattooed on his knuckles. He wakes one night, filled with restlessness, and runs outside, ready to take off. But when he gets to the highway, "he didn't find nothing but road." The highway now is just an empty image, not a symbolic path to freedom or fun. In this dark undercurrent of Springsteen's music, the highway is treacherous, a space of isolation and disconnection, at times veering into criminality.

This musical vein is matched in visual imagery connected to Springsteen's work. David Michael Kennedy's hauntingly dark landscape of a highway receding into the distance, seen through a car windshield, appeared on the cover of the *Nebraska* album and matches the mood of that cycle of songs. Arnold Levine's black-and-white video for "Atlantic City," from the same album, was shot from the window of a moving car, driving in and around that New Jersey resort city just after the casinos came in with legalized gambling. Released in 1982, shortly after MTV began broadcasting, the video presents a somber style that contrasted sharply with the flash and quick cutting of most early music videos.

Pamela Springsteen's black-and-white photographs, taken first for the thirty-second commercial and then the full music video for "The Ghost of Tom Joad," stand as the most fully realized body of visual images to match her brother's musical images and themes. For the video works, she shot hundreds of photographs along the highways in the Mojave Desert east of L.A., including views of the famous Route 66 (the highway the Joads traveled to California), showing it as a dusty dirt road in the middle of nowhere. Pamela Springsteen then edited these images together with scenes taken in poor neighborhoods of Los Angeles (some shot during the unrest after the Rodney King verdict in 1992). In Springsteen's own edit for the music video, her black-and-white stills dissolve one into the next, following the musical rhythms of the song. Arnold Levine later made the director's cut for the final music video, using Pam Springsteen's images.

Just as Bruce Springsteen yanks Steinbeck's story and John Ford's film of the novel out of the 1930s and into the 1990s—rendering Mexican immigrants as today's Okies, looking for a better life in California—Pamela Springsteen's work recalls the federal government's Farm Security Administration photos of the 1930s. Like such artists as Dorothea Lange, Ben Shahn, and Walker Evans, she shows a sympathetic regard in her portraits of the poor. Her evocative scenes of abandoned buildings and gas stations are equal parts Walker Evans, who was fascinated with soon-to-vanish, humble vernacular buildings, and Edward Hopper, the painter who created a powerful visual ode to American loneliness. Like the song, the photographs ask if the dream of a better life in the United States is still a viable vision.

In his recent release, *The Rising,* Bruce Springsteen has moved further into territory where image and language rather than narrative build his songs' lyrical structures. He retains a deft use of highway and car imagery that draws on earlier metaphors in "Further On Up the Road" and "The Fuse." Springsteen has talked about the genesis of these songs in the aftermath of the terrorists' attack on the World Trade Center on September 11, 2001. Images of rescue workers climbing stairs and of souls rising to the sky make the movement on *The Rising* vertical rather than horizontal, ascending rather than moving across a landscape. Nonetheless, the songs' compelling propulsion and marching rhythms drive the music forward and provide similar momentum as the music of Springsteen's "Born to Run" days.

Bruce Springsteen uses the car and the highway as a common language to comment on and to question American life. After all, Springsteen's music has always been about our civic life—what binds us, what divides us. In a 1978 interview, Springsteen commented that his car imagery was a means, not an end. "The heart of the action is beneath all that stuff," he said, comparing it to the way that certain film directors use genres such as Westerns or detective stories to make larger statements about the individual's relationship to society. The questions Springsteen poses in his lyrics come through in the tenor of his voice, marked most often by a sound of yearning that can be both exhilarating and heartbreaking. We hear it in "Born to Run," in "Thunder Road," in "Darkness on the Edge of Town," in "Backstreets," in "Streets of Fire," in "No Surrender," and countless other songs. Yet it's also in a seemingly inconsequential party song that Springsteen calls us to remember our better selves and bigger dreams. "My love is bigger than a Honda / It's bigger than a Subaru," he sings rockabilly style in "Pink Cadillac." And in that seemingly simple image, that rock 'n' roll status symbol, embodying all of the beauty, exuberance, and vulgarity of American appetites, he reminds us of our citizenship in an expansive nation with a generous spirit, no matter how fraught with doubt or disillusion we may sometimes be.

Alan Light

∎

Alan Light's piece that ran in the August 5, 2002, issue of *The New Yorker* nicely captures the friction in *The Rising* between hope and despair, faith and redemption—ongoing concerns of Springsteen over the decades. Light was a writer for *Rolling Stone* from 1990 to 1993, the editor of *Vibe* from 1993 to 1997, and the editor of *Spin* from 1997 to 2002. If *The Rising* disappointed some by lacking an urgent sense of political engagement,[1] a charge leveled by more than a few critics, it appealed to others for its resiliency, its perseverance, and its exploration of the variegated shades of love.

The Missing

The New Yorker

∎IF THERE WAS EVER a moment for Bruce Springsteen to take back his place at rock's center stage, this would be it. His last album of new work, *The Ghost of Tom Joad,* came out seven years ago, in 1995. After that—despite an extensive world tour in 1999 and 2000—he struggled to find a subject or a sound compelling enough to build an album around. Then came the September 11th attacks on the World Trade Center. In the months that followed, Springsteen wrote and recorded thirteen new songs; they have now been released, along with two tracks that were written earlier, as an album called *The Rising.* This seems to set the stage for a familiar scenario: the rock veteran's triumphant return to relevance, form, and, ultimately, Grammy recognition (see Bob Dylan, Santana, and U2). But instead of writing the album that would undoubtedly have put him back in the spotlight—a *Born in the U.S.A.* for a new era—Springsteen came up with something riskier and more surprising, something more than the country's archetypal living rock star fulfilling his obligation as America's rock-and-roll conscience.

From the start, Springsteen's songs have reflected a tension between his obsessive love of rock and his respect for the simple, direct power of folk music, leading to both the majestic scope of *Born to Run* and the quiet intensity and Woody Guthrie–inspired moralism of *Nebraska* and

The Ghost of Tom Joad. Anthemic, operatic epics like "Thunder Road" and "Jungleland" seemed, in their expansiveness, to invoke the complete history of rock and roll, and helped him break through to a mass audience. And songs like "The River" and "Badlands" achieved a near-perfect balance between despair and defiance, drawing as much on John Steinbeck and John Ford as on Chuck Berry. After *Born in the U.S.A.* (1984) sold fifteen million copies and established Springsteen as a pumped-up, dressed-down, blue-collar megastar, he pulled back, turning to honed parables of immigrant experience and small-town American life set against intimate musical backdrops. Today, he is among the world's greatest rock icons, but he has had only one album reach No. 1 on the charts since *Tunnel of Love* (1987), and it was a greatest-hits album released in 1995.

The Rising sounds like nothing Springsteen has ever done before. Although this is his first studio album in eighteen years to draw on the full power of the E Street Band, its producer, Brendan O'Brien, didn't go for a live, classic-rock-band approach. Instead, Springsteen sings over dense, constructed blocks of sound, heavy on strings and stacked guitars, light on Clarence (Big Man) Clemons barroom sax solos. His voice seldom rises to that strained, fever pitch familiar from his arena concerts. The lovely, gentle sway of "You're Missing" is one of the most delicate tracks he's ever recorded, whereas the Middle Eastern texture and slashing guitar of "Worlds Apart" bring to mind Sting or Peter Gabriel.[2] Even "Mary's Place," the one song on the album that sounds like a classic E Street "Rosalita"-style barn burner, never reaches the rave-up heights we expect. The song, which describes a gathering at a party or a bar, comes to a break about two-thirds of the way in, and turns into a chorus singing "Turn it up!" This is the part in a Springsteen song when the music should lift off irresistibly—but nothing happens. The chorus repeats for a few more minutes and then fades out, as if Springsteen just can't find a way to give in to joyous rock-and-roll release.

The lyrics are even more atypical than the sound. All the signature Springsteen narrative and detail has been stripped out: there is not a single Joe Roberts or Bill Horton wrestling with his conflicts, no Crazy Janey or Magic Rat, no working on the highway or racing in the street. The language is bare, almost generic; words and images repeat from song to song. The five songs that most explicitly evoke the attacks—"Into the Fire," "Empty Sky," "You're Missing," "The Rising," and "My City of Ruins"—reduce the events to an anonymous domestic fragment

("Just an empty impression / In the bed where you used to be," or "Coffee cup's on the counter, jacket's on the chair / Paper's on the doorstep, but you're not there"). Rather than tell individual stories as allegories of a broader social condition (the way the characters on *Born in the U.S.A.* and *Nebraska* chronicled the fallout from Reaganomics), Springsteen seems to be striving for something universal to capture the mood of the whole nation. Language that strives for universality can often lapse into imprecision, though, and in some cases Springsteen's decision to avoid fully fleshed-out stories plays away from his greatest strength: without his finely observed narratives, bouncy, doo-wop flavored cuts like "Waitin' on a Sunny Day" and "Let's Be Friends (Skin to Skin)" seem lightweight— pleasant, if minor, lookin'-for-love songs with dark undercurrents.

But, more often than not, Springsteen achieves moments of understated eloquence and grace. Sudden flashes of elevated symbolism recall the mystic vocabulary of early albums ("On the plains of Jordan, I cut my bow from the wood / Of this tree of evil, of this tree of good," he sings on "Empty Sky"); the dual mythologies of religion and rock and roll have long run together in Springsteen's work. On his last tour, he promised concertgoers "a rock-and-roll baptism." But now the language of faith and redemption seems to have assumed a more sober meaning for him; "Fire," "Ruins," and the title track all culminate in rousing, life-affirming prayer.

The Rising contains none of the political engagement we might have expected to find on a Bruce Springsteen 9/11 album. In fact, this is ultimately an album about love. "The Fuse" and "Let's Be Friends (Skin to Skin)" have a sexual heat that has mostly been absent from Springsteen's work. On songs such as "Worlds Apart" and "Lonesome Day," which address the limitations of relationships, we see more fully how the world after September 11th has lent an urgency to themes of independence that have often been present in Springsteen's writing. "You're afraid to love something so much, you're afraid to be in that love," Springsteen said in 1992, describing the tensions in his offstage life that surfaced on the albums *Lucky Town* and *Human Touch*. "Because a world of fear leaps upon you, particularly in the world that we live in. . . . My specialty was keeping my distance, so that if I lost something, it wouldn't hurt so much."

Despite the new sonic sound and lyrical direction of *The Rising*, there is no mistaking its resonances with Springsteen's earlier work. The indelible connection between grief and joy—an ongoing preoccupation of Springsteen's—lies behind every one of the songs, including those written before the attacks. ("My City of Ruins," which Springsteen performed during the *Tribute to Heroes* telethon on September 21st, was actually inspired by the disrepair of Asbury Park.) Springsteen has said the narrator of the first verse in the spare, haunting "Paradise" is a female suicide bomber, but it's easy to miss that. What's clear is the song's sense of yearning for human connection, and a wish to "get to that place where we really wanna go," which Springsteen has been singing about since *Born to Run*. "Worlds Apart" may refer to "Allah's blessed rain" and have a chanting chorus, sung by the Pakistani qawwali singer Asif Ali Khan and his group, but the troubled couple it describes could come straight off *Tunnel of Love*.

All the songs on *The Rising* reach a point where the singer warily considers a future of being alone, and concludes, as Springsteen has again and again over the years, that perseverance is the greatest heroism. This album reflects a new sense of what it's like to live with mortality—after all, Springsteen, at fifty-two, is no longer young. But for him music has always been about survival, not victimhood. Twenty-two years ago, the night after John Lennon was murdered, Springsteen took the stage in Philadelphia. "It's a hard world that makes you live with things that are unlivable," he said. "And it's hard to come out here and play tonight, but there's nothing else to do."

Notes

1. In *CounterPunch*, the biweekly newsletter edited by Alexander Cockburn and Jeffrey St. Clair, Alan Maass, editor of the Chicago-based *Socialist Worker*, takes Springsteen to task for not assuming a more active political stance. "There's nothing wrong with eulogies," he writes, but "a lot more needs to be said about September 11, and Springsteen, as much as any songwriter around, has the skills to say it." See Alan Maass, *"The Rising," CounterPunch*, September 9, 2002. Josh Tyrangiel agrees. "What's missing on *The Rising* is politics." See Josh Tyrangiel, "Bruce Rising: An Intimate Look at How Springsteen Turned 9/11 into a Message of Hope," *Time,* August 5, 2002.

2. In a lengthy interview with Adam Sweeting, Springsteen recalls the origin of "Worlds Apart." "I was trying to look outside the United States and move the boundaries of the record in some fashion. I think the song started when I saw a picture of the women in Afghanistan with the veils off a few days after they'd routed the Taliban out of Kabul, and their faces were so beautiful." See Adam Sweeting, "Into the Fire," *Uncut*, September 2002.

A. O. Scott

■

A. O. Scott is a film critic for the *New York Times* and the former book critic for *Newsday* as well as a regular contributor to the *New York Review of Books*. Here, in a review of *The Rising* that ran in the online magazine *Slate* (August 6, 2002), he discusses Springsteen's prophetic visions and the singer's ongoing obsession with finding redemption and salvation—and its often cathartic effect.

The Poet Laureate of 9/11: Apocalypse and Salvation on Springsteen's New Album

Slate

■VERY FEW RECENT albums have been anticipated with as much hunger or greeted with as much rapture as *The Rising*, Bruce Springsteen's new one. It is not only the Boss' first studio album with the E Street Band since *Born in the U.S.A.* back in 1984, but also his first rock 'n' roll record in a decade, and the first rock 'n' roll record in a very long time whose release has seemed like a cultural event. Rock 'n' roll, while not exactly dead, is decidedly middle-aged—no longer the dominant, organizing principle of youth-driven popular music. In a music industry given over to the various permutations of metal, hip-hop, neo-bubblegum, and the folk revival revival, rock 'n' roll survives mainly in cut-price CD back stock and in the drearily repetitive playlists of "classic rock" radio stations. Chuck Berry, Springsteen's great precursor, promised that the music would "deliver us from the days of old," but more often these days it transports us back to them.

Though his best-known songs are staples of the not-quite oldies format, Springsteen, now 52, has remained a stubborn, if sometimes melancholy romantic, indifferent to both fashion and nostalgia. "The church door's / thrown open / I can hear the organ's song / but the congregation's gone," Springsteen sings in "My City of Ruins," the last song on *The Rising*. His own congregation, of course, has remained remarkably steadfast in its faith. At his Madison Square Garden concerts with the newly reunited E Street Band two summers ago, Springsteen, midway through his medley of "Good Golly Miss Molly," "Devil with a Blue Dress," and other chestnuts, shouted and gesticulated like a fire-breathing Pentecostal preacher, invoking a "rock 'n' roll baptism." (Nothing if not ecumenical, he also called it a "rock 'n' roll bar mitzvah.") Since *Born to Run,* the album in which he first discovered his prophetic vocation, Springsteen's lyrics have often given a religious inflection to the durable rock 'n' roll themes of desire, frustration, and the longing for liberation, fusing Berry's vocabulary of cars, guitars, and pretty girls with the language of apocalypse and salvation, purgation and redemption. And these are more than just themes: The dialectic of despair and triumph is built into the musical structure and aural texture of the songs themselves, which enact, and induce in their listeners, the very emotions their words describe.

The songs, indeed, may be the only concrete manifestations of the abstractions—faith, freedom, "Born to Run's" everlasting kiss—they summon up. Consider, among many possible examples, "The Promised Land," from *Darkness on the Edge of Town.* Its lyrics begin, after a low-key, harmonica-tinged introduction, with a particular character in a specific place—a "rattlesnake speedway in the Utah desert." In the second verse, the character's malaise builds into thwarted rage and then, at the end, into a climactic vision of purifying destruction, "a twister to blow / everything down / that ain't got the faith / to stand its ground."

At this point, the song leaves the ground of realist narrative and ascends into metaphor: The storm is not an actual event in the narrator's life, but the figuration of his anger and his hope. And what delivers the metaphor— what makes its grandiose, Utopian imagery so powerful and vivid—is the music, with its thickly layered middle register (two guitars, two keyboards) carrying the voice through its litany of agony and defiance.

This is not Springsteen's only mode, of course. It evolved out of the shaggy-dog hipster surrealism of his first two records and has always coexisted with the more hedonistic and contemplative sides of his personality. For most of the past 15 years, the oracular strain of Springsteen's voice, at least in the recording studio, was all but silent. After *Born in the U.S.A.,* he preferred to bear witness—to his own romantic wounds (on *Tunnel of Love*) and to the travails of the forgotten and the dispossessed (on *The Ghost of Tom Joad*). He refashioned himself as the heir to Woody Guthrie and John Steinbeck, lonely avatar of a faded tradition of social conscience and left-wing populism.

And then there was Sept. 11, the overt or implicit subject of most of the songs on *The Rising* and one of the reasons its arrival has stirred up so much emotion. If any American artist could summon up an adequate, inclusive response to the events of that day, it would have to be Springsteen. This is not only because he has roots in the same Northeastern Catholic working-class soil from which so many of the local heroes of 9/11 sprouted, but because his songwriting idiom is almost uncannily attuned to the tangle of feelings—horror, grief, and rage, but also resolve, resilience, and solidarity—that that day left in its wake and is perhaps uniquely capable of clarifying them.

In the past, Springsteen has approached the disasters of history— Vietnam, deindustrialization, Third World poverty—obliquely and piece-meal, through the lens of individual first- and third-person narratives. While some of the songs on the new album adopt fictional personas—a lost fireman's widow ("Into the Fire"), a rescue worker suffering from post-traumatic depression ("Nothing Man"), even a suicide bomber ("Paradise")—the details of their lives have been almost entirely stripped away. There are no proper names and no place names (aside from generic markers like "Al's Barbecue" and "Mary's Place"); instead, the language is spare and elemental, with the same simple nouns recurring again and again: blood, fire, rain, sky; strength, hope, faith, love.

This is only fitting. Unlike the unemployed dockworkers and immi-grant farmers of *Ghost of Tom Joad,* we already know the names and the stories of many of the individual victims of 9/11. And in the face of a ter-rible and tremendous experience, too much eloquence is suspect, and we fall back on commonplaces. It takes more than mere sincerity to turn these utterances into poetry, but Springsteen, through the understated conviction of his voice and the precision of producer Brendan O'Brien's arrangement, manages something close on "Into the Fire," whose chorus expresses something every New Yorker has felt walking past the local firehouse since last fall.

> *May your strength give us strength*
> *May your faith give us faith*
> *May your hope give us hope . . .*

Similar words turn up in "Countin' on a Miracle" and "My City of Ru-ins" (a song written before Sept. 11 to lament the decay of Springsteen's beloved Asbury Park, N.J.). Repetition, psychologists say, is part of the work of grief, and over the course of the 15 songs on *The Rising* the re-iteration of key words and phrases—now sung in agony, now in resigna-tion, now in hope—has a cathartic effect. In the weeks and months after 9/11, people told and retold their stories almost compulsively and plunged again and again into their terror and confusion in a paradoxical effort to move beyond the experience and to keep it close. *The Rising*, listened to repeatedly—the only way true Springsteen fans know how—has a similar effect. It neither assuages the horror with false hope nor al-lows it to slip into nihilistic despair.

But rock 'n' roll is not all about grief and terror, and the song that has lodged most firmly in my head is "Mary's Place," an effusion of joy that comes two-thirds of the way through *The Rising*. Here, Clarence Clemons' saxophone, overshadowed on much of the album by Soozie Tyrell's violin, at last cuts loose, and the way the band stops short before plunging into the chorus is an E Street moment of pure (though highly disciplined) release the likes of which have not been heard on record for 20 years. "Meet me at Mary's place." I'll be there, Boss.

Kevin Coyne

∎

Kevin Coyne is a reporter for the *Asbury Park Press,* contributing editor of *New Jersey Monthly,* and Freehold's town historian. He is also the author of *A Day in the Night of America* (1992), *Domers: A Year at Notre Dame* (1996), and *Marching Home: To War and Back with the Men of One American Town* (2003), and teaches at the Graduate School of Journalism at Columbia University. "His Hometown" first appeared in the January 2003 issue of the *New Jersey Monthly.* In an earlier article,[1] which appeared in the *Asbury Park Press and the Home News Tribune,* Coyne mined much the same territory, discussing how Springsteen's songs echo the lives of so many people, both in his home state and elsewhere, but also observing how proprietary the town of Freehold is toward him. In both articles, he refers to the pedigree of the Springsteen name— Springsteens were among the original Dutch settlers of Monmouth County.

His Hometown
New Jersey Monthly

∎ON THE MORNING OF the first anniversary of the September 11 attacks, after my kids are safely on their way to school, I put on a blue shirt and a red tie and walk from my house to the interfaith service the local clergy association is holding at one of the stately Protestant churches that line Main Street in Freehold. I go not because I've lost anybody— mercifully, I haven't—but because it's what my town is doing to mark the day, and I think I should be there.

It's a service much like thousands of other services all over America this day—solemn and understated, simple and deeply moving. The weight of the event it's commemorating is sufficient so that no flourishes are necessary. As a rabbi intones the names of county residents who died that day, a minister reads a mournful litany of remembrance. There's a choral response led by a soloist:

> *"May your strength give us strength*
> *May your faith give us faith*
> *May your hope give us hope . . ."*

It's sung without comment or introduction, and it's repeated several more times throughout the litany and again after the reading of the 46th Psalm, as if it were a psalm itself, a refrain that everyone everywhere is saying today, a prayer that dates back centuries rather than the chorus of a song that was released barely a month ago, Bruce Springsteen's "Into the Fire." Springsteen's name is never mentioned; his words are simply absorbed into the fabric of the day.

The singing of the chorus is a fitting, seamless grace note in a somber ceremony, but it's also an almost perfect illustration of the complex, subtle, and powerful bonds between Springsteen and his hometown, between an artist and his art. I'm the town historian in Freehold Borough—where Springsteen was born in 1949, where he lived until he left to become a rock star, and which he revisits often in the lyrics of his songs—and I frequently get calls from reporters and fans plumbing his biography. Most of their questions are simple and easily answered: Where did he live? Where did he go to school? Where did his first band play? Where's Greasy Lake?

They end up coming to me because there's no other obvious place to go, and that often becomes their next question: Why aren't these spots marked? Why aren't there any tours? Why isn't there a museum, a monument, at least a sign somewhere? Why is there no public acknowledgment at all of your most famous native?

Proposals, in fact, surface occasionally in town—to rename South Street Bruce Springsteen Boulevard, to put up a statue in front of Borough Hall—but they've quickly died. Such conventional ways of honoring Springsteen miss the point of his relationship with his hometown and that of his hometown with him; they would memorialize it as something dead and distant—a historical curiosity, like Grover Cleveland's birthplace in Caldwell, say—rather than the deep and complicated thing it really is, alive and near. The reason we don't have any public acknowledgment of Springsteen in Freehold isn't because we don't love him here, but because we do.

People in New Jersey always have felt proprietary about Bruce Springsteen because he's always seemed to be so completely one of us. He's never pretended to be from New York or Philadelphia, never said he was anything but what he was. He proudly proclaimed where he was from at a time when many other people from New Jersey didn't. He doesn't set his songs in some generic landscape, some floating world detached from this one, but in a familiar territory you could navigate with the map of your own experience—the Turnpike, Madam Marie's, Highway 9, the boardwalk in Asbury Park, the auto plant in Mahwah. He knows the ragged cities, the faded factory towns, the seductive beaches, the guys who *"come home from work and wash up, and go racin' in the street."*

Local references like that go only so far, though, in explaining his saint-like stature here in his home state. Behind them is the larger sense that he knows what our lives are like and that he's telling our stories. Springsteen's music can be insistent, propulsive, ecstatic, tender, and indelible, but in the canon of popular culture it will never approach the formal innovation, the startling melodies, of a band like the Beatles. Springsteen's power is derived instead from his gifts as a writer. He's by far the best novelist rock-and-roll has yet produced,[2] and he's even better than most who have emerged from the novel-writing business itself.

In his songs—the chapters of his books—he draws characters, depicts scenes, and touches themes that have a quality sufficiently universal to make fans in Florida or Michigan or Sweden hear their own lives in them. That largeness of vision is what has made for the largeness of his appeal—why he sells out wherever he plays in the world. Here in New Jersey we can see the smallness too, the details that seem lifted almost whole from our own lives, that are rooted in the place we share with him—which is why he can sell out Continental Airlines Arena at the Meadowlands for fifteen nights, as he did in 1999.

Some writers get locked into writing about their home territories and never rise above the level of regional chroniclers. Others burrow so deeply into one place that they hit the stream running underneath all places— William Faulkner's Mississippi, John Steinbeck's California, Robert Frost's Vermont, Flannery O'Connor's Georgia. William Kennedy, the laureate of Albany, once described himself in a way that seems to fit Springsteen too: "a person whose imagination has become fused with a single place, and in that place finds all the elements that a man ever needs for the life of the soul."

Springsteen has the purest pedigree of almost any important New Jersey writer since Stephen Crane. There have been Springsteens in New Jersey almost as long as there has been a New Jersey; it's an old Dutch name that goes back to the colony's early settlers.[3] Springsteens from Monmouth County fought in the Revolution, the War of 1812, and the Civil War. His mother's side of Italian stock arrived much later, part of the wave of twentieth-century immigration that transformed the state into the polyglot culture of today.[4] *"I was born right here on Randolph Street in Freehold,"* he sang in "In Freehold," an alternately funny and bitter slice of autobiography that he debuted in a concert at his old parochial school gym in 1996. *"Well my folks all lived and worked right here in Freehold."*

That concert was his gift to all of us in his hometown, a benefit to raise money for a Hispanic community center the Catholic church was building, with admission restricted to residents of Freehold Borough. Imagine the intimacy that you, a resident of Plainfield or Montclair or even Asbury Park, feel when you see him perform at the Meadowlands, multiply it by, say, a hundred, and you'll get a glimmer of how we felt that night. It was like a conversation at a family reunion. He didn't have to explain to anybody what or where Caiazzo's was.

It was far from a sentimental lovefest, though, and more like a reunion for a family that had traveled a lot of rough roads but was still together. He sang darkly of the hard times the town had given his father, his sister, and him. Between songs he was at times profane, riffing on oral sex in a way calculated to offend the priests and nuns in the crowd. *"If you were different, black or brown, it was a pretty redneck town,"* he sang. And we nodded in recognition and cheered him loudly.

I thought back to that night recently, when a reporter asked me why Freehold seemed to embrace Springsteen so wholeheartedly when his portrait of our town often seems so unflattering. She was thinking mainly of "My Hometown," with its shuttered factory, its racial strife, its ghostly Main Street. Because we don't see it as unflattering, I told her. We see it as the truth. Freehold isn't like that anymore, but it once was. He was just being honest, and honesty is the basis of all good relationships. And while people on the outside assume that song is about leaving, we on the inside know it's really about staying.

When he sang "In Freehold" again several years later for a much larger audience at the Meadowlands, he added a verse about *"the statue of me in my hometown"* that had been proposed, and, to his relief, rejected:

> *"Well I'd like to thank the town council, my friends, for saving me from humiliation*
> *By demonstrating the good, hard common sense that we learned in Freehold . . ."*

Notes

1. Writes Coyne, "[I]t is the particularity of his songs, the portrait they offer of the real life of a place, that makes people in New Jersey—more especially at the Shore in general, and most especially of all in Freehold—proprietary about him. You can put him beside Elvis in the Hall of Fame, they say, but he will always belong to us." See Kevin Coyne, "The Faulkner of Freehold," *Asbury Park Press and Home News Tribune,* March 14, 1999. See also Bob Crane, *A Place to Stand,* in this volume.

2. "Almost uniquely in the annals of rock 'n' roll, Bruce Springsteen is a narrative artist. Line his songs up end to end over the three decades and they assume the shape and size and weight of a novel, an epic about the struggle to build a decent life in shifting sands of postwar America. . . . And like the best novels, his is rooted in a deep understanding of the world that made him. Charles Dickens walked miles through London by night, soaking up sights and sounds and smells. John Steinbeck traveled the migrant camps of his native California. Bruce Springsteen kept returning, again and again, to the streets of the town where he was once so desperate to escape." Coyne, ibid. Other scholars have arrived at a similar conclusion. See Jim Cullen, *Born in the U.S.A.* (New York: Viking, 1997), and Larry David Smith, *Bob Dylan, Bruce Springsteen, and American Song* (Westport, Conn.: Praeger Publishers, 2002).

3. The name is a combination of the Dutch words "spring," referring to the source of a body of water, and "steen," meaning "stone." In other words, the name literally means a stone from which a spring flowed. The earliest reference to the name in New Jersey dates as far back as circa 1664.

4. Coyne elaborates on Freehold's checkered past: "Freehold has always been distinguished by an uncommon mixture of village intimacy and city diversity—small enough, with never much more than 10,000 people, to constitute a knowable world, but large enough to contain the whole sweep of America. The black people who moved into town were followed by the Irish, who had first been drawn to the potato fields that stretched for a half-day's walk in every direction, and then the Eastern Europeans, who came to work in the factories, and finally by Puerto Ricans, Mexicans and the whole spectrum of more recent immigrants." See Coyne, "The Faulkner of Freehold," March 14, 1999.

Eric Alterman

■

Eric Alterman is a political and cultural columnist for the *Nation* and writes the "Altercation" Web log for MSNBC.com (www.altercation.msnbc.com). He is also the author of *Sound and Fury: The Making of the Punditocracy* (1992), *Who Speaks for America? Why Democracy Matters in Foreign Policy* (1998), and, most recently, *What Liberal Media? The Truth About Bias and the News* (2003). In 2004 he published, with Mark Green, *The Book on Bush: How George W. (Mis)Leads America.* The following selection is from the appendix to the Spanish edition (2003) of *It Ain't No Sin to Be Glad You're Alive: The Promise of Bruce Springsteen,* which was originally published in 1999.

from *It Ain't No Sin to Be Glad You're Alive: The Promise of Bruce Springsteen*

■TWENTY-FOUR HOURS or so after landing in Paris for a five-city tour in search of the new European anti-Americanism, I found myself in a big old ugly hockey arena on the outskirts of town, surrounded by 15,000 people waiting for Bruce Springsteen and the E Street Band to come on-stage. The concert turned out to be a pretty standard Springsteen concert. But it's always interesting to see him play abroad, and Paris enjoys a special place in Springsteen lore. It was here, back in 1980, that Bruce first talked politics with his fans. Largely self-educated, Springsteen had been given a copy of Allan Nevins and Henry Steele Commager's *A Short History of the United States.* He read it and told the crowd that America "held out a promise and it was a promise that gets broken every day in the most violent way. But it's a promise that never, ever dies, and it's always inside of you."

You can tell a lot about a continent by the way it reacts to Bruce Springsteen. Tonight, at the Bercy Stadium, the typically multigenerational, sold-out Springsteen audience could be from Anytown, U.S.A. Everybody knows all the lyrics, even to the new songs. Toward the end of the evening, Bruce announces, in French, "I wrote this song about the Vietnam War. I want to do it tonight for peace," and 15,000 Parisians, standing in the historic home of cultural anti-Americanism, scream out at the top of their collective lungs, "I was born in the U.S.A.," fists in the air.

You can't be anti-American if you love Bruce Springsteen. You can criticize America. You can march against America's actions in the world. You can take issue with the policies of its unelected, unusually aggressive and unthinking administration, and you can even get annoyed with its ubiquitous cultural and commercial presence in your life. But you can't be anti-American. George W. Bush is "like a cartoon stereotype" representing "the worst side of the U.S. culture," Jordi Beleta, 45, told Phil Kuntz of the *Wall Street Journal,* outside Barcelona's Palau Sant Jordi two nights after Paris. "Bruce is real. He's a street man."[1] A Reuters reporter found a similar story in Berlin: "America can keep Bush but Springsteen can come back here as often as he wants," said Rumen Milkov, 36.

Springsteen was touring Europe in support of his album, *The Rising,* and Europe, just like America, was loving him. The record entered the charts at the number one spot upon its release not only in the U.S., but also in Canada, the United Kingdom, Germany, Italy, Spain, Sweden, Belgium, Finland, Denmark, and Norway. Inspired by the horrific attacks of 9/11, *The Rising,* Robert Lloyd of the *L.A. Weekly,* wrote, "is not a work of rage or analysis, but rather a collection of love songs (or lost-love songs) and ghost stories, and not the least of its many virtues is that you can dance to just about all of it."[2] True, but too simple.

Springsteen described his goals on *The Rising* to a *New York Times* reporter in a manner consistent with the entire body of his work. He explained, "You have to come to grips with the real horrors that are out there," he told the reporter. "And then all people have is hope. That's what brings the next day and whatever that day may bring. You can't be uncritical, but just a hope grounded in the real world of living, friendship, work, family, Saturday night. And that's where it resides. That's where I always found faith and spirit. I found them down in those things, not some place intangible or some place abstract. And I've really tried to write about that basic idea my whole life."[3]

Abroad, Springsteen is widely understood to represent the best of America. Alessandro Portelli, a professor of American literature at the University of Rome, told me that in the wake of 9/11 many Europeans yearned to see Americans develop some empathy for the suffering of the rest of the world as a result of their own tragic experience. "You can hear this in *The Rising,*" explains Portelli, who is one of Italy's resident Springsteen experts, "as Bruce looks beyond the boundaries of the United States with moral courage and intelligence. But instead of Bruce we have Bush.

And the dominant rhetoric has been of the exceptionalism of American sorrow."[4]

In the United States, however, there is a strain of criticism that finds his work to be unworthy of hipster chic or ultra-leftist discourse. In what will go down in history as one of the stupidest comments ever made by a rock critic—or perhaps by anyone at all—the *Village Voice*'s Keith Harris opined of the record, "Because his vision of rock and roll is so grand, Springsteen requires a popular consensus as surely as any invasion of Iraq. And as we've learned yet again, nothing sparks phony consensus like national cataclysm. Maybe that's why, for the past few days, a nagging thought has burrowed into my brain that I wish was merely the snide aphorism I initially took it for: If there hadn't been a September 11, Bruce Springsteen would have had to invent one."[5]

Harris's comment was idiotic but instructive. Aside from its self-evident (and self-incriminating) silliness, what galls about the comment is its willful forfeiture of the common cultural ground upon which Bruce Springsteen plies his trade. Did 9/11 belong only to the Bush administration? Is American popular culture the exclusive preserve of Spielberg, and Britney?

While managing to keep both feet planted in the mainstream, Springsteen has done more than any American artist to give voice to the American "other" that pop culture would prefer to forget: the humiliated Vietnam veteran, the fired factory worker, the hunted illegal immigrant, the death-row inmate, the homeless person living beneath the bridge, and Amadou Diallo, the West African immigrant, accidentally murdered by 41 shots from New York's finest.

Springsteen is vulnerable to criticism on any number of grounds, artistic and commercial, but his willingness to offer solace in troubled times strikes me as pretty low on that list. Springsteen was literally stopped in his car after 9/11 by someone who cried out, "We need you."[6] Monmouth County, where he lives, lost 158 people in the towers. He played a couple of local benefits. He read, repeatedly, about the meaning of his work to his fans in the *New York Times*'s "Portraits of Grief." He called a few widows, shared their stories, and made a record. It's what he does. "I have a sense of what my service to my audience is going to be," he explains. "It's the true nature of work in the sense that you're filling a place. And that place comes with its blessings and its responsibilities."[7] So sue him.

It is a separate question as to whether one thinks the art that emanated from this impulse is wholly successful. But to take issue with the very idea that art can be a balm to those in pain—or, as Springsteen puts it, "music is medicine"—is cynicism itself. And to the degree that this is at all representative of leftist attitudes, it speaks for an impotent and self-defeating left: too smug and self-satisfied to engage the culture of the common people, preferring instead to smirk on the sidelines.

Granting both its sincerity and its (inconsistent) genius, *The Rising* does nevertheless raise some complicated questions about art, politics, and commerce. One has to go back to 1984—to Springsteen's own *Born in the U.S.A.*—to find a rock record that was marketed as energetically to mainstream America. And that one, as we all know, was more misunderstood than meaningful—at least initially. Here, after decades of relative reclusiveness, Springsteen was suddenly everywhere in the mass media: taking over the *Today* show in Asbury Park, on David Letterman two nights in a row, ditto Ted Koppel, on MTV, VH1, *Saturday Night Live*, simultaneous covers of *Time* and *Rolling Stone*, long interviews with the *New York Times*, the *LA Times*, and *USA Today*. I half expected him to duet with Elmo or Big Bird over breakfast. It should surprise no one that the record entered the charts at No. 1 in 11 countries. A year later, when the world tour was still going strong, Springsteen just about sold out ten shows at the Giants (football) Stadium in New Jersey. The roughly 500,000 seats sold proved to be more than any artist has ever sold in one place at one time—ever.

The problem arises—just as it did with *Born in the U.S.A.*—when the work's cultural signification overwhelms its artistic essence; what Nietzsche, in *Twilight of the Idols*, termed "the thing itself." The dilemma for anyone who seeks to use popular culture to communicate a message at odds with its market-driven heart of darkness is: who's using whom? Did Springsteen accidentally empower Reaganism back in the mid-1980s as he simultaneously denounced it? Is he somehow cheapening the individual tragedies of which he writes and sings by performing these haunting melodies at the ungodly hour of 8:30 A.M. in the happy-talk contest of a *Today* show beach party?

NBC's Matt Lauer asked Springsteen whether he feared being accused of exploiting the tragedy of 9/11, and Springsteen told him to listen to the music and make up his own mind. The same might be said of his willingness to embrace (and exploit) America's mighty mass-marketing machine.

The answer has to be a personal one. In Asbury Park, I did some random interviewing of people who had traveled many hours, and waited on overnight lines, in the hope of seeing Springsteen perform four songs in the Convention Hall for the *Today* broadcast. I spoke to a firefighter who had gone into the burning buildings, a 16-year-old girl who was repaying her mom for waiting 10 hours on line to get 'NSync tickets, a woman with her 5-year-old son, who, back in '85, enlisted her entire family in a week-long wait for tickets. Nobody mentioned the media. Nobody mentioned the marketing campaign. Nobody complained about the all-night wait and the uncertainty that they would be allowed inside the hall. They were there for Bruce because Bruce was there for them. In the midst of what Springsteen accurately terms "a theater of humiliation on TV and on the radio, a reflection of self-loathing,"[8] they had created a community around something better. This was their hometown.

Notes

1. See Phil Kuntz, "In Europe, Uncle Sam Has Lost Popularity, but the Boss Rocks," *Wall Street Journal*, October 18, 2002.
2. See Robert Lloyd, "Bruce Springsteen in the City of Ruins," *LA Weekly*, September 13–19, 2002.
3. See Jon Pareles, "His Kind of Heroes, His Kind of Songs," *New York Times*, July 14, 2002.
4. See Eric Alterman, "USA Oui! Bush Non!," *Nation*, February 10, 2003.
5. Quoted in Eric Alterman, "The Mayor of My Hometown," *Nation*, September 2, 2002.
6. According to Gregory J. Volpe, a staff writer for the *Asbury Park Press*, the "someone" in question was Rumson, New Jersey, resident Edwin R. Sutphin Jr. Sutphin happened to be attending a club in nearby Sea Bright. As he pulled into the club's parking lot, he saw Springsteen pulling out. Springsteen did not stop but nodded in acknowledgment and later told the story to Pareles. According to the article, Sutphin's childhood friend, David Bauer, also of Rumson, worked on the 105th floor of the World Trade Center's north tower and perished in the terrorist attacks. See Gregory J. Volpe, "Rumson Man Inspired Boss," *Asbury Park Press*, July 31, 2002.
7. Pareles, "His Kind of Heroes."
8. Ibid.

Christopher Phillips

■

Born in Pittsburgh, Christopher Phillips grew up in upstate New York and Maine before moving with his family to Georgia when he was ten. He attended Duke University, majoring in English and design, and in 1993 made the cross-country trek to Seattle, which happened to be the headquarters of *Backstreets*, the highly acclaimed Springsteen fanzine founded by Charles Cross in 1980. "I didn't move there for *Backstreets*," Phillips maintains, but as a longtime reader of the magazine, he soon wound up on board as managing editor. In 1998, he took over from Cross as editor and publisher and, two years later, moved the editorial offices to Washington, D.C. His writing has also appeared in *The Rocket, Seattle Magazine, Discoveries,* and *Revolver.* The following reflective piece, written especially for *Racing in the Street,* recalls Phillips's own Boss awakening.

The Real World

■For every Bruce Springsteen fan, there's an origin story. When we meet, it's chatter as unavoidable as "So what do you do?" at a cocktail party—the story of how we each discovered our passion is as integral a part of our personal histories as a first kiss. As editor of *Backstreets* magazine, a publication for Springsteen fans, I've heard plenty of 'em, and with Springsteen's performing career now spanning five decades and counting, these stories run the gamut. Happening by a club in 1972. Hearing "Born to Run" for the first time over a car's AM radio in 1975. Tuning in to David Letterman's last NBC show in 1993 to find a guitar slinger stomping on Paul Shaffer's piano. Downloading a live MP3 from the E Street Band's reunion tour to hear what all the fuss is about. These moments change lives. Considering my job for the past ten years—the only one I've held in the adult world—it's easy to say that my life was changed drastically.

I came in somewhere in the middle of that spectrum; my conversion came in early 1984, when I was 13, courtesy of a Maxell XLII 90-minute cassette. I was in my room—sitting on the floor in front of my Realistic stereo, as usual, with the "record" button in reach in case a good song came on the radio—when my older brother burst in with five of my favorite words: "You've got to hear this!" The way I remember it, although it couldn't have been this dramatic, he whipped the door shut behind him and jammed his back against it, as if he had smuggled in contraband. Of course, since we lived in a small town in the South, that's practically what it was. He held a Bruce Springsteen mix tape made by his girl-friend, with all of *Born to Run* as side B. As a Top 40 radio freak, I knew the name, but the glossy, throwback sound of "Hungry Heart" hadn't prepared me for what was about to come blasting out of my speakers—my brother had the tape cued up to "Jungleland." And that's all it took. As Tom Waits would later mutter, "Kid, you're hooked, heavy as lead."

They said that home taping was killing the music industry, but I bought every Bruce record I could get my hands on thanks to that hum-ble homemade cassette. I immersed myself. *The River* and *Darkness on the Edge of Town* first, courtesy of the Columbia House Record & Tape Club, and when *Born in the U.S.A.* was released that summer, total im-mersion was an easy task.

It's easy to say "and the rest is history." But when fandom stretches well over half a lifetime, the more interesting question may not be how we get there, but why we stay. Springsteen hasn't been releasing music in a vacuum, and it's been far from the only thing on my stereo—that crappy Realistic, or any other. I have new "You've got to hear this" mo-ments once a week. In 1987, I'm sure I listened to the Replacements' *Pleased to Meet Me* far more than Springsteen's live box set. The follow-ing year, my copy of *Appetite for Destruction* got more spins than *Tun-nel of Love;* in 1992, it was *Nevermind* and *Slanted and Enchanted* more than *Human Touch* and *Lucky Town.* But in the end, Springsteen's mu-sic has been the soundtrack of my life, the music I've returned to again and again. Why is it that I keep coming back to "Atlantic City," but could be happy never hearing "Paradise City" again?

Inducting Bob Dylan into the Rock and Roll Hall of Fame, Spring-steen recalled the first time he heard Dylan's "Like a Rolling Stone": "I was in the car with my mother listening to WMCA, and on came that snare shot that sounded like somebody'd kicked open the door to your mind." As a 13-year-old kid, getting in and out of my mind was the least of my problems—my head was where I spent most of my time, and that door was in constant use. The fantasyland of late-'70s/early-'80s radio was right there with me: Aldo Nova's life was just a "Fantasy," 38 Spe-cial had their "Fantasy Girl," and Bad Company their "Rock and Roll

Fantasy." Until that cassette found its way to my room, my musical obsessions were over-the-hills-and-far-away bands like Styx. Kansas. Yes. Rush. If they had songs with movements, numbered with Roman numerals and names like "Father Padilla Meets the Perfect Gnat," you could count me in. But "Jungleland," that opera out on the Turnpike, took the kind of romantic, overblown fantasia I was drawn to and set it down in the more earthly realm of jukeboxes, gas stations, cop cars, and, certainly not least of all, bedrooms. "Beneath the city" was a secret world, sure, but it was this world, our world, the real world. For me, Bruce blew that door off its hinges.

It's no coincidence that Springsteen's music hit me just as I was starting to care about girls and cars. But it was the landscape those cars traversed—where actions always have consequences, and where there are as many disappointments as thrills—that made me feel a mainline connection to the world around me. The story of the nameless guy and his nameless "baby" in "Racing in the Street" reverberated with truth. I remember listening to the song in my room, lit only by the blue light from my stereo's radio dial, and calling my mom in so she could hear what I heard, from start to finish. Lord knows what she thought at the time— of the song, or of me listening to it in the dark. But I heard the real world, loud and clear, like I'd heard no one express it before. I wanted her and everyone else to hear it, too. When it came down to it, I probably knew more people like John Cougar's characters Jack and Diane. I didn't know anyone who actually raced in the street; I didn't know what fuelie heads were. To be honest, I'm not sure I've ever seen anyone actually sucking on a chili dog, either. But even though the setting of "Racing in the Street" was worlds and years away, it was that song that hit me as real, and terrifying and true.

Having been less than half Springsteen's age when I discovered him, his songs came as missives from the front, imbued with the real wisdom of someone who had seen more of this world than I had. There's no question that in Springsteen's music I found a voice that reflected my frustrations and my hopes. At 17, feeling trapped in a small town, with nothing to do but drive around, there's a lot to be said for having *Born to Run* or *Darkness on the Edge of Town* to crank on the car stereo. And in the me-against-the-world mode of adolescence, songs like "Racing in the Street" and "The River" came to me as cautionary tales. But over time, the real value in those songs became not just in seeing myself reflected back to me, but also in the converse: to see what connected me to the rest of humanity. In Springsteen's music, I not only recognized myself, but also the larger world and the people around me. The obstacles, the small triumphs, the universal struggles with circumstances beyond control. A given character could be me, could be family, friends, someone on the street—and at a certain point, his music suggested, there's little difference. "Nobody wins unless everybody wins," he said. What affects others also affects us—and that means we have a responsibility to each other. Heartbreak and isolation—and their counterparts, faith and community—make the world of human experience turn.

Other music might tell you to have your dreams; Springsteen's music confronts the reality that dreams go unrealized, and explores what we do in the face of that fact. "You've got to learn to live with what you can't rise above." "God have mercy on the man who doubts what he's sure of." Lines like these have made me wince and ache, and still do. I've chuckled with Westerberg, marveled at Dylan, and sneered with Costello. But no one has comforted me and chilled me at the same time like Bruce. There are more clever songwriters, there are more subtle songwriters, but rock 'n' roll has had no finer, more sincere observer of universal human truths.

Before Springsteen there wasn't a precedent in rock music for growing up and everything that comes with it. Partly because rock 'n' roll itself was so young, it was traditionally the music of youth; it was born to be wild, to rock around the clock, to rave on, to sniff glue—it was music of rebellion, not acceptance. If rock 'n' rollers didn't die before they got old, they might just become country music fans. But Springsteen's rock 'n' roll came to embrace the roots of the genre—aspects of country, R&B, folk, gospel, and the blues—in a way that went beyond his music or his appropriated on-stage shtick. He blazed a trail, intentionally and deliberately, to bring the adult concerns of those other forms to rock 'n' roll. In *Songs,* his 1998 collection of lyrics, Springsteen mused on the shift in his songwriting following *Born to Run:* "I began to listen seriously to country music around this time. I discovered Hank Williams. I liked the fact that country music dealt with adult topics, and I wanted to write songs that would resonate down the road." Characters in his songs may be "ready to grow young again," or able to laugh at how fast the glory days pass, but they have to live with the uncertainty, the frustrations, the contradictions, and the compromises of an adult world.

Still, at root, Bruce Springsteen is a guy with a guitar who makes people happy. He's no stranger to joy and wild abandon, as anyone knows who has witnessed "Rosalita," the "Detroit Medley," or recent "Ramrod" concert marathons. Anyone who covers "Achy Breaky Heart" and "You Sexy Thing"—anyone who fills up half a double album with songs like *The River*'s "Sherry Darling," "Crush on You," and "Out in the Street"—clearly isn't immune to the power and the glory of the frivolous three-minute pop song. But it's rare that such fun-loving moments in Springsteen's music won't be earned, tempered, and offset. From the deliberate peaks and valleys of his live performances, to the other half of *The River*, with songs like "Stolen Car" and "Wreck on the Highway," what seems to define Springsteen's art is the complexity of experience, of the world as a combination of elements in tension. "Love" tattooed on one hand, and "Fear" on the other. *MOJO*, a brilliant music magazine from the U.K., regularly asks celebrities to name a favorite Saturday night record and a favorite Sunday morning record. Depending on where you set the needle down, a Springsteen record can be both: celebratory and melancholy, earthly and ethereal. His music is large. It contains multitudes.

The author David Foster Wallace has remarked that the biggest thing that screwed up his generation was that, somewhere along the line, people got the idea that the point of life is to be happy. If anything saved me from that delusion, it was listening to Springsteen's music, in which life is struggle. We're bound to find ourselves places we'd never imagined; it's what we do when we get there that makes the difference. Don't you lose heart. Show a little faith. Man, the dope's that there's still hope. These never come across as easy sentiments—it's not optimism so much as a hard-earned awareness of what it takes to make it through.

Just outside of Boston, in February 2003, Springsteen played a pair of intimate shows at the Somerville Theatre, taking questions from the audience at the end of each show. One fan requested "Real World," a song Springsteen hadn't played in years. Bruce was dismissive, saying "I thought everybody hated that one." There was just a moment to hear the requester's voice say "the Christic version . . ." before it was drowned out by others clamoring to get a word in. The show went on. But for the record: no, no, no, we don't hate "Real World"! Fans have objected to the treatment recorded for 1992's *Human Touch*, a slick production gooped up with bells and synthesizers. But the song itself was a long-awaited destination point, a touching-down of the story arc that his music had been moving toward for years. Particularly in the incarnation Springsteen debuted at a 1990 benefit for the Christic Institute, it's a raw declaration of love, hope, acceptance, and defiance, best expressed in the turn-on-a-dime last verse: "And if love is hopeless, hopeless at best / Come on put on your party dress, it's ours tonight." And from that threat of hopelessness, just a few lines later bring the final refrain, "It's just me and you and the hope we're bringing into the real world."

I've vacationed in the stratosphere, too; and in the cartoon world of the Ramones; with the street-fighting men of Jagger and Richards and Strummer and Jones; on the Mothership and the Sunset Strip. But Springsteen's music continues to connect me more closely with a landscape that I recognize as my own, that pulses with life and with wisdom, and provides me tools with which to navigate. The grass ain't always green, and the girls ain't always pretty. But that's all right with me.

Afterword

■

Robert Santelli

Glancing over the names of contributors to *Racing in the Street: The Bruce Springsteen Reader*, I am struck by a personally intriguing possibility: it seems I might well be the writer who owns the longest relationship with Bruce Springsteen and his music. I use the word "relationship" loosely. What I mean is that of all the critics, journalists, and music historians represented here, I was the first, I believe, to witness Springsteen's rock and roll genius, as well as the first of the bunch to write about him.

To the reader that doesn't mean much. After all, I am not making any claims here that I discovered Springsteen or had any role in revealing him to the rest of the world. But for me, my long-term connection to Springsteen confirms a couple of striking things in my self-history. First, it means that Springsteen's music has touched me, deeply and powerfully, for thirty-five years, bringing me countless hours of joy and rock and roll truth. Second, I realize that Springsteen and his music have had more impact on me than any other person in popular music, past or present, or, for that matter, in any of the other arts. Over the years, much of what I've come to think and love about American music, in all its forms, as well as what I do today—namely write about music, teach music history, and head a music museum, Seattle's Experience Music Project— comes largely from the inspiration of Bruce Springsteen.

I *know* I am the most fortunate of those who have chronicled Springsteen's career. In late 1997, I was chosen to work with Springsteen on the only book he's ever authored: *Songs*.[1] The book, as many of you undoubtedly already know, is a beautiful journey into Springsteen's artistic soul. In the concise essays that precede the lyrics to the songs of his albums, Springsteen takes the reader on a tour of his songwriting process and unveils the ideas and inspirations that led to a body of work that is now a vital part of the American music canon. My role in *Songs* was to help Springsteen organize his thoughts and give structure to them. In truth, Springsteen did all the heavy lifting while I got to spend quality time with him, listening in on his autobiography, asking all the questions I've always wanted to ask him, and getting to know the man behind the music better than I ever imagined.

We often worked in Springsteen's study in his house in New Jersey. But there were also motorcycle rides to his country retreat, jaunts to the beach, and the occasional drive to Asbury Park. Although I lived in Cleveland at the time, working for the Rock and Roll Hall of Fame and Museum, I regularly made the hour-long flight back to Jersey on weekends to work on *Songs*. There hasn't been a more rewarding writing project that I have been involved in than this one.

All of this has given me a privileged, panoramic view of Springsteen's career that I've never taken lightly. Historians often long for the opportunity to see history unfold in front of their eyes, to be there when history is actually made, instead of having to research it, read about it, and wonder what it really was like. As a music historian, I've satisfied that craving, for I've watched Springsteen find his path to stardom from a front row seat and then travel it to the Promised Land.

I first saw Bruce Springsteen in early 1969 in a coffeehouse for teens in Red Bank, New Jersey. Performing solo, he was a scrawny hippie with a mane of long hair and a confident command of both his guitar and his music. I remember being struck by a Tim Buckley song he covered, but I can't recall the title. (Neither could Springsteen when I brought it up during the writing sessions for *Songs*.) At the time, I was a seventeen-year-old wanna-be folk-rock musician, and Tim Buckley, a '60s singer-songwriter of uncommon talent (and the father of the late Jeff Buckley), was a big influence. Three years earlier my family had moved from West New York, N.J., just across the Hudson River from Manhattan, down to the Jersey Shore, to the town of Point Pleasant Beach, some six miles as the crow flies from Asbury Park. My best friend had given me a Tim Buckley album, *Hello/Good-Bye*, on a visit back home, and at once it became a record that rarely left my phonograph.

I didn't know who Springsteen was, but most of the young people at the club did. By this time on the Jersey Shore, there was already a Bruce buzz in the air. He had surfaced as a member of the Freehold-based band the Castiles, which had gained a reputation beyond Bruce's hometown by playing area high school and CYO dances in addition to the teen clubs that sprouted on the Shore in the middle and late '60s.

When the Castiles broke up in early 1968, Springsteen formed two other bands, Earth and Child, and occasionally played solo, before the creation of Steel Mill—according to many longtime fans the best Springsteen band of the pre–E Street era.

Back then, the Jersey Shore was little more than a string of resort towns that came to life in the summer as hordes of tourists descended on its beaches and boardwalks, and went back to sleep after Labor Day. Caught between the energy and excitement of Philadelphia and New York, the Jersey Shore had no musical identity of its own, save for its reputation as having the largest collection of boardwalk beer joints on the East Coast and more bar bands per square mile than anywhere else in America. If you were a musician and had ambition beyond the bar stage, the Jersey Shore, in 1969, was not the place to launch a career. You had to go to New York or to California. Everyone knew that.

Springsteen went to both. Tinker West, Steel Mill's manager and surfing partner, convinced the band to take its music to San Francisco, a trip that didn't pan out, despite good reviews and attention from legendary impresario Bill Graham. Upon returning to Jersey, Steel Mill imploded, and Springsteen began making trips to New York to play as a solo artist in Greenwich Village clubs, where he made an impression on legendary talent scout John Hammond, leading to Springsteen's contract with Columbia Records in 1972. In between Steel Mill's demise and his recording contract, Springsteen had formed the Bruce Springsteen Band, an absolutely ripping soul-rock revue that mostly played an Asbury Park club, the Student Prince, where students from nearby Monmouth College (today Monmouth University) hung out, played pool, and drank cheap beer. I was a freshman at Monmouth in the fall of 1969 and later became somewhat of a regular at the Student Prince.[2]

The summer before I started college I had heard about an after-hours musician's club called the Upstage, located above a shoe store on Cookman Avenue in Asbury Park. If you hoped to be taken seriously as a musician at the Shore, it was essential that you be asked to jam at the Upstage. Musicians still wired from their bar or teen club gigs arrived at the Upstage ready to fill what was left of the night and early morning hours with blues-based jams on the club's stage. When the sun began to rise, some of the musicians went down to the beach a few blocks away and got some shut-eye in the sand before the lifeguards nudged you and asked where your beach badge was.

More times than not, Springsteen was the jam leader at the Upstage. Almost always he was the one who selected the songs, picked the players, and shouted out the solos. Other Upstage regulars included drummer Vini Lopez, bass player Garry Tallent, keyboards-guitarist David Sancious, and organist Danny Federici, all of whom, in a couple of years, would join Springsteen in the first edition of the E Street Band. Steve Van Zandt, known as Miami Steve, also logged time at the Upstage, as did Southside Johnny and other assorted Jersey Shore music characters such as Big Danny, Little Danny, and Albany Al.

Nicknames were common at the Shore back then, especially in the music and surfing circles. Being knighted with a nickname gave you a certain stature; it meant that you now had an identity that more accurately reflected who you were and what you were about. Johnny Lyon got his nickname out of respect for his vast blues knowledge and particular love of Chicago blues. Danny Gallagher, Springsteen's Irish-American roommate, was big—in height and girth—and could only have "Big" as his nickname. Vini Lopez was known as "Mad Dog." If anyone back then had seen his temper grow hot and explode, they'd know why the nickname fit.

Springsteen wasn't yet called the Boss, but he could have been. He was certainly the boss of the burgeoning Jersey Shore rock scene. He was the best guitarist, although my recollection is that Sancious routinely gave Springsteen a run for his money whenever he stepped away from the keyboards and strapped on his guitar. Springsteen was also the best rock, blues, and soul singer at the Upstage, except when the occasional black singer from the other side of the Asbury Park railroad tracks, literally speaking, showed up and taught the white boys how to wail into the microphone.

The Upstage lasted only a couple of years before racial tensions in Asbury Park forced it to close, leaving local musicians without a place to exchange ideas and compete onstage. Without the Upstage the local music scene quickly fragmented, but Springsteen remained focused on his dream, which was to do something of consequence with his music. Rather than leave Jersey after getting his Columbia Records contract and relocate to New York, which is what everyone expected him to do—after all, that's what everyone from Count Basie to Frank Sinatra did once they got their break—Springsteen went back to Asbury Park and formed the E Street Band with Upstage friends and a black saxophonist, Clarence

Clemons, who had been playing Shore clubs in soul bands after a career in pro football proved unattainable.

By this time I had begun writing for the Monmouth College newspaper, *The Outlook,* reviewing records and local concerts and doing occasional features on area bands. Not surprisingly, Springsteen was quite popular on campus and played there often in the late '60s and early '70s. I had seen Springsteen perform solo, at the Upstage as a jam-master, and leading the bands Child, Steel Mill, and the Bruce Springsteen Band. I had even seen one of a handful of performances by a deliriously quirky ensemble called Dr. Zoom and the Sonic Boom that Springsteen put together for a brief period. The experimental outfit included a full horn section, backup singers, a dozen or so other musicians, and, incredibly, a Monopoly game centerstage while a drum majorette twirled a baton nearby. One of Dr. Zoom's gigs—the one I saw—occurred at Asbury Park's dumpiest club, the Sunshine In. Dr. Zoom and the Sonic Boom opened for a hot new band out of Macon, Georgia: the Allman Brothers.

While at Monmouth I signed up for a journalism course taught by an editor, Tom Jobson, from the *Asbury Park Press,* the Jersey Shore's top newspaper. When not enough students enrolled in it, the course was cancelled. Jobson recognized my disappointment and was intrigued with what I wanted to do: become a music journalist. He invited me to freelance for the *Press,* writing articles on popular music—and get paid for them. I took him up on his offer. My very first Springsteen articles, aside from those in *The Outlook,* were published in the *Asbury Park Press.* Dozens and dozens more would follow.

While all this was going on, Springsteen had taken the songs he'd been working on, taught them to his new band, and led them into the studio to make his debut album. Columbia was concerned that Springsteen insisted on calling the record *Greetings from Asbury Park, N.J.,* after a popular boardwalk postcard with the same name. Columbia believed Springsteen needed a New York connection and tried to persuade him to cut away from his Jersey roots and retitle the album. Springsteen resisted, saying that he was from Jersey and not afraid to admit it. The album title and his Asbury Park address wouldn't be changed.

That decision had profound implications for musicians on the Jersey Shore and eventually for everyone living in New Jersey. Not only did Springsteen proudly proclaim his roots, he celebrated the very things virtually every other artist and entertainer from the state sought to sep-

arate himself from. Jersey jokes routinely poured from the mouths of co-
medians. It was easy to poke fun at a state with no identity of its own except that which derived from the Jersey Turnpike, wise guys, and the
refineries that made the air stink and sky turn gunmetal gray.

Springsteen found lyrical currency and musical inspiration in the
street and boardwalk subcultures that thrived in Asbury Park and other
Jersey Shore towns. He made their colorful characters leading men in
his songs, and with delightful detail he depicted his neighborhood as a
kooky carnival, where lovable crazies ran rampant and sought the meaning of love under the boardwalk, cheap thrills on the Tilt-a-Whirl, and
the promise of the future, if there was such a thing, at Madam Marie's.

Most important though, *Greetings from Asbury Park, N.J.*, its follow-
up album, *The Wild, the Innocent & the E Street Shuffle*, and the masterpiece, *Born to Run*, ultimately were about us. Springsteen taught all
of us at the Jersey Shore things about ourselves we never knew. He was
our Faulkner, our Emerson. But most important, he was ours.

It's difficult to describe to an outsider the impact Springsteen made
not only at the Shore, but in all of Jersey. Back then the state hadn't any
cultural heroes to speak of, save those who had left it and represented us
from afar. Theirs was a cheap way to claim connection to Jersey without
actually having to live there. Springsteen stayed on. Even when he
moved to California many years later, he returned home, he settled in
and began his family. In a place that had been abused so much on late-
night television, a state that was home to two football teams, the Giants
and the Jets, though both arrogantly proclaimed themselves from New
York, Springsteen was Jersey, and proud of it. And he made all of us feel
exactly the same way.

After *Born to Run*, his monumental breakthrough album in 1975,
Springsteen began to write less about New Jersey and more about
America. When Jersey did reappear in Springsteen's songs, as on the album *Nebraska*, then in gems such as "My Hometown" and "Tunnel of
Love," and even in interpretations of other artists' songs, like Tom
Waits's "Jersey Girl," it was enough to keep him our rock poet laureate,
though we now shared him with the rest of the world. Unlike his earlier
work—when he described New Jersey as a unique place—Springsteen
now wrote about the state as if it were a microcosm of America, which,
in all probability, it had always been.

❈ ❈ ❈

I'm grateful that Springsteen's commitment to New Jersey has never wavered. Certainly it has rewarded him with a loyalty so deep and intense that going to see Springsteen perform is now practically a rite of passage in the state. Today, parents take their kids to a Springsteen concert so that they can participate in a Jersey rock and roll ritual and seemingly be exposed to some sacred truth. I confess: I did the same for my three kids a few years ago, when we lived in Cleveland. My wife, my two daughters, and my son already had seen Springsteen perform live, met him, and had pictures taken with him. But now it was important that we go to see Springsteen in concert as a *family*. We flew to Jersey—it had to be in Jersey—and took in a Meadowlands concert, one of the best I had seen in a long time. I just had to do it.

All these years, all the albums, all the concerts, and all the writing about both—and yet I still take nourishment from Bruce Springsteen. I don't expect things to be changing, either.

Note

1. The updated and expanded edition of *Songs,* including lyrics and a new chapter on *The Rising,* was published by HarperCollins in 2003.

Appendix

■

Discography

■ ALBUMS ■

Greetings from Asbury Park, N.J.
(Columbia, 1973)
Highest chart ranking: 60

Springsteen's debut: words, words, and more words. Loose and wild, it features Springsteen's patented flights of lyrical fancy as well as an impressive display of musical styles from jazzy funk to straight-ahead rock, from acoustic to electric.

Tracks: Blinded by the Light; Growin' Up; Mary Queen of Arkansas; Does This Bus Stop at 82nd Street?; Lost in the Flood; The Angel; For You; Spirit in the Night; It's Hard to Be a Saint in the City

The Wild, the Innocent & the E Street Shuffle
(Columbia, 1973)
Highest chart ranking: 59

Springsteen's second album still retains its Dylanesque wordplay but with more narrative detail. An exuberant display of Springsteen at his most youthfully passionate.

Tracks: The E Street Shuffle; 4th of July, Asbury Park (Sandy); Kitty's Back; Wild Billy's Circus Story; Incident on 57th Street; Rosalita (Come Out Tonight); New York City Serenade

Born to Run
(Columbia, 1975)
Highest chart ranking: 3

What's to say? One of the great releases of the rock era.

Tracks: Thunder Road; Tenth Avenue Freeze-Out; Night; Backstreets; Born to Run; She's the One; Meeting Across the River; Jungleland

Darkness on the Edge of Town
(Columbia, 1978)
Highest chart ranking: 5

Springsteen digs deeper on this disturbing but undeniably engrossing release. Includes the ineffable "Racing in the Street."

Tracks: Badlands; Adam Raised a Cain; Something in the Night; Candy's Room; Racing in the Street; The Promised Land; Factory; Streets of Fire; Prove It All Night; Darkness on the Edge of Town

The River
(Columbia, 1980)
Highest chart ranking: 1

Springsteen's most eclectic effort: rock and roll, pop songs, rockabilly, folk, country, blue-eyed soul. In this double album, Springsteen takes the rock narrative form to new heights in songs like the title cut, "Independence Day," and "Point Blank." In many ways, The River *is a prelude to* Nebraska, *with its mournful ballad "Stolen Car" and the country-inflected "Wreck on the Highway." It also features the wistful "I Wanna Marry You" and the pleading vocals of "Fade Away"—two songs that wear their '60s influences well.*

Tracks: The Ties That Bind; Sherry Darling; Jackson Cage; Two Hearts; Independence Day; Hungry Heart; Out in the Street; Crush on You; You Can Look (But You Better Not Touch); I Wanna Marry You; The River; Point Blank; Cadillac Ranch; I'm a Rocker; Fade Away; Stolen Car; Ramrod; The Price You Pay; Drive All Night; Wreck on the Highway

Nebraska
(Columbia, 1982)
Highest chart ranking: 3

Springsteen's stark, mostly acoustic masterpiece is haunted by many ghosts: Woody Guthrie most prominently but also Hank Williams, Chuck Berry, and the anonymous singers of America's darkened past.

Tracks: Nebraska; Atlantic City; Mansion on the Hill; Johnny 99; Highway Patrolman; State Trooper; Used Cars; Open All Night; My Father's House; Reason to Believe

Born in the U.S.A.
(Columbia, 1984)
Highest chart ranking: 1

Bruce's huge crowd-pleaser. At turns angry (the misunderstood title cut), playful ("Darlington County"), paranoid ("Cover Me"), plain scary ("I'm on Fire"), dark ("Downbound Train"), defiantly exuberant ("No Surrender"), and bittersweet (the lovely "My Hometown"). And, of course, it contains the synthesizer hit, "Dancing in the Dark."

Tracks: Born in the U.S.A.; Cover Me; Darlington County; Working on the Highway; Downbound Train; I'm on Fire; No Surrender; Bobby Jean; I'm Goin' Down; Glory Days; Dancing in the Dark; My Hometown

Bruce Springsteen & the E Street Band Live/1975–85
(Columbia, 1986)
Highest chart ranking: 1

This three-CD boxed set almost does justice to Springsteen and the band live, or as close as one can get without actually being in the front row. It features most of the big hits, as well as terrific cover versions of Guthrie's "This Land Is Your Land" and Tom

*Waits's "Jersey Girl" and alternate versions of "Thunder Road" (stripped bare to pi-
ano), early classics, and the previously unreleased "Paradise by the 'C.'"*

Tracks: Thunder Road; Adam Raised a Cain; Spirit in the Night; 4th of July, Asbury
Park (Sandy); Paradise by the "C"; Fire; Growin' Up; It's Hard to Be a Saint in the
City; Backstreets; Rosalita (Come Out Tonight); Raise Your Hand (*Steve Cropper,
Eddie Floyd, and Alvertis Isbell*); Hungry Heart; Two Hearts; Cadillac Ranch; You
Can Look (But You Better Not Touch); Independence Day; Badlands; Because the
Night (*Bruce Springsteen and Patti Smith*); Candy's Room; Darkness on the Edge of
Town; Racing in the Street; This Land Is Your Land (*Woody Guthrie*); Nebraska;
Johnny 99; Reason to Believe; Born in the U.S.A.; Seeds; The River; War (*Barrett
Strong and Norman Whitfield*); Darlington County; Working on the Highway; The
Promised Land; Cover Me; I'm on Fire; Bobby Jean; My Hometown; Born to Run;
No Surrender; Tenth Avenue Freeze-Out; Jersey Girl (*Tom Waits*)

Tunnel of Love
(Columbia, 1987)
Highest chart ranking: 1

*A moody, introspective journey into the lonely heart of darkness. A virtual one-man
show (Springsteen plays most everything), Tunnel of Love is his most mature work.*

Tracks: Ain't Got You; Tougher Than the Rest; All That Heaven Will Allow; Spare
Parts; Cautious Man; Walk Like a Man; Tunnel of Love; Two Faces; Brilliant Disguise; One Step Up; When You're Alone; Valentine's Day

Human Touch
(Columbia, 1992)
Highest chart ranking: 2

*An uneven effort about taking chances, but, to this listener, Human Touch is Spring-
steen's least satisfying release.*

Tracks: Human Touch; Soul Driver; 57 Channels (and Nothin' On); Cross My Heart
(*Bruce Springsteen and Sonny Boy Williamson*); Gloria's Eyes; With Every Wish; Roll
of the Dice (*Bruce Springsteen and Roy Bittan*); Real World (*Bruce Springsteen and
Roy Bittan*); All or Nothin' at All; Man's Job; I Wish I Were Blind; The Long Good-
bye; Real Man; Pony Boy (*traditional; arranged with additional lyrics by Bruce
Springsteen*)

Lucky Town
(Columbia, 1992)
Highest chart ranking: 3

*A complete turnaround. Lucky Town, unlike the simultaneously released Human
Touch, is sheer joy: infectious rockers, touching ballads, along with ample doses of
self-deprecating humor.*

Tracks: Better Days; Lucky Town; Local Hero; If I Should Fall Behind; Leap of
Faith; The Big Muddy; Living Proof; Book of Dreams; Souls of the Departed; My
Beautiful Reward

Greatest Hits
(Columbia, 1995)
Highest chart ranking: 1

The Greatest Hits *package may strike hard-core Springsteen fans as redundant and a bit anticlimactic. Nevertheless, it does include several new songs and material not previously available on CD (the hit single "Streets of Philadelphia" as well as the pretty "Secret Garden," the incendiary "Murder Incorporated," "Blood Brothers," and "This Hard Land").*

Tracks: Born to Run (acoustic version); Thunder Road; Badlands; The River; Hungry Heart; Atlantic City; Dancing in the Dark; Born in the U.S.A.; My Hometown; Glory Days; Brilliant Disguise; Human Touch; Better Days; Streets of Philadelphia; Secret Garden; Murder Incorporated; Blood Brothers; This Hard Land

The Ghost of Tom Joad
(Columbia, 1995)
Highest chart ranking: 11

The dark side of the new American Dream. Springsteen at his most luminous.

Tracks: The Ghost of Tom Joad; Straight Time; Highway 29; Youngstown; Sinaloa Cowboys; The Line; Balboa Park; Dry Lightning; The New Timer; Across the Border; Galveston Bay; My Best Was Never Good Enough

MTVPlugged
(Sony, 1997)

For hard-core fans only or people wishing to complete their Springsteen collection.

Tracks: Red Headed Woman; Better Days; Atlantic City; Darkness on the Edge of Town; Man's Job; Human Touch; Lucky Town; I Wish I Were Blind; Thunder Road; Light of Day; If I Should Fall Behind; Living Proof; My Beautiful Reward

Tracks
(Columbia, 1998)
Highest chart ranking: 64

This boxed set of 66 tracks spanning 25 years offers a fascinating musical tour of Springsteen's remarkable career. Contains previously unreleased material, early demos, B-sides of hit singles, alternate takes ("Stolen Car," "Born in the U.S.A."). A must for the serious Springsteen fan.

Tracks: Mary Queen of Arkansas; It's Hard to Be a Saint in the City; Growin' Up; Does This Bus Stop at 82nd Street?; Bishop Danced; Santa Ana; Seaside Bar Song; Zero and Blind Terry; Linda Let Me Be the One; Thundercrack; Rendezvous; Give the Girl a Kiss; Iceman; Bring on the Night; So Young and in Love; Hearts of Stone; Don't Look Back; Restless Nights; A Good Man Is Hard to Find (Pittsburgh); Roulette; Dollhouse; Where the Bands Are; Loose Ends; Living on the Edge of the World; Wages of Sin; Take 'Em as They Come; Be True; Ricky Wants a Man of Her Own; I Wanna Be with You; Mary Lou; Stolen Car; Born in the U.S.A.; Johnny Bye-Bye; Shut Out the Light; Cynthia; My Love Will Not Let You Down; This Hard

Land; Frankie; TV Movie; Stand on It; Lion's Den; Car Wash; Rockaway the Days; Brothers Under the Bridge ('83); Man at the Top; Pink Cadillac; Two for the Road; Janey Don't You Lose Heart; When You Need Me; The Wish; The Honeymooners; Lucky Man; Leavin' Train; Seven Angels; Gave It a Name; Sad Eyes; My Lover Man; Over the Rise; When the Lights Go Out; Loose Change; Trouble in Paradise; Happy; Part Man, Part Monkey; Goin' Cali; Back in Your Arms; Brothers Under the Bridge

18 Tracks
(Sony, 1999)
Highest chart ranking: 64

The cuts that got away from the 1998, four-CD set of outtakes, B-sides, and various rarities. Springsteen makes up for the omission by including such longtime fan favorites as "The Fever" (covered most famously by Southside Johnny and the Asbury Jukes), "The Promise," and "Trouble River," an outtake from the Human Touch *sessions.*

Tracks: Growin' Up; Seaside Bar Song; Rendezvous; Hearts of Stone; Where the Bands Are; Loose Ends; I Wanna Be with You; Born in the U.S.A.; My Love Will Not Let You Down; Lion's Den; Pink Cadillac; Janey Don't You Lose Heart; Sad Eyes; Part Man, Part Monkey; Trouble River; Brothers Under the Bridge; The Fever; The Promise

Bruce Springsteen & the E Street Band/Live in New York City
(Sony, 2001)
Highest chart ranking: 5

This 20-song collection is culled from the two Madison Square Garden shows during the E Street Band's 1999–2000 tour. It features the big hits as well as two new songs, "Land of Hope and Dreams" and the controversial "American Skin (41 Shots)," as well as a darker, slow blues version of "Born in the U.S.A." and a rarely performed early Springsteen classic, "Lost in the Flood."

Tracks: My Love Will Not Let You Down; Tenth Avenue Freeze-Out; Land of Hope and Dreams; Prove It All Night; Two Hearts; American Skin (41 Shots); Lost in the Flood; Atlantic City; Mansion on the Hill; Born in the U.S.A.; Don't Look Back; The River; Youngstown; Jungleland; Ramrod; Murder Incorporated; Badlands; If I Should Fall Behind; Out in the Street; Born to Run

The Rising
(Columbia, 2002)
Highest chart ranking: 1

Springsteen's often sublime, spiritually searching reply to the World Trade Center attacks. Includes the heartbreaking "You're Missing."

Tracks: Lonesome Day; Into the Fire; Waitin' on a Sunny Day; Nothing Man; Countin' on a Miracle; Empty Sky; Worlds Apart; Let's Be Friends (Skin to Skin); Further On (Up the Road); The Fuse; Mary's Place; You're Missing; The Rising; Paradise; My City of Ruins

The Essential Bruce Springsteen
(Columbia, 2003)

This three-CD set is a career-spanning collection that includes never-before-released songs and live recordings, such as "From Small Things (Big Things One Day Come"); *"None but the Brave," recorded during the* Born in the U.S.A. *sessions; "County Fair," recorded after the* Nebraska *sessions; and "Code of Silence," cowritten with Joe Grushecky and recorded live in 1999.*

Tracks: Blinded by the Light; For You; Spirit in the Night; 4th of July, Asbury Park (Sandy); Rosalita (Come Out Tonight); Thunder Road; Born to Run; Jungleland; Badlands; Darkness on the Edge of Town; The Promised Land; The River; Hungry Heart; Nebraska; Atlantic City; Born in the U.S.A.; Glory Days; Dancing in the Dark; Tunnel of Love; Brilliant Disguise; Human Touch; Living Proof; Lucky Town; Streets of Philadelphia; The Ghost of Tom Joad; The Rising; Mary's Place; Lonesome Day; American Skin (41 Shots); Land of Hope and Dreams; From Small Things (Big Things One Day Come); Big Payback; Held Up Without a Gun (live); Trapped (live); None but the Brave; Missing; Lift Me Up; Viva Las Vegas; County Fair; Code of Silence (live); Dead Man Walking; Countin' on a Miracle (acoustic)

▓ EP ▓

Chimes of Freedom
(Columbia, 1988)

Originally released from Springsteen's Amnesty International shows in 1988, it features live versions of "Tougher Than the Rest," "Be True," Dylan's "Chimes of Freedom," and an acoustic "Born to Run."

▓ SELECTED SINGLES ▓

Blinded by the Light/The Angel (1972)
Spirit in the Night/For You (1973)
Born to Run/Meeting Across the River (1975)
Tenth Avenue Freeze-Out/She's the One (1976)
Prove It All Night/Factory (1978)
Badlands/Streets of Fire (1978)
Hungry Heart/Held Up Without a Gun (1980)
Fade Away/Be True (1981)
Dancing in the Dark/Pink Cadillac (1984)
Cover Me/Jersey Girl (live) (1984)
Born in the U.S.A./Shut Out the Light (1984)
I'm on Fire/Johnny Bye-Bye (1985)
Glory Days/Stand on It (1985)
I'm Goin' Down/Janey Don't You Lose Heart (1985)
My Hometown/Santa Claus Is Comin' to Town (live) (1985)
War/Merry Christmas Baby (live) (1986)
Fire/Incident on 57th Street (live) (1987)

Brilliant Disguise/Lucky Man (1987)
Tunnel of Love/Two for the Road (1988)
One Step Up/Roulette (1988)
Human Touch/Better Days (1992)
57 Channels (and Nothin' On)/Part Man, Part Monkey (1992)
Streets of Philadelphia/Atlantic City (1992)
Secret Garden/Thunder Road (1995)
The Rising/Land of Hope and Dreams (2002)

Filmography

Baby, It's You (1983)
Directed by John Sayles
Cast: Rosanna Arquette, Vincent Spano, Tracy Pollan,
Matthew Modine, Robert Downey Jr.

Tracks: "Adam Raised a Cain"; "She's the One";
"It's Hard to Be a Saint in the City"

Ruthless People (1986)
Directed by David Zucker and Jim Abrahams
Cast: Bette Midler, Danny DeVito

Track: "Stand on It"

The Indian Runner (1991)
Directed and written by Sean Penn
Inspired by Springsteen's "Highway Patrolman" from *Nebraska*
Cast: Viggo Mortensen, David Morse, Patricia Arquette, Dennis Hopper,
Sandy Dennis, Charles Bronson

Peter's Friends (1992)
Directed by Kenneth Branagh
Cast: Kenneth Branagh, Emma Thompson

Track: "Hungry Heart"

The Crossing Guard (1995)
Directed by Sean Penn
Cast: Jack Nicholson, David Morse, Anjelica Houston, Robin Wright

Track: "Missing"

Philadelphia (1993)
Directed by Jonathan Demme
Cast: Tom Hanks, Denzel Washington, Antonio Banderas

Track: "Streets of Philadelphia"

Dead Man Walking (1995)
Written and directed by Tim Robbins
Cast: Susan Sarandon, Sean Penn

Track: "Dead Man Walking"

Jerry Maguire (1996)
Directed by Cameron Crowe
Cast: Tom Cruise, Cuba Gooding Jr., Renée Zellweger

Track: "Secret Garden"

Limbo (1999)
Directed by John Sayles
Cast: Mary Elizabeth Mastrantonio, David Strathairn,
Vanessa Martinez, Kris Kristofferson

Track: "Lift Me Up"

High Fidelity (2000)
Directed by Stephen Frears
Cast: John Cusack, Jack Black, Catherine Zeta-Jones, Joan Cusack, Tim Robbins
Features a cameo by Springsteen.

25th Hour (2002)
Directed by Spike Lee
Cast: Edward Norton, Philip Seymour Hoffman, Barry Pepper

Track: "The Fuse"

Selected Compilations Featuring Various Artists

No Nukes
(Asylum, 1979)

Tracks: "Stay" (with Jackson Browne),
"Devil with the Blue Dress Medley"

We Are the World
(Columbia, 1985)

Track: "Trapped"

Folkways: A Vision Shared:
A Tribute to Woody Guthrie and Leadbelly
(Columbia, 1988)

Tracks: "I Ain't Got No Home," "Vigilante Man"

Harry Chapin Tribute
(Relativity, 1990)

Track: "Remember When the Music"

The Last Temptation of Elvis
(NME, 1990)

Track: "Viva Las Vegas"

United Artists for the Poet: A Tribute to Bob Dylan
(Columbia, 1991)

Track: "Chimes of Freedom"

Sampler Claus
(Columbia, 1992)

Track: "Merry Christmas Baby"

A Tribute to Curtis Mayfield: All Men Are Brothers
(Warner Brothers, 1994)

Track: "Gypsy Woman"

Christmas of Hope
(Columbia, 1995)

Track: "Santa Claus Is Coming to Town"

Concert for the Rock and Roll Hall of Fame
(Columbia, 1996)

Tracks: "Shake, Rattle, and Roll"; "Great Balls of Fire" with Jerry Lee Lewis; "Whole Lotta Shakin' Goin' On" with Jerry Lee Lewis

'Til We Outnumber 'Em
(Righteous Babe, 1996)

Tribute CD to Woody Guthrie by the Rock and Roll Hall of Fame and Museum in Cleveland. Springsteen performs "Riding in My Car" and "Plane Wreck at Los Gatos (Deportee)."

Diamond Cuts: A Compilation of Baseball Songs and Poetry
(HFM, 1997)

Track: "Glory Days"

Diana, Princess of Wales—Tribute
(Sony, 1997)

Track: "Streets of Philadelphia"

Where Have All the Flowers Gone?: The Songs of Pete Seeger
(Appleseed Records, 1998) Two-CD set

Tribute to Pete Seeger. Includes Springsteen singing "We Shall Overcome," accompanied by a ten-piece band. Other performers include Billy Bragg, Nanci Griffith, Indigo Girls, Bruce Cockburn, Jackson Browne, Bonnie Raitt, Roger McGuinn, and Pete Seeger himself.

The Spirit of Asbury Park: Rockin' the Jersey Shore
(Halcyon, 1999)

Volume 1 of a planned two-CD set. Includes artists from the Jersey Shore's glory days: Glen Burtnick, Cats on a Smooth Surface, Sonny Kenn, and others.

America: A Tribute to Heroes
(BMG/EMI/Sony/Universal/WB, 2001)

Track: "My City of Ruins"

Kindred Spirits: A Tribute to the Music of Johnny Cash
(Sony, 2002)

Collection of Cash covers by rock and country artists. Springsteen contributes "Give My Love to Rose." Other artists include Mary Chapin Carpenter, Sheryl Crow, and Emmylou Harris ("Flesh and Blood"); Bob Dylan ("Train of Love"); Steve Earle ("Hardin Wouldn't Run"); and Dwight Yoakam ("Understand Your Man").

Tributes

One Step Up/Two Steps Back: The Songs of Bruce Springsteen
(The Right Stuff, 1997)

Two-CD set of Springsteen covers. Includes notes from the artists themselves. Among the highlights (and oddities): "Atlantic City" by Kurt Neumann; "Jackson Cage" by John Wesley Harding; "Wreck on the Highway" by Nils Lofgren; "Johnny 99" by John Hiatt ("This song has it all . . . crime, punishment, drama, mama and a one way ticket to hell."); "Seeds" by Dave Alvin; "Light of Day" by Joe Grushecky and the Houserockers; "All or Nothin' at All" by Marshall Crenshaw; "Meeting Across the River" by Syd Straw; "4th of July, Asbury Park (Sandy)" by Ben E. King; "Protection" by Donna Summer; "Stolen Car" by Elliott Murphy; "It's Hard to Be a Saint in the City" by David Bowie; "The Fever" by Southside Johnny and the Asbury Jukes; "If I Was the Priest" by Allan Clarke.

Badlands: A Tribute to Bruce Springsteen's Nebraska
(Sub Pop, 2000)

Features Chrissie Hynde and Adam Seymour's "Nebraska," Hank Williams III's "Atlantic City," Crooked Fingers's "Mansion on the Hill," Los Lobos's "Johnny 99," Dar Williams's "Highway Patrolman," Deanna Carter's "State Trooper," Ani DiFranco's "Used Cars," Son Volt's "Open All Night," Ben Harper's "My Father's House," Aimee Mann and Michael Penn's "Reason to Believe," and three bonus tracks: "I'm on Fire" by Johnny Cash, "Downbound Train" by Raul Malo of the Mavericks, and "Wages of Sin" by Damien Jurado and Rose Thomas. Liner notes by Robert Santelli.

Light of Day: A Tribute to Bruce Springsteen
(Schoolhouse Records, 2003)

Springsteen as songwriter is showcased in this 2-CD tribute. The songs featured include "Better Days" by Elliott Murphy, "Thunder Road" by Dan Bern, "Candy's Room" by Crazysloth, "Johnny 99" by The Mystic Knights of the Sea, "If I Should Fall Behind" by Cindy Bullens, "Something in the Night" by Matthew Ryan, "Highway Patrolman" by Sid Griffin, "Badlands" by Joe D'Urso and Stone Caravan, "State Trooper" by Steve Wynn, "I Ain't Got You" by Gary Lucas's Gods and Monsters, "Bobby Jean" by Jennifer Glass, "The River" by the Clarks, "E Street Shuffle" by Jersey Shore bar veterans John Cafferty and the Beaver Brown Band, "Brilliant Disguise" by Elvis Costello, "New York City Serenade" by Pete Yorn, "Streets of Philadelphia" by Garland Jeffreys, "Lucky Town" by Rosie Flores, "I'm on Fire" by Willie Nile," "Souls of the Departed" by the Paradise Brothers, "The Promise" by the "Italian Springsteen" Graziano Romani, "For You" by the Format, "Hungry Heart" by Jess Malin, "Secret Garden" by Tom Cochrane and Damhnait Doyle, and "Working on the Highway" by Joe Ely.

Highlights, of which there are many, include Dion's doo-wop version of "Book of Dreams," Lucky 7's zydeco waltz on "Valentine's Day," Nils Lofgren's acoustic "Man at the Top," Mike Rimbaud's spirited "Atlantic City," and Billy ("Springsteen makes me keep my faith in America") Bragg and the Blokes' countrified "Mansion on the Hill." Marc Broussard gives "Back in Your Arms" a Louisiana feel and a gospel touch; Graham Parker's "Pink Cadillac" has a funky groove; Jason Ringenberg offers a sensitive rendering of "My Hometown"; and Joe Grushecky and the Houserockers swing on "Light of Day." There's also Patty Griffin's haunting "Stolen Car" and Mark Wright's lovely "Two Hearts." On the other hand, Kirk Kelly's ukulele version of "Downbound Train" is totally wrong, and Cowboy Mouth's take on the iconic "Born to Run" is simply dreadful. Includes terrific photographs of the Asbury Park boardwalk.

All sales from the CD will be split between the Parkinson's Disease Foundation (www.pdf.org) and the Kristen Ann Carr Fund (www.sarcoma.com).

Related Artists (A Sampling)

■ ROY ACUFF ■

The Essential Roy Acuff (1936–1949)
(Sony, 1992)

Gospel, old-time string-band, and hillbilly music from the "King of Country Music." Includes "Night Train to Memphis," "Prodigal Son," "Wabash Cannonball," and "Wreck on the Highway" (Springsteen modeled his own song of the same name after Acuff's somber original).

■ GARY U.S. BONDS ■

Dedication
(Razor & Tie, 1981)

Features Springsteen's vocals on the title track and the Cajun classic "Jole Blon." He also wrote "This Little Girl," "Your Love," and the title track.

On the Line
(Razor & Tie, 1982)

Follow-up to *Dedication,* it features seven Springsteen songs: "Hold On," "Out of Work," "Club Soul City," "Love's on the Line," "Rendezvous," the Cajun-flavored "Angelyne," and the ballad "All I Need."

■ BILLY BRAGG AND WILCO ■

Mermaid Avenue
(Elektra/Asylum, 1998)

The first collaboration of English roots rocker/erstwhile socialist Billy Bragg and alternative rock band Wilco, setting Woody Guthrie's unrecorded lyrics to their own music. Includes "Walt Whitman's Niece," "California Stars," "Way Over Yonder in the Minor Key," "Christ for President," "Another Man's Done Gone." Natalie Merchant adds her wonderfully distinctive voice.

Mermaid Avenue, Vol. II
(Elektra/Asylum, 2000)

Bragg and Wilco do it again—the second time around. Features guest artist Natalie Merchant. Much more musically diverse—and rocking harder—than the first volume, it includes "Secrets of the Sea," "Blood of the Lamb," "All You Fascists Are Bound to Lose," and "Black Wind Blowing."

▨ THE CARTER FAMILY ▨

Anchored in Love: Their Complete Victor Recordings, 1927–1928
(Rounder, 1993)

Appalachian folk ballads at their starkest. Includes "Storms Are on the Ocean," "Wildwood Flower," "Wandering Boy," "River of Jordan," "Bury Me Under the Weeping Willow," "John Hardy Was a Desperate Little Man," and "Will You Miss Me When I'm Gone."

Worried Man Blues: Their Complete Victor Recordings, 1930
(Rounder, 1995)

The Carter Family sing about perennial themes—family, love, motherhood, faith—in their timeless voices with luminous guitar playing. They performed murder ballads, gospel songs, love songs, and Appalachian folk tunes. Includes the title track, "On the Rock Where Moses Stood," "On My Way to Canaan's Land," "Weary Prodigal Son," and "When I'm Gone."

Can the Circle Be Unbroken?: Country Music's First Family
(Sony, 2000)

Simple vocals, haunting harmonies, stark guitar chords. The history of American-roots music lies here. The 20 selections were recorded from 1935 to 1940. Includes the title track, "My Clinch Mountain Home," "Wildwood Flower," "Worried Man Blues," "Gospel Ship," "River of Jordan," "Storms Are on the Ocean," "On the Rock Where Moses Stood," and "Black Jack David."

▨ JOHNNY CASH ▨

American Recordings
(Universal, 1994)

Considered one of Cash's masterpieces, it features the singer shorn of all pretenses. It's just Cash and his acoustic guitar. Includes covers of Kris Kristofferson, Nick Lowe, Leonard Cohen, Tom Waits, and Loudon Wainwright songs. Highlights include "Delia's Gone," "Why Me Lord," "Thirteen," and "Redemption."

Johnny 99
(Koch Records, 1999)

Originally released in 1983, this fine CD features two Springsteen songs—"Highway Patrolman" and the title cut, which Cash turns into a rowdy rockabilly ode—a Civil War ballad, and a duet with June Carter Cash.

The Essential Johnny Cash
(Sony, 2002)

Two-disk set features Cash's most memorable recordings for the Sun, Columbia, and Mercury labels, from 1955 to 1993. Includes "Ring of Fire," "Were You There

(When They Crucified My Lord)," a live version of "Folsom Prison Blues," Kris Kristofferson's "Sunday Morning Coming Down," and, accompanied by U2, the gospel-tinged "The Wanderer."

American IV: The Man Comes Around
(Universal, 2002)

Includes a heart-wrenching version of Trent Reznor's "Hurt" and the Cash-penned title cut, a chilling piece of apocalyptic imagery.

■ CLARENCE CLEMONS ■

Live in Asbury Park
(Valley, 2002)

The E Street Band's main sax man recorded live at Asbury Park's famed Stone Pony. Includes three original compositions and several Springsteen compositions ("Savin' Up," "Paradise by the 'C,'" "Small Things").

■ BOB DYLAN ■

The Freewheelin' Bob Dylan
(Sony, 1963)

Dylan's second album features some of his best-known work, timeless songs that reek of the '60s and the civil rights and peace movements: "Blowin' in the Wind," "Masters of War," "Hard Rain's a-Gonna Fall," "Don't Think Twice, It's All Right," and "I Shall Be Free."

Bringing It All Back Home
(Sony, 1965)

Half-electric, half-acoustic Dylan, it includes such classics as "Subterranean Home-sick Blues," "Love Minus Zero/No Limit," "Mr. Tambourine Man," "It's Alright, Ma (I'm Only Bleeding)," and "It's All Over Now, Baby Blue."

Highway 61 Revisited
(Sony, 1965)

The summer of 1965 saw the release of this surrealistic masterpiece—Dylan's first all-electric album. Features "Like a Rolling Stone," "From a Buick 6," "Ballad of a Thin Man," "Just Like Tom Thumb's Blues," "Desolation Row," and the amazing title track.

Blonde on Blonde
(Sony, 1966)

Originally released in 1966, *Blonde on Blonde* redefined the boundaries of rock. Includes one great song after another: the sublime "Sad Eyed Lady of the Lowlands," "Visions of Johanna," "I Want You," and "Rainy Day Women #12 and 35."

John Wesley Harding
(Sony, 1967)

Perhaps Dylan's starkest album, with such haunting ballads as the title track, "I Dreamed I Saw St. Augustine," "Ballad of Frankie Lee and Judas Priest," and the Guthriesque turns of "I Am a Lonesome Hobo" and "I Pity the Poor Immigrant." A great accompaniment to Springsteen's *Nebraska*.

◼ STEVE EARLE ◼

Guitar Town
(MCA, 1986)

Earle's debut album announced the arrival of a major talent who did things his own way—and damn the consequences. Includes "My Old Friend the Blues" and "Someday."

Train a' Comin'
(Warner Brothers, 1995)

Earle's return to basics—with masterful results.

Ain't Ever Satisfied
(Hip-O, 1996)

Two-disc set is essentially a greatest hits package, but it does include a live version of Springsteen's "State Trooper."

El Corazón
(Warner Brothers, 1997)

Love and politics, folk and bluegrass, and fire-in-the-belly rock. "Christmas in Washington" is Earle's paean to Woody Guthrie.

The Mountain
(E-Squared, 1999)

Earle's bluegrass album and a love letter to the father of bluegrass, Bill Monroe. A truly great album that one can listen to over and over again. "Pilgrim" is heartbreakingly beautiful.

Transcendental Blues
(Artemis, 2000)

Earle's eclecticism is on full display on this wonderful record. Every cut is a winner. The highlight to this listener, though, is the stunning "Over Yonder (Jonathan's Song)," about a condemned man's last tortured hours on earth.

Jerusalem
(Artemis, 2002)

Earle's most political recording, it includes the controversial "John Walker's Blues," about John Walker Lindh, the Marin County teenager turned Taliban fighter, but also the hopeful title track.

■ JOE ELY ■

Letter to Laredo
(MCA, 1995)

The great West Texas country rocker turns to Latino influences here: cowboy music of the West Texas ranch country, mariachi music of Mexico, and even the gypsy music of Spain. The instrumentation ranges from flamenco guitar to harmonica to steel guitar to Tex-Mex accordions. Springsteen, a longtime Ely fan, sings background vocals on "All Just to Get to You" and "I'm a Thousand Miles from Home."

■ DANNY FEDERICI ■

Danny Federici
(Hip-O, 2001)

Reissue of Federici's 1997 solo debut, *Flemington,* with an extra track, "Erica."

■ JOE GRUSHECKY AND THE (IRON CITY) HOUSEROCKERS ■

American Babylon
(Razor & Tie, 1995)

Includes the terrific title track as well as "Homestead," cowritten by Bruce Springsteen, about a hardscrabble Kentuckian who moves to Pittsburgh in 1973 to work in the steel mills of Homestead amid the ghosts of Henry Clay Frick and Andrew Carnegie.

Coming Home
(Viceroy, 1998)

Follow-up to *American Babylon.* Includes four tracks written by Springsteen: "Cheap Motel," "I'm Not Sleeping," "1945," and "Idiot's Delight."

Down the Road Apiece
(Schoolhouse Records, 1999)

Live CD includes Springsteen on three tracks: "Talking to the King," "Pumping Iron," and the title cut.

Fingerprints
(Schoolhouse Records, 2002)

Grushecky's solo release. Guitar-based rock from the Pittsburgh native.

▪ WOODY GUTHRIE ▪

This Land Is Your Land: The Asch Recordings, Vol. 1
(Smithsonian/Folkways, 1997)

Guthrie at his all-time best has provided fodder for generations of musicians from Dylan to Springsteen. Includes "This Land Is Your Land," "Hobo's Lullaby," "Pastures of Plenty," "Gypsy Davy," "Jesus Christ," "Do-Re-Mi," "Jesse James," and "Sinking of the Reuben James."

Dust Bowl Ballads
(Buddha, 2000)

Guthrie's tale of the devastating effects of the Dust Bowl and the arduous ordeal experienced by its refugees. Includes "Talking Dust Bowl Blues," "Pretty Boy Floyd," "Tom Joad," "Do-Re-Mi," "Dust Bowl Refugee," "I Ain't Got No Home," and "Vigilante Man."

▪ JOHN WESLEY HARDING ▪

Awake
(Appleseed, 2001)

This reissue includes a cover of "Jackson Cage" plus a live acoustic duet with Springsteen on "Wreck on the Highway."

▪ ROBERT JOHNSON ▪

The Complete Recordings
(Sony, 1990)

This two-CD boxed set contains bluesman Robert Johnson's entire recording output (including alternate takes), featuring such classics as "I Believe I'll Dust My Broom," "Stones in My Passway," "Hellhound on My Trail," "Me and the Devil Blues," and "Love in Vain." Recorded in Dallas and San Antonio in 1936–1937. Rock and roll truly starts here.

▪ LITTLE STEVEN (VAN ZANDT) ▪

Born Again Savage
(Pachyderm, 1999)

Little Steven without the Disciples of Soul (this time around, he is accompanied by Jason Bonham and Adam Clayton of U2). Van Zandt's powerful musical homage to the '60s rockers who influenced him so much, from the Kinks to Cream, but with Van Zandt's patented political edge.

■ LITTLE STEVEN & THE DISCIPLES OF SOUL ■

Men Without Women
(Razor & Tie, 1982)

Van Zandt's debut solo album. The wall of sound production nicely augments this bluesy rock and soul gem. Complete with Stax-like horns.

■ JOHN (COUGAR) MELLENCAMP ■

Lonesome Jubilee
(Polygram, 1987)

Fiddles, accordions, and mandolins give this record a decidedly rustic and rural feel, Midwestern style. Includes "Hard Times for an Honest Man" and "Cherry Bomb" and the exquisite fiddling of Lisa Germano.

Scarecrow
(Polygram, 1990)

A haunting and poignant musical homage to Mellencamp's native Indiana. Includes such Mellencamp classics as "Rain on the Scarecrow," "Small Town," "Minutes to Memories," and "You've Got to Stand for Somethin'." Themes range from the plight of small farmers to the hardships of rural life and other social commentaries. Straight-ahead love songs, too.

Trouble No More
(Columbia, 2003)

A collection of mostly American blues, folk, country, and gospel classics, including Robert Johnson's "Stones in My Passway," Lucinda Williams's "Lafayette," and Woody Guthrie's "To Washington" with new lyrics by Mellencamp.

■ JIMMIE RODGERS ■

The Essential Jimmie Rodgers
(RCA, 1997)

Classic country by the "Blue Yodeler." Includes "Brakeman's Blues," "I'm Lonely and Blue," "Mule Skinner Blues (Blue Yodel No. 8)," "T.B. Blues," "Frankie and Johnny," and the plaintive "Waiting for a Train."

Songs of Jimmie Rodgers: A Tribute
(Sony, 1997)

The likes of Bono, Alison Krauss, Bob Dylan, Steve Earle, John Mellencamp, Van Morrison, Aaron Neville, and Dwight Yoakam pay their musical respects to the country giant.

■ PATTI SCIALFA ■

Rumble Doll
(Sony, 1993)

Scialfa's solo debut showcases her beautiful—and underrated—voice. Hubby Bruce is on hand to lend support.

■ HARRY SMITH ■

Anthology of American Folk Music
(Smithsonian/Folkways, 1997)
Various Artists

Originally released in 1952 on vinyl, this six-CD reissue was painstakingly researched and annotated by filmmaker, music collector, and musicologist Harry Smith. It includes a massive amount of material from country blues to Appalachian murder ballads, from Clarence Ashley's rendition of "House Carpenter" to "Fishing Blues" by Henry Thomas. They're all here: Buell Kazee, Carolina Tar Heels, Charlie Poole and the North Carolina Ramblers, Mississippi John Hurt, Furry Lewis, Eck Robertson, Alabama Sacred Harp Singers, Bascom Lamar Lunsford, Blind Willie Johnson, Ernest Phipps and the Holiness Singers, Dock Boggs, the Stoneman Family, Blind Lemon Jefferson, Sleepy John Estes. Includes the Carter Family's "John Hardy Was a Desperate Little Man" and Julius Daniels's "99 Year Blues," which influenced Springsteen's *Nebraska*. Includes a substantial 68-page booklet that features an essay by Greil Marcus. Indispensable.

■ PATTI SMITH ■

Easter
(Arista, 1978)

The priestess of punk at her most accessible. Features the great rock classic "Because the Night," cowritten by Smith and Springsteen.

■ SOUTHSIDE JOHNNY AND THE ASBURY JUKES ■

I Don't Want to Go Home
(Sony, 1975)

Springsteen wrote the liner notes as well as "The Fever."

Hearts of Stone
(Sony, 1978)

Springsteen wrote the title track as well as "Talk to Me" and, with Southside Johnny and Steve Van Zandt, "Trapped Again." Classic Jersey Shore rock and soul.

Better Days
(MCA, 1991)

A terrific comeback album. Southside is joined by the likes of Max Weinberg, Garry Tallent, Steve Van Zandt, Jon Bon Jovi, and even a fellow named Bruce.

The Best of Southside Johnny and the Asbury Jukes
(Sony, 1992)

Blue-eyed soul, Jersey style.

I Don't Want to Go Home/This Time It's for Real/Hearts of Stone (boxed set)
(Sony, 1997)

Three discs of the great Jersey Shore bar band in all its glory.

▓ TOM WAITS ▓

Heartattack & Vine
(Elektra/Asylum, 1990)

Bluesy ballads, street-smart poetry, wickedly funny lyrics, and of course *that* voice. Includes the original version of the song that Springsteen made famous, "Jersey Girl."

▓ MAX WEINBERG ▓

Max Weinberg 7
(Hip-O, 2000)

Springsteen drummer Weinberg and his septet from *Late Night* with Conan O'Brien show strut their stuff.

▓ HANK WILLIAMS ▓

The Ultimate Collection
(Universal, 2002)

This two-disc set is a solid introduction to the country icon. Features "A Mansion on the Hill," "I'm So Lonesome I Could Cry," "Alone and Forsaken," "Lost Highway," and "Long Gone Lonesome Blues" (Springsteen reportedly modeled "The River" on this Williams classic).

▓ WARREN ZEVON ▓

Bad Luck Streak in Dancing School
(Elektra/Asylum, 1980)

Features "Jeannie Needs a Shooter," cowritten by Bruce Springsteen.

The Wind
(Artemis, 2003)

Zevon's final recording, it features numerous guest artists, including Springsteen on the incendiary "Disorder in the House."

Videos

Bruce Springsteen
Video Anthology, 1978–1988
(Columbia, 1989)

Includes a collection of 18 videos.

Bruce Springsteen & the E Street Band
Blood Brothers
(Columbia, 1996)

Documentary of the 1995 E Street reunion tour.

Bruce Springsteen
The Complete Video Anthology: 1978–2000
(Columbia, 2000)

Includes the original 18 videos as well as 15 additional post-1988 clips. Two-DVD/VHS set.

Bruce Springsteen & the E Street Band/Live in New York City
(SMV Enterprises, 2001)

Culled from the last shows of the 1999–2000 Madison Square Garden tour, this is an expanded version of the HBO concert film. Two-DVD/two-VHS set.

Bruce Springsteen & the E Street Band: Live in Barcelona
(Columbia, 2003)

A two-DVD set contains almost three hours of footage, including interviews with Springsteen and the Band.

Literary Influences

The following books, an eclectic bunch, have profoundly influenced or inspired Springsteen—each in its own distinctive way.

JAMES AGEE
Photographs by **WALKER EVANS**
Let Us Now Praise Famous Men
(Mariner, 2001)

Features Walker Evans's evocatively stark portraits of Great Depression–era share-croppers in the South, accompanied by the vivid prose of James Agee.

NINETTE BEAVER, B. K. RIPLEY, *and* PATRICK TRESE
Caril
(Lippincott, 1974)

Inspiration for *Nebraska*. A biography of Caril Fugate, who, along with partner Charles Starkweather, went on a killing spree in the American heartland in the late 1950s.

ROBERT COLES
The Secular Mind
(Princeton University Press, 1999)

The Harvard professor's thoughtful meditation on the relationship between religion and science in Western intellectual culture, which was inspired partly by conversations with such figures as Paul Tillich, William Carlos Williams, Dorothy Day, and Walker Percy.

MORRIS DEES
A Season for Justice: The Life and Times of Civil Rights Lawyer Morris Dees
(Scribner's, 1991)

The grandson of a Ku Klux Klansman, Dees, in this colorful autobiography, relates how he used the proceeds from a business venture to cofound the Southern Poverty Law Center in Montgomery, Alabama. The book was a considerable influence on Springsteen's *The Ghost of Tom Joad*.

WILLIAM PRICE FOX
Dixiana Moon
(Viking, 1981)

Fox's third novel is the picaresque tale of a New York salesman who joins forces with a fast-talking Southern con man on the Jubilee Crusade and Famous Life of Christ Show, part gospel revival meeting and part traveling circus.

JOE KLEIN
Woody Guthrie: A Life
(Ballantine, 1990)

The definitive Guthrie biography and a seminal influence on the direction of Springsteen's music.

RON KOVIC
Born on the Fourth of July
(Pocket Books, 1981)

Kovic's brutally frank memoir of the Vietnam War.

DALE MAHARIDGE
Photographs by **MICHAEL WILLIAMSON**
Journey to Nowhere: The Saga of the New Underclass
(Doubleday, 1985/Hyperion, 1996)

A contemporary version of *The Grapes of Wrath*. Springsteen wrote the introduction to the revised edition. The stories told in the book directly influenced the writing of "Youngstown" and "The New Timer," both of which appear on *The Ghost of Tom Joad*.

ALLAN NEVINS *and* HENRY STEELE COMMAGER
A Pocket History of the United States
(1943; Pocket Books, 1992)

The classic history of the United States that so influenced Springsteen during The River tour.

FLANNERY O'CONNOR

The short stories of Flannery O'Connor made a huge impact on Springsteen. "There was something in those stories of hers," he said, "that I felt captured a part of the American character that I was interested in writing about . . . some sort of meanness." *The Complete Stories* collection (Noonday Press, 1996) includes "A Good Man Is Hard to Find," "Revelation," "The Life You Save May Be Your Own," and other O'Connor classics. *Wise Blood* (Noonday Press, 1996), O'Connor's first novel, is a savagely wicked satire about goodness, redemption, and repentance that was adapted into a film by John Huston, which highly impressed Springsteen. Her second novel, *The Violent Bear It Away* (Noonday Press, 1960), covers similarly dark terrain—duty, self-doubt, and individualism being among its themes. For anyone wishing to learn about her personal faith and the role religion played in the creation of her art, see *Flannery O'Connor: Spiritual Writings* (Orbis Books, 2003), which is part of Orbis's Modern Spiritual Masters Series and is edited by Robert Ellsberg with an introduction by Richard Giannone.

WALKER PERCY
The Moviegoer
(Knopf, 1961; Vintage, 1998)

The portrait of a New Orleans stockbroker and lost soul on the eve of his 30th birthday, who, through movies and fleeting relationships, tries to escape from the responsibilities and drudgery of real life. Percy's *The Message in the Bottle: How Queer Man Is, How Queer Language Is, and What One Has to Do with the Other* (Farrar, Straus & Giroux, 1954; Picador, 2000) is a collection of essays that addresses the greatest of philosophical dilemmas: Why are we so unhappy in the world?

PHILIP ROTH

During interviews on *The Rising* tour, Springsteen had mentioned reading several recent Philip Roth novels. Three in particular—*American Pastoral* (1998), *I Married a Communist* (1998), and *The Human Stain* (2001)—examine themes that are familiar to anyone with even a cursory interest in Springsteen's work: how life doesn't always turn out as expected, the destruction of the American Dream, self-discovery, betrayal and loss, the spiritual and physical collapse of communities across the country (in Roth's case, Newark, New Jersey). *American Pastoral* (Vintage) is set in the 1960s.

JIM THOMPSON
The Killer Inside Me
(Vintage, 1991)

Springsteen's "My Best Was Never Good Enough" on *The Ghost of Tom Joad* was inspired by the character of Lou Ford, the cliché-spouting Texas sheriff's deputy in Thompson's *The Killer Inside Me* (originally published in 1952), who also happens to be a sociopath.

ROBERT JOHNSON

Bluesman Robert Johnson had a considerable influence on Springsteen, especially during the making of *Nebraska*. The following titles may be of interest to anyone seeking to learn more about the man, his life, and his music:

ACE ATKINS
Crossroad Blues: A Nick Travers Mystery
(St. Martin's Press, 1998)

A detective mystery involving an ex–football player, a quest for nine previously unknown Robert Johnson recordings in the Mississippi Delta, a missing professor, and a teenage Elvis look-alike hit man. What more could you ask for?

T. CORAGHESSAN BOYLE
T. C. Boyle Stories
(Penguin, 1999)

Includes "Stones in My Passway, Hellhound on My Trail," Boyle's take on the death of Robert Johnson.

SAMUEL CHARTERS
Robert Johnson
(Music Sales Corp., 1992)

ALAN GREENBERG
Love in Vain: A Vision of Robert Johnson
(Da Capo Press, 1994)

Introduction by Stanley Crouch, foreword by Martin Scorsese; this is the as-of-yet unfilmed script of Robert Johnson's life that was written in the early 1980s and follows the bluesman's life from cotton fields to juke joints.

PETER GURALNICK
Searching for Robert Johnson
(Obelisk, 1989)

A slender but fascinating rumination on the legendary bluesman's life.

WALTER MOSLEY
R. L.'s Dream
(Pocket Books, 1996)

The spirit of Robert Johnson lives on in Greenwich Village.

BARRY LEE PEARSON AND BILL MCCULLOCH
Robert Johnson: Lost and Found
(University of Illinois Press, 2003)

Part of the Music in American Life series. Pearson and McCulloch expertly separate fact from fiction.

ALAN RODGERS
Bone Music
(Longmeadow Press, 1995)

This horror novel combines the African-inspired Santeria religion, Robert Johnson, and other assorted blues and rock figures, including Leadbelly, Ma Rainey, the mythical John Henry, and even Elvis, and settings that range from New York City to Mississippi to contemporary New Orleans.

ROBERT WOLF
Hellhound on My Trail: The Life of
Robert Johnson, Bluesman Extraordinaire
(Creative Editions, 2003)

Miscellaneous

The Bruce Springsteen Special Collection
Asbury Park Public Library
500 First Avenue
Asbury Park, NJ 07712

The Bruce Springsteen Special Collection was donated to the library by the editors of the Springsteen fanzine *Backstreets*. Additional contributions have been received from around the world. The collection was formally presented to the library by *Backstreets* editor Christopher Phillips at a dedication ceremony on December 8, 2001. Mayor Kevin Sanders also participated in the proceedings. Later that evening at the city's Convention Hall, Bruce Springsteen remarked: "I want to thank all you folks who showed up at the library today for our little section there. . . . The collection has almost 1,000 books and magazines on my-self and the band—more stuff than every place except my mother's basement!"

The collection includes books, periodicals, song books, tour books, fanzines, and comic books dating from the early 1970s to the present. As of December 2002, donations have been received from 24 countries: Argentina, Australia, Brazil, Canada, Denmark, Finland, France, Germany, Greece, Holland, Italy, Japan, Malaysia, Mexico, Poland, Portugal, Singapore, Spain, Sweden, Thailand, Turkey, the U.K., the United States, and Yugoslavia.

Web Sites

■

There are countless Springsteen Web sites—too many to list here. The following are among the best.

www.brucespringsteen.net   Official Springsteen site.

www.greasylake.org   Springsteen tribute page with access to articles, features, reports, as well as great links.

www.theboots.net   Flynn McLean's Springsteen Web connection, including information on albums, videos/DVDs, compilations, books, tributes, and related artists.

www.backstreets.com   *Backstreets* magazine Web site consists of regular updates with the latest Springsteen news, including recording news, performances, set lists, and much more. It also contains an online shop of official and authorized Springsteen merchandise: tour T-shirts, books, magazines, posters, and CDs and records.

www.pointblankmag.com   Online version of the Spanish-based bilingual magazine (English and Spanish) that is devoted entirely to Springsteen.

www.luckytown.org   Internet e-mail list for Springsteen fans and an important fan forum.

www.candysroom.freeservers.com   Rambling Springsteen site with photos, mailing lists, discussion groups, and links.

www.missingtracks.com   Online archive of all the songs Springsteen has written and performed during his career.

www.springsteen.org.uk/intro.htm   John Leach's On the Tracks Web site is devoted to both official releases and unreleased outtakes and demos of Springsteen songs.

www.orel.ws   Matt Orel's Bruce Springsteen pages list all the official releases of covers of Springsteen songs, display single sleeves and album covers, and provide a complete Springsteen discography.

www.brucebase.com   The Springsteen bootleg discography.

www.brucespringsteen.it   Complete database of Springsteen set lists, lyrics, and studio sessions.

Related Web Sites

www.maxweinberg7.com   Web site for E Street Band drummer Max Weinberg.

www.littsteven.com   Official Web site for E Street Band guitarist Steve Van Zandt.

www.nilslofgren.com   Official website for E Street guitarist Nils Lofgren.

www.clarenceclemons.com   Web site for E Street sax player Clarence Clemons.

www.southsidejohnny.org   Official Web site for Southside Johnny and the Asbury Jukes.

www.grushecky.com Web site for the Pittsburgh-based band Joe Grushecky and the Houserockers.

www.welcometofreehold.com Web site of Freehold history and terrific Springsteen links. Features a faded color copy of Bruce's library card, a photograph of the lime-green "Born to Run" Freehold fire truck, and early family photos.

www.asburypark.net Asbury Park—past, present, and future.

www.asburypark.lib.nj.us Official site of the Asbury Park Public Library with links to the library's Bruce Springsteen Collection, or go directly to **www.asbury-park.lib.nj.us/bruce.htm**.

www.app.com Web site for the *Asbury Park Press*.

www.members.aol.com/monandsue/njtour.htm Extensive history and background information on Jersey Shore and area towns, including Asbury Park, Long Branch, Freehold, Ocean Township, Ocean Grove, Neptune, Red Bank, Holmdel, Belmar, Point Pleasant and Point Pleasant Beach, Seaside Heights and Seaside Park, Sea Bright, and Routes 9, 88, 33, and 35.

www.njrockmap.com Web site of Stan Goldstein and Jean Mikle, coauthors of *Rock & Roll Tour of the Jersey Shore*. They have given walking tours of Springsteen-related sites in Asbury Park, Belmar, and Freehold since 1999.

www.rothenbergphoto.com Website of photographer Debra L. Rothenberg, who has taken a plethora of Springsteen photographs over the years.

www.homestead.com/savetillie The official Web site of the Palace Preservation Campaign, better known as the Save Tillie Campaign.

CREDITS

Grateful acknowledgment is made for permission to reprint the following copyrighted works:

Eric Alterman: Selection from Spanish-language edition of *It Ain't No Sin to Be Glad You're Alive: The Promise of Bruce Springsteen* (*Nacido para el rock*, Ma Non Troppo, Barcelona, 2003) by Eric Alterman. Used by permission of the author.

Lester Bangs: "Hot Rod Rumble in the Promised Land," *CREEM*, November 1975. Copyright CREEM Media, Inc., 2003. Used by permission.

Dave Barry: "Glory Days," *The Miami Herald*, July 10, 1994. Used by permission of the author.

T. Coraghessan Boyle: "Greasy Lake" from *Greasy Lake and Other Stories* by T. Coraghessan Boyle. Copyright © T. Coraghessan Boyle, 1982. Used by permission of Viking Penguin, a division of Penguin Group (USA) Inc.

Jay Cocks: "Rock's New Sensation: The Backstreet Phantom of Rock," *Time*, October 27, 1975. © 1975 Time Inc. Reprinted by permission.

Kevin Coyne: "His Hometown," *New Jersey Monthly*, January 2003. Used by permission of the author.

Bob Crane: Selection from *A Place to Stand: A Guide to Bruce Springsteen's Sense of Place* (Palace Books, 2002). Used by permission of the author.

Charles R. Cross: "The Promise," *Backstreets*, Winter 1991. Used by permission of the author.

Jim Cullen: Selections from *Born in the U.S.A.: Bruce Springsteen and the American Tradition* by Jim Cullen. Copyright © 1996 by Jim Cullen. Reprinted by permission of HarperCollins Publishers Inc.

Pellegrino D'Acierno: "Roll Over, Rossini: Italian American Rock 'n' Roll" and "After the Long Goodbye: From Frank Zappa to Bruce Springsteen and Madonna" (excerpted from "Italian American Musical Culture and Its Contribution to American Music" by Robert Connolly and Pellegrino D'Acierno) appearing in *The Italian American Heritage: A Companion to Literature and Arts* edited by Pellegrino D'Acierno (Garland Publishing, 1999). Used by permission of the author.

Nicholas Dawidoff: "The Pop Populist" (also titled "Steinbeck in Leather"), *The New York Times Magazine*, January 26, 1997. © 1997 Nicholas Dawidoff. Distributed by The New York Times Special Features. Reprinted by permission of The New York Times.

Hope Edelman: From "Bruce Springsteen and the Story of Us," *The Iowa Review*, January 1996. Reprinted by permission of The Iowa Review.

Nadine Epstein: "Asbury Park, My Hometown," *The Christian Science Monitor*, August 23, 1999. Used by permission of the author.

Simon Frith: "The Real Thing—Bruce Springsteen" from *Music for Pleasure: Essays in the Sociology of Pop* by Simon Frith (Routledge, 1988). Used by permission of the author.

Bryan K. Garman: "The Ghost of History: Bruce Springsteen, Woody Guthrie, and the Hurt Song," *Popular Music and Society*, Summer 1996. Used by permission of the publisher. The version appearing in this book has been edited by the author.

Mikal Gilmore: "Bruce Springsteen's America" from *Night Beat: A Shadow History of Rock & Roll* by Mikal Gilmore. Copyright © 1998 by Mikal Gilmore. Used by permission of Doubleday, a division of Random House, Inc.

Andrew Greeley: "The Catholic Imagination of Bruce Springsteen," *America*, February 6, 1988. Used by permission of the author.

Robert Hilburn: "Out in the Streets," *Los Angeles Times*. Copyright 1980 Los Angeles Times. Reprinted with permission.

Nick Hornby: "Thunder Road" from *Songbook* by Nick Hornby (McSweeney's Books, 2002). Used by permission of the author.

Peter Knobler with Greg Mitchell: "Who is Bruce Springsteen and Why Are We Saying All These Wonderful Things about Him?" *Crawdaddy!*, March 1973. Copyright © 1973 by Peter Knobler. Reprinted by permission of International Creative Management, Inc.

Gene Lazo: "Newark by the Sea." Used by permission of the author.

Alan Light: "The Missing," *The New Yorker*, August 5, 2002. Used by permission of the author.

Kevin Major: Selection from *Dear Bruce Springsteen* by Kevin Major. Copyright © 1988 by Kevin Major. Used by permission of Dell Publishing, a division of Random House, Inc.

Greil Marcus: "The Next President of the United States," *New West*, December 22, 1980. Used by permission of the author.

Bibliography

Editor's note: Entries marked with an asterisk are included in this volume.

Agee, James, and Walker Evans. *Let Us Now Praise Famous Men.* New York: Mariner Books, 2001.

Allister, Mark. "'There's a Meanness in This World': Bruce Springsteen's *Nebraska* and Folk Music." *John Edwards Memorial Foundation Quarterly* 19, no. 70 (Summer 1983): 130–34.

Allsop, Kenneth. *Hard Travelin': The Hobo and His History.* London: Hodder and Stoughton, 1967.

*Alterman, Eric. *It Ain't No Sin to Be Glad You're Alive: The Promise of Bruce Springsteen.* New York: Little, Brown, 1999.

———. "Presleyites, Dylanists and Springsteenians." *New York Times,* January 30, 2000.

Altschuler, Glenn C. *All Shook Up: How Rock 'n' Roll Changed America.* New York: Oxford University Press, 2003.

Anderson, Nells. *The Hobo: The Sociology of the Homeless Man.* Chicago: University of Chicago Press, 1923.

Andrews, Betsy, and Randi Gollin, eds. *Zagatsurvey Music Guide: 1,000 Top Albums of All Time.* New York: Zagat Survey, 2003.

Arax, Mark, and Tom Gorman. "California's Illicit Farm Belt Export." *Los Angeles Times,* March 13, 1995.

Badger, Anthony J. *The New Deal: The Depression Years, 1933–1940.* Chicago: Ivan R. Dee, 2002.

Banashek, Mary-Ellen. "Bruce Springsteen: Why He Makes Us Feel So Good." *McCall's,* November 1985.

*Bangs, Lester. "Hot Rod Rumble in the Promised Land." *CREEM,* November 1975.

Banks, Russell. "The Devil and Robert Johnson: The Blues and the 1990s." *New Republic,* April 29, 1991.

Barlow, Rich. "Exploring Springsteen's Spirituality." *Boston Globe,* March 22, 2003.

Barol, Bill. "He's on Fire." *Newsweek,* August 5, 1985.

Barreca, Regina, ed. *Don't Tell Mama! The Penguin Book of Italian American Writing.* New York: Penguin, 2002.

Barry, Dave. "Glory Days." *Miami Herald,* July 10, 1994

Berry, Jason. "Pimp Slays Bully: Exploring the History and Significance of a Famous R&B Song." *New York Times,* April 27, 2003.

Binelli, Mark. "Bruce Springsteen's American Gospel." *Rolling Stone,* August 22, 2002.

Bird, S. Elizabeth. "'Is That Me Baby?': Image, Authenticity, and the Career of Bruce Springsteen." *American Studies* 35, no. 2 (1994): 39–57.

Blake, Richard A. *Afterimage: The Indelible Catholic Imagination of Six American Filmmakers.* Chicago: Loyola Press, 2000.

Bonca, Cornel. "Save Me Somebody: Bruce Springsteen's Rock 'n' Roll Covenant." www.killingthebuddha.com.

Bottum, J. "The Soundtracking of America." *Atlantic Monthly,* March 2000.

°Boyle, T. Coraghessan. "Greasy Lake." In *Greasy Lake & Other Stories.* New York: Viking, 1985.

Bradley, Bill. "He's New Jersey and He Is Ours." *USA Today,* August 5, 1985.

Brown, Cecil. *Stagolee Shot Billy.* Cambridge, Mass.: Harvard University Press, 2003.

Bruce Springsteen: The Rolling Stone *Files: The Ultimate Compendium of Interviews, Articles, Facts and Opinions from the Files of* Rolling Stone. Introduction by Parke Puterbaugh. The editors of *Rolling Stone.* New York: Hyperion, 1996.

Callow, Philip. *From Noon to Starry Night: A Life of Walt Whitman.* Chicago: Ivan R. Dee, 1990.

Cantwell, Robert. *When We Were Good: The Folk Revival.* Cambridge, Mass.: Harvard University Press, 1996.

Cara, Holly. "John Hammond: A Vision Shared." *Backstreets,* Winter 1991.

Cavicchi, Daniel. *Tramps Like Us: Music and Meaning Among Springsteen Fans.* New York: Oxford University Press, 1998.

Chantal-Pike, Helen. *Asbury Park.* Images of America series. Charleston, S.C.: Arcadia Publishing, 1997.

Charlie Rose: The Music Interviews. Bruce Springsteen, October 2, 1999. New York, VH1.

Charters, Samuel. *Robert Johnson.* New York: Oak, 1973.

Clarke, Donald. *The Rise and Fall of Popular Music.* New York: St. Martin's/Griffin, 1995.

Clausen, Christopher. *Faded Mosaic: The Emergence of Post-Cultural America.* Chicago: Ivan R. Dee, 2000.

Cocks, Jay. "Against the American Grain." *Time,* November 15, 1982.

———. "Along Pinball Way." *Time,* April 1, 1974.

———. "Riding High with the Hard-Luck Guys: Joe Ely Keeps the Faith with the Past and Makes Good Music." *Time,* May 11, 1981.

°———. "Rock's New Sensation." *Time,* October 27, 1975.

———. "Round the World: A Boss Boom." *Time,* August 26, 1985.

———. "There's Magic in the Night." *Time,* November 10, 1986.

Coles, Robert. *Bruce Springsteen's America: The People Listening, A Poet Singing.* New York: Random House, 2003.

————. *The Secular Mind.* New York, Princeton, N.J.: Princeton University Press, 1999.

Connolly, Robert, and Pellegrino D'Acierno. "Italian American Musical Culture and Its Contribution to American Music." In *The Italian American Heritage: A Companion to Literature and Arts.* Edited by Pellegrino D'Acierno. New York: Garland Publishing, 1999.

Constant, Chantal, trans. "Jon Landau: The Man Behind the Boss." *Backstreets,* Summer 1987.

Corn, David. "The Boss' Other America." *In These Times.* September 28– October 1, 1985.

————. "Bruce Springsteen Tells the Story of the Secret America." *Mother Jones,* March–April 1995.

————. "Guthrie's Ghost." *Nation,* December 11, 1995.

Cotter, K. J. "Springsteen's Life, Music Inextricably Entwined." *Asbury Park Press,* November 27, 1996.

Cowie, Jefferson. "Fandom, Faith, and Bruce Springsteen." *Dissent,* Winter 2001.

Coyne, Kevin. "The Faulkner of Freehold." *Asbury Park Press/Home News Tribune,* March 14, 1999.

°————. "His Hometown." *New Jersey Monthly,* January 2003.

°Crane, Bob. *A Place to Stand: A Guide to Bruce Springsteen's Sense of Place.* Silver Springs, Md.: Palace Books/Save Tillie, Inc., 2002.

————. "Beyond the Palace: Saving Tillie." *Backstreets,* Spring 1999.

Cross, Charles R. "The Ghost and Mr. Springsteen." *Backstreets,* Late Fall 1995.

————. "It Was 20 Years Ago Today." *Backstreets,* Fall/Winter 2000.

————. "Mansion on the Hill: The Fred Goodman Interview." *Backstreets,* Spring 1997.

°————. "The Promise." *Backstreets,* Winter 1991.

Cross, Charles R., and the editors of *Backstreets* magazine. *Backstreets: Springsteen—The Man and His Music.* New York: Harmony Books, 1989; Crown, 1992.

°Cullen, Jim. "Tom Joad's Children," and "The Bars of Graceland." In *Born in the U.S.A.: Bruce Springsteen and the American Tradition.* New York: HarperCollins, 1996.

————. "Bruce Springsteen's Ambiguous Musical Politics in the Reagan Era." *Popular Music and Society* 16, no. 2 (Summer 1992): 1–22.

————. "Good Men through the Ages: August '81 in Context." *Backstreets,* Fall 2001.

°D'Acierno, Pellegrino. "Roll Over, Rossini: Italian American Rock 'n' Roll," and "After the Long Good-Bye: From Frank Zappa to Bruce Springsteen and Madonna." In *The Italian American Heritage: A Companion to Literature and Arts.* Edited by Pelligrino D'Acierno. New York: Garland Publishing, 1999.

Dalton, Joseph. "My Hometown." *Rolling Stone,* October 10, 1985.

Dansby, Andrew. "Stone Pony Faces Demolition: Music Fans Rally to Save the Club That Launched Springsteen." *Rolling Stone,* January 11, 2002.

Davis, Francis. "Blues Walking Like a Man: The Complicated Legacy of Robert Johnson." *Atlantic Monthly,* April 1991.

———. *The History of the Blues: The Roots, the Music, the People—from Charley Patton to Robert Cray.* New York: Hyperion, 1995.

———. "Napoleon in Rags." *Atlantic Monthly,* May 1999.

Dawidoff, Nicholas. *In the Country of Country: A Journey to the Roots of American Music.* New York: Pantheon, 1997; Vintage, 1998.

°———. "The Pop Populist." *New York Times Magazine,* January 26, 1997.

DeCurtis, Anthony. *Rocking My Life Away: Writing About Music and Other Matters.* Durham, N.C.: Duke University Press, 1998; 1999.

———. "Springsteen Returns." *Rolling Stone,* January 10, 1991.

DeCurtis, Anthony, and James Henke, with Holly George-Warren. *The Rolling Stone Illustrated History of Rock & Roll: The Definitive History of the Most Important Artists and Their Music.* New York: Random House, 1992.

Dees, Morris. *A Season for Justice: The Life and Times of Civil Rights Lawyer Morris Dees.* New York: Scribner's, 1991.

DeLillo, Don. *Great Jones Street.* New York: Penguin, 1973.

Denisoff, R. Serge. *Great Day Comin': Folk Music and the American Left.* Urbana, Ill.: University of Illinois Press, 1971.

Denisoff, R. Serge, and David Fandray. "'Hey, Hey Woody Guthrie I Wrote You a Song': The Political Side of Bob Dylan." *Popular Music and Society* 5, no. 1 (1977): 31–42.

DeRogatis, Jim. *Let It Blurt: The Life and Times of Lester Bangs.* New York: Bantam Doubleday, 2000.

DeVault, Russ. "Springsteen and Seger: They're Older, Tamer, and on the Road Again." *Atlanta Journal-Constitution,* January 26, 1996.

Dollar, Steve. "Springsteen Plugs in to Nation's Longings." *Atlanta Journal-Constitution,* January 29, 1996.

Douglas, Ann. "Bruce Springsteen and Narrative Rock: The Art of Extended Urgency." *Dissent,* Fall 1985.

Draper, Robert. Rolling Stone *Magazine: The Uncensored History.* 1990. New York: HarperPerennial, 1991.

Droney, Maureen. "Classic Tracks: Bruce Springsteen's 'The River.'" *Mix,* October 1, 2003.

Duffy, John, ed. *Bruce Springsteen: In His Own Words.* London: Omnibus, 1992.

Duffy, Thom. "Landau's Creative Touch with Springsteen." *Billboard,* June 13, 1992.

Duncan, Robert. "Bruce Springsteen Is Not God (and Doesn't Want to Be)." *CREEM,* January 1976.

°Edelman, Hope. "Bruce Springsteen and the Story of Us." *Iowa Review,* January 1996.

Edwards, Henry. "If There Hadn't Been a Bruce Springsteen, Then the Critics Would Have Made Him Up." *New York Times,* October 5, 1975.

Ehrenreich, Barbara. *Fear of Falling: The Inner Life of the Middle Class.* New York: HarperPerennial, 1985.

———. *Nickel and Dimed: On (Not) Getting By in America.* New York: Henry Holt, 2001.

———. *The Worst Years of Our Lives: Irreverent Notes from a Decade of Greed.* New York: HarperPerennial, 1991.

Eidus, Janice, and John Kastan, eds. *It's Only Rock and Roll: An Anthology of Rock and Roll Short Stories.* Jaffrey, N.H.: David R. Godine, 1998.

Eliot, Marc, with Mike Appel. *Down Thunder Road: The Making of Bruce Springsteen.* New York: Simon & Schuster, 1992.

Elledge, Jim, ed. *Sweet Nothings: An Anthology of Rock and Roll in American Poetry.* Bloomington, Ind.: Indiana University Press, 1994.

°Epstein, Nadine. "Asbury Park, My Hometown." *Christian Science Monitor,* August 23, 1999.

Ewing, Tom, ed. *The Bill Monroe Reader.* Urbana and Chicago: University of Illinois Press, 2000.

Farber, David, ed. *The Sixties: From Memory to History.* Chapel Hill, N.C.: University of North Carolina Press, 1994.

Feinberg, Cara. "Poised for Possibility: Interview with Bobbie Ann Mason." The Atlantic Online (Atlantic Unbound), September 19, 2001.

Ferraro, Thomas J. "Catholic Ethnicity and Modern American Arts." In *The Italian American Heritage: A Companion to Literature and Arts.* Edited by Pellegrino D'Acierno. New York: Garland Publishing, 1999.

Filene, Benjamin. *Romancing the Folk: Public Memory and American Roots Music.* Cultural Studies of the United States. Chapel Hill, N.C.: University of North Carolina Press, 2000.

Finnegan, Jim. "Earle and Springsteen Duke It Out." *Backstreets,* Spring 1998.

Fischer, Stanley. "3M Plant Is Shut Down but Fight Goes On." *Backstreets,* Spring 1987.

Fisher, James T. "Clearing the Streets of the Catholic Lost Generation." *South Atlantic Quarterly,* Summer 1994.

Flanagan, Bill. "Ambition, Lies, and the Beautiful Reward: Bruce Springsteen's Family Values." *Musician,* November 1992.

———. *Written in My Soul: Rock's Great Songwriters Talk About Creating Their Music.* New York: Contemporary, 1986.

Flippo, Chet. "Blue Collar Troubadour." *People,* September 3, 1984.

———. "Bruce Springsteen: A Rock 'n' Roll Evangelist for Our Times Crusades for Patriotism and Puritanism of a Different Stripe." *Musician,* November 1984.

Fox, William Price. *Dixiana Moon.* New York: Viking, 1981.

°Frith, Simon. "The Real Thing—Bruce Springsteen." In *Music for Pleasure: Essays in the Sociology of Pop.* New York: Routledge, 1988.

Fusilli, Jim. "The Selling of Bruce Springsteen." *Wall Street Journal,* July 2, 1984.

Gaines, Donna. *A Misfit's Manifesto: The Spiritual Journey of a Rock & Roll Heart.* New York: Villard, 2003.

Gardner, Elysa. "Springsteen's 'Rising.'" *USA Today,* July 14, 2002.

°Garman, Bryan K. "The Ghost of History: Bruce Springsteen, Woody Guthrie, and the Hurt Song." *Popular Music and Society* 20, no. 20 (Summer 1996): 69–120.

———. *A Race of Singers: Whitman's Working-Class Hero from Guthrie to Springsteen.* Chapel Hill, N.C.: University of North Carolina Press, 2000.

Gill, Andy. "Thunder Road: The Power and the Glory." *Independent,* January 17, 2003.

Gillett, Charlie. *The Sound of the City: The Rise of Rock and Roll.* New York: Da Capo Press, 1996.

Gilmore, Mikal. "Bruce Springsteen: What Does It Mean, Springsteen Asked, to Be an American?" *Rolling Stone,* December 15, 1990.

———. "Interview with Bruce Springsteen." *Rolling Stone,* December 10, 1987.

°——— "Bruce Springsteen's America." In *Night Beat: A Shadow History of Rock & Roll.* New York: Anchor, 1998.

———. "Springsteen on Life in the U.S.A." *Los Angeles Herald Examiner,* June 1, 1984.

———. "Springsteen's 'Nebraska': One from the Heartland." *Los Angeles Herald Examiner,* September 24, 1982.

———. "Star Spangled Rock 'n' Roll." *Los Angeles Herald Examiner,* September 25, 1984.

Goldstein, Stan, and Jean Mikle. *Rock & Roll Tour of the Jersey Shore.* Privately printed, 2002.

Goodman, Fred. *The Mansion on the Hill: Dylan, Young, Geffen, Springsteen and the Head-On Collision of Rock and Commerce.* New York: Vintage, 1998.

°Greeley, Andrew. "The Catholic Imagination of Bruce Springsteen." *America,* February 6, 1988.

———. *The Catholic Myth: The Behavior and Beliefs of American Catholics.* New York: Collier, 1990; Touchstone Books, 1997.

Greenberg, Alan. *Love in Vain: The Life and Legend of Robert Johnson.* Garden City, N.Y.: Dolphin Doubleday, 1983.

Greenway, John. *American Folksongs of Protest.* Philadelphia: University of Pennsylvania Press, 1953.

Gregory, James. *American Exodus: The Dust Bowl Migration and Okie Culture in California.* New York: Oxford University Press, 1989.

Grimm, T. L. "Joe Grushecky: Coming Home." *Backstreets,* Winter 1997.

Grossberg, Larry. "Pedagogy in the Age of Reagan: Politics, Postmodernity, and the Popular." *Curriculum and Teaching* 3, 1988.

Gunderson, Edna. "In 'Joad,' Springsteen Answers Ghost of His Past." *USA Today,* December 1, 1995.

Guralnick, Peter. *Feel Like Going Home: Portraits in Blues and Rock 'n' Roll.* New York: HarperCollins, 1989.

———. *Lost Highway: Journeys and Arrivals of American Musicians.* New York: Harper & Row, 1989.

———. *Nighthawk Blues: A Novel.* New York: Back Bay, 2003.

———. *Sweet Soul Music: Rhythm and Blues and the Southern Dream of Freedom.* New York: Harper & Row, 1986.

———. *A Vision Shared: A Tribute to Woody Guthrie and Leadbelly.* Liner notes. CBS Records, 1988.

Guralnick, Peter, Robert Santelli, Holly George-Warren, and Christopher John Farley, eds. *Martin Scorsese Presents: The Blues—A Musical Journey.* New York: HarperCollins/Amistad Press, 2003.

Guthrie, Woody. *Pastures of Plenty: A Self-Portrait.* Dave Marsh and Harold Leventhal, eds. New York: HarperCollins, 1990.

Hagen, Mark. "Interview." *MOJO,* January 1999.

Hajdu, David. *Positively Fourth Street: The Lives and Times of Joan Baez, Bob Dylan, Mimi Baez Fariña, and Richard Fariña.* New York: Farrar, Straus & Giroux, 2002.

Halker, Clark. *For Democracy, Workers, and God: Labor Song-Poems and Labor Protest, 1865–1895.* Urbana, Ill.: University of Illinois Press, 1991.

Hampton, Wayne. *Guerrilla Minstrels: John Lennon, Joe Hill, Woody Guthrie, and Bob Dylan.* Knoxville, Tenn.: University of Tennessee Press, 1987.

Harnes, John A. "Painter of 'Tillie' Dies at 90." *Asbury Park Press,* March 15, 2003.

Hemphill, Michael R., and Larry David Smith. "The Working American's Elegy: The Rhetoric of Bruce Springsteen." In *Politics in Familiar Contexts: Projecting Politics Through Popular Media.* Edited by Robert L. Savage and Dan Nimmo. Norwood, N.J.: Ablex, 1990.

Henke, James. "Bruce Springsteen: The *Rolling Stone* Interview." *Rolling Stone,* August 6, 1992.

Hepworth, David. "Bruce Springsteen: The Q Interview." *Q Magazine,* August 1992.

°Hilburn, Robert. "Out in the Streets." *Los Angeles Times,* October 1980.

———. *Springsteen.* New York: Rolling Stone Press, 1985.

———. "A Storyteller Returns: Springsteen Defines Musical Focus with Images of Steinbeck in Solo Concert." *Los Angeles Times,* November 28, 1995.

———. "Under the Boss' Skin." *Los Angeles Times,* April 1, 2001.

Hilferty, John. "A Song Debate Blooms in the Garden State." Knight-Ridder newspapers, July 6, 1980.

Himes, G. "Springsteen's Music Is Mature, Personal." *Baltimore Sun,* August 26, 1984.

Holden, Stephen. "Springsteen Scans the American Dream." *New York Times,* May 27, 1984.

°Hornby, Nick. "Thunder Road." In *Songbook*. San Francisco: McSweeney's Books, 2002; New York: Riverhead Books, 2003.

Humphries, Patrick. *The Complete Guide to the Music of Bruce Springsteen*. London: Omnibus, 1996.

Humphries, Patrick, and Chris Hunt. *Springsteen: Blinded by the Light*. New York: Henry Holt, 1986.

Johnson, Nunnally. *The Grapes of Wrath*. Screenplay. Hollywood, Calif.: Script City, 1940.

Judge, Mark Gauvreau. "The Cult of Bruce." *Wall Street Journal*, August 23, 2002.

Kahn, Ashley, et al. *Rolling Stone: The Seventies*. New York: Little, Brown, 1998.

Kaplan, James. *Two Guys from Verona: A Novel of Suburbia*. Boston: Atlantic Monthly Press, 1998.

Kihn, Greg, ed. *Carved in Rock: Short Stories by Musicians*. New York: Thunder's Mouth Press, 2003. Includes short fiction from Ray Manzarek of the Doors, David Byrne, Graham Parker, Lydia Lunch, Larry Kirwan of Black 47, Dee Dee Ramone, Eric Burdon, Richard Hell, Joan Jett, Suzzy Roche, Robyn Hitchcock, Steve Earle, Suzanne Vega, Tom Verlaine, Pete Townsend, and Kinky Friedman.

Kimmel, Michael. *Manhood in America: A Cultural History*. New York: Free Press, 1996.

King, Wayne. "The Apprenticeship of John Cougar Mellencamp." *Backstreets*, Summer 1986.

———. "In a Wide Open Country." *Backstreets*, Spring 1986.

———. "A Self-Made Man." *Trouser Press*, October 1980.

———. "Till All the Rivers Run Dry." *Backstreets*, Summer 1986.

Klein, Joe. *Woody Guthrie: A Life*. New York: Knopf, 1980.

Klein, Joshua. "Light of Day: The Rebirth of Bruce Springsteen." *Onion*, December 16, 1999.

Kot, Greg. "Ghost Stories." *Chicago Tribune*, November 21, 1995.

———. "Working-Class Heroes: Bruce Springsteen Returns with the E Street Band to Chronicle Sept. 11, but *The Rising* Finds the Most Power in Its Subtleties." *Chicago Tribune*, July 28, 2002.

Knobler, Peter. "Running on the Backstreets with Bruce Springsteen." *Crawdaddy!*, October 1975.

°Knobler, Peter, with Greg Mitchell. "Who Is Bruce Springsteen and Why Are We Saying All These Wonderful Things About Him?" *Crawdaddy!*, March 1973.

Knobler, Peter, and Greg Mitchell, eds. *Very Seventies: A Cultural History of the 1970s, from the Pages of Crawdaddy!*. New York: Fireside/Simon & Schuster, 1995.

Knopper, Steve. "Influencing the Boss: Springsteen Mines Many Sources for Inspiration." *Milwaukee Journal Sentinel*, September 27, 2002.

Kovic, Ron. *Born on the Fourth of July*. New York: Pocket Books, 1981.

Krist, Gary. *The Garden State: Short Stories*. New York: Vintage, 1989.

Kusmer, Kenneth L. *Down and Out, on the Road: The Homeless in American History.* New York: Oxford University Press, 2003.

Landau, Jon. "Growing Young with Rock and Roll." *Real Paper,* May 22, 1974.

———. *It's Too Late to Stop Now: A Rock 'n' Roll Journal.* San Francisco: Straight Arrow Books, 1972.

Lapham, Lewis H. "Who and What Is American?" *Harper's,* January 1992.

Lasch, Christopher. *The Culture of Narcissism: American Life in an Age of Diminishing Expectations.* Rev. ed. New York: W. W. Norton, 1991.

Leach, William. *Country of Exiles: The Destruction of Place in American Life.* New York: Vintage Books/Random House, 1999.

Lewis, David L., and Laurence Goldstein, eds. *The Automobile and American Culture.* Ann Arbor, Mich.: University of Michigan Press, 1983.

Liebermann, Robbie. *My Song Is My Weapon: People's Songs, American Communism, and the Politics of Culture, 1930–1950.* Music in American Life Series. Urbana, Ill.: University of Illinois Press, 1989.

°Light, Alan. "The Missing." *New Yorker,* August 5, 2002.

Lind, Michael. *The Next American Nation: Nationalism and the Fourth American Revolution.* New York: Free Press, 1995.

Lingeman, Richard. *Small Town America: A Narrative History, 1620 to the Present.* Boston: Houghton Mifflin, 1980.

Loder, Kurt. "Bruce!" *Rolling Stone,* February 28, 1985.

———. "Bruce Springsteen: The *Rolling Stone* Interview." *Rolling Stone,* December 6, 1984.

Lomax, Alan. *The Land Where the Blues Began.* New York: Pantheon Books, 1993.

Lomax, John A., and Alan Lomax. *Folksong U.S.A.* New York: Signet, 1947.

Lombardi, John. "The Sanctification of Bruce Springsteen and the Rise of Mass Hip." *Esquire,* December 1988.

Loving, Jerome. *Emerson, Whitman, and the American Muse.* Chapel Hill, N.C.: University of North Carolina Press, 1982.

Lynch, Kate. *Springsteen: No Surrender.* New York: Proteus, 1984.

Lyons, Julie, and George H. Lewis. "The Price You Pay: The Life and Lyrics of Bruce Springsteen." In Timothy E. Scheurer, ed. *The Age of Rock: Readings from the Popular Press.* Bowling Green, Oh.: Bowling Green State University Popular Press, 1989.

Maass, Alan. "The Boss on Bush: 'A War Well Handled'—What's Missing from *The Rising.*" *CounterPunch,* September 9, 2002.

———. "Songs of the New Oakies: The Ghost of Tom Joad." *Socialist Review,* March 1996.

McConnell, Frank. "A Rock Poet: From Fitzgerald to Springsteen." *Commonweal,* August 12, 1983.

McGee, David. "Bruce Springsteen Claims the Future of Rock & Roll." In *Bruce*

Springsteen: The Rolling Stone *Files.* The editors of *Rolling Stone.* New York: Hyperion, 1996.

°McLeese, Don. "Abdicating the Rock 'n' Roll Pedestal: Bruce Springsteen Gets Down." *Chicago Reader,* October 24, 1980.

————. "Springsteen Shows His Dark Side." *Rocky Mountain News,* April 18, 1988.

McMurtry, Larry. *Roads: Driving America's Great Highways.* New York: Simon & Schuster, 2000.

Maharidge, Dale, and Michael Williamson. Introduction by Bruce Springsteen. *Journey to Nowhere: The Saga of the New Underclass.* New York: Hyperion, 1996. (Doubleday, 1985)

°Major, Kevin. *Dear Bruce Springsteen.* New York: Delacorte, 1988.

Makin, Robert. "Developmentally Challenged: Asbury Landmarks in Trouble." *Backstreets,* Winter 2001/2002.

————. "The Life and Times of Steve Van Zandt." *Backstreets,* Spring 2000.

Malone, Bill C. *Country Music U.S.A.* Austin: University of Texas Press, 1985.

————. *Singing Cowboys and Musical Mountaineers: Southern Culture and the Roots of Country Music.* Athens, Ga.: University of Georgia Press, 1993.

————. *Southern Music, American Music.* Lexington, Ky.: University Press of Kentucky, 1979.

Marcus, Greil. "Bruce Springsteen: In Your Heart You Know He's Right." *Artforum,* November 1984.

————. *The Dustbin of History.* Cambridge, Mass.: Harvard University Press, 1997.

————. *Lipstick Traces: A Secret History of the 20th Century.* Cambridge, Mass.: Harvard University Press, 1989.

————. *Mystery Train: Images of America in Rock 'n' Roll Music.* 3rd ed. 1975; New York: Plume, 1990.

°————. "The Next President of the United States." In *In the Fascist Bathroom: Punk in Pop Music, 1977–1992.* Cambridge, Mass.: Harvard University Press, 1999.

————. "Springsteen's Thousand and One American Nights." *Rolling Stone,* October 9, 1975.

Marcus, Greil, ed. *Stranded: Rock and Roll for a Desert Island.* New foreword by Robert Christgau. New York: Da Capo Press, 1996.

Marling, Karal Ann. *The Colossus of Roads: Myth and Symbol Along the American Highway.* Minneapolis: University of Minnesota Press, 2000.

————. *Graceland: Going Home with Elvis.* Cambridge, Mass.: Harvard University Press, 1997.

————. "Nightmare Highways." In *Springsteen: Troubadour of the Highway.* Edited by Laura Westlund. Minneapolis: Weisman Art Museum, 2002.

Marquat, Debra. *The Hunger Bone: Rock & Roll Stories.* Minneapolis: New Rivers Press, 2001.

Marqusee, Mike. *Chimes of Freedom: The Politics of Bob Dylan's Art.* New York: New Press, 2003.

°Marsh, Dave. "Thunder Road." In *Born to Run: The Bruce Springsteen Story.* New York: Doubleday, 1979; Thunder's Mouth Press, 1996.

°————. "Bruce Springsteen: A Rock 'Star Is Born.'" *Rolling Stone,* September 25, 1975.

————. "Bruce Springsteen Raises Cain." *Rolling Stone,* August 24, 1978.

————. *Bruce Springsteen: Two Hearts, The Story.* New York: Routledge, 2003.

————. *Glory Days: Bruce Springsteen in the 1980s.* Vol. 2. New York: Pantheon, 1987.

Marsh, Dave, ed. *Mid-Life Confidential: The Rock Bottom Remainders Tour America with Three Chords and an Attitude.* Photographs by Tabitha King. New York: Viking, 1994.

Marshall, Scott, and Marcia Ford. *Restless Pilgrim: The Spiritual Journey of Bob Dylan.* Lake Mary, Fla.: Relevant Books, 2002.

Martin, Gavin. "Hey Joad, Don't Make It Sad . . . (Oh, Go On Then)." *New Musical Express,* March 9, 1996.

°Mason, Bobbie Ann. *In Country.* New York: Harper & Row, 1985.

Miller, James. *Flowers in the Dustbin: The Rise of Rock and Roll, 1947–1977.* New York: Fireside, 1999.

————. "Return of the Rock Heroes." *Newsweek,* June 18, 1984.

Millman, Joyce. "To Sleep, Perchance to Dream About the Boss." *Salon,* August 8, 1997.

°Morley, Jefferson. "Darkness on the Edge of the Shining City." *New Republic,* March 23, 1987.

Morone, James A. *Hellfire Nation: The Politics of Sin in American History.* New Haven, Conn.: Yale University Press, 2003.

Morse, Steve. "Bruce Looks Back: Springsteen Talks About Life, Changes, and His New Boxed Set." *Boston Globe,* November 20, 1998.

Morthland, John, ed. *Main Lines, Blood Feasts, and Bad Taste: A Lester Bangs Reader.* New York: Anchor Books, 2003.

Naughton, John. "Interview with Bruce Springsteen." *MOJO,* June 1994.

Nelson, Chris. "Reason to Believe." *Village Voice,* April 4–10, 2001.

Nelson, Paul. "Is Springsteen Worth the Hype?" *Village Voice,* August 25, 1975.

————. "Let Us Now Praise Famous Men" (review of *The River*). *Rolling Stone,* December 11, 1980.

————. "The Year's Ten Best Albums." *Real Paper,* December 17, 1975.

Nevins, Allan, and Henry Steele Commager, with Jeffrey Morris. *A Pocket History of the United States of America.* 1943. Reprint. New York: Pocket Books, 1992.

Newall, Michael. "Between What's Flesh and What's Fantasy." *Backstreets,* Summer 2000.

Newfield, Jack. "Reasons to Believe." *Backstreets,* Spring 1986.

O'Connor, Flannery. *The Complete Stories.* New York: Noonday Press, 1996.

———. *Wise Blood.* New York: Noonday Press, 1996.

°Orth, Maureen, Janet Huck, and Peter S. Greenberg. "Making of a Rock Star." *Newsweek,* October 27, 1975.

Ortner, Sherry B. *New Jersey Dreaming: Capital, Culture, and the Class of '58.* Durham, N.C.: Duke University Press, 2003.

Palmer, Robert. *Deep Blues.* New York: Viking, 1981.

———. "Springsteen's Music Hits Chord of America." *New York Times,* August 6, 1985.

°Pardini, Samuele F. S. "Bruce Springsteen's 'American Skin.'" *Artvoice,* June 2000.

Pareles, Jon. "Bruce Springsteen—Rock's Populist." *New York Times,* August 18, 1985.

———. "His Kind of Heroes, His Kind of Songs." *New York Times,* July 14, 2002.

———. "John Mellencamp Records Antiwar Song." *New York Times,* March 5, 2003.

Parsons, Tony. "Bruce: The Myth Just Keeps on Coming." *New Musical Express,* October 14, 1978.

Peabody, Richard, ed. *Mondo Elvis: A Collection of Stories and Poems About Elvis.* New York: St. Martin's Press, 1994.

Pearson, Barry Lee, and Bill McCulloch. *Robert Johnson: Lost and Found.* Music in American Life Series. Urbana, Ill.: University of Illinois Press, 2003.

Percy, Walker. *The Message in the Bottle: How Queer Man Is, How Queer Language Is, and What One Has to Do with the Other.* New York: Picador USA/Farrar, Straus and Giroux, 2000.

———. *The Moviegoer.* New York: Knopf, 1961; Vintage, 1998.

°Percy, Will. "Rock and Read." *DoubleTake,* Spring 1998.

Perrotta, Tom. *Bad Haircut: Stories of the Seventies.* New York: Berkley, 1997.

———. *Joe College.* New York: Griffin, 2001.

°———. *The Wishbones.* New York: Berkley, 1998.

Petersen, James R. "The Ascension of Bruce Springsteen." *Playboy,* March 1976.

Phillips, Christopher. "41 Shots: The Sound and the Fury." *Backstreets,* Summer 2000.

Podhoretz, Norman. "Springsteen *Is Not* in Tune with a Patriotic Vision." *Los Angeles Times,* August 29, 1985.

Pond, Steve. "*Nebraska* Album Review: Springsteen Delivers His Bravest Record Yet." *Rolling Stone,* October 28, 1982.

———. "*Tunnel of Love* Album Review: Bruce's Hard Look at Love." *Rolling Stone,* December 3, 1987.

Pont, Jonathan B. "Better Angels: The *Backstreets* Interview with Jim Cullen." *Backstreets,* Summer/Fall 1997.

Porterfield, Nolan. *The Jimmie Rodgers Story: The Life and Times of America's Blue Yodeler.* Urbana, Ill.: University of Illinois Press, 1992.

Potter, David M. *People of Plenty: Economic Abundance and the American Character.* Chicago: University of Chicago Press, 1954.

Pratt, Ray. "'Is a Dream a Lie If It Don't Come True, or Is It Something Worse?': A Commentary on Political Implications of the Springsteen Phenomenon." *Popular Music and Society* 11 (1987): 51–74.

Primeau, Patrick. *The Moral Passion of Bruce Springsteen.* Bethesda, Md.: International Scholars Publications, 1996.

Puterbaugh, Parke, ed. *Bruce Springsteen: The* Rolling Stone *Files—The Ultimate Compendium of Interviews, Articles, Facts and Opinions from the Files of* Rolling Stone. New York: Hyperion, 1996.

Puterbaugh, Parke, and Alan Bisbort. *Life Is a Beach: A Vacationer's Guide to the East Coast.* New York: McGraw-Hill, 1986.

Putnam, Robert D. *Bowling Alone: The Collapse and Revival of American Community.* New York: Simon & Schuster, 2000.

Rauch, Alan. "Bruce Springsteen and the Dramatic Monologue." *American Studies Journal* (Spring 1988): 29–49.

°Reiken, Frederick. *The Lost Legends of New Jersey.* New York: Harcourt, 2000.

Richards, Barry. "Bruce Springsteen and the Crisis of Masculinity." *Free Associations* 9, 1987.

Ridl, Jack. *Between.* Fulton, Mo.: Dawn Valley Press of Westminster College, 1988.

°———. "Video Mama." In *Sweet Nothings: An Anthology of Rock and Roll in American Poetry.* Jim Elledge, ed. Bloomington and Indianapolis: Indiana University Press, 1994.

°Ringer, R. C. "Asbury Park." In *Shore Stories: An Anthology of the Jersey Shore.* Edited by Rich Youmans. Harvey Cedars, N.J.: Down the Shore Publishing, 1998.

"Rock and Remembrance." *Economist,* August 1, 2002.

Rockland, Michael, and Angus Kress Gillespie. *Looking for America on the New Jersey Turnpike.* Brunswick, N.J.: Rutgers University Press, 1993.

Rockwell, John. "'Hype' and the Springsteen Case." *New York Times,* October 24, 1975.

———. "New Dylan from New Jersey? It Might as Well Be Springsteen." *Rolling Stone,* October 9, 1975.

———. "The Rocky Road to Stardom." *New York Times,* August 15, 1975.

°———. "Springsteen's Rock Poetry at Its Best." *New York Times,* August 29, 1975.

Rodnitzky, Jerome L. *Minstrels of the Dawn: The Folk Protest Singer as a Cultural Hero.* Chicago: Nelson Hall, 1976.

Roediger, David. *The Wages of Whiteness: Race and the Making of the American Working Class.* New York: Verso, 1991.

Rotella, Sebastian. "Children of the Border: Caught in a Makeshift Life, Immigrants, Youths Eke Out a Living in San Diego's Balboa Park." *Los Angeles Times,* April 3, 1993.

Russell, Tony. *The Blues from Robert Johnson to Robert Cray.* New York: Schirmer Books, 1997.

Samway, Patrick, S.J. *Walker Percy: A Life.* Chicago: Loyola Press, 1999.

Sanders, Scott Russell. *Staying Put: Making a Home in a Restless World.* Boston: Beacon Press, 1994.

Sandford, Christopher. *Springsteen: Point Blank.* New York: Da Capo Press, 1999.

Santelli, Robert. "Asbury Museum Up for Sale." *Backstreets,* Spring 1990.

———. *Guide to the Jersey Shore: From Sandy Hook to Cape May.* 6th ed. Guilford, Conn.: Globe Pequot, 2003.

———. "Rock 'n' Roll Highway." In *Springsteen: Troubadour of the Highway.* Edited by Laura Westlund. Minneapolis: Weisman Art Museum, 2002.

———. "'Thunder Road': The First Bruce Fanzine." *Backstreets,* Summer 1987.

°———. "Twenty Years Burning Down the Road: The Complete History of Jersey Shore Rock 'n' Roll." *Backstreets: Springsteen—The Man and His Music.* Edited by Charles R. Cross and the editors of *Backstreets* magazine. New York: Harmony Books, 1989; Crown, 1992.

Santelli, Robert, and Emily Davidson, eds. *Hard Travelin': The Life and Legacy of Woody Guthrie.* American Music Masters series. Hanover, N.H.: Wesleyan University Press, 1999.

Santelli, Robert, Holly George-Warren, and Jim Brown, eds. *American Roots Music.* Foreword by Bonnie Raitt. New York: Abrams, 2001.

Santoro, Gene. "Hey, He's Bruce." *Nation,* September 16, 2002.

———. "Robert Johnson." *Nation,* October 8, 1990.

Scaduto, Anthony. *Bob Dylan.* New York: New American Library, 1979.

Scheurer, Timothy E., ed. *The Age of Rock: Readings from the Popular Press.* Bowling Green, Oh.: Bowling Green State University Popular Press, 1989.

Schoemer, Karen. "Heart of Darkness." *Newsweek,* April 1, 1996.

Schoenberg, Tom. "Professor's Research Inspires a Rock Star." *Chronicle of Higher Education,* January 19, 1996.

Schruers, Fred. "Bruce Springsteen and the Secret of the World." *Rolling Stone,* February 5, 1981.

°Scott, A. O. "The Poet Laureate of 9/11: Apocalypse and Salvation on Springsteen's New Album." *Slate,* August 6, 2002.

°Sheehy, Colleen. "Springsteen: Troubadour of the Highway." In *Springsteen: Troubadour of the Highway.* Edited by Laura Westlund. Minneapolis: Weisman Art Museum, 2002.

———. "Staging Springsteen: Drive All Night . . . to the Great White Way?" *Backstreets,* Spring/Summer 2002.

Shelton, Robert. *No Direction Home: The Life and Music of Bob Dylan.* New York: Morrow, 1986.

Smith, Larry David. *Bob Dylan, Bruce Springsteen, and American Song.* Westport, Conn.: Praeger Publishers, 2002.

Smith, Martha Nell. "Sexual Mobilities in Bruce Springsteen: Performance as Commentary." *South Atlantic Quarterly* 90, no. 4 (Fall 1991): 833–54.

Springsteen, Bruce. Rock and Roll Hall of Fame Speech. In *The Dylan Companion*. Elizabeth Thomson and David Gutman, eds. New York: Da Capo Press, 2001.

———. *Songs.* New York: Avon, 1998; New York: HarperCollins, 2003.

Stefanko, Frank. *Days of Hope and Dreams: An Intimate Portrait of Bruce Springsteen*. Introduction by Bruce Springsteen. Preface by Chris Murray. New York: Billboard Books, 2003.

Strauss, Neil. "The Springsteen Interview." *Guitar World*, October 1995.

°———. "Springsteen Looks Back but Keeps Walking On." *New York Times*, May 7, 1995.

Steinbeck, John. *The Grapes of Wrath*. 1939. New York: Penguin, 1987.

Steinberg, Jacques. "A Rocker and a Revered Author Bond for a Cause: Robert Coles and Bruce Springsteen, Pundits and Pals." *New York Times*, March 20, 2003.

Streissguth, Michael, ed. *Ring of Fire: The Johnny Cash Reader*. New York: Da Capo Press, 2002.

°Swartley, Ariel. "The Wild, the Innocent & the E Street Shuffle." In *Stranded: Rock and Roll for a Desert Island*. Edited by Greil Marcus. New foreword by Robert Christgau. New York: Da Capo Press, 1996.

Sweeting, Adam. "Into the Fire." *Uncut*, September 2002.

Sylvan, Robin. *Traces of the Spirit: The Religious Dimensions of Popular Music*. New York: New York University Press, 2002.

Tate, Greg. "Tear the Roof Off Jungleland." *Village Voice*, August 11–17, 1999.

Taylor, Lori Elaine. "The Politicized American Legend of the Singing Hero: Joe Hill, Woody Guthrie, Pete Seeger, Bob Dylan, and Bruce Springsteen." Master's thesis, George Washington University, 1990.

Thompson, Jim. *The Killer Inside Me*. New York: Vintage Books, 1991.

Thomson, Elizabeth, and David Gutman, eds. *The Dylan Companion: A Collection of Essential Writings About Bob Dylan*. New York: Da Capo, 2001.

Tichi, Cecelia. *High Lonesome: The American Culture of Country Music*. Chapel Hill, N.C.: University of North Carolina Press, 1994.

Tonelli, Bill, ed. *The Italian American Reader: A Collection of Outstanding Fiction, Memoirs, Journalism, Essays, and Poetry*. Foreword by Nick Tosches. New York: William Morrow/HarperCollins, 2003.

Tosches, Nick. *Country: The Twisted Roots of Rock 'n' Roll*. New York: Da Capo Press, 1998.

Tracy, David. *The Analogical Imagination: Christian Theology and the Culture of Pluralism*. New York: Crossroad Publishing, 1981.

Tucker, Ken. "Springsteen: Beyond the Music, A Challenge to Better the USA." *Philadelphia Inquirer*, August 16, 1985.

———. "Springsteen: The Interview." *Entertainment Weekly*, February 28, 2003.

Tyrangiel, Josh. "Bruce Rising: An Intimate Look at How Springsteen Turned 9/11 into a Message of Hope." *Time,* August 5, 2002.

Volpe, Gregory J. "Rumson Man Inspired Boss." *Asbury Park Press,* July 31, 2002.

Walsh, Jim. "Baptism by Bruce." *St. Paul Pioneer Press,* October 27, 1999.

White, Timothy. *Rock Lives: Profiles and Interviews.* New York: Henry Holt, 1990.

°Wieder, Judy. "Bruce Springsteen: The *Advocate* Interview." *Advocate,* April 2, 1996.

Wien, Gary. Photos by Debra L. Rothenberg. *Beyond the Palace.* Victoria, B.C.: Trafford, 2003.

Wilentz, Sean. *Chants Democratic: New York City and the Rise of the American Working Class, 1788–1850.* New York: Oxford University Press, 1984.

°Will, George F. "Bruuuuuce" In *The Morning After: American Successes and Excesses, 1981–1986.* New York: Free Press, 1986.

Williams, Richard. *Long Distance Call: Writings on Music.* London: Aurum Press, 2002.

Williams, Roger M. *Sing a Sad Song: The Hank Williams Story.* Urbana, Ill.: University of Illinois Press, 1981.

°Wolcott, James. "The Hagiography of Bruce Springsteen." *Vanity Fair,* December 1985.

°Wurtzel, Elizabeth. *Prozac Nation: Young and Depressed in America.* Boston: Houghton Mifflin, 1994; New York: Riverhead Books, 1995.

Wuthnow, Robert. *All in Sync: How Music and Art Are Revitalizing American Religion.* Berkeley, Calif.: University of California Press, 2003.

Youmans, Rich, ed. *Shore Stories: An Anthology of the Jersey Shore.* Harvey Cedars, N.J.: Down the Shore Publishing, 1998.

Zengerle, Jason. "Questions for Steve Earle: Sympathy for a Rebel." *New York Times Magazine,* August 25, 2002.